Making the Novel

Fiction and Society in Britain, 1660–1789

Brean Hammond

and

Shaun Regan

First published in 2006 by
PALGRAVE MACMILLAN
Houndmills, Basingstoke, Hampshire RG21 6XS and
175 Fifth Avenue, New York, N.Y. 10010
Companies and representatives throughout the world.

PALGRAVE MACMILLAN is the global academic imprint of the Palgrave Macmillan division of St. Martin's Press, LLC and of Palgrave Macmillan Ltd. Macmillan® is a registered trademark in the United States, United Kingdom and other countries. Palgrave is a registered trademark in the European Union and other countries.

ISBN-13: 978–0–333–62853–9 hardback
ISBN-10: 0–333–62853–5   hardback
ISBN-13: 978–0–333–62854–6 paperback
ISBN-10: 0–333–62854–3   paperback

This book is printed on paper suitable for recycling and made from fully managed and sustained forest sources.

A catalogue record for this book is available from the British Library.

A catalog record for this book is available from the Library of Congress.

10 9 8 7 6 5 4 3 2 1
15 14 13 12 11 10 09 08 07 06

Printed in China

MAKING THE NOVEL

To Ian Bell and
In Memoriam *Anne-Marie Taylor*

Contents

Acknowledgements

The idea for this book began many years ago, as a collaboration between Brean Hammond and Ian Bell, formerly Professor of English at University of Wales, Swansea. When Ian's health deteriorated, and his wife's health also worsened, he had to withdraw from the project. Anne-Marie Taylor's poignantly early demise followed in 2003, and this book is dedicated to Ian and to the memory of Anne-Marie.

In time, Shaun Regan came on board as a new collaborator, and we reconceived the study in the light of the ever-growing body of scholarship being published on its subject: the eighteenth-century novel. The collaboration has been a happy one for us, and we hope that the pleasure of writing together is reflected in the book itself.

Amongst those we would like to thank are: the students of the University of Nottingham and University College Dublin, who have taken courses with us on the novel and have contributed more to the final product than they will ever imagine; Paul Goring, Moyra Haslett, and Valerie Pedlar, for their careful and generous readings of drafts; our editors at Palgrave, for their patience and support, and also the anonymous readers for the Press, who offered numerous useful suggestions for improving the typescript, many of which we have adopted; and finally the Arts and Humanities Research Council, for granting a term's leave to Brean in Spring 2004, which greatly facilitated the project's completion.

Preface

This book offers students of literature and readers of prose fiction an account of the creation and early development of the novel – the most modern of literary genres. In University taught courses, the period 1660–1789 is relatively neglected, squeezed as it is between two juggernaut competitors: the Renaissance at one end, the Romantic and Victorian period at the other. One consequence of this situation is that, even in departments of English literature, the earliest novels with which readers engage often date not from the eighteenth but from the nineteenth century – the novels of Jane Austen and the Brontës, Charles Dickens and George Eliot. Such readers may acquire very little sense of the artistic, social and economic forces that first brought the novel into being. The uncertain nature of early experiments in prose fiction, and the difficulties that were faced by the pioneers of the genre, are not always easily perceived by those who take up the story of the novel only later, when the genre had already secured its status as a distinct form of writing and a marketable commodity.

Today, the novel is conspicuously the most successful literary genre. Unlike drama, the novel is primarily the product of print; and because it deploys the potent technology of print, it touches the lives of most people in developed, literate societies. The central place of the genre in twentieth-century life was strongly expressed in 1936 by the novelist D.H. Lawrence, in an essay entitled 'Why the Novel Matters'. As Lawrence wrote:

> The novel is the one bright book of life. Books are not life. They are only tremulations on the ether. But the novel as a tremulation can make the whole man alive tremble. Which is more than poetry, philosophy, science, or any other book-tremulation can do.[1]

One of the central purposes of *Making the Novel* is to enable an under-standing of the distance that had to be travelled by the novel genre, in order to arrive at such a powerful assertion of its significance as Lawrence here offers. Retracing this journey is an important enterprise, because our answer to the question, 'why does the novel matter?', depends partly on an awareness of how the novel came about – of the social and economic determinants that brought it into being, the purposes that it evolved to serve, and the ways in which it was shaped by the expectations of those who consumed it. Recapturing a sense of the novel's early history – of its struggle for recognition and authority in eighteenth-century Britain – will lead us to a richer appreciation of the novel's importance to our own cultural moment.

There can be no single, definitive account of the way in which a recognizably 'modern' genre of the novel emerged out of ancestral forms of imaginative prose writing. There is, however, a notable 'market leader' in the field: Ian Watt's *The Rise of the Novel*, which was first published nearly 50 years ago. It is extremely important for those who wish to engage with the novel to understand why Watt's thesis about the genre's evolution has proved so enduring; but also how subsequent generations of critics, sometimes proceeding from different theoretical assumptions, have challenged and modified it. This is the business of Chapter 1, in which we outline our own perspective on the novel's emergence. Our own approach takes more account than did Watt of the eighteenth-century market for fiction, of female writers of novels, and of the genre's relationship to forms of imaginative literature not written in prose. While we try to keep the ideas coined in that theoretical opening chapter in circulation throughout the book, it has not been our intention to apply them as a template for the analyses of individual novels that we offer in subsequent chapters. Neither has it been our intention to provide a *comprehensive* history of the eighteenth-century novel, though we do believe that our selection of texts and writers is considerably wider than is the case in many books on the subject, particularly those that replicate Watt's rather narrow focus upon the 'big three' early novelists: Daniel Defoe, Samuel Richardson, and Henry Fielding. While our chapters proceed chronologically, we also want to resist the idea that the novel itself progressed inexorably, onwards and upwards, from uncertain beginnings in the early eighteenth century to the works of the great Victorian novelists and beyond. Rather, our readings seek to show how the early novelists operated in contested fields of discourse, grappling with a verbal, printed medium whose rules and conventions existed in an ongoing process of formation and modulation. More generally, our approach might be characterized as bi-focal: viewing individual novels as far as possible as their contemporaries might have viewed them, but without neglecting their continuing relevance to modern debates about – in Lawrence's words – 'books' and 'life'.

To conclude, a few words are necessary on the editions we have used and on spelling conventions in our quotations. Wherever possible, we have used what we consider to be the best, widely accessible editions of the novels that we analyse in detail. In such cases, our quotations are generally given in standard, modern English. In the absence of accessible modern editions, we have used either the first printed edition or a close alternative; in such cases, our quotations will be presented as they appear in these eighteenth-century texts. It is worth bearing in mind, therefore, that eighteenth-century printing conventions dictated that the first letters of most nouns were capitalized, and that during the eighteenth century words were often spelt slightly differently, and with slightly less consistency, than they are in modern dictionaries.

BREAN HAMMOND AND SHAUN REGAN

1
Introduction: Modelling the Novel

To see how sophisticated today's browsers in the fiction sections of bookshops and on the internet have become, it is necessary only to look at the astonishingly fine discriminations that are made by commentators on and consumers of one single sub-genre: science fiction. Science fiction is already a specialized generic niche within the broader category of fiction, and it is often further distinguished into the broad subcategories of science fiction and science fantasy. Then the fun really starts. A glance at the available literature will yield the following further discriminations (and the list is far from exhaustive):[1]

cyberpunk	utopias/dystopias	Edisonade
genre SF	hard SF	soft SF
new wave	slash fiction	sci-fi/skiffy
scientifiction	slipstream	space opera
heroic fantasy	planetary romance	science fantasy
steampunk	speculative fiction	magic realism
Sword and sorcery		

Such discriminations seem to be made on a 'not exactly X, more Y' basis, where the point of making the judgement is perhaps to show how familiar with the subject one is: how sophisticated and discriminating one can be with respect to its subject matter. There is a cultish dimension to this minute taxonomizing – almost a one-upmanship involved in being able to perceive small inflections in literary subtypes.

An annual paperback bestseller list published in *The Guardian* at the end of 2001 records that of the fictional titles listed, only around a third are given the designation 'novel'. Novels, on this list, come in an A-class and a B-class, where category A novels are smaller sized paperbacks designed for a 'mass market', and B novels are larger-sized, 'middle-to-highbrow' publications. Jilly Cooper would be category A; Rose Tremain category B. What of the two-thirds of fictional titles not designated 'novel'? It seems that the reader can distinguish between a variety of generic designations: 'thriller' (John Grisham, Tom Clancy), distinguished from 'mystery', 'adventure' and 'crime' (Ian Rankin, Nicci French); 'romance' (successful romance writers include Danielle Steele and Charlotte Bingham); 'saga' (Catherine Cookson), which appears not to be the same as the 'historical novel', written by authors such as Bernard Cornwell. The modern reader presumably knows what to expect when s/he buys a novel under one of the above designations. At whatever point one consults such a classified bestseller list, there are also a number of nonce generic labels that would be very difficult to define, and seem to have a more ephemeral existence. Examples in 2001 included 'city girl', covering Bridget Jones books and titles by Robyn Sisman, Jane Green and Lisa Jewell (and its male counterpart, 'town boy'), with another major label being 'juvenile', to include Harry Potter and J.R.R. Tolkien – though their readership is certainly not entirely juvenile, and the term 'kiddult' has also been coined to cover the transfer of books intended primarily for children to an adult readership.

To those interested in the history of the novel, some questions and observations might arise. What exactly is a 'mass market' novel and how is it distinguished from its middle-brow rival? Has the middle-brow/low-brow split always been perceptible? How and when did such a complicated system of labelling arise? Which of those designations are of long duration? Romance, for example, is a label that seems to have been around for a very long time. When did it first come into use and to what sort of fiction was it first applied? When did it all begin? More importantly, when did the generic category 'novel' first emerge into English consciousness and become recognizable to readers? Turning to an influential present-day guide, *The Oxford Illustrated History of English Literature* (1987), we read that 'of several claimants to the title of our first true novel, the strongest is Daniel Defoe's *The Life and Strange Surprizing Adventures of Robinson Crusoe*', which was first published in 1719.[2] This is the conventional wisdom among literary scholars, but it ought to prompt some questions. Why is *Robinson Crusoe* the strongest claimant to being the 'first true novel'? Why are some pieces of prose fiction published before this *not* true novels? What was there *before* there was a novel? A very long and important recent book on the subject, Margaret Doody's *The True Story of the Novel* (1996), gives the minimalist definition of a novel that 'a work is a novel if it is fictional, if it is in prose, and if it is of a certain length' – which, if satisfactory, would entail that the first true novel must have been written long before 1719 and certainly not by an Englishman.[3] After all, long works of prose fiction had been produced in Europe throughout the sixteenth and seventeenth centuries, by such leading writers as Rabelais (*c.*1484–1553) and Cervantes (1547–1616). And if we accept Doody's argument, there are a host of ancient Greek and Roman examples, like *Apollonius of Tyre*, Heliodorus, Apuleius and Petronius Arbiter. If Defoe himself had been accosted on the street as 'father of the novel', he would, one suspects, have made off at speed, convinced that someone was trying to bring a paternity suit against him. He would certainly not have recognized himself under that description. So what is behind the Oxford *History*'s guidance?

The Oxford *History*'s hedged sponsorship of Defoe's *Robinson Crusoe* reflects the influence of one of the most powerful models of the novel's rise currently available: Ian Watt's *The Rise of the Novel*. Published in 1957, Watt's study offered a charismatic account of the development of the most popular genre of imaginative writing, with which entire generations of literary students grew up and still grow up. With its use of the 'rise' metaphor, Watt's title deliberately echoes R.H. Tawney's epoch-making sociological study, *Religion and the Rise of Capitalism* (1926), because he argues that the conditions out of which the modern novel emerged were the same conditions that produced the Protestant religion, early capitalism and the middle class, a set of developments that have in common a new emphasis on individual experience. At the heart of Watt's explanation for the emergence of the novel is what he calls 'formal realism'. For Watt, the novel proper is distinguished from earlier fictional forms by narrative procedures that are designed to secure the objectives of formal realism. The modern novel encapsulates the experience of individual protagonists, particular people in particular circumstances, using original plots, as against the repetitive conventionalities of older romance traditions – such as are familiar to us from the many versions of the Arthurian legend. Of Daniel Defoe, Watt states that his 'total subordination of the plot to the pattern of the autobiographical memoir' is a 'defiant assertion of the primacy of individual experience'.[4] There is a new emphasis on the exploration of personality in relation to categories of time and space: characters are set in solidly imagined milieux and there is a concern for the effect of the past upon present and future events, as well as a minutely discriminated timescale, as the novel tries to approximate the texture of everyday happenings. Defoe's fiction, says Watt, 'presents us with a picture both of individual life in its larger perspective as a historical process, and in its closer view which shows the process being acted out against the historical background of the most ephemeral thoughts and actions'.[5] 'Formal realism', then, is a set of procedures through which the novel specifies the setting, the time, and the individuality of the events and personalities that it imagines.

The novel emerged when and where it did – in England in the early eighteenth century – argues Watt, because at that time the feudal, aristocratic elite was being challenged by a new bourgeois commercial element, whose values were those of empiricism and individualism. Individualism is the result of the economic specialization produced by a pre-capitalist economy (division of labour, breakdown of traditional communities, urbanization) and by a Protestant emphasis on the primacy of individual conscience. Political conditions were ripe for economic individualism, which requires relative liberty (such as was secured for English people after 1688 through the so-called 'Revolution Settlement', that bent the King's will to that of Parliament), and a mobile and heterogeneous society, in order to flourish. Merchants, successful tradesmen and shopkeepers, manufacturers, financial brokers and urban professionals: these groups were swelling the ranks of the book-buying public and were achieving the social clout to demand that their leisure time be filled by representations of themselves in action. (Apprentices and household servants might also have become more literate, concedes Watt, and although not middle class, they might also have bought and read novels.) The literary taste of this emergent reading public was more secular and less highbrow than that of their predecessors in the seventeenth century. In Watt's reading, the novel was supremely well fitted to supply the leisure time needs of readers who required to be entertained, for growing periods of time, with stories about individuals whom they could recognize, identify with, and profit from. Watt's 'triple rise' theory – the rise of the middle class, of Protestantism and of the novel – has proved highly durable. There have, however, been challenges to it from several different quarters. Today, nearly half a century on, we might say that it is bloody but unbowed. We must now consider some of those critiques, and the alternative accounts that they have generated.

To start with, what of Watt's controlling metaphor, the 'rise' of the novel? Characterized by 'realism' and starting with Defoe, the idea of the novel's 'rise' speaks, to some, of an irresistible tide of progress – a linear, teleological historical development culminating in the triumph of nineteenth-century realist fiction as practised by George Eliot, later to be recycled in even more aesthetically pleasing form as theorized by Henry James. Whatever is inconvenient to this grand narrative – whether it be those writers whose work doesn't easily fit the model, or the considerable evidence of contestation and struggle, which would render the story less bland – is simply omitted. Some of the difficulties of this model are raised in one of the earliest sustained critiques of Watt, which was made by John Richetti in *Popular Fiction Before Richardson* (1969), in a chapter entitled 'The Rise of the Novel Reconsidered'. Among Richetti's criticisms of *The Rise of the Novel* are: that it incorporates a 'teleological bias', an assumption of a progressive movement from the immature origins of the novel to the 'rise' and 'dominance' of the fully formed genre; that the canon of authors upon which it focuses is 'drastically selective'; and, importantly, that Watt possesses an over-developed sense of the middle-class' influence upon contemporary narrative forms. As Richetti pointedly remarks: 'It is by no means certain that the early eighteenth century can be entirely summed up in terms of the advancing practicality and incipient democratic attitudes of the middle classes.'[6] To some sceptical historians, the 'middle class' has been rising since the medieval period, and there is nothing distinctive about the early eighteenth century in its emergence. For 'revisionist' scholars like Jonathan Clark, by contrast, there never was any rise of the middle class in this period because, virtually until the Reform Act of 1832, England remained a rural society dominated by the aristocracy and the Established Church.[7] To some extent, these historians argue that the term 'class' itself is a concept inapplicable to English society prior to the full swing of the Industrial Revolution, because it relates to the solidarity shared by wage-earning factory workers in industrial cities. 'Class', they argue, is a category referable to socio-economic criteria, whereas early eighteenth-century society was organized around stratifications based on status that did not map directly onto wealth. To our minds, however, there *is* a broadly tripartite division of English society during this period, which separates into the following groupings: first, the aristocracy and gentry, landowners with private incomes who did not work; then, the 'middling sort' who did work but who did not dirty their hands – commercial or industrial investors who had a stock of money or goods that they sought to improve, and whose goals were accumulation and self-improvement; and finally the 'mechanick part of mankind', those labourers without capital who depended on their hands for a living. Such a division is implicit in Robinson Crusoe's account of his rebellion against his father's counsel, at the opening of Defoe's novel:

> [My father] bid me observe it, and I should always find, that the calamities of life were shared among the upper and lower part of

mankind: but that the middle station had the fewest disasters, and
was not exposed to so many vicissitudes as the higher or lower part
of mankind.[8]

In our view, Watt is broadly correct to say that the second tier, the
'middling sort', was growing in this period. To be wholly persuasive,
however, an account of the middle station's role in promoting novel-
writing and novel-reading would need to be considerably more
nuanced than Watt's.

Next, there is the question of 'formal realism' itself. How do we
evaluate Watt's contention that what separates the writing of those
novelists that he considers to be fully fledged – Defoe, Richardson and
Fielding – from earlier English and French prose fictions is its greater
capacity to render plausibly in language what readers experienced as
'real life'? Here, the various challenges of literary historians and cultural
critics can be divided into two broad paradigms of approach, though
most participants in the discussion draw upon both: (1) is 'formal
realism' actually the defining characteristic of the novel? (2) what are
the appropriate texts and pre-texts to bring forward in arriving at
the 'true story of the novel'? An important related question is: how
does the novel proper distinguish itself from the romance? Why is
Fielding's *Tom Jones* (1749) a novel whereas, say, Thomas Lodge's
Rosalynde (1590) – the source for Shakespeare's *As You Like It*, usually
termed a 'pastoral romance' – is not a novel? Claims to realism tend to
be historically relative, and are not borne out by any criterion intrinsic
to language itself. Would we say that a soap opera, for example, is 'realistic'? What is judged realistic by one generation or community of readers might be regarded as laughably artificial by another. William Warner
makes the point thus: 'no text ... once transported from the space or
time of its production, and no matter how earnest its aspirations to
facticity or truth, can bear a mark in its own language that verifies its relation to something outside itself'.[9] In *Crime and Defoe* (1993), Lincoln
Faller argues that the concrete particularity so celebrated by Watt as a
quintessential feature of Defoe's fiction is actually more apparent in his
non-fictional writing. To Faller, Defoe's fiction is distinguished not by
its quiddities of particular experience but by the arresting complexities
of the narrative point of view.[10] There are qualitative assumptions at
work here. Defoe is deemed to be better, because his works are more
complex, than any previous prose writer, and that is why we mark him
out as a pioneer. Watt himself, we might note, was very aware of the
difficulties raised by arguments about 'realism'. Commenting on his

achievement in *The Rise of the Novel* some 20 years after its publication, he wrote:

> The semantic difficulty with realism here seems to be insuperable, largely because we are all – and equally – experts on 'reality', and therefore feel authorized to handle its terminology in whatever way we like. As a result the present debate, or rather non-debate, about realism is essentially a form of shadow-boxing in which no blows are ever landed because the ring of reality is so large: in fact there are no ropes.[11]

This moves us on nicely to the broader question of the relationship between the novel and the older genre of romance, which many would say is the one most relevant to the novel's development. To come into its own, Watt argues, the novel had to evolve out of, or cut itself free from, the romance form above all – not least because the world evoked by romance is tested to destruction by such realist assumptions as those outlined earlier. In *Factual Fictions* (1983), Lennard Davis proposes that the key difference between the romance and the novel is that the former derives from the epic tradition of Homer and Virgil – with its distant, idealized settings and characters, aristocratic focus, and lengthy, episodic looseness of structure – whereas the latter derives from history and journalism, is middle class, and is concerned with present-day actualities, usually treated in the first-person or epistolary form. For Davis, the essential task of novelistic discourse was to distinguish itself from romance on the one hand – which it did by claiming certain kinds of documentary, factual significance not assumed by romance – and from newspaper journalism on the other, which it achieved by preserving fictionality and thus evading the provisions of the 1712 Stamp Act, which rendered purveyors of false news liable to prosecution.[12] Ingenious though this argument is, it is entirely possible to argue that the novel never *did* distinguish itself from romance in such a neat and wholesale manner. Shifting the focus from Defoe to Henry Fielding, we might well argue that Fielding's novels are *not* realistic in form. The use of a self-conscious, intrusive narrator; the preface to *Joseph Andrews* (1742), which associates the novel with the epic; the clear manipulation of narrative content through coincidence and careful management of plot information – all this gives Fielding's writing a texture entirely different from that of Defoe, and shows it to be more indebted to older narrative forms. Neither does the content of Fielding's novels express a clear ideological commitment to the struggling urban poor and bourgeois – figures like Moll Flanders and Robinson Crusoe, who benefit from Defoe's special pleading. If anything, rather than promoting the rise of the middle classes, Fielding patronizes the commercial and trading sectors of society, from the elevated standpoint of the gentry.

One further consequence of this critical demarcation of the novel from the romance tradition is that by focusing on Defoe, Richardson and Fielding, critics following Watt have been embarrassed by the love-centred or 'amatory' fiction produced by writers such as Aphra Behn, Delarivier Manley, Eliza Haywood and Penelope Aubin. Some feminist-inspired critiques of Watt have advanced the argument that upholding this split between romance and novel is part of a masculinist project designed to devalue those pre-Defovian writers whose main topics were love and sexual desire. As Laurie Langbauer writes:

> The sudden break between the novel and romance that Watt highlights in his argument confirms the male privilege tacit in that argument by inserting it in a key feature of formal realism: plot.[13]

Deborah Ross' *The Excellence of Falsehood: Romance, Realism and Women's Contribution to the Novel* (1991) suggests that in working this tactic – in creating the romance = trivial = female, novel = serious = male equation – Watt was recapitulating procedures adopted by male satirists and critics in the period itself.[14] For Langbauer, Ross and others, the 'true story' of the novel can only emerge when this damaging binarism between the serious and the trivial in early fiction is removed. Both below and in Chapter 2, we will return to this problem of a gendered blind spot that has persisted into a number of the post-Wattian accounts of the 'rise' and 'origins' of the novel genre.

It was the durability of romance conventions in the characterization and structure of novels such as those of Richardson and Fielding, and Watt's manifest refusal to see this in his single-minded promotion of formal realism, that encouraged Michael McKeon to produce his monumental study, *The Origins of the English Novel* (1987).[15] Marxist in its inspiration and complex in its expression, McKeon's book was not rapturously received in all quarters. Lennard Davis' review, for instance, states that 'to attempt to trace the *origins* of the English novel by discussing political theory from the Greeks and Romans, through medieval and Renaissance writers, and finally to Enlightenment thinkers is rather like trying to write a book on the origins of the cinema by reviewing all the theories of optics for the last 2,000 years'.[16] For McKeon, however, the main problem with Watt is that he gives a static, one-dimensional account of a very sudden 'rise' or emergence of the novel – now you don't see it, now you do. By contrast, McKeon aims to provide a more dialectical view of a fluid and unstable process. It is a wild goose chase, thinks McKeon, to try to pinpoint the very *first* novel. Instead, McKeon describes a series of 'dialectical engagements' out of which the novel arose, enabling us to comprehend the ideological work that the novel was developed to perform. Underlying his thesis is the discernment of two defining 'crises' in the early modern period: a crisis over how it is possible to use narrative to tell the truth, and a crisis over the relationship between the external social order and internal moral values. (An example of the latter might be Moll Flanders' confrontation with a society that is determined to make a dishonest woman of her, however morally she tries to act.) In McKeon's analysis, the novel was developed to mediate these twin questions of truth and virtue to a community of readers for whom they had become increasingly problematic.

It is difficult in a short précis to do justice to the full complexity of McKeon's argument, but it might be summarized as follows. As the seventeenth century progressed, romance writing – as exemplified, say, by Sir Philip Sidney's *Arcadia* (1590/1593) – was discredited because of its idealism and implausibility. 'Romance idealism' was gradually replaced by a narrative mode of 'naïve empiricism' that was committed to truth-telling, as in travel books, spiritual autobiographies and scientific writings. This in turn was called into question by a mode of 'extreme scepticism' which challenged the truth-claims of naïve empiricism, often by calling attention to the artificiality of *all* writing (in a way that actually recalls aspects of romance idealism). We can detect in society itself a process of transformation and change that mirrors this generic instability of narrative. During the seventeenth century, an aristocratic ideology that places emphasis on landowning and codes of honour, considering personal merit and virtue to be a consequence of social rank (in some quarters this might be called 'civic humanism'), begins to give way to a progressive ideology that challenges the assumption that rank always equals virtue. In this new ideology, individual worth is measured not by social rank and its associated obligations, but by enterprise, intelligence, survival instinct and the amassing of wealth. Daniel Defoe's novels might speak to this ideology. In turn, though, this progressive view generates a backlash of conservative contempt for the circulation of money and accumulation of capital, such as we find in Swift's *Gulliver's Travels* (1726) and in Fielding's hatred for dishonest land stewards, racketeers, money men and corrupt public functionaries.

Drawing this together, we might represent McKeon's complex argument in diagrammatic form thus:

Generic instability (questions of truth)	Social instability (questions of virtue)
Romance idealism Romance gradually distinguishes itself from novels. History/literature split in terms of fact/fiction.	*Aristocratic ideology* Land-based. Wealth=honour. Status conferred by rank and inheritance. Genealogy and social position signifies intrinsic moral worth.
↓	↓
Naïve empiricism Scientific revolution, spread of print and Reformation creates works (like Defoe's) making new claims to realism and factuality.	*Progressive ideology* Personal virtue more important than social rank. Money replaces land as economic criteria replace status. Business, 'projects', investment.
↓	↓
Extreme scepticism Claims to truthfulness of writers like Defoe are subjected to parody and sceptical backlash.	*Conservative ideology* Market exchange of commodities and invisible earnings lead only to corruption. Aristocracy is debased, but the land stewards and money men are no better.

Thus McKeon tries to establish a relationship between ideological formations and literary forms, and puts the novel into a richer dialogue with a wealth of other kinds of writing than Watt had attempted to do. Significantly, McKeon's 'dialectical' model also entails the idea that the category of the novel in this period cannot be reduced to the style or achievement of any one novelist alone. Rather, in this model the genre emerges in debates *between* different prose fictions, and the assumptions about the world to which they correlate. For McKeon, the novel exists only *within* the competition between *Robinson Crusoe* and *Gulliver's Travels*, or between Richardson's *Pamela* (1740) and Fielding's *Shamela* (1741) – oppositions that we will discuss in more detail in subsequent chapters. Is some *Crusoe–Gulliver hybrid*, then, the 'first true novel'? If such a question seems facetious, we need at least to register the difficulty that is presented to actual readers by this idea that *individual* prose fictions from the early eighteenth century cannot in themselves be defined as 'novels'.

As this focus upon dialectical relationships between Defoe and Swift, and Richardson and Fielding, might suggest, for all the critical sophistication of his study McKeon himself replicates one of the further problems in Watt's original thesis. For isn't McKeon's account also a rather phallocentric one? In her pointedly titled *The Rise of the Woman Novelist* (1986), published the year before McKeon's study, Jane Spencer focuses attention on a host of writers – Delarivier Manley, Jane Barker, Penelope Aubin, Elizabeth Rowe, Eliza Haywood, Mary Davys, Catherine Trotter, and others – who were all writing fiction during the period 1690–1725, and who should perhaps have some part to play in the story. Watt's account is of the founding fathers of the novel; were there not also founding mothers? Spencer stresses the importance not only of female writers but also of female readers in the early development of the novel. More upper- and middle-class women were joining the ranks of the consuming public, and were indeed very prominent within it. Although the legal position of the married woman had changed very little (a wife remained her husband's chattel, without any independent property-owning rights), her former importance in both the home and the workplace was eroded as the workplace became increasingly separated from the domestic hearth and apprentices took over tasks traditionally undertaken by the wives of businessmen and tradesmen. Suburbanization, the increasing availability of luxury goods, and increasing standards of living resulted in a more decorative purpose for many women, who were required to become their husbands' status symbols, and settled into an existence of hostessing and reading. Accompanying this change in social role was an ideological shift, whereby women began to be considered as inhabiting a separate sphere of emotional expertise. It was in the early eighteenth century that women were first constructed as custodians of moral and emotional virtue, as homemakers with a monopoly on sensitivity. Cast as experts in the domain of sensibility, finer feelings, and moral refinement, and offered a vision of themselves as discreet, soft, reserved and understanding, women were encouraged to think of themselves as queens in a domestic realm. Thus, women of suitable ambition found themselves with a subject to write about and an audience to write for. Novel-writing, Spencer suggests, 'may be seen as the literate middle-class household's substitute for the declining home industries which had once enabled the housewife to contribute to the support of the family'. It would be attempted by women who, while moderately well-educated,

were not educated in Greek and Latin; and the epistolary novel in
particular seemed an accessible extension to forms of writing already
being undertaken by such women in their leisure time.[17]

The sudden rash of female creativity, then, has a sociological explanation. Nancy Armstrong's *Desire and Domestic Fiction: A Political
History of the Novel* (1987) takes this argument as far as it can go in
arguing that the Wattian 'rise' thesis must be understood in gendered
terms.[18] At the very heart of the novel, she contends, are *female*, not
male, structures of feeling. For Armstrong, conduct books, educational
treatises and domestic novels in the eighteenth and nineteenth
centuries together created an ideal form of femininity based on emotional development, which replaced aristocratic conceptions of fortune
and rank. To explain the vast increase in production and consumption
of fiction by women, Armstrong argues that women's domestic experience, especially with respect to sexual desire, love, courtship and
marriage, promoted and was promoted by the novel. The desirable
woman became the domestic goddess, sophisticated in the technology
of feeling and supremely well fitted to impart values to children.
In Armstrong's account, the novel part-created and part-reflected this
emergent cultural shift. And yet, as other scholars have noted, literary
creation for women was from the outset a somewhat paradoxical
endeavour. As Kathryn Shevelow has shown with respect to early periodical writing, it was unacceptable for women to seek literary fame
through authorship: they had to relinquish at least that aspect of male
ambition.[19] Publication is not the most demure and passive of vocations
and, from the first, there was a tension between the new ideology of
femininity and the upsurge in women's literary productivity.

Watt's neglect of women writers, to which the above critics respond,
is a subset of a larger question regarding the precursors of the novel's
development. Watt spends too little time, some have argued, considering
earlier claimants: only John Bunyan – author of *The Pilgrim's Progress*
(1678/84), the most reprinted religious allegory in modern times – is
seriously entertained as a contender for the title 'novelist' prior to
Defoe. Doesn't this make Watt's account not merely a phallocentric,
but also a very anglocentric one? What about Cervantes, Rabelais and,
if we consider the case made by Margaret Anne Doody, a host of
ancient Greek and Roman writers? On this issue of which texts are to be
considered as part of the prehistory of the novel, we would draw attention to J. Paul Hunter's important account in *Before Novels* (1990).
The novel's emergence from other forms of discourse has often been
regarded as a process of *secularization*, whereby casuistry (the application

of moral principles derived from religion to human conduct) and soteriology (the discourse surrounding the salvation of the soul) are rhetorics taken over from religious writing and privileged in the early novel, as the cornerstone of faith moved from belief to conduct, from theology to ethics. Hunter, though, considers a much wider swathe of non-imaginative writing as relevant to the process. Hunter would concur with McKeon that we can't actually pinpoint the first novel. In Hunter's own account, the emergence of the novel is a two-phase process. The first phase occurred in the period from the 1690s to the 1720s, culminating in Defoe's novels and *Gulliver's Travels*, while the second was a much more self-conscious period during the 1740s and 1750s, when writers like Richardson and Fielding actually knew that it was novels they were writing and began to theorize self-consciously about the process. For Hunter, romance, as well as religious writing, has been artificially privileged in the ancestry of the novel. Novels should be perceived distinctly against numerous forms, many of them minor and non-literary, which Hunter goes on to discuss. He covers late seventeenth-century journalism (by which he means not only newspapers but also the various broadsheets and ephemeral publications that offered 'true accounts', 'strange and surprising adventures', 'horrid tales', and the like); the Protestant practice of 'Occasional Meditation' designated 'meletetics' by Robert Boyle (the practice of educing mean ing out of rocks, trees, clouds, comets or strange and wonderful prodigies, such as a whale being found in the river Humber); travel books, both real and imaginary; criminal biography; conduct manuals; and an entire wealth of didactic literature, on which he places particular emphasis. Beside the diversity of the material he considers, Hunter's most distinctive contribution is to make his case in terms of a reconstruction of contemporary reader-expectations. What was available to readers before there were novels? What developing needs did these readers have that the novel had to satisfy? Readers themselves, argues Hunter, 'gain the power to create texts by communicating, though not necessarily consciously or directly, their needs and desires to those in a position to make books'. There is not, in his view, much crossover between the reading public for novels and that for imaginative writing in more traditional genres such as poetry. From the first, novel-reading was perceived to be a less elite, less intellectually challenging form of entertainment, which carried with it moral dangers and was capable of leading young readers off the beaten track. Novel-reading was conducted in the solitude of a reader's own space, permitting a young reader to construct a realm of privacy both physical and imaginative, over which the parental generation had diminished control. In his exploration of who those readers were who wanted to consume novels, Hunter finds a group of 'ambitious, aspiring, mobile, and increasingly urban young people, both men and women' to have been the target group for this new form of fiction.[20]

To conclude this review of the 'origins' debate post-Watt, we single out two further accounts that approach the phenomenon from very different angles, but which both try to imagine what the process must have looked like to those immersed within it. William Warner's *Licensing Entertainment: The Elevation of Novel Reading in Britain* (1998) is one of the most original and inspiring books about the novel to have been written in recent years. Perceiving the novel's early development as a function of the need to satisfy new markets for forms of entertainment, to give new kinds of readers what they wanted, Warner sees the elevation of Richardson and Fielding in the 1750s not as a founding *truth* about the history of the novel – as though the novel had now come of age and achieved the degree of higher seriousness and respectability that later literary historians would ask of it – but as part of a market-driven competition to come up with a successful product. In this perspective, novels of amatory intrigue such as those written by Behn, Manley and Haywood (and neglected by Watt) developed the formulaic fictions that were 'overwritten' with a more responsible and conventional ethical system by the later writers:

> The very elements of these [amatory] novels that drew the scorn of cultural critics – their shallowness, their opportunistic seriality and shameless repetition, and their absence of compelling ethical justification – all fitted this new commodity so as to thrive on an urban print market of diverse buyers ready to pay cash for entertainment.

Notably, Warner combats the traditional literary-critical view of novels of amorous intrigue as constantly failing to be truly novelistic. Instead, he argues, these novels should be seen as 'instigators of a new contagion of reading deemed a threat in early modern Britain'. Intriguingly, Warner does not accept the feminist case for a gendered re-visioning of Watt. Readers are not addressed, in his view, under the category of their separate genders. Rather, early novels address female and male readers alike, apprehending them as indistinguishable units within a hazily perceived 'market'.[21]

Finally in our survey, we consider a group of commentators led by Homer Obed Brown, and including Alan Downie and Robert Mayer, who would regard even 1750 as a date too early to mark the stabilization and 'market visibility' of the novel genre. This trio puts enormous pressure on any straightforward sense that Defoe was the first English novelist, and teases out a number of the complexities involved in the process of canon-formation. As Mayer puts the case: 'Defoe presented his texts to readers as works of history and only gradually and very problematically were they read into the tradition of the novel.'[22] In Downie's view, it is impossible simply to ignore or to dismiss the fact that most of the early novelists that we are looking at either rejected the term 'novel' (along with 'romance') as inadequate to describe their own endeavour, or simply failed to refer to their novels *as* 'novels'.[23] Readers of Defoe in Defoe's own era, who did not have the benefit of clearly signed bookshops, would not have known whether his major works were fact or fiction, given that their title-pages didn't make this clear. These readers would not even have known whether any two of the works were written by the same author, given that Defoe's name itself didn't appear on the title-pages. In *Institutions of the English Novel* (1997), Homer Brown asks what it is that entitles us to say that the novel has truly emerged as a cultural institution. 'What is clear', he writes, 'is that the linear history of the novel as having an "origin" and "rise", the history we have been brought up on, with its genealogies, lines of descent and influence, family resemblances, is itself a fictional narrative – a kind of novel about the novel'.[24] In Brown's view, we can only say that the novel is a cultural institution when it is collected and available on library bookshelves. Anna Laetitia Barbauld's 50-volume collection of 1810, *The British Novelists*, and Sir Walter Scott's *Ballantyne's Novelists' Library*, a 10-volume collection of 1821–24, alongside critical histories of the novel as a genre written at this time, are the acts of canonization that really enable us to speak of the novel as having gained cultural acceptability. For Brown, then, the eighteenth-century novel was actually stabilized at the beginning of the nineteenth century, rather than around 1750, as more conventional accounts would suggest:

> What we now call 'the novel' didn't appear visibly as a recognized single 'genre' until the early nineteenth century, when the essentially heterogeneous fictional prose narratives of the preceding century were grouped together institutionally under that name … it can with some accuracy be said that the eighteenth-century novel was invented at the beginning of the nineteenth century.[25]

We will return to this question of the 'institutional' conditions that affected the development and cultural consolidation of the novel genre in Chapter 8 of our study.

For the moment, let us draw a line under what others think, the better to set out our own model of the novel's emergence. If we have pointed out some of the problems with the metaphor of the 'rise' of the genre, what might be our own preferred analogy? We might liken the novel's emergence to a scene from a 1950s horror movie set in Egypt, entitled, for instance, *The Curse of the Mummy's Tomb*. There's a pool of bubbling mud and as our clean-cut, shorts-clad Egyptologist watches in fascination, a shape slowly emerges from it, at first and for some time indistinguishable from the mud that is its element. Only very gradually are the contours of a bandaged mummy separable from the muddy amniotic fluid of its birth. And there it is, the novel. It is a thing of shreds and patches, carbon-dateable to the later seventeenth century, as Chapter 2 will contend. The mud is a kind of typographical primal soup, an amniotic fluid that includes very many ingredients: romances and various modifications of romance (popular chivalric romance, political and allegorical romance, French heroic romance); novellas; 'picaresque' fiction (called after the Spanish term 'picaro', meaning 'rogue'), a form of fiction that takes an unscrupulous protagonist through a long series of scrapes, crimes, confidence-tricks and the like; criminal biography; spiritual autobiography; imaginary voyages; and utopias. And of course, following J. Paul Hunter, we can add to this a wealth of non-fictional material: sermons; memoirs; scandalous chronicles or secret histories; broadsheets; pamphlets; newspapers; letters; diaries; conduct manuals – in truth, it is difficult to exclude any form of printed material as being wholly irrelevant to the story. Defoe has been privileged in this story by critics considering the matter in retrospect, partly because of the sheer popularity of *Robinson Crusoe*, an early bestseller, but partly also because of the kinds of fictional work that were subsequently discerned as culturally valuable. Our account will discuss Defoe as actually a very awkward writer to choose to inaugurate the new genre. His differences with the amatory writers on the one hand, and with conservative cultural critics such as Jonathan Swift on the other, render him very difficult to place on the map of the novel. 'The novel', though, is not a category intrinsic to the material itself, and it is therefore open to contestation and debate. Our perception of phenomena alters depending on the vantage point that we adopt, and the 'true story' of the novel partly depends on when and where one chooses to begin it.

Before elaborating further on our own vantage and starting points, we need to dwell for a moment on the vexed term 'realism'. In *The Rise of the Novel*, Watt provides a useful summary of what he means by the term. 'Formal realism', he writes, is

> the narrative embodiment of a premise that Defoe and Richardson accepted very literally, but which is implicit in the novel form in general: the premise, or primary convention, that the novel is a full and authentic report of human experience, and is therefore under an obligation to satisfy its reader with such details of the story as the individuality of the actors concerned, the particulars of the times and places of their actions, details which are presented through a more largely referential use of language than is common in other literary forms.[26]

Although Watt recognizes here that realism is a 'convention' or set of conventions, it is fair to say that he sometimes seems to forget this in seeking to define the novel genre in terms of its manner of representing the world. In his recently published *The English Novel: An Introduction* (2005), Terry Eagleton offers a characteristically arch account of the difficulties involved in deploying a term such as 'realism':

> To call something 'realist' is to confess that it is not the real thing. False teeth can be realistic, but not the Foreign Office ... [Realism] is the form which seeks to merge itself so thoroughly with the world that its status as art is suppressed. It is as though its representations have become so transparent that we stare straight through them to reality itself. The ultimate representation, so it seems, would be one which was identical with what it represented. But then, ironically, it would no longer be a representation at all. A poet whose words somehow 'become' apples and plums would not be a poet but a greengrocer.

For all the sceptical tone of this passage, Eagleton nevertheless accepts that realism is 'the dominant style of the modern English novel'. If the word 'style' here protects him from making the mistake of confusing representation with reality, it is a line that even he finds hard to hold, as when he goes on to declare that 'the extraordinarily radical achievement of Defoe's novels is to tell the stark, unvarnished truth about this world, without posture or pretension'.[27] Surely the term 'truth' here is far too unqualified? As Eagleton evidently discovered, the notion of 'realism' is not easily done away with in discussions of the novel. However difficult it might be to establish that Richardson's fictions are more 'realistic' than, say, Eliza Haywood's, such was certainly perceived to be the case by the majority of eighteenth-century readers. While we recognize the very considerable difficulties attaching to 'realism', then, we have not altogether expunged it from our vocabulary in this study.

Returning to our own model of the making of the genre: from the outset, we would emphasize that there is no *single* true story of the novel. If Watt tried to plant a flag in the novel and claim it for England, subsequent critics have laid bare the ideological import of his inclusions and exclusions. European precursors, especially novellas and romances written in France and Spain, and the English amatory fictions inspired by them, were in fact occluded from the beginning, as it became necessary in the eighteenth century to assert English superiority over France and emphasize a *native* tradition of achievement. The story that the present authors will tell is itself Anglophone in emphasis, not only for reasons of space and expertise, but because we believe that there is an important story here to be told. There are, we would argue, very good reasons for commencing our account in Britain, although we don't leave it as late as the eighteenth century to get the story started. We agree with those who think that the female-authored early novel plays a significant part in the story, and with those who argue that market forces also do, even if we are not quite content to reduce achievements such as those of Richardson and Fielding to shrewd appraisals of what would sell.

If our textual survey is not primarily European, our theoretical underpinnings are more so. As J. Paul Hunter's work makes evident, the novel is not a pure genre. It is a very capacious form, a generic mixture that 'contains multitudes' (in Whitman's evocative phrase) of earlier kinds of writing. It took some time for that mixture to settle, so that it could be perceived as having a distinctiveness of its own. We intend to make some use here of the theoretical writing of Mikhail Bakhtin. Our deployment of his approach to the novel will assist us in putting forward the case that the novel is not only or entirely 'made' of prose. In our view, the novel is influenced by cultural trends so broad that they embrace even poetry and writing for the theatre: imaginative writing, that is, which is not expressed in prose. As we will argue, then, certain developments within poetry and theatre at this time are both relevant and significant to the story. Who then is Bakhtin? The Russian critic Mikhail Bakhtin is perhaps the most influential theorist of the novel as loose, baggy monster. His major work was done in the 1940s and 1960s, but in the Anglophone world his importance has only been recognized more recently, partly through the translation of four magnificent essays, which were published in 1981 under the title *The Dialogic Imagination*. Bakhtin's vantage point is the Russian novelist, Dostoevsky, who plays the role for Bakhtin that one might describe George Eliot playing for Ian Watt and the Anglo-American critical tradition. For Bakhtin, the prehistory of the novel does indeed include fiction written in ancient Greece and Rome, and he sees the emergence of the modern novel not as an eighteenth-century English phenomenon but as a characteristic cultural creation of Renaissance Europe, with Rabelais and Cervantes as the major players. Bakhtin has important ideas on the nature of the novel and on the cultural conditions in which it flourishes. He argues, for instance, that when the linguistic conditions that obtain in a society make for what he terms 'polyglossia', the use of several languages, then all language use becomes interestingly self-conscious. Straightforward uses of language become subject to parody and travesty, and all serious language-use generates comic doubling, which provides the corrective of laughter and criticism.

In an essay entitled 'Epic and Novel', the first of the four essays published as *The Dialogic Imagination*, Bakhtin offers an account of the nature and development of the novel in terms of a comparison with epic. For Bakhtin, the epic and the novel lie at opposite ends of the mimetic spectrum. Whereas epic is monologic and monoglossic, dominated by a single authoritative voice, the novel is dialogic and polyglossic, representing an orchestra of diverse discourses and giving to no one of these a position of authority over the others. Epic represents an absolute closure and impersonality: its world is untouchable, located in an unchangeable past that is called to memory but that we have no genuine capacity to inhabit. Whereas epic is 'structured in the zone of the distanced image, a zone outside any possible contact with the present in all its openendedness', the novel is 'associated with the eternally living element of unofficial language and unofficial thought (holiday forms, familiar speech, profanation)'. The roots of the novel are folkloric, and all genres that permit laughter have a contribution to make to its development. Epic, by contrast, has no such contribution to make. Indeed, epic discourse takes itself so seriously that 'it is precisely laughter that destroys the epic', to the extent that laughter dissolves the distanced detachment upon which epic writing depends. The 'plane of laughter' allows us to walk disrespectfully around objects, perceiving them in undignified postures and from unorthodox vantage points, and it is the novelist's privilege to operate in a contemporaneous, non-hierarchical relationship to the material reality that s/he represents. Bakhtin's polarized model of the epic and the novel also has important consequences for the way in which we respond to the individuals that these literary forms portray. With regard to characterization, Bakhtin argues that the epic hero is 'complete', but that he is

> hopelessly ready-made ... he is, furthermore, completely externalized. There is not the slightest gap between his authentic essence and its external manifestation. All his potential, all his possibilities are realized utterly in his external social position.[28]

For the period that we are discussing, the distinction that Bakhtin conceptualizes here between epic and novelistic characters might be illustrated in the difference between, say, the strutting, posturing, attitudinizing heroes of seventeenth-century heroic tragedies, and a Moll Flanders or a Robert Lovelace – both of whom have a sense of the self as a series of social roles, requiring different modifications of persona. Whereas the social situation of many novelistic characters remains open to determination, and is frequently very different at the end of the novel from the beginning, then, epic characters are entirely lacking in this flexible capacity for social and personal development.

Bakhtin's own model of the historical movement from epic to novel is primarily linguistic. In the Renaissance, there was a shifting away from Latin as a master-language towards the use of different European vernaculars, creating the conditions of parody and travesty, dialogue and conversation, that help to constitute the novel. The language that is used in novels (the speech of a character or narrator, say) is represented language, that interacts with the narrator/author's viewpoint, and a conversation is carried on between that 'language-image' and the arguing, eavesdropping, ridiculing, parodying function of the narrator. For Bakhtin, all novelistic language is 'dialogic', part of a system of intersecting languages that interanimate each other. The novel, rather like a Renaissance fairground, is thus a meeting-place for a heterogeneous collection of discourses that operate on each other and on extra-novelistic language by parody. Unlike the sealed-off, impermeable language of epic, language in the novel is in touch with the 'reality' of the people.

For Bakhtin, then, the novel is a comic, relativistic, socially orientated, contemporaneous and heterogeneous form. For our own purposes, Bakhtin is more suggestive than authoritative. There are many aspects of Bakhtin's theory with which one might wish to take issue. Is the contrast between epic and the novel, in terms of dialogism, really so stark as he contends? Some would argue that theatrical discourse must surely be more dialogic than novelistic discourse – plays, after all, have multiple voices as a basic condition of the art-form; while others would argue that the epic itself is far less monologic than Bakhtin allows. Within the novel genre, some novels might also seem to be more dialogic than others. Early first-person novels retain the authority of a single voice, and later novels often confer that authority upon a narrator. While Richardson's novels might contain a plurality of letter-writers, they also incorporate a *dominant* voice, which cannot be subverted except through subversive acts of reading. Bakhtin's idealism in celebrating the absence of any authoritative, privileged voice in the novel, and in freeing us from the austerity of the classical body, is determined in part by the repressive political circumstances in which he was formulating his theories. One can see only a limited applicability of an analysis like this to the English material that is our main concern in this study. The comic novels that Henry Fielding, Tobias Smollett and Laurence Sterne write in eighteenth-century Britain do certainly owe something to their Rabelaisian and Cervantic precursors, and Sterne in particular might be considered a writer of 'dialogic' narratives, which are not clearly dominated by a single, authoritative voice. This model works less well, though, for the more pious and didactic works of Sarah Fielding, Samuel Richardson and Frances Sheridan, where the spirit of carnivalesque parody and folksy misrule seems less apparent, and where the narrator seems anxious to hold on to authority rather than to permit the mischief of parody.

We would want to employ Bakhtin in a somewhat broader way, however. We shall be using his term 'novelization' to refer to a cultural process which, we will argue, took place in post-1660 England, making for the mingling and mixing of different literary modes within and between all the major genres. We would accept the conclusions of recent historical and sociological analysis, that the growth of the English book market is an aspect of the 'commercial capitalism' that transformed pre-industrial Britain into a consumer society in the period between the English Civil War and the mid-eighteenth century.[29] Demand for printed materials is recognized to have been stimulated by the Civil War itself, and literacy rates, steadily rising throughout the early modern period, are thought to have been rising especially quickly, particularly amongst women, in the decades following the Restoration. In a society becoming capable of delivering a standard of living considerably above that of mere subsistence to an increasing number of its members, books were amongst the possessions that these improving individuals most wanted to consume. They were high on the list of such consumables because, as people grew richer, they required the trappings of what David Hume would call 'refinement', both to distance themselves from those who could not afford to acquire it, and to narrow the gap between themselves and those who had possessed it effortlessly for several generations. By the 1690s, when newspapers and periodicals had become a permanent part of the publishing scene, when women were entering the literary workplace as consumers and producers, when theatre was becoming big business, and when arguments had begun to be made about the unique status of 'wit' as a form of intellectual property, we can speak of the beginnings of a mass market for literature. Publishers were trying to locate this market with ever-greater precision and directness, writers were responding to their sense of what comprised it and trying to stimulate it, and readers were eager to participate in it.

The growth of this market, and the parallel rise in the number of professional writers who sought to make a living by satisfying it, had a profound effect on what was actually written. The generic mutations that we wish to specify to Bakhtin's rubric of 'novelization' speak to altering standards of plausibility. New generations of readers, deriving from different social provenances, wanted to read new kinds of stories – not stories with remote, ramrod-stiff heroes, but stories coloured by humour and concerned with individuals whose destinies might conceivably resemble their own. As expertise in classical languages became diluted, readers would increasingly turn to translations when they wanted to access the great epics. More and more, though, these readers also wanted their *own* plots. The kinds of stories that Aphra Behn, Delarivier Manley, Eliza Haywood, Daniel Defoe and others wanted to tell do differ from epic stories in the ways described by Bakhtin. In the last decades of the seventeenth century and the early decades of the eighteenth, much imaginative writing was aspiring to a new condition of narrativity, privileging the telling of relevant, domestic, and contemporaneous stories. In the theatre, the plots of comedies and tragedies began to resemble one another as the classic genres lost their distinctiveness; and the new tragicomic mixture itself became more domestic and bourgeois in scope. Even in poetry, the long-cherished conception of epic as the pinnacle of achievement was compromised as the epic increasingly came to seem like a remote and vanishing ideal. In the hands of writers such as Alexander Pope, epic is now parodied by mock-epic. In Pope's *The Rape of the Lock*, for instance, the epic becomes the domestic, and the storyline resembles the kind of amorous skirmish that is going to become the stuff of novel plots. To help exemplify the point that we are making here, consider the following extract from the third canto of Pope's poem. In this well-known episode, the war of the sexes is played out through the symbolism of the fashionable card game, ombre:

> *Belinda* now, whom Thirst of Fame invites,
> Burns to encounter two adventrous Knights,
> At *Ombre* singly to decide their Doom;
> And swells her Breast with Conquests yet to come ...
>
>   Behold, four *Kings* in Majesty rever'd,
> With hoary Whiskers and a forky Beard;
> And four fair *Queens* whose hands sustain a Flow'r,
> Th' expressive Emblem of their softer Pow'r;
> Four *Knaves* in Garbs succinct, a trusty Band,
> Caps on their heads, and Halberds in their hand;
> And Particolour'd Troops, a shining Train,
> Draw forth to Combat on the Velvet Plain.
>   The skilful Nymph reviews her Force with Care;
> *Let Spades be Trumps!* she said, and Trumps they were ...
>
>   Thus far both Armies to *Belinda* yield;
> Now to the *Baron* Fate inclines the Field ...
>
>   The *Baron* now his *Diamonds* pours apace;
> Th' embroider'd *King* who shows but half his Face,
> And his refulgent *Queen*, with Pow'rs combin'd,
> Of broken Troops an easie conquest find.
> *Clubs, Diamonds, Hearts*, in wild Disorder seen,
> With Throngs promiscuous strow the level Green.
> Thus when dispers'd a routed Army runs,
> Of *Asia*'s troops, and *Africk*'s Sable Sons,
> With like Confusion different Nations fly,
> Of various Habit and of various Dye,
> The pierc'd Battalions dis-united fall,
> In Heaps on Heaps; one Fate o'erwhelms them all.
>   The *Knave of Diamonds* tries his wily Arts,
> And wins (oh shameful Chance!) the *Queen of Hearts* ...[30]

Pope's poem, first published in 1712, augmented in 1714, and revised in 1717, was written to intervene in a high-society quarrel between the

Fermor and Petre families, that was caused by Lord Petre publicly cutting off a lock of hair from the back of Arabella Fermor's head. In the poem, Lord Petre becomes the predatory Baron, with Arabella cast as the coquette, Belinda. In literary criticism, the above extract would normally be produced as an example of mock-heroic verse, that is to say, verse that applies to contemporary situations the underlying conventions of the Greek and Roman epics. As such an analysis would suggest: by inflating the tone of a high-society spat between a young lady and gentleman from wellborn families and comparing it, through personified playing cards, to military combat as it might be described by Homer or Virgil, Pope subjects to graceful satire the essential triviality of the quarrel.

In the context of this book's argument, however, we would wish to make a different set of points. First, the fact that *mock*-epic poetry came to be written at all in this period itself suggests the weakening hold of classical literature on the reading public. Mock-epic might be deployed to satirize Belinda and the Baron, and thus contemporary eighteenth-century life, but the mockery also reflects back on the epic universe itself. Society ladies and gentlemen nowadays, Pope's poem is saying, concern themselves with fashionable trivia. One way to ridicule this is to describe genteel society in language more suitable to the warrior society depicted in the great ancient epics. However, one *effect* of doing so is to tarnish the dignity of the Virgilian and Homeric worlds themselves. It is just that bit harder to take *The Iliad* seriously once one has read Pope's poem. *The Rape of the Lock* is a prime example of the process of 'novelization' that we are outlining; of the gradual domestication of the literary agenda. The subject matter of Pope's poem, the erotic intrigues of the *beau monde*, will become the material of the amatory novel from the 1720s onwards, and there is much that is novelistic in Pope's own treatment of it. Card-playing, the specific substance of Pope's satire here, is an excellent example of a 'novelistic' topic, a topic that was pervasively treated across all of the literary genres. Before, during, and after Pope's poem, card-playing and its attendant evils of gambling featured in prose tracts such as Richard Steele's *The Christian Hero* (1701), in plays such as Susanna Centlivre's *The Gamester* and *The Basset-Table* (1705), and in poetry such as Edward Young's *Satire* VI, in his *Love of Fame* series (1728); and by mid-century, it becomes central to Henry Fielding's final novel, *Amelia* (1751). Card-playing takes its place as one of a wide set of social issues that begin to fuel imaginative writing across all genres: duelling; prostitution; master/servant protocols; social rank; love-marriages as against marriages of convenience or property – and so forth. Our point here is that, in many critical accounts, only prose forms of imaginative writing are considered to be relevant to the story of the novel's rise. In our own view, by contrast, 'the novel' is characterized more by certain kinds of discourses with particular ideological agendas, than it is by specific formal features associated with genre.

What we are suggesting here is that there are cultural shifts in post-Restoration English society that relate to the emergence of the novel as a literary form, and that require a fairly broad brush to sketch in. Not only are many species of prose writing relevant to the story, but drama and poetry also have to be included in the discussion. To describe the topography of the terrain in more detail than this would require a specialist study of its own, and we are sure that the reader who has followed us thus far is impatient with ground-clearing and eager to start engaging with novels themselves. Until now, we have been summarizing various challenges to Ian Watt's seminal account, and using Bakhtin to theorize a process of 'novelization' that we do not think most of Watt's challengers have quite put their fingers on. Particular social and cultural conditions stimulated the growth of a literary market, and where there is a market there will be entrepreneurs to satisfy it. Imaginative writing designed for this literary marketplace would necessarily be different to the kind of writing that had developed to meet pre-market conditions, the literature produced for aristocratic patrons and circulation in manuscript or limited print-runs within narrow coteries. Literary artefacts having the properties of what we now call 'novels' were the products of the new market conditions.

So let us now give a brief overview of the position on the novel's 'rise' that this book proposes to take, bearing in mind that this is only one possible way of seeing the matter. In our view, the question 'what is the first novel?' is the wrong question to ask. To search for a first novel is to give imaginative writing the mode of being that one attributes to an invention like the telephone. As a result, we have been saying, of deep structural changes in society, the implications of which can be studied through sociological, political and cultural analysis, imaginative literature in the post-1660 period became 'novelized'. Imaginative writing in many modes took on a more domestic, more contemporaneous colouring. In *Before Novels*, J. Paul Hunter offers a checklist of features that he discerns in writing that is the product of the processes we are terming 'novelization'. The most important of these features can be summarized thus:

1. *Contemporaneity.* Novels are stories of now, rather than of the far-away in place and time.

2. *Credibility and probability.* People and events are believable, and the laws governing fictional events are like those that govern our everyday world.
3. *Familiarity.* People are of a social rank similar to that of the majority of readers, rather than being heroes, kings and the like.
4. *Rejection of traditional plots.* Stereotypes in plots, character and naming typical of earlier, more aristocratic forms, are abandoned.
5. *Individualism, subjectivity.* There is a greater degree of self-consciousness and awareness of the processes of thought and feeling that affect individuals.
6. *Empathy and vicariousness.* Novels give the reader a sense of what it would be like to be another individual. Readers can 'identify' or 'empathize' with characters.
7. *Coherence and unity of design.* The incidents and action of the novel are drawn together by a guiding design and by a serious engagement with ideas that adds up to a presiding 'theme'. Novels engage ideologies: systems of belief.
8. *Inclusivity, digressiveness, fragmentation.* Within the coherence described under [7], novels also digress and parenthesize, but in a way that relates to a print medium rather than to the oral patterns of earlier romance.[31]

This set of identifiers issues, for us, in the conclusion that there were bursts of novelistic activity initiated by Aphra Behn in the 1680s. Behn, we would argue, was the first writer to exploit the market with a fictional product that has some of the characteristics, though not all and not incontestably, that are listed here. Delarivier Manley, Eliza Haywood, Penelope Aubin and Daniel Defoe were her most prolific successors, the first publishing in a 10–15 year period at the beginning of the eighteenth century and the others in an intense burst between roughly 1719 and 1730. There is then a hiatus. Defoe dies in 1731, by which time Haywood has worked out the seam of amatory formula fiction that she began to mine in 1719 with the publication of *Love in Excess.* It is a decade before Samuel Richardson works up a pair of 'familiar letters' – advice on conduct for young persons – into the epoch-making *Pamela; or Virtue Rewarded* (1740). *Pamela* might have remained a one-off literary phenomenon had it not been for the fact that Henry Fielding found himself with time on his hands. His career in the theatre ended prematurely as a result of the passing, in 1737, of a Stage Licensing Act that was partly designed to curtail his own satirical dramas. Objecting to the implied moral scheme of *Pamela,* infuriated by the kind of reader and reading that this fiction seemed to posit, he worked up his parody *Shamela* (1741) and, soon afterwards, published *Joseph Andrews* (1742), which outgrew the *Shamela* satire, and which contains an important preface theorizing a new species of writing: the 'comic Epic-Poem in Prose'. *Shamela* soon became only one single shot, if the most effective, in a controversial battle between writers dubbed 'Pamelists' and 'anti-Pamelists', the effect of which was to push imaginative fiction onto a higher plane of explicit theorization. Earlier writers had certainly written of their intentions with respect to their writing – Congreve had in the 1690s, Defoe had, and Swift had – but their main concern had been to address its basis in truth or fact. In the 1740s, Richardson and Fielding took the fictionality of fiction more for granted, and were much more concerned with the achievement of higher moral truth. When he poses as the editor rather than the composer of Pamela's letters, Richardson's concern is not to *occlude* the fiction, but to render it the more convincing.

Ian Watt, we have seen, neglected women writers in his account of the early novel. For Watt, the superiority of Defoe over Manley and Haywood lay partly in the fact that, in inventing characters such as Robinson Crusoe, Moll Flanders and Roxana, he had interrogated the nature of the modern *subject*. Defoe had, in short, produced psychologically convincing characters, of whom it made sense to ask: why do they do what they do? What motivates them? How do we understand them? The rise of the novel was an account of the rise of modern subjectivity, carried on by Richardson and Fielding. Authors of amatory fiction had, it must have seemed to Watt, nothing to contribute to such a project. Their characters, devoid of any real personality, were simply counters to be shuffled on a narrative backgammon board created by their plots. In certain respects, our own account concurs with this line of reckoning. As we would broadly agree, the only real interest afforded by such works as Haywood's *Love in Excess* is: 'what happens next?' Who will seduce whom? What duels might ensue? Who might die? Many of the amatory fictions produced by women writers at this time were simply too *absorptive*, and when their formulas became recognizable and tired, there was no reason to go back to them.[32] Defoe's texts, by contrast, could stand up to closer scrutiny; they had much to say about some of the most important aspects of contemporary cultural life. All the same, we would also argue that Watt paid insufficient attention to an imaginative recreation of the appetites of early fiction readers, and so did not conceive an adequate account of the emerging literary market. As Catherine Ingrassia observes, 'Haywood thrived in the open market and her rapid rate of composition suited the immediacy and topicality of her texts'.[33] Ingrassia's words capture both the significance and the problem of early eighteenth-century amatory writing. The strikingly immediate may be swiftly disposable; much of this writing was the entertainment of an evening. And yet, the amatory writers of the early eighteenth century were some of the canniest players in the emerging marketplace for fiction. Our next chapter will give detailed consideration to some examples of amatory fiction, and address the question of what it might have had to offer to the early modern reader. Our starting-point, though, is a work that orients itself rather differently to this fiction: William Congreve's *Incognita*.

2
Missing Parts: Fiction to Defoe

William Congreve, Incognita

By way of preface to *Incognita; or, Love and Duty Reconcil'd* (1692), which he refers to as a 'novel', William Congreve, best known as the dramatist who gave us *The Way of the World* (1700), draws a distinction between 'romances' and 'novels' that has been cited many times subsequently. The distinction is made in terms of the greater 'familiarity' of novels, their superior credibility and down-to-earth quality:

> Romances are generally composed of the Constant Loves and invincible Courages of Hero's, Heroins, Kings and Queens, Mortals of the first Rank, and so forth; where lofty Language, miraculous Contingencies and impossible Performances, elevate and surprize the Reader into a giddy Delight, which leaves him flat upon the Ground whenever he gives of, and vexes him to think how he has suffer'd himself to be pleased and transported, concern'd and afflicted at the several Passages which he has Read, *viz.* these Knights Success to their Damosels Misfortunes, and such like, when he is forced to be very well convinced that 'tis all a lye. Novels are of a more familiar nature; Come near us, and represent to us Intrigues in practice, delight us with Accidents and odd *Events*, but not such as are wholly unusual or unpresidented, such which not being so distant from our Belief bring also the pleasure nearer us. Romances give more of Wonder, Novels more Delight.[1]

As we observed in our introduction, qualities like familiarity and plausibility are, to some extent, relative. To the twenty-first century reader, Congreve's story in *Incognita* might not appear to perform particularly strongly on either count. Compared with the productions of contemporaneous French writers, such as Madeleine de Scudéry's

Artamenes; or, The Grand Cyrus (1690–91), though, Congreve's tale can certainly be said to be operating on an altogether more approachable level of experience. There are two enamoured young couples, Aurelian and Juliana (the 'Incognita' of the title), and Hippolito and Leonora. The two males have exchanged identities for various pressing reasons of plot. Far from assisting them to unite as it is supposed to do, this expedient actually places obstacles in the way of their unions. From the outset, the plot is an ironic reversal of the usual romance plot, familiar from Shakespeare's comedies, in which young lovers are prevented from consummating their love by an older generation that is determined to frustrate their natural inclinations, thereby forcing the youngsters to devise witty ruses to gain their ends. The lovers in Congreve's story are actually frustrating themselves by unnecessary complication. Here there is no conflict between love and duty: what the lovers *ought* to do is for once what they *want* to do.

This fundamental joke at the expense of the romance plot is carried into the narrative voice of *Incognita*. The story is told by a narrator who is familiar with romance descriptions and story-telling strategies, and who is determined to have fun with them. It is this flexible, approachable tone, and the re-positioning of the reader that results from it, that marks the crucial distinction between Congreve's 'novel' and French romance. Consider the narrator's description of nightfall:

> You must know, that about the fall of the Evening, and at that time when the *aequilibrium* of Day and Night, for some time, holds the Air in a gloomy suspence between an unwillingness to leave the light, and a natural impulse into the Dominion of darkness. About this time our Hero's, shall I say, sally'd or slunk out of their Lodgings, and steer'd toward the great Palace, whither, before they were arrived, such a prodigious number of Torches were on fire, that the day, by help of these Auxiliary Forces, seem'd to continue its Dominion; the Owls and Bats apprehending their mistake, in counting the hours, retir'd again to a convenient darkness; for Madam Night was no more to be seen than she was to be heard; and the Chymists were of Opinion, That her fuliginous Damps rarefy'd by the abundance of Flame, were evaporated.
>
> Now the Reader I suppose to be upon Thorns at this and the like impertinent Digressions, but let him alone and he'll come to himself; at which time I think fit to acquaint him, that when I degress, I am at that time writing to please my self, when I continue the Thread of the Story, I write to please him; supposing him a reasonable Man,

I conclude him satisfied to allow me this liberty, and so I proceed. (10–11)

Here, the 'poetic' description of nightfall, rendered in periphrastic or 'roundabout' language, is subverted by the deliberately 'low' verb 'slunk', and this conscious breach of literary decorum is continued into the scientific terminology of 'fuliginous' (sooty). The narrator then self-consciously intervenes to point up the comedy of the passage, in case any reader should be foolish enough to take its description of nightfall at face value. Readers familiar with Henry Fielding's novels may well recognize an ancestral voice here. Throughout *Incognita*, Congreve parodies the formulae of romantic fiction, guying the 'phatic' conversations that young lovers have with each other – a sublime form of talking about absolutely nothing just to establish communication – and exaggerating romantic conventions into a mannered comedy: 'I should by right now describe her Dress, which was extreamly agreeable and rich, but 'tis possible I might err in some material Pin or other, in the sticking of which may be the whole grace of the Drapery depended' (21–2). A reader who is in league with the narrator is inscribed or 'built into' the story, which naturalizes itself by continually invoking a kind of romance narrative by contrast to which it is indeed the apogee of the credible. At one point in the story, Aurelian loses his way in attempting to keep an appointment with his Incognita, but then inadvertently rescues her (she is in drag, so that he does not recognize her) from the murderous attentions of a villain. This is how Congreve evokes Aurelian's gradual sense of having strayed into unfamiliar territory:

> Now because it is possible this at some time or other may happen to be read by some Malicious or Ignorant Person, who will not admit, or does not understand that Silence should make a Man start; and have the same Effect, in provoking his Attention, with its opposite Noise; I will illustrate this Matter, to such a diminutive Critick, by a Parallel Instance of Light; which ... should it immediately cease, to have a Man left in the Dark by a suddain deficiency of it, would make him stare with his Eyes, and though he could not see, endeavour to look about him. (89)

The matter-of-fact, somewhat bullying tone that the narrator adopts here, towards an inscribed reader who is carefully distinguished from the *actual* reader of the text, again offers an intriguing anticipation of strategies that Fielding would adopt in his own novels, half a century later. Even before the end of the seventeenth century, Congreve has made available a tonality that would become extremely important in the subsequent development of what we now call 'the novel' – a tone of arch, self-conscious literariness. In order to establish the plausibility of *Incognita*, Congreve sets his tale against a form of romance fiction that he brands as both inherently *implausible* and, in its overblown verbal register, decadently *artificial*.

Aphra Behn, Love-Letters between a Noble-Man and his Sister

The accomplished, aristocratic ease of manner of *Incognita* is not a voice that Aphra Behn ever adopts, but she is no less important than Congreve in providing the early blueprints for the novel. If some of the critics discussed in Chapter 1 had been searching for *mothers* rather than fathers of the novel, Behn would surely have figured more prominently than she has done in modern accounts of the early novel. If the narrative voice of *Incognita* can be regarded as a dry run for Fielding's, Behn's formal technique in *Love-Letters between a Noble-Man and his Sister* (1684–87) might be viewed as a progenitor of Samuel Richardson's. The first part of this very long prose narrative, which in its original 3-volume publication ran to 1000 pages, is written entirely in the epistolary form, as an exchange of letters between Silvia and her brother-in-law, Philander, with whom she has fallen madly in love. In other respects, though, *Love-Letters* offers an entirely different reading experience to that afforded by Richardson's novels. The characters and events of Behn's narrative are based upon the circle of Whig enemies to King Charles II that centred on James Scott, Duke of Monmouth (Caesario in Behn's fiction). Silvia and Philander represent Lady Henrietta Berkeley and Ford Lord Grey, the protagonists in a celebrated kidnapping trial of 1683. As a Tory Royalist, part of Behn's aim in *Love-Letters* is doubtless to show the moral nullity of this circle who were capable of hatching plots against their rightful monarch, though the texture is complicated by the representation of Silvia as herself a Tory Royalist who attempts, in part one, to persuade Philander to abandon Caesario's faction. Noticeably, Behn sacrifices some of the plausibility of her love story in order to make this point. The political differences between the couple are so extreme that it is quite difficult for the reader to imagine them actually getting along. Nevertheless,

Behn's deployment of the epistolary method in part one of her narrative demonstrates the incipient strength of this manner of story-telling through letters. The correspondents here are supposedly 'writing from the heart', baring their souls in an unmediated form of communication that gives the reader direct, intimate access to their innermost thoughts and feelings. In the process, however, the letter-writers sometimes give themselves away, indulging in rhetorical excesses that betray their insincerity. In an early letter written to Silvia before their relationship has been consummated, for instance, Philander elaborates a fantasy of gender-reversal and abasement:

> I know not what opinion Men generally have of the weakness of Women; but 'tis sure a vulgar error, for were they like my adorable *Silvia!* had they her wit, her vivacity of spirit, her Courage, her generous fortitude, her command in every graceful look and Action, they were most certainly fit to rule and Reign, and Man was only born robust and strong to secure 'em on those Thrones they are form'd (by Beauty, Softness, and a Thousand Charms which men want) to possess. Glorious Woman! was born for command and Dominion; and though custom has usurpt us the name of Rule over all; we from the beginning found our selves, (in spight of all our boasted prerogative) slaves and Vassals to the Almighty Sex. Take then my share of Empire ye Gods! and give me Love! let me toyl to gain, but let *Sylvia* Triumph and Reign. I ask no more! no more than the led slave at her Chariot Wheels, to gaze on my Charming Conqueress, and wear with joy her Fetters![2]

For all the grandeur of the rhetoric here, which casts Silvia as a Cleopatra, dominatrix to her grovelling love-slave Antony (and *All for Love* (1677), John Dryden's popular stage adaptation of *Antony and Cleopatra*, may well be behind this), this letter reveals Philander's true level of opportunism and desperation. He remains in Caesario's band of rebels, he tells Silvia, first because he is in too deep to get out, and second because he might possibly manage to displace Caesario and win power for himself. The letter ends, though, with a character assassination of Caesario which confesses that there are actually no rational grounds for supporting him, and that those who do are part of a pathetic, self-deluded rabble.

Behind Philander's evaluation of Caesario lies another of John Dryden's works, his famous Royalist poem, *Absalom and Achitophel* (1681). The rhetorical postures of this poem – notably Dryden's hatred of figurehead heroes and the malleable mob, who are so easily manipulated by politicians – are at many points echoed by Behn:

> Neither is there one part of fifty (of the Fools that cry him up) for his Interest, though they use him for a Tool to work with, he being the only great Man that wants sense enough to find out the cheat, which they dare impose upon. Can any body of reason believe if they had design'd him good, they would let him bare fac'd have own'd a party so opposite to all Laws of Nature, Religion, Humanity and Common gratitude? ... no believe me, *Silvia*, the Politicians show him to render him odious to all men of tolerable sence of the Party, for what reason soever they have who are disoblig'd (or at least think themselves so) to set up for Liberty, the world knows *Cesario* renders himself the worst of Criminals by it, and has abandon'd an interest more Glorious and Easy than Empire to side with and aid People that never did or ever can oblige him: and he is so dull as to imagine that for his sake (who never did us service or good, unless Cuckolding us be good) we should venture life and fame to pull down a true Monarch, to set up his Bastard over us. *Cesario* must pardon me, if I think his Politicks are shallow as his Parts, and that his own Interest has undone him; for of what advantage soever the design may be to us, it really shocks ones nature to find a Son engag'd against a Father. (1:146–8)

In subtler hands than Behn's, self-revelation through letters will become a sharper instrument than it is here. Individuals will differ from themselves in a more nuanced way than does Philander, who proves himself to be a worthless, unprincipled hypocrite. At this moment, moreover, it is not at all clear that Behn is in full control of her discourse. It is unclear, for instance, whether Behn actually *wants* the reader to make this damning judgement of Philander's character. Such, certainly, is not Silvia's own conclusion. Quite possibly, Behn simply could not resist the temptation to put these arch-Tory sentiments into Philander's mouth, notwithstanding the effect that this might have on what we now think of as a coherent, novelistic 'character'.

In other respects also, *Love-Letters* is a curious work. Even today, readers might well be struck by the extraordinary candour of its testimony to the terrifying power of sexual desire. Whereas, in stage tragedies of this period, heroes and heroines analyse their love-versus-honour dilemmas in high-sounding phrases, striking attitudes that seem far distant from the *immediacies* of physical passion, in *Love-Letters* there is simply no contest between desire and duty. For all its high-society gloss, much of what happens in the work is venereal and sordid, more Jilly Cooper than Samuel Richardson. Desire wins out every time, making a mockery of the very idea of a moral code by which one might conceivably be able to live. Desire thus breaks down every barrier to its own satisfaction – except, occasionally, those barriers created by desire itself. When Philander finally conquers all of his sister-in-law's objections to intercourse and gains access to her boudoir, he is frustrated not by Silvia but by his own inability to act upon his desire. In the letter that he writes to Silvia following this fiasco, the idealized lover becomes the impotent male, ludicrously attempting to explain away his failure to perform. Philander's excuses pick up on poems written around the same time by the sexually explicit poet, John Wilmot, Earl of Rochester, and also by Behn herself – poems concerning 'imperfect enjoyment' which play upon the psychological and physiological complexities involved when minds fail to communicate adequately with bodies. There can, certainly, be no doubting Philander's sexual hunger:

> I saw (Yes *Silvia* nor all your Art and Modesty could hide it) I saw the Ravishing Maid as much inflam'd as I; she burnt with equal fire, with equal Languishment ... her hands that grasp'd me trembling as they clos'd, while she permitted mine unknown, unheeded to traverse all her Beauties. (1:183)

There is, indeed, no doubt about the *mutuality* of the desire between these characters. And yet, as Philander continues:

> I rusht upon her, who all fainting lay beneath my useless weight, for on a sudden all my power was fled swifter than Lightning hurryed through my infeebled veins, and vanisht all: Not the dear lovely Beauty which I prest, the Dying Charms of that fair face and eyes, the Clasps of those soft Arms, nor the bewitching accent of her voice that murmur'd Love half smother'd in her Sighs, nor all my Love, my vast, my mighty passion, could call my fugitive vigor back again: Oh no, the more I look – The more I touch'd and saw, the more I was undone. Oh pity me my too too lovely Maid, do not revile the faults which you alone create. Consider all your Charms at once expos'd, consider every sense about me ravisht, o'ercome with joys too mighty to be supported: No wonder if I fell a shameful sacrifice to the fond Deity ... I want [i.e., lack] Philosophy to make this out, or faith to fix my unhappiness on any chance or natural accident, but this my

Charming *Silvia* I am sure, that had I lov'd you less, I'd been less wretched. (1:184–5)

One can perhaps sense here the female author's enjoyment of Philander's discomfiture, and of the ridiculous figure that he makes as he declares the potency that he cannot prove, and is forced back upon claiming that it is the very intensity of his love for Silvia that has confounded his physical prowess. The episode concludes in a kind of slapstick comedy reminiscent of Chaucer and Boccaccio, and of more recent stage comedies, as Philander makes his escape from Silvia's closet disguised as Melinda the maid. Unluckily for Philander, whilst still disguised he runs into Silvia's father, who has been hoping to have his wicked way with Melinda and who, inevitably, takes Philander to be his intended prey. Behn delights in the contrast between Philander's impotence and the workmanlike 'briskness' of the Count, as well as in the homoerotic overtones of the fumbling that Philander is now forced to endure, as he adopts a high-pitched whisper in response to the Count's addresses:

I am no Whore, Sir, – No crys he, but I can quickly make thee one, I have my Tools about me Sweet-heart, therefore let's lose no time but fall to work ... with that he clapt fifty Guinnies in a Purse into one hand, and something else that shall be nameless into the other. (1:190)

At several points in the narrative, Behn creates this *Carry On*-style texture of bawdy slapstick, in order to puncture the pretensions of the characters and to bring the whole story down to earth. Throughout part two, for example, Philander's steward Briljard, who has been forced into a marriage of convenience with Silvia, plots to gain sexual satisfaction from his legal wife. When he finally manoeuvres himself into a position to take this satisfaction, however, he finds himself *hors de combat* because he has taken an overdose of aphrodisiac and is, as a consequence, too sick to perform.

What are we to make, then, of this curious mixture of a text? In the final analysis, we would suggest, *Love-Letters* fails to make the most of its opportunities because it brings together a group of characters whose amoralism and atheistical hedonism progressively alienates the reader. What exactly is the *point* of assembling this cynical and manipulative cast of power-hungry egotists? Even the apparent political message (Tory Royalists good, Whig Republicans bad) is blurred, because Silvia the Tory has, by the end of the narrative, lost all vestiges of credibility as an ethical touchstone. Later writers of prose fiction would develop much more satisfactory ways of directing readers' sympathies and attaching them to, or detaching them from, their characters. Some would even take on board the point that novels have to be *about* something; that there needs to be an overall theme that orchestrates the storyline into some exemplary significance. Indeed, from the standpoint of what would later be termed 'unity of design', a more significant pretext in the history of novelistic development is provided by a work that was published shortly after the concluding part of *Love-Letters*: Behn's short prose fiction, *Oroonoko*.

Aphra Behn, Oroonoko

Perhaps the first thing that needs to be said about *Oroonoko; or, The Royal Slave* (1688) is that it is an exceptionally controversial text. In his important study of the history of the slave trade, Hugh Thomas assesses the work in the following manner:

> Aphra Behn's contribution to the preparation for the abolitionist movement can scarcely be exaggerated. She helped to prepare literary people's minds for a change on humanitarian grounds. She was more influential than popes and missionaries.[3]

For Richard Kroll, by contrast, *Oroonoko* is barely about slavery at all – nor, for that matter, is it a novel:

> *Oroonoko* is ... not a novel; nor is it a quasi-sociological account of the conditions of slavery or emerging colonialism. It is in fact Behn's desperate attempt between 10 and 29 June 1688 to warn James II that if he continues on the path he has described since his accession, he risks suffering the same fate as his father [Charles I, who was executed by Parliament].[4]

In Kroll's view, to approach *Oroonoko* as a novel about slavery is to confuse the 'formal meaning' of the work with its later reception. As readers have often noted, Oroonoko's death is a type of martyrdom, which deliberately calls to mind the execution of King Charles I. Kroll highlights the Christological significance of the (female) narrator's mother and sister being present at the event, 'which emblematically

reproduce[s] the Passion when the crucified Christ is accompanied by
three women including his own mother and Mary Magdalene'. There
is, then, some encouragement to the reader to regard Oroonoko as a
divinely sanctioned royal martyr. Kroll supplies compelling evidence for
arguing that *Oroonoko* is a specific intervention into the political events
of 1688 – the period of King James II's desertion of the English throne
and the calling over of William of Orange from Holland to assume it; a
time when the putting on trial of the Seven Bishops for refusing to read
in church the Declaration of Indulgence exposed the English monarchy
to rebellion and takeover by the Dutch. If we interpret *Oroonoko* as a
novel, complains Kroll, we are likely to end up viewing it as confused
and botched. It is, rather, a work of 'parallel history', a story made out
of many generic elements that is rhetorically designed to enforce a comparison between the events represented in the narrative and events in
the real, extra-fictional world.

If Kroll's analysis is sufficiently engaging to merit the above summary, we do not ultimately concur with his arguments regarding either
the generic status or the actual meaning of *Oroonoko*. Even if the work
did constitute a 'desperate' political move on Behn's part, we would
argue that authorial aims or intentions cannot entirely prescribe how
such complex verbal artefacts as *Oroonoko* will actually be read, either
immediately or by future generations. For readers in Behn's own time,
we would argue, Oroonoko's blackness would necessarily have registered
as a signifier of otherness, even if not of racial difference as currently
understood. Casting their minds back to Shakespeare's *Othello*, Behn's
late-seventeenth-century readers could hardly have avoided viewing the
work as dramatizing a clash of racial, cultural and ethico-religious
codes. To endure beyond their moment, moreover, literary works have
to be re-interpretable by subsequent generations of readers in accordance with their current interests. For modern readers, *Oroonoko*
presents a fascinating account of the confrontation and intersection of
three different social groupings: white plantation-owners, their African
slaves, and the South American native tribesmen with whom they trade
and try to live. It is concerned with the cultural and ethical relativities
that emerge from this mingling of societies, and from the institution of
slavery itself. Our reading of *Oroonoko*, then, cannot be limited to its
precise political meaning in a particular fortnight in June 1688. While
the specific party politics of the period should certainly inform interpretation, they do not fully comprehend our present interest in the work.

Oroonoko is the story of an African prince whose wife, Imoinda, has
been forced by his grandfather the King to become a royal concubine.

She is sold into slavery when it becomes known that Oroonoko has consummated his relationship with her (thus breaking a tribal incest taboo) and when her continued existence at court has become an inconvenience. Oroonoko himself is captured into slavery under the cloak of hospitality by an unscrupulous English slave-trader and, by a considerable coincidence, ends up on the same plantation as Imoinda, in Surinam in South America. Although the enlightened planter, Trefry, does not treat them like other slaves (those slaves, that is, who lack royal pedigree), Oroonoko is repeatedly frustrated in his attempt to secure the freedom that he has been promised. When Imoinda falls pregnant, Oroonoko becomes more militant, unable to endure the idea that their child will be born into slavery. Having led a revolt that proves unsuccessful, he is recaptured and savagely beaten – a dishonour that he is unable to support. He tries finally to take his own life (having first despatched his beloved Imoinda), but his heroic strength is such that he survives self-laceration, only to meet an appallingly violent death by mutilation at the hands of the bloodthirsty Deputy-Governor, Byam.

Part of the fascination of *Oroonoko* lies in the way in which a variety of novelistic and pre-novelistic ingredients can be observed struggling for priority within it. A number of romance motifs and assumptions are strong contenders in this struggle. In a manner characteristic of romance fiction, Oroonoko himself is represented as supremely virtuous and noble. This nobility of character, which is a function of his high birth, shines through even in slavery. When his owner, Trefry, first sees Oroonoko, for instance, he perceives something 'so extraordinary in his face, shape and mien, a greatness of look, and haughtiness in his air' that 'he began to conceive so vast an esteem for him that he ever after lov'd him as his dearest brother'.[5] Judging by what we know of the empirical history of slavery, such a reaction on the part of a British plantation-owner to a black slave is almost unimaginable. It derives more from the kind of romance conventions that also operate in Shakespeare's late plays. In *The Winter's Tale*, for instance, Perdita, although brought up as a shepherdess, displays a majesty about her bearing, a natural grace of expression and deportment, that immediately sets her apart, and that bears witness to her royal lineage. *Oroonoko*'s equation of high rank and moral virtue is, then, carried over from the aristocratic assumptions that had informed much earlier writing. Also inherited from romance is the scale of plot coincidence that allows Oroonoko to arrive at the very same plantation where Imoinda is enslaved (and where she is already marked out, Perdita-like, as a special individual whom even the white men cannot bear to treat as a slave).

As the novel genre develops and strives for greater plausibility and fidelity to lived experience, it will seek to naturalize itself by focusing upon more *ordinary* individuals than these, leading more ordinary lives; and by banishing coincidences of such a massive order as Behn seems happy to allow.

At the same time, *Oroonoko* also incorporates a number of more 'realistic' elements that exist in a state of tension with the carry-overs from romance. The story is presented to us as a truthful account, and the South American section may indeed have some basis in fact. Although the evidence here is far from conclusive, it is possible that Behn herself spent some time in Surinam, and that she actually witnessed a slave revolt there.[6] At the outset of *Oroonoko*, Behn's narrator attempts to guarantee the story's veracity by stepping outside the frame of the fiction and evoking a familiar context that is shared by its readers. Artefacts and specimens from Surinam are now to be found at 'His Majesty's Antiquaries', she relates, while the native costume that the narrator herself brought back from the colony has been given to the King's Theatre company and is now in use to dress John Dryden and Sir Robert Howard's play, *The Indian Queen* (1664). In this way, elements of the fictional world are brought into continuity with the non-fictional experience of the contemporary reader (75–6).

More important than these early gestures towards documentary authentication are the respects in which the colony of Surinam is itself convincingly evoked in the text. By stark contrast to the part of the story that is set in West Africa, which reads more like an Arabian Nights or 'eastern tale' fiction, the Surinam section incorporates topographical descriptions and accounts of native customs and habits that might well strike readers as convincingly authentic. Even here, though, there is a fascinating and complex interplay between the plausible and the less plausible, between 'realistic' and overtly fictional material. In the reading, *Oroonoko* taxes and manipulates the reader's credulity. A useful illustration of this point is provided by the episode in which Oroonoko accompanies a party of white settlers (including the narrator) into the hinterland, where they encounter a native tribe. The narrator's description of this encounter nicely evokes the meeting of mutually strange peoples, the whites resplendent in their rich garments, the natives naked. As she relates:

> From gazing upon us round, they touched us, laying their hands upon all the features of our faces, feeling our breasts and arms, taking up one petticoat, then wondering to see another, admiring

our shoes and stockings, but more our garters, which we gave them, and they tied about their legs. (121)

As might also be expected, though, the narrator's own attitude to the tribespeople is somewhat ambivalent. While she makes an affectionate and entranced attempt to understand their language, customs and gestures, her perception of these alien others is informed by the kind of cultural condescension that characterizes a colonizing mentality:

> I soon perceived, by an admiration that is natural to these people, and by the extreme ignorance and simplicity of them, it were not difficult to establish any unknown or extravagant religion among them, and to impose any notions or fictions upon them. (122)

Yet the most astonishing construction of alterity is presented not *by* but *to* the Europeans, through the spectacle of the native 'war captains':

> For my part I took them for hobgoblins, or fiends, rather than men. But however their shapes appeared, their souls were very humane and noble, but some wanted their noses, some their lips, some both noses and lips, some their ears, and others cut through each cheek, with long slashes, through which their teeth appeared; they had several other formidable wounds and scars, or rather dismemberings. (123)

The war captains have come by their horrible mutilations, it seems, via a virility contest for potential generals in which each contender has to prove his bravery by inflicting an ever-more-painful wound upon himself. For the European reader, this pointless and illogical custom, that would render the successful candidate unfit for active service, is barely credible. As the reader might well wonder then: is this itself a 'notion or fiction' being imposed upon the narrator and, through her, upon the reader? Just what is credible in this story, and what is not?

From the beginning, it is apparent that the narrator views both the African and the South American native peoples through a Eurocentric cultural filter. To the narrator, for instance, the native South Americans convey 'an absolute idea of the first state of innocence, before man knew how to sin; and 'tis most evident and plain, that simple Nature is the most harmless, inoffensive and virtuous mistress' (77). Overlaying them with a template of Biblical and Miltonic conceptions of Eden, the narrator uses the tribespeople to represent a purity that contrasts with the perfidiousness, lack of honour and failure to keep promises that characterizes European society. Oroonoko himself is also deployed for the same purpose. By generalizing this point, Behn seeks to organise the reader's point of view regarding the relationship between (so-called) 'civilized' and 'savage' peoples. Oroonoko's confrontation with the slave-captain who deceitfully entraps him into slavery is a case in point. Oroonoko has been given the slave-captain's word that he will be set free, and because he cannot comprehend the notion of untruthfulness, he demands to be released from his chains on a promise of good behaviour:

> This was delivered to the still doubting captain, who could not resolve to trust a heathen he said, upon his parole, a man that had no sense or notion of the God that he worshipped. Oroonoko then replied he was very sorry to hear that the captain pretended to the knowledge and worship of any gods who had taught him no better principles, than not to credit as he would be credited; but they told him the difference of their faiths occasioned that distrust: for the captain had protested to him upon the word of a Christian, and sworn in the name of a great God, which if he should violate, he would expect eternal torment in the world to come. 'Is that all the obligation he has to be just to his oath?' replied Oroonoko. 'Let him know that I swear by my honour, which to violate, would not only render me contemptible and despised by all brave and honest men, and so give myself perpetual pain, but it would be eternally offending and diseasing all mankind, harming, betraying, circumventing and outraging all men; but punishments hereafter are suffered by oneself; and the world takes no cognizances whether this god have revenged them, or not, 'tis done so secretly, and deferred so long; while the man of no honour suffers every moment the scorn and contempt of the honester world, and dies every day ignominiously in his fame, which is more valuable than life.' (104)

For Oroonoko, truth-telling is sanctioned not by eternal punishment, but by the worldly sanction of shame. He can scarcely imagine telling lies because this is not the action of a rational man. In several places in the text, lip-service Christianity is counterposed to a rational morality which seems to have been absorbed quite naturally, without the need for any theological back-up. To a large extent, confrontation between Christianity, and a heathenism that in some ethical respects is superior to it, is the main theme of *Oroonoko* – what it is primarily *about*. Behn's ideological approach to this subject is not, though, at all consistent. It is riven by what the critic Alan Sinfield has taught us to call 'faultlines'.[7]

While the text tries to do justice to the alterity or 'otherness' of African and native Indian peoples, its anthropological impulse is reined in by an Europeanism that simply *has* to domesticate this strangeness. Nowhere is this more apparent than in the physical descriptions of Oroonoko and Imoinda themselves. Oroonoko is surely the only West African who ever lived who has a Roman nose, does not have thick lips, speaks in French and English, is sympathetic to neo-classicism, and is a Jacobite sympathizer. Moreover, as Catherine Gallagher argues, 'The reader is frequently invited to marvel at the fact that Oroonoko, *although black*, behaves just like a perfectly conventional European tragic hero.'[8] To this we would add that Behn perceives Oroonoko and Imoinda partly through the canonical cultural reference of the Othello story – a filter that is perhaps most apparent in the discourse surrounding Oroonoko's killing the thing he loves most.

Ideological ambivalence, then, characterizes Behn's handling of race and slavery in *Oroonoko*. This ambivalence is partly responsible for the complex patterning of the credible and the incredible in the work, which we referred to earlier. It is convincing, for instance, that what should finally precipitate Oroonoko and Imoinda into rebellion is the thought that their child will be born into slavery. As is emphasized in recent fictional accounts of slave societies, such as Toni Morrison's *Beloved* (1987), it was this consideration, more than the immediate harshness of their treatment, that pushed slaves into open conflict. By contrast, the speech that Oroonoko makes to his fellow slaves, inciting them to rebel, reads like an unconvincing slab of rhetorical fashioning – the more unconvincing because Oroonoko has himself been a supplier of slaves in West Africa and has had no previous objection to the institution of slavery. As the narrator notes, most of the slaves on Trefry's plantation are only there because Oroonoko supplied them in the first place. Oroonoko does, it is true, draw a distinction between being enslaved as a result of being vanquished in war, and as an act of commerce; but this is hardly a root-and-branch objection to the practice. Oroonoko is a noble savage, a Hercules figure capable of killing tigers in hand-to-hand combat; but the narrator's attitude towards him is one of severely qualified admiration: 'I neither thought it convenient to trust him much out of our view, nor did the country who feared him' (115). Symbolic of this ideological ambiguity towards slavery and the African, of an Occidentalism that reins in and complicates sympathy, are the frequent passages that deal with physical mutilation, which we touched upon earlier in relation to the native tribesmen. Oroonoko's sacrifice of Imoinda, for instance, is handled with a poetical tenderness reminiscent of Desdemona's *Liebestod* in *Othello*. When the (unpoetical) stink of Imoinda's decaying corpse leads Byam's party to Oroonoko, however, he 'cut a piece of flesh from his own throat, and threw it at them' (138), after which he rips up his belly and pulls out his own bowels. On the one hand, this illustrates the incredible physical courage and stoicism of the 'savage'. On the other, the manner of Oroonoko's death emphasizes the strangeness, the near inhumanity of a creature who is able to endure such appalling physical torture. Oroonoko may be admirable, the narrative implies, but he is not like 'us'. To that extent, he is barbaric. He dies smoking a pipe, as an executioner cuts off his 'members', ears and nose with a blunt knife, giving up the ghost only when he loses his second arm (140).

To the twenty-first-century reader, *Oroonoko* offers a succinct, dense, and highly suggestive proto-novel on the topic of racial difference and the enslavement of other races. There is, assuredly, no fundamental objection here to slavery itself. Behn's concern with Oroonoko is more that he is a *royal* slave than that he is a royal *slave*. The slave trade was still in its infancy in 1688. Horrors such as those associated with the Middle Passage across the Atlantic were not yet extensively reported. Later writers such as Defoe, and even ex-slaves who wrote their own stories, such as Olaudah Equiano towards the end of the century, would remain highly circumspect in their objections to it. Equiano's 'official' view, like Defoe's, is that slavery is a commercial necessity but that with good treatment and conditions of work, slaves would yield much greater profit.[9] Turnover, the endless re-supply of slaves, is usurping their profitability in commercial development, concentrating profit in the hands of suppliers rather than owners. (One would concede that Equiano's view as expressed in his letters is somewhat different, and that he had an eye for politics as the art of the possible.) Behn's treatment of slavery owes a great deal more to romance and heroic drama than to any sustained sociological analysis of its evils. She did, however, enable new ways of thinking about racial exploitation and new possibilities for prose fiction in analysing such social evils. She is legitimately to be discussed in the same frame of reference as Defoe, Richardson and Fielding and the maturer eighteenth-century writers of imaginative fiction.

Delarivier Manley, The New Atalantis

In the early years of the eighteenth century, Aphra Behn found a natural successor in Delarivier Manley, whose *Secret Memoirs and*

*Manners of several Persons of Quality, of both Sexes. From the New
Atalantis. An Island in the Mediterranean* was published in 1709 and
landed its author in the dock. This long work of prose fiction is
episodic, containing no obvious plot or single narrative thread. Here is
an example of the kinds of narrative pleasure to be gained from
Manley's scandalous book:

> [The beautiful Diana] had nothing on but a nightdress, one
> petticoat, and a rich, silver-stuff nightgown that hung carelessly
> about her. It was the evening of an excessive hot day; she got into a
> shade of orange flowers and jassamine, the blossoms that were fallen
> covered all beneath with a profusion of sweets. A canal run by which
> made that retreat delightful as 'twas fragrant. Diana, full of the
> uneasiness of mind that love occasioned, threw her self under the
> pleasing canopy, apprehensive of no Acteon to invade with forbid-
> den curiosity her as numerous perfect beauties as had the goddess.
> Supinely laid on that repose of sweets, the dazzling lustre of her
> bosom stood revealed, her polished limbs all careless and extended,
> showed the artful work of nature Roderiguez ... with softly tread-
> ing steps, stole close to the unthinking fair and, throwing him at his
> length beside her, fixed his lips to hers with so happy a celerity that
> his arm was round her to prevent her rising and himself in possession
> of her lovely mouth before she either saw or heard his approach. Her
> surprise caused her to shriek aloud but there was none in hearing.
> He presently appeased her and, with all the artful address of power
> ful love, conjured her not to remove from him that enchanting
> prospect of her beauties! He vowed he would not make himself
> possessor of one charm without her willing leave. He sighed, he
> looked with dying! wishing! soft regards! the lovely she grew calm
> and tender! the rhetoric of one beloved, his strange bewitching
> force. She suffered all the glowing pressures of his roving hand, that
> hand, which with a luxury of joy wandered through all the rich
> meanders of her bosom. She suffered him to drink her dazzling
> naked beauties at his eyes! to gaze! to burn! to press her with
> unbounded rapture! taking by intervals a thousand eager short-
> breathed kisses, whilst Diana, lulled by the enchanting poison love
> had diffused throughout her form, lay still, and charmed as he! – she
> thought no more! – she could not think! – let love and nature plead
> the weighty cause! – let them excuse the beauteous frailty! – Diana
> was become a votary to Venus – obedient to the dictates of the
> goddess![10]

Unusually in the case of eighteenth-century literature, such writing is probably *more* familiar to us now than it would have been to readers in 1709, whom it would have impressed as new and daring. Anyone who has read a Mills & Boon or Harlequin romance will have come across writing lineally descended from this kind of material, which the critic Ros Ballaster first termed 'amatory fiction'.[11] Manley's writing is erotic, not pornographic. It preserves a hotline to respectability by employing a classical frame (Actaeon, Venus) that simultaneously assists in creating sensuality. Diana's body is displayed to the male gaze against a backdrop of perfume and the rich tactile sensation evoked by the materials of her night attire. Manley perceives that in representing the seduction of a woman earlier described as virtuous, it is useful to preserve an ambiguity of the 'did she fall or was she pushed?' variety. If Roderiguez has 'his arm ... round her to prevent her rising', he also vows that 'he would not make himself possessor of one charm without her willing leave'. This equivocation between rape and seduction becomes a standard device in amatory fiction, beautifully encapsulated in the locution 'she suffered'. Mimetic punctuation, the machinery of dashes and exclamation marks that enacts the breathless submission of reason to passion, also becomes a standard typographical means of indicating sexual surrender.

For the eighteenth-century reader, this passage would also have had an additional source of interest. There are real-life characters behind the romantically named Diana and Roderiguez: respectively, Frances, Countess Scudamore and Thomas, the first Earl of Coningsby. Like Behn's *Love-Letters*, *The New Atalantis* is a work that claims to uncover the conduct of the English aristocracy at its present time. It also has an allegorical framework: Astrea, the Goddess of Justice (and daughter of Zeus) revisits 'Atalantis' in the company of Virtue, guided by Intelligence, 'to see if humankind were still as defective, as when she in a disgust forsook it' (4). Since 'Astrea' was one of Aphra Behn's nicknames, by which she was frequently addressed, Manley's publication was partly an act of homage. Like Behn, Manley's work has a Tory bias, and the roll call of the greatest villains in the book consists of the Whig potentates who supported William of Orange in his takeover of the English throne after 1688, and who, in the first decade of the eighteenth century, could appear to be threatening the moral fabric of society with their vast war profits and belief that they could buy anything or anyone with their wealth. Manley did not, we would emphasize, conceive of her text as a 'novel'. When she reflects on her project in the opening to volume 2, she allies it rather with the satire of Varro and Lucian, identifying with John Dryden's late-seventeenth-century defence of satire. Her business is to scourge the vices of the times and to point out those individuals who are indulging in them. It is this Varronian or Lucianic impulse that drives the structure of *The New Atalantis*, which is, so to speak, 'processional'. Astrea and Virtue are squired by Intelligence from vantage point to vantage point, where they observe and interact with a succession of people – numbered in the hundreds – whose true motives and conduct the figure of Intelligence exposes. This is an entirely open-ended process that has no necessary conclusion. *The New Atalantis* possesses nothing resembling a plot or the satisfactory sense of closure (or even the inventive *suspension* of closure) that modern readers have come to expect from their novels.

Not content with story-for-story's-sake, though, Manley also wished to conduct a philosophical enquiry about the relationship between reason and the passions in the human psychosomatic constitution, a theme that becomes explicit at the outset of volume 2. Here, Virtue condemns those freethinkers, Epicureans and libertines whose philosophy has corrupted God-given freedom of choice and pushed humans in the direction of sensuality and libidinousness. Indeed, throughout *The New Atalantis*, scandal-mongering and the exposure of vice are held in check by didactic impulses that condemn such practices, and by philosophical impulses that present the entire pageant of human vice and folly as a laboratory for testing out theories of the human personality. This, for instance, is how the story of Diana's adultery concludes·

As soon as she reached her [husband's] presence who received her with tears in his eyes! tears of tenderness and commiseration! she fell upon her knees more convicted by that unwearied, unexpected, ungrounded goodness of his than she could have been by any ill usage or reproaches! Indeed her very aspect was enough to raise compassion. The fire of her eyes seemed quite extinguished by the opposite element, water had gained the ascendant, her air was dejected, her habit forlorn, fitted to represent distress. The briars and bushes through which she had passed, had not only torn and sullied the fashion of her garment, but the lovely face and hands had suffered by their outrage. Add to this her being great with child and the conviction of her own conscience with her indignation at the baseness of her lover and grateful sorrow at the tenderness of her husband, which gave her a remorse so becoming and inexpressible that it was impossible for any eye to have seen a beauty dazzling as hers in such distress without wishing to acquit her of her fault.

'I am come my lord', (says she with a languishing sorrow), 'and willingly to meet whatever punishment you can inflict … If you take away my life I cannot complain because I have deserved from you the cruellest death! … Let me never again converse, or look abroad into a world, which I have so justly armed with occasion to destroy my fame … I will forever mourn! forever lament! My fairest hours shall be wasted in penitence! I will incessantly count my prayers and my tears and say 'em all for you.' The Conde granted her request. (250)

And why wouldn't he? Diana is a woman taken in adultery and placed in a condition of wholesale abjection, a Madonna/saint figure who gains Christ-like overtones from the detail of her face and garments having been rent by thorns, and whose very grief heightens her sexuality, making her an even more gratifying object to the male gaze. (There is a relatively short distance, one might think, between Manley's Diana and Hardy's Tess of the D'Urbervilles. Here, even if Hardy himself would have disowned her, is one of Tess' ancestors.) In a welter of sentimental forgiveness, Diana is thus welcomed back into the fold by her lord and master, her husband. Although some critics have found feminist icons in female writers of early fiction, didactic passages such as this, which both objectify and abjectify women, must surely give us cause for further reflection.

Emphasizing the didactic element in *The New Atalantis* should not, though, obscure the sense in which the text nevertheless takes on a primary function of the emerging novel: the articulation of forms of experience that are social taboos and that, *until* the novel, had no socially acceptable means of wide dissemination. This can be illustrated via the early episode involving 'the Duke' and 'Mlle. Charlot'. This story of the corrupting love of a much older man for his young ward is the first of many in *The New Atalantis* to deal with incestuous (or in this case, quasi-incestuous) passion – a topic that fascinates Manley (who had, we might note in passing, married her own cousin). The focus throughout this tale is on the way in which culture – especially the performing and the literary arts – can foster the erotic passions and therefore needs to be carefully policed. The Duke is first attracted to Charlot when he sees her acting the part of the chaste Diana in some amateur theatricals. Kissing and embracing her, the Duke at once recognizes the immorality of his feelings for her and thrusts her from him. In words that emphasize the incestuous dimension of the innocent Charlot's response, Manley relates that she 'comes nearer, spreads her fond arms about him and in her usual fawning language calls him dear papa, joins her face, her eyes, her cheeks, her mouth, close to his' (32). Thereafter, the Duke gives Charlot free rein in his library, selecting for her Ovid's *Metamorphoses* and directing her attention to 'the love of Myrra for her father'. He observes 'the young swelling breasts just beginning to distinguish themselves' as they heave with emotion at Cinyras' angry rejection of Myrra after he has possessed her (35). The Duke draws her attention to the most amatory of the ancient authors – Ovid, Petrarch, Tibullus – and even to sex manuals which are not named, but which are likely to have been similar to the infamous *Aristotle's Master-piece*, an anonymous sex manual that first appeared around 1680 and became the period's major source of illicit knowledge for young people. By implication, Manley distinguishes her own writing from such corrupting influences as the Duke places before Charlot:

> There are books dangerous to the community of mankind, abominable for virgins, and destructive to youth; such as explain the mysteries of nature, the congregated pleasures of Venus, the full delight of mutual lovers and which rather ought to pass the fire than the press. (37)

Although Manley's own writing would soon be regarded in a light not very different from this, she makes here a pre-emptive claim that her work is not pornographic or otherwise damaging. As we shall see in Chapters 3 and 4, such attempts to secure respectability for early fiction, by distinguishing it from other fictional forms that are not edifying or improving, become embodied in the writings of many later novelists, and play an important role in legitimating novel-writing as the serious art that it is now taken to be. Conceding that reading may be dangerous to the young, Manley implies that reading her *own* writing has a tendency to promote virtue. At the same time that she represents forms of experience (such as incestuous passion) that were hitherto unrepresented in fiction aspiring to be polite, Manley thus endeavoured to legitimate her own representations and to police her audience's reading of them.

This did not, of course, prevent her from actually *representing* the taboo. A similar narrative trajectory to that of the Duke/Charlot episode is later enacted in the story of Hernando and Louisa, where again an older man engages in a formal, protective, quasi-incestuous relationship with a younger woman and deploys a combination of sensuous and intellectual weapons in order to seduce her. Louisa is rendered pliable by being taken to the theatre to see an emotionally powerful tragedy, before being persuaded by Old Testament arguments in support of polygamy and concubinage that surrendering herself to a married man is no sin. Another example of breaching taboos, of saying the unsayable, is found in the section dealing with the Cabal of ladies. This bohemian group is first presented as travelling rowdily in stagecoaches, laughing uproariously and leaving behind the cares of the world. The figure of Intelligence is immediately at pains to deny the suggestion that the ladies of the Cabal are lesbians. Rumours to this effect, it is suggested, are spread by cynical and vicious people who cannot conceive of sexual innocence, and who are even capable of believing that Socrates and Alcibiades, the protagonists of Plato's *Dialogues*, were homosexually involved. Clearly, this is ambivalent: *everyone* believed that Alcibiades and Socrates' relationship was more than merely platonic. This ambivalence increases as the activities of the Cabal are described and the real-life women involved become easier and easier to identify (the poet Catherine Trotter, one of Manley's rivals, for instance, has her name linked to the Cabal). They are virtually a secret society: communistic in structure (all of their property is held in common), cut off from contact with the outside world, exchanging kisses and embraces, and fuelled by excessive wine-drinking. Within a short space, Intelligence is defining the members of the Cabal as opposed to nature – as unnatural. When they take in a novice, for instance, they 'strictly examine her genius, whether it have fitted her for the mysteries of the Cabal, as if she may be rendered insensible on the side of Nature. Nature, who has the trick of making them dote on the opposite improving sex, for if her foible be found directed to what Nature inspires, she is unanimously excluded' (156). Some of the women are rather masculine and several of them turn out to be cross-dressers, who 'wander through the gallant quarter of Atalantis in search of adventures. But what adventures? Good heaven! none that could in reality wound [their] chastity' (157). The tone here skirts dangerously close to outright irony, seeming to suggest that the women are in fact 'cruising' for sex. By the end of Intelligence's narration, Astrea finds herself just as confused and uncertain about the morality of this clique as does the reader:

> It is something so new and uncommon, so laudable and blameable, that we don't know how to determine, especially wanting light even to guess at what you call the mysteries of the Cabal. If only tender friendship, inviolable and sincere, be the regard, what can be more

meritorious or a truer emblem of their happiness above? ... But if they carry it a length beyond what nature designed and fortify themselves by these new-formed amities against the hymeneal union, or give their husbands but a second place in their affections and cares, 'tis wrong and to be blamed. (161)

Here again we see Manley's formula at work: using the narrative to air a topic normally considered salacious and denied to polite conversation (and of course to expose particular individuals with whom she wants to get even); treating it ambivalently, even ironically; and drawing from it a moral lesson that upholds the conventional norms of heterosexual decency and monogamous marriage.

It is not difficult to see why *The New Atalantis* should have been such a commercial success. Its efficacy as scandalous gossip about real people is readily apparent, but the reader also obtains purer fictional satisfactions where Manley is less committed to pillorying her enemies and gives a story its head. An example here is the tale that ends the first volume, regarding the dalliance between a young gallant, Mosco, and a Quaker girl, Zara. This is a tale of strong, elemental passion, powerfully told. What is so impressive is the convincing way in which Zara's naïve religious beliefs lay her open to exploitation by the worldly and cynical Mosco. According to Quaker doctrine, cohabitation is sufficient to constitute a marriage, so that although Mosco is already married, Zara is prepared to accept that his cohabiting with her constitutes an overriding commitment *to* her. Mosco manipulates her Quaker faith to make his adulterous lust appear as a sincere expression of love – though for him it is simply a rake's charter. When he is surfeited and sick of her, he is forced to explain, with some embarrassment, that the law of the land does not permit bigamy. In the treatment of Zara, Manley invents a plain form of speech that might be appropriate to her education. Dialogue is differentiated in an attempt to discern character:

Alas I was innocent! I knew none of those arts by which, I am since informed, the women of the world prolong and heighten the lover's passion. I thought it was a merit in me to love what seemed so meritorious. I should have believed it a fault unpardonable to have dissembled it. I was bred up in the plain road of sincerity; my heart corresponds with my manners. I know nothing so base and guilty as dissimulation, therefore speak to you for the last time. Things are come to that height, I can't bear to live and not possess you all. Will you do as you promised? Will you live with me? (125)

This idiom contrasts with the weasel words of Mosco, and although Zara's later suicide speech is melodramatic and theatrical, the reader senses that here there is an urge to develop character – to take a more *internalized* approach to personality. All too often, Manley's approach to character involves little more than employing assumed names as flags of convenience for pillorying immoral behaviour.

Eliza Haywood, Love in Excess *and* *Daniel Defoe,* Moll Flanders *and* Roxana

As we noted in Chapter 1, the year 1719 is often viewed as a momentous one in the history of the novel because in that year was published Daniel Defoe's *The Life and Strange Surprizing Adventures of Robinson Crusoe*. But 1719 also saw the commencement of an equally prolific career in fiction writing, that of Eliza Haywood. By June, *Robinson Crusoe* had gone through three editions of 1000 copies each. Also published in 1719 were parts 1 and 2 of Haywood's debut novel, *Love in Excess; or, The Fatal Enquiry*. Although *Love in Excess* was a somewhat slower burner than *Robinson Crusoe*, it too was a major seller, running into six editions by 1725. Haywood published no fewer than 36 titles in the 1720s alone, and in terms of quantity at least was a dominant voice in the development of the eighteenth-century novel. Why is it, then, that this state of affairs is not usually recorded in standard literary histories of the period? We have already touched upon this topic in Chapter 1, where the masculinist bias of all but very recent criticism was discerned, and where the influence of Ian Watt's account of the novel's rise, which foregrounds 'realism' as the primary criterion of novelistic achievement, was emphasized. Haywood and Defoe were, though, involved in a similar project to capture a market for their works. As John Richetti argues, the early fiction writers 'helped to constitute, quite simply, a new kind of marketplace for a newly aggressive fictional product'. As he continues:

> A commodity produced by cheap labour hired by booksellers and publishers to satisfy a growing market, popular fiction is nothing less than the central and initiating line of the novel. To varying degrees, the art novel written by talented individuals is only an occasionally successful protest against this marketing strategy.[12]

And yet, there are also important differences between the ways in which Haywood and Defoe set about trying to satisfy the marketplace. It is possible to discern that Defoe and Haywood were in specific competition with one another, and that they themselves viewed their writing in these terms. After Haywood published *Idalia; or, The Unfortunate Mistress* in 1723, Defoe felt compelled to respond with *The Fortunate Mistress* (the novel popularly known as *Roxana*) the following year. Obliquely in the Preface, Defoe refers to *Idalia* when he writes:

> This *Story* differs from most of the Modern Performances of this Kind, tho' some of them have met with a very good Reception in the World: *I say*, It differs from them in this Great and Essential Article, *Namely*, That the Foundation of This is laid in Truth of *Fact*; and so the Work is not a Story, but a History.

In the body of the work, Defoe takes further opportunities to distance himself from those who were writing in what he considered to be the less valuable mode of romance. As Roxana states when she is being wooed by her French Prince, for instance: 'it wou'd look a little too much like a Romance here, to repeat all the kind things he said to me, on that Occasion'.[13] Evidently, the standards of plausibility and verisimilitude that operate in Defoe's text are different from those that prevail in works such as *Idalia*. If Haywood and Defoe resemble each other in their competition for a market, their fictional products nevertheless entailed different ways of satisfying that market and of succeeding within it.

Since we will be exploring *Robinson Crusoe* more thoroughly in Chapter 3, we concentrate here on those of Defoe's novels that feature female protagonists, in order to bring out the different strategies that Haywood and Defoe adopted for capturing the imaginations of their readers. We begin with Haywood's *Love in Excess*. In the third part of this work, which was published in 1720, the narrator grows philosophical about the nature of love:

> When love once becomes in our power, it ceases to be worthy of that name; no man really possest with it, *can* be master of his actions; and whatever effects it may enforce, are no more to be condemned, than poverty, sickness, deformity, or any other misfortune incident to humane nature. Methinks there is nothing more absurd than the notions of some people, who in other things are wise enough too; but wanting elegance of thought, delicacy, or tenderness of soul, to receive the impression of that harmonious passion, look on those to be mad, who have any sentiments elevated above their own,

and either censure, or laugh, at what they are not refined enough to comprehend. These *insipids*, who know nothing of the matter, tell us very gravely, that we *ought* to love with moderation and discretion, – and take care that it is for our interest, – that we should never place our affections, but where duty leads, or at least, where neither religion, reputation, or law, may be a hindrance to our wishes. – Wretches! We know all this, as well as they; we know too, that we both do, and leave undone many other things, which we ought not; but perfection is not to be expected on this side the grave.[14]

The attractions of this message for youthful readers are not difficult to fathom. Desire, it seems, knows no limits; it cannot be controlled. Rational knowledge – the moral constraints learned through upbringing – simply cannot compete with the stirrings of the heart and the loins. Those who try to put old heads on young shoulders are '*insipids*', who lack 'elegance of thought, delicacy, or tenderness of soul'. It is difficult to conceive any message more welcome to those who wished to give full rein to the transgressive potential of erotic love.

The story that *Love in Excess* has to tell reinforces this message powerfully. In the world depicted by Haywood, a man's being married is no barrier to his desiring, and perhaps gaining, any woman who enchants him. Haywood's characters, certainly, do not feel themselves bound to resist their illicit urges. Just prior to the passage quoted in the previous paragraph, we are informed of the character Young Frankville's belief that 'it would be meer madness, as well as ill nature, to say a person was blame-worthy for what was unavoidable'. Love, as defined by Haywood and acted upon by her characters, is a form of laudable excess, which overpowers any possibility for the moral evaluation of actions. Via this permissive sexual ideology and the sensuousness of its descriptions, Haywood thus licenses the sexual fantasies of her readers. Given the private nature of novel-reading, the opportunities that it affords for auto-erotic reverie, readers can find endorsement here for their sexual fantasies in the imposing medium of print. Consider for instance the following passage. At this point in the narrative, the novel's hero, D'Elmont, has quarrelled with his wife, Alovysa, and takes refuge in the company of the new object of his affections, Melliora:

'You have done well madam,' said D'elmont looking on her with eyes sparkling with indignation, 'you have done well, by your impertinent curiosity and imprudence, to rouze me from my dream of

happiness, and remind me that I am that wretched thing a husband!'
"'Tis well indeed', answered Alovysa, who saw now that there was no
need of farther dissimulation, 'that any thing can make you remember
both what you are, and what I am'. 'You', resumed he, hastily
interrupting her, 'have taken an effectual method to prove your self
a wife! – a very wife! – insolent – jealous – and censorious! But
madam', continued he frowning, 'since you are pleased to assert
your priviledge, be assured, I too shall take my turn, and will exert
the – husband!' In saying this, he flung out of the room in spite of
her endeavours to hinder him, and going hastily through a gallery
which had a large window that looked into the garden, he perceived
Melliora lying on a green bank, in a melancholy but a charming
posture ... her beauties appeared if possible more to advantage than
ever he had seen them, or at least, he had more opportunity thus
unseen by her, to gaze upon 'em; he in a moment lost all the rage of
temper he had been in, and his whole soul was taken up with
softness. (104)

Here, readers can enjoy first the voyeuristic pleasure of access to a
private marital quarrel, and then, from the male perspective, the contrast between the harshness of a wife and the downy compensations of
a potential mistress. Opening Melliora to the male gaze, displaying her
as an erotic object, Haywood is an early exponent of what escapist
romantic fiction will continue to offer its readers through the centuries,
down to the airport departure lounges of our own time. A little later in
this episode, the narrator gives the reader the further benefit of her
quasi-philosophical generalizations on the subject of love:

Ambition, envy, hate, fear, or anger, every other passion that finds
entrance in the soul, art and discretion may disguise, but love, tho'
it may be feigned, can never be concealed; not only the eyes ... but
every feature, every faculty betrays it! It fills the whole air of the person possest with it; it wanders round the mouth! plays in the voice!
trembles in the accent! and shows it self a thousand different, nameless
ways! (105)

There may be little enough *truth* in this statement, but it is certainly
what many youthful readers might have wanted to hear. Lectures on
morality can have very little effect if love is as powerful as Haywood's
novel proclaims it to be. Blame, moral opprobrium, sermons from the
pulpit – all such attempts at ethical or religious guidance are beside the
point once amorous passion comes into play.

Haywood's fiction, we would argue, is Manley's without the psychological or philosophical self-awareness. As Ros Ballaster notes, both authors incorporate into their writings devices that set some distance between the narratives themselves and the level of narration.[15] Whereas we have seen earlier Manley's interest in tracking the relationship between a character's religious faith and upbringing and her subsequent erotic development, however, Haywood is interested only in the erotic biographies of her characters, as though these exist in a vacuum. As John Richetti observes, by contrast to the narrative voice in Behn and Manley, which 'distinguishes itself as a moral intelligence from the thoughtless, merely hedonistic characters in the fiction itself', Haywood's writing offers its readers an 'intense' but 'uncritical involvement in passion's white-hot excitements and deliciously unbearable tragedies'.[16] In Haywood, moreover, any discourse that could plausibly be ascribed to 'character development' or 'psychology' – or whatever else one wants to call the writing that, in novels, tells us more about characters than they can tell us about themselves – has gone absent without leave. As we shall now go on to argue, the crucial distinction between Haywood and Defoe can be made in terms of the different conceptions of selfhood that underlie their narratives, and the distinct narratological procedures that this entails.

Potential consumers of Defoe's *The Fortunes and Misfortunes of the Famous Moll Flanders* (1722), who picked up a copy of the work in an early-eighteenth-century bookshop, might certainly have been enticed by the prospect of a thrilling read. As the book's title-page declares, Moll Flanders was 'born in Newgate, and during a Life of continu'd Variety for Threescore Years, besides her Childhood, was Twelve Year a *Whore*, five times a *Wife* (whereof once to her own Brother) Twelve Year a *Thief*, Eight Year a Transported *Felon* in *Virginia*, at last grew *Rich*, liv'd *Honest*, and died a *Penitent*'. Yet generations of readers have found *Moll Flanders* considerably less sensational than its prospectus suggests. It turns out to be an extended, and deeply serious meditation on the idea of having a 'second chance', taking as its case-study a female protagonist who, from the point of view of conventional morality, has committed every sin in the book. Close observation of Moll's conduct, certainly, will not confirm the ecstatic hypothesis about love offered by Eliza Haywood. There is no emotion here that cannot be disguised, and no degree of amatory transport that is not tempered by pragmatic material considerations. Just as, in *Robinson Crusoe*, there is a kind of 'original sin' involved in Crusoe's desire to go to sea, Moll Flanders' founding 'sin' might be said to be her very early ambition to be a gentlewoman. Following her subsequent ruin, Moll offers the plea of 'Necessity' or need as mitigation for her unlawful conduct. It is her desperate circumstances, rather than mere personal 'inclination', that has forced her into these sexual indiscretions and criminal activities.[17] She claims, in effect, to be in a 'sin or starve' predicament – not always entirely convincingly, given that she never seriously entertains the possibility of gaining legitimate employment. Nevertheless, Moll's predicament is highly plausible, and her dilemmas realistic enough to draw the reader's ethical engagement. 'What would you do', the narrator seems to ask, 'given this same set of options?' Having once fallen from grace, and having embarked upon a criminal career, there seems to be no way back for Moll, according to the absolute moralities of the period. Defoe himself, though, has enough sympathy for the career-criminal to propose repentance as a somewhat creaky mechanism that enables Moll to have a second chance, to start again on the road to respectability. However ironic it can sometimes appear to modern readers, Moll's repentance in Newgate jail at least passes the test of being distinct from the kind of 'gallows repentance' that involves merely fear of punishment, rather than a genuine loathing of one's crime and a desire for a clean slate. Indeed, as Lincoln Faller contends, 'If Moll is not truly repentant, her situation at the end of the novel might seem unimaginably horrible.'[18]

Defoe, we would argue, gives very serious consideration to the question of how one could lead a virtuous life in such straitened circumstances as Moll finds herself. In Defoe's hands, the narrative exploration of this question is embodied in characterization of considerable subtlety. Much has been written about the part played in shaping his fiction by Defoe's Protestantism, by habits of Bible-reading that would stress the comparison of one passage with another, by his inherited interest in Calvinist soteriology that provided him with 'case-work' files extensible into novelistic situations, and (more broadly) by the accommodation of moral absolutes to the realities of life among the poorer classes. Our particular concern here is to address, and to attempt to account for, the differences between Defoe's own fiction and the contemporaneous writings of Eliza Haywood. Consider the following, extended extract from *Moll Flanders*. During this passage, Moll recalls how she stole from a child who was on her way home from dancing lessons:

> I WENT out now by Day-light, and wandred about I knew not whither, and in search of I knew not what, when the Devil put a

Snare in my way of a dreadful Nature indeed, and such a one as
I have never had before or since; going through *Aldersgate-Street*
there was a pretty little Child had been at a Dancing-School, and was
going home, all alone, and my Prompter, like a true Devil, set me
upon this innocent Creature; I talked to it, and it prattl'd to me
again, and I took it by the Hand and led it a long till I came to a
pav'd Alley that goes into *Bartholomew Close*, and I led it in there;
the Child said that was not its way home; I said, yes, my Dear it is,
I'll show you the way home; the Child had a little Necklace on of
Gold Beads, and I had my Eye upon that, and in the dark of the Alley
I stoop'd, pretending to mend the Child's Clog that was loose, and
took off her Necklace and the Child never felt it, and so led the
Child on again: Here, I say, the Devil put me upon killing the Child
in the dark Alley, that it might not Cry; but the very thought
frighted me so that I was ready to drop down, but I turn'd the Child
about and bade it go back again, for that was not its way home; the
Child said so she would, and I went thro' into *Bartholomew Close*,
and then turn'd round to another Passage that goes into *Long-lane*,
so away into *Charterhouse Yard* and out into *St. John's-street*, then
crossing into *Smithfield*, went down *Chick-lane* and into *Field-lane*,
to *Holbourn-bridge*, when mixing with the Crowd of People usually
passing there, it was not possible to have been found out; and thus
I enterpriz'd my second Sally into the world.

In this extract, Moll seeks to pin the blame for her dreadful deed upon
the Devil, her 'Prompter'. She divorces the act from her own agency,
rather as a slightly lunatic member of a radical Protestant sect might
have done. The impersonal pronoun 'it', which Moll uses to refer to her
prey, gives the impression of genuine colloquial speech but also involves
a disturbing objectification of the child-victim. Is Moll at the mercy of
a satanic 'Prompter', then, or is she driven only by her own, callous self-
interest? As the episode develops, a more materialistic explanation for
Moll's act displaces the spiritual one just given. Now, it is *poverty*, rather
than the Devil, that has forced her to commit the offence; and we see
Moll inventing an entirely fictional mini-narrative in a vain attempt to
justify her actions:

THE thoughts of this Booty put out all the thoughts of the first, and
the Reflections I had made wore quickly off; Poverty, as I have said,
harden'd my Heart, and my own Necessities made me regardless of
any thing: The last Affair left no great Concern upon me, for as I did

the poor Child no harm, I only said to my self, I had given the Parents a just Reproof for their Negligence in leaving the poor little Lamb to come home by it self, and it would teach to take more Care of it another time.

THIS string of Beads was worth about Twelve or Fourteen Pounds. I suppose it might have been formerly the Mother's, for it was too big for the Child's wear, but that, perhaps, the Vanity of the Mother to have her Child look Fine at the Dancing School, had made her let the Child wear it; and no doubt the Child had a Maid sent to take care of it, but she, like a careless Jade, was taken up perhaps with some Fellow that had met her by the way, and so the poor Baby wandred till it fell into my Hands.

HOWEVER, I did the Child no harm, I did not so much as fright it, for I had a great many tender Thoughts about me yet, and did nothing but what, as I may say, meer Necessity drove me to. (193–5)

Here, Moll proposes a series of moral justifications for her crime: the parents were negligent; the mother was justly punished for her vanity in sending the child to dancing school in her finery; there was probably a maid whose attention was captivated by her 'Fellow'. By the end of the episode, she is also speaking of the child in orthodox Christian imagery as a 'poor little Lamb' and a 'poor Baby', casting herself as a good shepherdess, rather than as an agent of the devil. How, finally, are we to assess Moll's oscillating yet self-justifying account of her most recent crime? The reader of this passage is, we would suggest, offered a complex depiction of personality in action. Such, Defoe seems to say, are the ways in which criminals rationalize their conduct, ranging from an almost schizophrenic claim of hearing voices, through a momentary acceptance of personal responsibility, to a materially based sense of *societal* responsibility, to a psychological self-justification that turns the vice into a virtual virtue.

Both in its circumstantial particularity of description and its evocation of an individual consciousness, this passage from *Moll Flanders* exemplifies what readers of novels respond to as 'realistic'. Recent critics, especially feminist critics, have wished not to distinguish between Haywood and Defoe on the Wattian grounds of 'realism' because, as we have agreed, it is a notoriously slippery term to define and has sometimes been used as a means of suppressing women's writing. There is, nevertheless, an enormous difference in the experience of reading these authors, which it is our critical duty to try to explain. Defoe invites us to read, not only for the story, but for the involved reflections to which that story gives rise. Defoe's next novel featuring a female protagonist, *Roxana* (1724), is structured around *relationships* rather than plot-events – five significant heterosexual bonds, to each of which substantial discourse is apportioned: relationships with her first husband, her landlord the English jeweller, a French Prince, a Dutch merchant and an English Lord. Three of them, the first husband, the French Prince and the merchant, exert an influence on the narrative beyond the termination of their relationships with Roxana; indeed the Dutch merchant later marries her. This marriage puts an end to the novel's interest in the socio-sexual economy of partnerships and its last phase is dominated by Roxana's daughter Susan's obsessive search for identity, her single-minded quest to make Roxana own up to maternity. For the last third of the narrative, Roxana's Magwitchian desire to benefit her children, counterbalanced by what she experiences as an absolute requirement of anonymity, develops as a powerful nemesis – the price she has to pay for her material prosperity. The merchant's first proposal of marriage to the pregnant Roxana involves her in articulating views about matrimony very far indeed from the cultural norms of her own era, and forces the reader to pose questions that are quite shocking from those normative perspectives:

> I told him, I had, perhaps, differing Notions of Matrimony, from what the receiv'd Custom had given us of it; that I thought a Woman was a free Agent, as well as a Man, and was born free, and cou'd she manage herself suitably, might enjoy that Liberty to as much Purpose as the Men do; that the Laws of Matrimony were indeed, otherwise, and Mankind at this time, acted quite upon other Principles; and those such, that a Woman gave herself entirely away from herself, in Marriage, and capitulated only to be, at best, but *an Upper-Servant*, and from the time she took the Man, she was no better or worse than the Servant among the *Israelites*, who had his Ears bor'd, *that is*, nail'd to the Door-Post; who by that Act, give himself up to be a Servant during Life.[19]

Roxana's articulation of the view that a married woman is in effect a slave is one that she herself condemns as wilful and inauthentic: she confesses that she only takes this position in order to protect her separate property. Here, the retrospective first-person narrative articulates this self-division in a way that Haywood's omniscient tale-telling is neither able to do nor intends to do. The entire novel is about the incongruence between Roxana's outward reality – her material circumstances – and her inner state of being. She is rich, but she is not happy. In *Roxana*, the self splits into a series of social roles as the individual is forced to protect her past history and her innermost feelings from those closest to her. Even penitence is not a potent enough magic to cure this self-division: hence the novel's insistence at various points on a distinction between genuine and fake penitence that is much more anguished than anything to be found even in *Moll Flanders*. Where Haywood drives on her fast-moving plots, Defoe writes more static 'scenes' that permit the attribution of considerable discourse to discussion, reflection and self-analysis. The retrospective narrative permits Roxana both to represent her ideology and to comment on it from the vantage point of maturity and experience.

Defoe's whore-protagonists are delineated with sufficient nuance and complexity to contribute to an ongoing debate about how the social problem of prostitution is to be treated. Whereas in pre-novelistic Britain, unchaste women were typically represented as rupturing acceptable moral norms, perversely and irreligiously privileging the needs of the body over those of the soul, Defoe's extended treatment of their predicament transfers some of the burden of guilt onto the social structures within which they lived. Haywood's aristocratic protagonists, by contrast, appear largely autonomous with respect to moral and legal laws, able to flout them at will, as the power of love requires that they must. Defoe's circumstantial and material account of the whore-figure contributed greatly to the perception that women were often prostituted by circumstances beyond their control. Here is another example of what we earlier called 'novelization' at work: novels contributing to a process that the historian Paul Langford describes as a shift, in the later eighteenth century, from private individual acts of charity, to the setting up of charities on a public, institutional foundation, of which the establishment of corrective facilities for 'penitent prostitutes' was an important facet.[20] A measure of the difference between the fictions of Defoe and Haywood resides in the difficulty one finds in thinking that Haywood's fiction could have contributed so signally to such an exchange of cultural energy between the novel and extra-fictional institutions. It was Defoe's understanding of these new conditions of selfhood, and in particular his novelistic manipulation of the distinction between the public and the private self – which adds up to the invention of a psychological 'depth model' for novelistic characterization – that distinguished his fictional writing most clearly from that of Eliza Haywood.

3
Novels and Anti-novels:
Contesting Fictions

A recent newspaper survey published in *The Guardian* recorded the finding that 81 per cent of a sample of young people between the ages of 18–24 could not name 3 novels by Charles Dickens. This was taken to be an index of educational failure, a clear indication that today's youths are know-nothings, ignorant of the 'classic' landmarks of their cultural heritage. Such a view is somewhat ironic given that, in the early phase of its development, the novel had to struggle hard against a powerful anti-novelistic discourse in order to gain *any* kind of cultural respectability. When did this situation begin to change? When did the novel begin to be taken seriously as an art form, to the extent that, by the millennium, ignorance of its most esteemed practitioners can be regarded as a touchstone of national malaise? The year 1884 was clearly significant, because in that year Sir Walter Besant gave a lecture at the Royal Institution setting out the proposition 'that Fiction is an Art in every way worthy to be called the sister and the equal of the Arts of Painting, Sculpture, Music, and Poetry'.[1] Besant's proposition is less important in itself than for the fact that it stimulated Henry James to write his landmark essay 'The Art of Fiction' (1884), in which he advances a manifesto for serious fiction:

> Only a short time ago it might have been supposed that the English novel was not what the French call *discutable*. It had no air of having a theory, a conviction, a consciousness of itself behind it – of being the expression of an artistic faith, the result of choice and comparison… During the period I have alluded to there was a comfortable, good-humoured feeling abroad that a novel is a novel, as a pudding is a pudding, and that our only business with it could be to swallow it … [The novel] must take itself seriously for the public to take it so.[2]

It took a long time for the novel either to take itself seriously, or to be taken seriously. Throughout most of the eighteenth century, there was a powerful discourse of opposition to the reading and writing of prose fiction that represented it as dangerously disturbing to established social hierarchies, associating it with rebellion and sexual promiscuity. In Alexander Pope's satirical poem, *The Dunciad* (1728), for instance, Eliza Haywood, whose writing we discussed in Chapter 2, is iconically represented as having 'Two babes of love close clinging to her waste.'[3] Her profession, clearly, has loosened her morals. She is offered as first prize in the high-pissing contest between the publishers Edmund Curll and Thomas Osborne. Shortly afterwards, Haywood also became one of Fielding's satiric targets in *The Author's Farce* (1730). In the play, Haywood appears as the ghost of 'Mrs Novel', who delivers an aria informing us, improbably, that she has died a maid for love, but admitting, more probably, that she would rather have lost her maidenhead and kept her breath. Many visual as well as verbal representations attest to the continuing influence of the bias against novel-reading. In Hogarth's 1736 paired illustrations *Before* and *After*, the sexual availability of the young woman is connected to the fact that she has on her dressing-table volumes entitled 'Novels' and 'Rochester' (the libertine poet), outperforming one called *The Practice of Piety*. As we will explore more fully in our conclusion, Richard Brinsley Sheridan's *The Rivals* (1775) shows the character Lydia Languish ordering her maid, Lucy, to hide the books that she has just acquired from a circulating library before the entrance of her aunt, Mrs Malaprop. This action in Sheridan's play is evidence of changing times. On the side of youth against age as the comic dramatist invariably is, Sheridan in the 1770s can send up the anti-novel discourse, associating it with killjoy fuddy-duddies and maiden aunts.

In truth, the novel had been inoculating itself against the anti-novel discourse almost from its earliest days. Michael McKeon registers the important point that 'the novel is, with the essay, the only genre to have emerged under the conditions of epistemological and historiographic self-consciousness that characterise the modern period'.[4] From the start, it was a narcissistic form, always looking at itself and taking itself more seriously than some hostile readers could be persuaded to. As we have already begun to observe, in its earliest phase in England the novel laid claims to its own importance by separating itself from previous kinds of fiction, particularly those that, at the time, were often imprecisely labelled as 'romances' or 'novels', or even as both. In Chapter 2, we saw how Congreve made just such a distinction between the new 'novel' and the old 'romance' in the last decade of the seventeenth century, and that the same distinction is implicit in *The New Atalantis*, where Manley uses a narrative metalanguage to distinguish her own prose fiction from the corrupting erotic works that the Duke recommends to the innocent Charlot. Examples, indeed, abound. An intriguing instance of such generic negotiation is provided by Lewis Theobald's *The History of the Loves of Antiochus and Stratonice* (1717). In putting together a potboiling account of an ancient exemplar of paternal tenderness – the Emperor Seleucus giving his wife Stratonice to his own son, Antiochus – Theobald not surprisingly became concerned that the story did not sit well with Christian notions of morality. His own version of the story therefore bent the historical facts, by placing Seleucus only on the *brink* of marriage to Stratonice. Significantly, Theobald's escape route was furnished by a sleight of genre. As the author reflected: 'In this Tract ... which I propos'd as a *Novel* rather than *History*, I accounted my self a Master of my Story.'[5] For Theobald, the term 'novel' thus licensed a radical departure from historical fact – though only, perhaps, in the interests of sound morality.

It is in the context of the novel/anti-novel discourse that we need to set the productive rivalry between Daniel Defoe and Jonathan Swift for mastery over the early phase of the novel's development. Surprisingly, the two authors appear never to have met. However, as Defoe's most recent biographer, Maximillian Novak, makes clear, a complex system of rivalry developed between them:

> Defoe considered Swift a member of the High Church and an enemy of the Dissenters. Defoe was also one of Swift's early targets, and took mortal offence at Swift's attacks on his learning and intelligence. He accused Swift of lacking manners as well as real learning in matters of economics, and boasted of his own knowledge of five languages, mathematics, logic, geography, and astronomy.[6]

All of Defoe's prose fiction was written in a short, intense burst between December 1718 and February 1724, *Robinson Crusoe* not being the first of these works. Despite the repeated claims that are made for it as the very first novel, *Crusoe* was not, it might be argued, even *Defoe's* first novel. His *Memoirs of Major Alexander Ramkins*, published in December 1718, possibly deserves that honour. *Crusoe* was, though, the work of a well-rounded, universally talented writer. Competing for readers against Haywood's *Love in Excess*, *Crusoe* went into four authorized editions between its date of publication, 25 April 1719, and 7 August of that year. Novak's biography lends support to the view that Defoe's market share was based on the appeal of a new kind of serious realist fiction.[7] Developing the discussion of *Moll Flanders* and *Roxana* in Chapter 2, in what follows we analyse *Robinson Crusoe* as a novel that developed a new account of subjectivity; a representation of selfhood that is recognizably 'modern'. In that very modernity lay the novel's challenge to writers such as Jonathan Swift, whose temperament and ideology were set entirely against it. As we will go on to argue, Swift's *Gulliver's Travels* is something of a paradox: a novel that sets itself up as an anti-novel. As this paradox also implies, however: had Swift had his way, *Gulliver's Travels* would have put an early end to the history of the novel.

Daniel Defoe, Robinson Crusoe

For the purposes of analysis, we begin by suggesting that the existential journey that is made by Robinson Crusoe can be divided into seven phases, which we might entitle Disobedience, Slavery, Solitude, Faith, Doubt, Society and Deliverance. The opening phase of the novel is dominated by what Crusoe later calls his 'original sin' – his refusal to obey his father's will and settle comfortably in the middle station of life. This is described partly in terms of psychomachia – 'tho' I had several times loud calls from my reason and my more composed judgment to go home, yet I had no power to do it' – and partly in terms of predestination – 'a secret overruling decree'.[8] Crusoe's becoming a seafarer is considerably overdetermined. Does it constitute a supreme act of will, which overrides his 'judgment'? Or is it a 'decreed unavoidable misery ... which it was impossible ... to escape', and thus the very *extinction* of will? Crusoe's first Captain distinguishes between himself and Crusoe in terms of his 'calling': the Captain has a vocation, and therefore a duty to put to sea, whereas Crusoe does not. The misfortunes of his first voyage are so great as to be 'a plain and visible token' that he should *not* become a seafarer – so much so that his decision to become one marks him out as a modern Jonah, an 'unhappy wretch' who will bring misfortune upon any ship's crew because he opposes the 'visible hand of Heaven'. By the end of the first phase of his journey, the reader is unsure whether Crusoe's departure from his paternal home is the result of personal determination, religious *pre*determination (the hand of fate or Providence), or an irreligious 'evil influence' (37–8). T' initial uncertainty over his motivating force will have ongoing conse quences in Crusoe's story.

Phase two of the story concerns Crusoe's enslavement and escape, his sale of Xury, and his setting himself up as a planter in Brazil. This phase is unremarkable, except for some possible ironies of circumstance. It is mainly his isolation, as an expatriate planter, that precipitates Crusoe into going to sea again. As he reflects: 'I had no body to converse with ... and I used to say I lived just like a man cast away upon some desolate island, that has no body there but himself' (56). One might imagine, therefore, that when Crusoe actually *is* shipwrecked on a desolate island, his principal terror will be isolation. In the event, it turns out to be other human beings. Having been enslaved by Moors, one might also imagine that it will not be a voyage 'related to the buying negroes' that takes Crusoe aboard another ship (59). He is though, at this point, remarkably obtuse. Selling Xury to the Portuguese sea-captain ought perhaps to be a moral dilemma for Crusoe, but it is not presented as such. Xury, we are told, is willing to go under new management and does not object to turning Christian; while the Portuguese captain has given abundant evidence of his humanity. Significant here is Defoe's own attitude to slavery, as expressed for instance in the second volume of *The Family Instructor* (1718). As Novak emphasizes in relation to this work, while Defoe advocated the slave trade as a way of increasing national prosperity, he insisted on good treatment of individual slaves.[9] On this issue, and on the issue of colonialism itself, Defoe's views would count as 'enlightened' in the period. If he was in favour of both, he also stressed the need for humanity in their administration. And so Crusoe sets off for Guinea, only to be shipwrecked on an island that turns out to be somewhere in the Caribbean, within sight of Trinidad.

What we are calling the novel's third phase is the one in which a familiar and enduring representation of Crusoe is formed: Crusoe the DIY hero. Equipped only with primitive tools to transform his spatial environment, Crusoe seems to travel back in time also, to a stage prior to the division of labour. 'By making the most rational judgement of things', the text flatters the reader, 'every man may be in time master of every mechanick art' (85). Do-it-yourself extends beyond the boundaries of the 'mechanick arts', however. Crusoe sets about building from scratch his own do-it-yourself religion. His early attempts at theodicy are manifestly crude:

Well, you are in a desolate condition, 'tis true, but pray remember, where are the rest of you? Did not you come eleven of you into the boat? where are the ten? Why were not they saved and you lost? Why were you singled out? Is it better to be here or there? and then I pointed to the sea. All evils are to be considered with the good that is in them, and with what worse attends them. (80)

What kind of God is it who saves one and allows ten to drown? Is that evidence for evil or for good in the universe? Throughout this third phase, Crusoe is haunted and harassed by the question of whether he was in fact singled out for the special attention of Providence. Are his circumstances evidence for the persistence or for the absence of a benevolent deity? Calling bookkeeping to his assistance, Crusoe lists the evil that has befallen him in the left-hand column of the 'ledger', and the good in the right, but can of course come to no clear conclusion as to profit or loss. At one point during this phase, Crusoe thinks he may have the answer when he sees 'some few stalks of something green shooting out of the ground' (94). Surely this green shoot is a miraculous interposition of Providence, evidence of a personal intervention by God on his behalf, a precise equivalent to the Biblical miracle of the manna from heaven? He recalls, however, that there is a more mundane explanation: he had shaken a few husks of shoot out of a bag of poultry feed. At this point, the text becomes a site for the meeting of the discourses of religion and science. Finding out that it is not a miracle momentarily lessens Crusoe's faith, but maybe it should not have done. As the mature, narrating Crusoe points out, the *probability* against 10 or 12 grains of corn being unspoilt and finding hospitable conditions for growth was so high that it might very well be called 'miraculous' (94).

Miracles unforthcoming, Crusoe's developing religious faith makes its next advance by means of a terrifying vision. Suffering from ague, Crusoe witnesses a flaming man appearing from a 'great black cloud', threatening him with a spear and pronouncing, in a terrible voice: 'Seeing all these things have not brought thee to repentance, now thou shalt die' (102). Whether the vision is a feverish hallucination or some kind of ambassador from the deity, Crusoe has no way of knowing; but it is now that his conscience first begins to awaken. It is at this moment that he first perceives a connection between his present reduced state and his act of filial disobedience, and that he sees the blasphemous impertinence of the Job-like questions, 'Why has God done this to me? What have I done to be thus used?' (107). Prayer and Bible-reading follow in short order, as Crusoe moves towards an ever more adequate construction of texts such as '*Call on me, and I will deliver you*' (111). This, he begins to understand, is not a promissory note, an insurance policy against durance and isolation. It is, rather, a promise to deliver him from a sinful condition into repentance and redemption.

The reward of Crusoe's crescent faith is instantaneous, and it is bread. More discourse is expended upon Crusoe's attempts to bake bread than upon any of the other practical vexations he faces – as if to defamiliarize the plea from the Lord's Prayer to 'Give us this day our daily bread' by showing that in his circumstances it is no trivial request. God does indeed '*spread a table in the wilderness*' for him when, travelling a little further than usual up-country, Crusoe finds melons and grapes, 'abundance of cocoa trees, orange and lemon, and citron trees', and determines on this green and pleasant area in which to build his 'country house' (113). Thus begins the period of Crusoe's greatest prosperity, as the analogies between his condition and that of a substantial property-owner or colonizer begin to multiply. Now, he understands 'what particular providences had attended me since my coming into this place, and how God had dealt bountifully with me' (142). Boastfully, Crusoe tells his reader that he has two plantations, both beautified and defended. His main dwelling has several apartments, a store of earthenware pots and woven baskets, and two corn fields. His policies extend to a 'country seat' featuring a 'tollerable bower', a tent with a comfortable couch, and a cattle enclosure to furnish 'a living magazine [storehouse] of flesh, milk, butter, and cheese' (161). Even an estate agent would be hard pressed to think of calling goats 'living magazines'. Recognizing that his life amongst unregenerate seafaring folk has been dreadful, and that God has extended many mercies by casting him adrift on such a well-appointed island, Crusoe can now vouch for the interposition of Providence. He is a parody-monarch, attended by his parrot, dog and cats, lord of all he surveys:

> It would have made a stoick smile to have seen me and my little family sit down to dinner; there was my majesty the prince and lord of the whole island; I had the lives of all my subjects at my absolute command; I could hang, draw, give liberty, and take it away, and no rebels among all my subjects. (157)

His construction of a home-made religion seems to be complete. He has worked hard and God has blessed his labours. He has Faith.

This faith is underwritten by what Crusoe perceives to be a tissue of coincidences so patterned that they cannot *be* coincidences. Each in itself random, the concurrence adds up to a kind of divine cipher, God's handwriting there to be discerned:

> And first by casting up times past, I remember that there was a strange concurrence of days in the various providences which befel me; and which, if I had been superstitiously inclined to observe days

as fatal or fortunate, I might have had reason to have looked upon
with a great deal of curiosity.

First, I had observed that the same day I broke away from my
father and my friends, and run away to Hull, in order to go to sea,
the same day afterwards I was taken by the Sallee man of war, and
made a slave.

The same day of the year that I escaped out of the wreck of that
ship in Yarmouth roads, that same day year afterwards I made my
escape from Sallee in the boat.

The same day of the year I was born on, viz. the 30th of
September, that same day I had my life so miraculously saved
twenty-six year after, when I was cast on shore in this island, so that
my wicked life and my solitary life begun both on a day. (143–4)

It is significant that at the height of Crusoe's material well-being and
self-confidence, when he thinks he can actually perceive Divine destiny
writing his lifelines, an event occurs that is so disturbing and inexplicable that it completely destroys Crusoe's security, pitching him into what
we can call the fifth phase of his life – the phase of Doubt:

It happened one day about noon going towards my boat, I was
exceedingly surprized with the print of a man's naked foot on the
shore, which was very plain to be seen in the sand. I stood like one
thunder-struck, or as if I had seen an apparition; I listened, I looked
around me, I could hear nothing, nor see any thing; I went up to a
rising ground to look farther; I went up the shore and down the
shore, but it was all one, I could see no other impression but that
one. I went to it again to see if there were any more, and to observe
if it might not be my fancy; but there was no room for that, for
there was exactly the very print of a foot, toes, heel, and every part
of a foot; how it came thither I knew not, nor could in the least
imagine. (162)

There have been, it is true, some curious events proleptic (i.e., eerily
anticipatory) of this cataclysmic one. Attentive readers would already
have registered the impregnation of his female cat and the apparently deliberate destruction of his store of grapes: but the suspense that
might have mounted from such narrative openers had been dissipated
by the comic incident of his awakening to hear what turns out to be his lost
parrot calling 'Robin, Robin, Robin Crusoe, poor Robin Crusoe, where
are you, Robin Crusoe? Where are you? Where have you been?' (152).

After the discovery of the single footprint, however, it is fair to say that Crusoe no longer knows where he is.

In the juxtaposition of the two passages of text quoted in the last paragraph, we can view the head-on collision of a distinctively pre-modern, and a distinctively modern, sensibility – a clash of *mentalités* that structures the entire novel and that imparts to *Robinson Crusoe* its importance in the history of the genre. Scott Paul Gordon's recent study of the 'passivity trope' within English Protestant thought quotes from William Haller's *The Rise of Puritanism* (1938) a passage that describes very accurately the pre-modern strand in Crusoe's attitude to his fate:

> Men in the Puritan age were taught to follow by intense introspec-
> tion the working of the law of predestination within their own
> souls. Theoretically, there was nothing they could do but watch,
> nothing they could of their own will do to induce or further the
> process of regeneration. They were only the witnesses of a drama
> which moved to its predetermined end according to a law they could
> do no more than marvel at.[10]

This catches very well Crusoe's early poring on the evidences of grace – his attempts to descry whether or not he is acted upon by the external agency of Providence. When Crusoe finds himself safe on his island, his first reflection, as we have observed, is upon his drowned comrades and his unique salvation. Much of the novel's project will be to evaluate the significance of Crusoe's escape from death – to discover whether it is a particular act of Providence or whether, on the contrary, it is a chance occurrence. These alternatives might be said to structure Crusoe's experience of the world, creating an oscillation in his psychological state between security, and terror at security breached. If he is the particular care of Providence, he can relax; but what if he is not?

The sad metonymies of his lost comrades, and metaphors of his own isolation, are the men's beached personal effects: 'three of their hats, one cap, and two shoes that were not fellows' (66). The items have some of the poignancy of the piles of effects left by the victims of concentration camps; the unmatched shoes in particular are oddly proleptic of the incident that is the most memorable in the novel. Crusoe is at the high-point of his physical security, replicating the life of a gentleman in his country seat and his 'tolerable' plantation, when he comes across the ominous footprint, all the more terrifying for not hav-ing a match. This inexplicable event, implicitly contrasted to that earlier example of the uncanny when he hears a voice calling him by name that turns out, harmlessly, to be a parrot, signals the destruction of Crusoe's peace of mind and psychological security. Thereafter, as he notes, he calls his 'bower' his 'castle'. It is not an exaggeration to say that this moment represents the very *discovery* of the psyche in the English novel:

> How strange a chequer work of providence is the life of man! and by what secret differing springs are the affections hurry'd about as differing circumstances present! To day we love what to morrow we hate; to day we seek what to morrow we shun; to day we desire what to morrow we fear, nay, even tremble at the apprehensions of; this was exemplify'd in me at this time in the most lively manner imaginable; for I whose only affliction was, that I seemed banished from human society, that I was alone, circumscribed by the boundless ocean, cut off from mankind, and condemned to what I called silent life; that I was as one who Heaven thought not worthy to be numbered among the living, or to appear among the rest of His creatures; that to have seen one of my own species would have seemed to me a raising from death to life, and the greatest blessing that Heaven it self, next to the supreme blessing of salvation, could bestow; I say, that I should now tremble at the very apprehensions of seeing a man, and was ready to sink into the ground at but the shadow or silent appearance of a man's having set his foot in the island. (164)

Fear and trembling sees the engendering of self-consciousness in Crusoe. He perceives the strange up-and-down barometer of human psychological states, and discovers the existentialist insight that hell is other people. He measures his own footprint against the one in the sand, observes that they are not identical, and is never again able to enjoy his solitude. The weakening of his religious faith during this fifth phase of his journey is extensively documented. As the grip on Crusoe of a Providential theodicy weakens, however, he develops a new capacity for self-scrutiny, for exploring the basis of all his inbuilt prejudices – a new capacity, that is, for psychological change. Having seen the horrible evidence of human sacrifice on the beach, Crusoe forms a murderous design against the 'savages' who have perpetrated such acts. Very soon, though, he finds himself examining the ethical basis for such action, and in a passage that anticipates later Enlightenment developments in early anthropology, Crusoe discovers in himself a capacity for cultural relativism that is distinctly modern and progressive:

> How do I know what God himself judges in this particular case? It is
> certain these people either do not commit this as a crime; it is not
> against their own consciences reproving, or their light reproaching
> them. They do not know it to be an offence, and then commit it in
> defiance of divine justice, as we do in almost all the sins we commit.
> They think it no more a crime to kill a captive taken in war, than
> we do to kill an ox; nor to eat humane flesh, than we do to eat
> mutton. (177)

Meditation on the genocide perpetrated by the Spanish *conquistadores*
upon the native peoples of America helps Crusoe to recognize that his
revulsion against alien customs was not warranted. Gradually, he fights
through to a renewed reliance upon Providence and upon 'those secret
hints or pressings of my mind' through which Providence operates on
the human psyche to make us act 'instinctively' for the good (181). The
self possessing such renewed faith is, though, greatly enlarged.

Crusoe is now ready to become a sociable being, a leader and a
teacher of others. His sixth phase begins when the desire for human
society becomes such a powerful yearning in him that he is ready to take
on the cannibals. This yearning is satisfied by the rescue of Friday.
In recent criticism, much is made of the fact that, after naming him, the
first word that Crusoe teaches Friday to say is, predictably, 'Master'.
It is the love and loyalty that develops between Crusoe and Friday,
however, and Crusoe's generous confession that Friday's capacity for
such virtues outstrips his own, that is more remarkable. The final stage
in Crusoe's religious education is reached when he becomes Friday's
theology teacher, discovering through this didactic role his own beliefs
and the limits of what he can explain. What foxes Crusoe is the problem at the very heart of any theodicy: the existence of evil in a universe
created by an omnipotent, omnipresent, and benevolent deity. He has
found it relatively easy to extrapolate from nature to a 'great First Cause
and over-ruling Power, a secret directing Providence' (219), but this
does not explain the existence of an evil spirit or devil:

> 'Well', says Friday, 'but you say, God is so strong, so great, is He not
> much strong, much might as the devil?' 'Yes, yes', says I, 'Friday,
> God is stronger than the devil, God is above the devil, and therefore
> we pray to God to tread him down under our feet, and enable us to
> resist his temptations and quench his fiery darts'. 'But', says he

again, 'if God much strong, much might as the devil, why God no kill the devil, so make him no more do wicked?' (220)

This moment might be characterized by Homi Bhabha's post-colonial term, 'mimicry'.[11] Friday's mimicry of his master's rational religion contains the seeds of subversion: it threatens to bring down the white man's house of cards. Thus naively expressed, the problem of evil is too difficult for the inexperienced theologian Crusoe. Friday's innocent questioning completes Crusoe's do-it-yourself religious fabrication by showing him the limits of rationality and forcing him to part company with deists and all other apostles of a purely rational religion:

> it was a testimony to me, how the meer notions of nature, though they will guide reasonable creatures to the knowledge of a God, and of a worship or homage due to the supreme Being, of God as the consequence of our nature; yet nothing but divine revelation can form the knowledge of Jesus Christ, and of a redemption purchased for us, of a Mediator of the new covenant, and of an Intercessor at the foot-stool of God's throne; I say, nothing but a revelation from heaven can form these in the soul, and that therefore the gospel of our Lord and Saviour Jesus Christ, I mean, the word of God ... are the absolutely necessary instructors of the souls of men. (220–1)

Crusoe's soul-making is complete. The novel's final unfoldings represent Crusoe's battle with the cannibals and his assumption of the role of a benevolent despot who allows 'liberty of conscience' to his motley crew of subjects (a passage to which we shall return). This final phase in his journey witnesses Crusoe's building from isolation into sociability and eventual escape from the island. Prospero-like, he enacts for three prisoners on an English ship the same workings of Providential salvation from which, by analogy, we must assume that he himself benefited. From obdurate and irreligious breaker of commandments, Crusoe has become a very agent of Providence, believed by the mariners he has saved to be an angel sent directly from heaven for their Deliverance.

What conclusions should we draw from this reading of *Robinson Crusoe*? Ostensibly, the novel constructs a theodicy every bit as smug and comfortable as that of Pope's *Essay on Man* (1733–34), so mercilessly mocked in Voltaire's *Candide* (1759):

> All Nature is but Art, unknown to thee;
> All Chance, Direction, which thou canst not see;

All Discord, Harmony, not understood;
All partial Evil, universal Good:
And, spite of Pride, in erring Reason's spite,
One truth is clear, 'Whatever IS, is RIGHT'.[12]

In Defoe's novel, the secret, benevolent workings of Providence are
evidenced in the tissue of seeming coincidences through which Crusoe
becomes aware of himself as a special case, and in the various portents
and prodigies that he believes to be 'certain discoveries of an invisible
world, and a converse of spirits' (249). Running entirely counter to
this, however, is an event such as the occurrence of the single footprint,
so *non-coincidental* that it does not even correspond to another
footprint, which is why it seems impossible to rationalize as any kind of
Providential sign. This is an event so bereft of rational explanation that
it destroys Crusoe's inner security and fledgling faith, its psychological
effect being out of all proportion to its merely narrative function.
The discovery of the self, then, is made in *Robinson Crusoe* through an
incident that is the apogee of the non-coincidental, of the categorically
inexplicable. Providence and the naked individual psyche are, one
might say, set at odds by the footprint: one signalized by the patterning
of coincidence, the other by the absolutely random. In his fictional
writing, as Carol Flynn observes, Defoe 'addresses obsessively the loneliness of the modern condition'.[13] The footprint in the sand stands as
the very sign of this condition, symbolizing the loneliness of the
individual psyche in a threatening and hostile environment for which
the older certainties of Providentialism and theodicy do not offer any
consolation.

Jonathan Swift, Gulliver's Travels

In the first book of *Gulliver's Travels* – the voyage to Lilliput, land of
the little people – Gulliver describes how the Lilliputian ministers of
state gradually turned against him. Despite his heroic status as the saviour of the nation, Articles of Impeachment are drawn up against
Gulliver. Things take a decisive turn when a rumour spreads that he has
been intimately involved with the Treasurer's wife: 'the Court-Scandal
ran for some Time that she once came privately to my Lodging'. In an
effort to salvage this lady's reputation, Gulliver provides a circumstantial account of his dealings with her – which, he protests, were always in
public and normally involved conversations conducted while her coach

drove round a table with a five-inch rim, that he had specially adapted for the purpose. The passage ends with Gulliver inadvertently betraying the extent to which living in this trivial, petty-minded society has degraded and corrupted his own way of thinking. He resorts to pulling rank over his accuser: he was a '*Nardac*', Gulliver declares, while the Treasurer was a mere '*Clumglum*'.[14] What it never occurs to Gulliver to say is that the lady in question can only have been a few inches tall, so that it would have been biologically impossible to take with her the sexual liberties of which he stands accused. The whole idea is palpably ludicrous, and in defending himself Gulliver colludes in the absurdity of a society that gives the rein to worthless gossip. In the author's sights here, we would suggest, is the kind of scandalous fiction that was discussed in Chapter 2: works like Manley's *The New Atalantis* that, under the cloak of fiction, made exaggerated and improbable accusations against identifiable individuals. Combining this with the earlier observation that the fire in her Imperial Majesty's apartment in the palace (the conflagration that Gulliver douses with his urine) was caused by 'the Carelessness of a Maid of Honour, who fell asleep while she was reading a Romance' (43), and the point made in Book 4 that the Houyhnhnms – the rational horses – do not have a literate culture, we might suspect that the implied author of *Gulliver's Travels* is not entirely in favour of prose fiction. Although it is frequently taken to be a novel, *Gulliver's Travels* actually loses no opportunity to satirize the tastes and reading habits of those who were creating a demand for such material. From the frontispiece portrait in the 1726 Motte edition (which depicts Lemuel Gulliver where the distinguished author should be) onwards, Swift targets the credulity of those who read only for the plot – who wish to be titillated, surprized, shocked, put into a state of suspense, and taken out of themselves. In this manner, Swift contributed to the dominant contemporary sense that reading fiction was a dangerously private activity that could slacken the morals of young people, causing them to be inattentive to their duty and discontented with their lot.

On the face of it, this presents a paradox, because for some literary historians *Gulliver's Travels* represents the high-water mark of the early novel's development. Swift did, after all, have the commercial acumen to charge his publisher, Benjamin Motte, £200 for the copyright (which was at the time the highest price ever paid for a work of prose fiction), despite the fact that the manuscript was delivered to him anonymously in a cloak-and-dagger fashion. If J. Paul Hunter is broadly correct to discuss the 'rise of the novel' in terms of two phases, the first culminating in the 1720s and the second getting off the ground in the 1740s, then we should be looking to *Gulliver's Travels*, published in 1726 as *Travels into several Remote Nations of the World*, to represent the acme of achievement in the first phase. Yet in crucial respects this does not seem to be an adequate placing of the *Travels*. If it is correct to regard the English novel as a distinctively *modern* form, related to social, political and demographic developments occurring at a particular historical juncture, Swift's writing is, in so far as it is aware of them, set against those developments. Although *Gulliver's Travels* is a long work of prose fiction (and thus, in Margaret Anne Doody's minimalist definition, a novel), we prefer to see it as an *anti*-novel – a work of prose fiction that was at least partly designed to summarize novelistic developments to date and to call a halt to them. This is not to deny that the text is steeped in fictionality. Doody herself has argued that on a structural level, as well as on a more precise level of direct influence, *Gulliver's Travels* belongs to a tradition deriving from ancient and Renaissance romance. She draws attention to motifs present in *Gulliver's Travels* that recur in romance – the Curious Traveller, Metamorphosed Man, Man in Skins, Enslaved Person, Imprisoned Courtier – to mount the argument that Swift's narrative 'draws upon the deep traditions of prose fiction in the West and is itself a virtuoso performance within that tradition'.[15] In our view, however, these age-old stories are organized in the overall discourse of the work by a satirical voice, the object of which is to ridicule and dismiss such storytelling as a frivolous activity of dubious moral efficacy.

There are some complex dimensions to Swift's hostility to the incipient prose fiction industry. One aspect of this is his Irishness. Swift lived most of his literary life in Ireland, and he was, in that sense, writing from the colonial periphery against the English centre. He made his reputation as an Irish patriot during the 1720s, writing a series of letters in the persona of a draper (*The Drapier's Letters*) that were designed to prevent the English coin-manufacturer, William Wood, from flooding Ireland with a debased currency – a project that was merely one symptom of the state of colonial dependence into which Ireland had been manoeuvred since the early seventeenth century. At several points, the narrative of *Gulliver's Travels* testifies to its author's specifically Irish perspective. Of particular import here is its ongoing attack on the trade in luxury goods, which reflects the various proposals that Swift made to the Irish people in the 1720s to the effect that they should use only goods manufactured in Ireland, rather than bolstering the English economy by importing finished 'luxury' items. Because Swift could see his native Ireland being stripped of its raw materials at knockdown prices, *Gulliver's Travels* develops a critique of luxury well before this becomes standard in writing in England. In the process of explaining his culture to his Houyhnhnm master, for instance, Gulliver writes: 'I assured him, that this whole Globe of Earth must be at least three Times gone round, before one of our better Female *Yahoos* could get her Breakfast, or a Cup to put it in' (244). Our analysis of Smollett's *Humphry Clinker* in Chapter 7 will have more to say about the anti-luxury discourse, and about the way in which it is specifically invested in the female of the species. At this point, we note Swift's considerable distance from Defoe on the issue of trade, and the extent to which this was informed by the off-centred and anti-metropolitan nature of his perspective.

This Hibernian perspective is particularly evident in book 3 of the *Travels*. Gulliver has been travelling in the Balnibarbian countryside with Lord Munodi (the Latin means 'I hate the world'). Everywhere, Gulliver sees a spectacle of ruin, poverty and devastation, until he arrives at Munodi's own estate:

> During our Journey, he made me observe the several Methods used by Farmers in managing their Lands; which to me were wholly unaccountable: For except in some very few Places, I could not discover one Ear of Corn, or Blade of Grass. But, in three Hours travelling, the Scene was wholly altered; we came into a most beautiful Country; Farmers Houses at small Distances, neatly built, the Fields enclosed, containing Vineyards, Corngrounds and Meadows. Neither do I remember to have seen a more delightful Prospect. His Excellency observed my Countenance to clear up; he told me with a Sigh, that there his Estate began, and would continue the same till we should come to his House. That his Countrymen ridiculed and despised him for managing his Affairs no better, and for setting so ill an Example to the Kingdom; which however was followed by very few, such as were old and wilful, and weak like himself. (167–8)

The phrase 'Ear of Corn, or Blade of Grass' here recalls the King of Brobdingnag's dictum, that 'whoever could make two Ears of Corn, or two Blades of Grass to grow upon a Spot of Ground where only one grew before; would deserve better of Mankind, and do more essential Service to his Country, than the whole Race of Politicians put together' (124–5). Munodi is linked with the King of Brobdingnag as one of the normative characters in the work, a figure whose opinions represent a positive moral standard by which other forms of conduct are to be judged. Munodi goes on to explain that the current ruinous state of Balnibarbi is the result of an influential governing elite who have absorbed ideas from the Flying Island of Laputa. This explanation probably encodes a reference to the class of Anglicized governors that Swift believed were the ruin of contemporary Ireland. As Declan Kiberd observes, '*Gulliver's Travels* reads at times as if England had been placed, palimpsest-like, atop of Ireland', so that Swift's satire can be read as 'a study in avoidable suffering brought on by projectors and professors, with Ireland cast in the role of a spectacular victim of *theory*'.[16] In the Academy of Lagado, Swift presents the state of contemporary science and technology as a counter-intuitive anti-utopia of inventors and projectors, whose impracticality and arsy-versy experimentation completes the country's economic ruin. The Lagadan projectors endeavour to reverse excrement into its original food, extract sunbeams from cucumbers, breed naked sheep, and build houses from the roof downwards. In the 'speculative' part of the Academy, they also write books using a machine that makes an entirely arbitrary selection of letters:

> Every one knew how laborious the usual Method is of attaining to Arts and Sciences; whereas by his Contrivance, the most ignorant Person at a reasonable Charge, and with a little bodily Labour, may write Books in Philosophy, Poetry, Politicks, Law, Mathematicks and Theology, without the least Assistance from Genius or Study. (175–6)

For Swift, we would suggest, romances and novels such as *Robinson Crusoe* fell into the category of books that could be written 'without the least assistance from Genius or Study'.

Wrapped up in this satire is a deeply ingrained opposition to the kind of 'creative' endeavour that seems to be spun out of the writer's own entrails. Swift's most important prose work prior to the *Travels* was *A Tale of a Tub. Written for the Universal Improvement of Mankind* (1704). Centred on a fictionalized persona – a hack author who spews out ceaseless verbiage in a self-validating torrent – the *Tale* offered a nightmarish vision of the modern bookmaking industry. We are witness here to the dawning of the age of ephemerality. As the Hack observes:

> To affirm that our Age is altogether Unlearned, and devoid of Writers in any kind, seems to be an Assertion so bold and so false,

that I have been sometimes thinking, the contrary may almost be proved by uncontroulable Demonstration. 'Tis true indeed, that altho' their Numbers be vast, and their Productions numerous in proportion, yet are they hurryed so hastily off the Scene, that they escape our Memory, and delude our Sight.[17]

The writer of these words in the *Tale* has a sensibility that Swift wished to designate 'modern': arrogant, self-regarding and ahistorical. The reader can infer that a superior sensibility is that of the 'ancient': the author who is aware of writing in a long and distinguished tradition, and whose desire is to emulate valued forms of ancient writing such as epic, georgic and elegy, rather than to supersede these forms with worthless modern fiction. There is an important social dimension to this cultural critique. Authors of the 'ancient' stamp will have the more distinguished pedigrees, and will not be writing for shallow commercial reasons. Writing had once been a noble calling, undertaken by gentlemen for the edification of others. As the star of the '*Grub-street* Brotherhood' rose, however, the public could look forward to an inundation of print, to which *A Tale of a Tub* is a kind of Noah's ark. If Swift was himself steeped in fiction and romance, his set towards it was nevertheless an alienating and defamiliarizing one. As J. Paul Hunter has argued, *A Tale of a Tub* can be read as an attack on the energies that would culminate in the first wave of true novel-writing, in the 1720s:

> To isolate the attitudes and features of contemporary writing that Swift attacks as reprehensible involves making a comprehensive list of features that found their labyrinthine way into the novel as it emerged in the half century after the *Tale* – subjectivity, novelty, contemporaneity, interest in individual lives, digressiveness, circumstantiality, the eccentric, and the bizarre. *A Tale of a Tub* is not exactly a parody of the novel – it is hard to parody something that has as yet no concrete form, tradition, or definitive example – but it is an exposure of the cast of mind and set of values that ultimately produced novels, and its attack upon the tastes and desires of contemporary audiences suggests that Swift understood modern readers early and well.[18]

What is true of *A Tale of a Tub* is even more apparent in *Gulliver's Travels*. Swift's 'novel' is ideologically opposed to the set of attitudes and beliefs that was fuelling the development of the genre.

Swift's ideological standpoint can, then, be broadly characterized as Irish, conservative, anti-progressive and 'ancient'. Defoe's attitudes to literature and life, by contrast, were those of a literary professional, deriving from the configuration of attitudes to trade, commerce and politeness, and to the literary forms most capable of *expressing* them, that were responsible for promoting the growth and development of the novel as a literary genre. Defoe was, in short, a progressive. He favoured some degree of democratization, criticized lazy élites, and celebrated the virtues and productive energies of the middling sort: the tradesmen, economists, and 'projectors' who had ideas to air and schemes to advance, all manner of business and social proposals. This 'modern' value-system is encapsulated in Defoe's fictional enterprises. As we suggested in Chapter 2, both Defoe and Haywood sought after commercially successful deployments of narrative. Defoe found his own solution in the creation and exploration of character, in the discussion of pressing social issues through the agency of a literary approximation to a living human being. In Moll Flanders, Roxana and Robinson Crusoe, he constructed convincing identities, characters to whom events occur and who react to those events on an inner as well as an outer level. Admittedly, the interior lives of Moll and Crusoe are not likely altogether to satisfy sophisticated modern readers, used as we are to reading novels written in the post-Freudian psychologistic era. Maybe Crusoe is never as terrified as he should be of the extreme isolation in which he finds himself. Did he never find himself becoming sexually frustrated? Maybe Moll should have some *feelings* rather than merely opinions about what she does with her life. Yet these characters are fully fleshed out and enduring consciousnesses. That all the events in these novels happen to Moll or to Crusoe is an important aspect of the sense of aesthetic wholeness and satisfaction that the reader can obtain from these works.

Swift, by contrast, deploys a parasitic system of characterization and narrative ordering that we might designate by Bertolt Brecht's term 'epic', a word that in this context refers not to the literary masterpieces of Greece and Rome but to a non-realist way of constructing character. Lemuel Gulliver does not have an autobiographically based consistency of character. In Lilliput, Gulliver is both physically and morally superior to the natives: his gigantism affords a bird's-eye view of the society, which exposes it as no longer operating according to the pure forms of its constitution. In this environment, Gulliver comes out looking rather good, expressing noble pacifist sentiments and refusing to put into practice a bloodthirsty Lilliputian plan to subdue the neighbouring

Blefuscu. In Brobdingnag (the land of the giants), however, Gulliver ends up defending the indefensible. Admitted to the corridors of power but lacking his former vantage point, he becomes a Lilliputian Englishman to the Brobdingnagian King. Now, he is no pacifist. Instead, he tries to gain status by imparting to the King the secret of gunpowder. Whereas in the fiction of Defoe (and in the later fiction of Richardson and Fielding), the author attempts to convey moral issues through the *experiences* of characters, Gulliver is Swift's satiric mouthpiece, a strategic device that shifts inconsistently between a range of viewpoints, according to satiric need. Whereas, in book 1, Gulliver is the vehicle of the satire, he is in book 2 the victim of it. In book 3, he is more of a social commentator, only minimally involved in the societies he visits. Notoriously, in book 4 the question of whether he is satiric vehicle or satiric victim becomes disturbingly undecidable, and critics have argued for decades over how far the misanthropic Gulliver speaks for the author. As Michael Seidel contends, then, regarding the characterization of Gulliver: 'Swift's satire tends to suck the lifeblood right out of the novel, to ignore the nuances of character, to present human response as reflexive, to doubt the unique and individual working of the human mind.'[19]

The final Book of *Gulliver's Travels* can be read as an almost-intentional parody of *Robinson Crusoe*. Readers familiar with both works might well find themselves haunted by a sense of *déjà lu*. In relation to Defoe's novel, the *Travels* offers an insistent subtext of the familiar that never quite articulates itself as clear parody. Gulliver arrives in Houyhnhnmland through the same mechanism of mutiny that brings the English captain and his crew to Crusoe's island; and Defoe's Providential disposition of significant dates is also mimicked by Swift. Gulliver's infuriatingly easy acceptance of the term 'Master' for the Houyhnhnm who discovers him and rescues him from the Yahoos, is surely an ironic comment upon Crusoe's usage for Friday, whom he likewise saves from mortal danger: 'I likewise taught him to say Master, and then let him know, that was to be my name.'[20] More generally, the educative process that Crusoe undertakes with respect to Friday, instilling in him the principles of natural religion, is ironically inverted in the comparative education that Gulliver gains at the hands of his own 'Master'. Playing Man Friday to this equine Crusoe, Gulliver learns that European culture is to Houyhnhnm as Friday's belief in Benamuckee is to Christian revelation. In both narratives, kindly and humane Portuguese sea-captains play a crucial role in ensuring the safety and prosperity of the protagonists, though again, Swift's deployment of this narrative token is not as straightforward as Defoe's, and can be read as an ironic comment on Gulliver's developing misanthropy. Whereas Crusoe's most fervent wish is to gain deliverance from his solitary island, Gulliver tells us that 'I had not been a Year in this Country, before I contracted such a Love and Veneration for the Inhabitants, that I entered on a firm Resolution never to return to human Kind' (250). At times, this *sotto voce* conjuring with *Crusoe* is more clearly enunciated, as for instance when Gulliver spends some time explaining to us how he makes a rudimentary form of oat-cake. Crusoe's struggle to make an acceptable bread was expounded at a length that meets here with Swiftian reproach:

> This is enough to say upon the Subject of my Dyet, wherewith other Travellers fill their Books, as if the Readers were personally concerned, whether we fare well or ill. However, it was necessary to mention this Matter, lest the World should think it impossible that I could find Sustenance for three Years in such a Country, and among such Inhabitants. (225)

With insouciant economy, Swift allows this one instance to stand as a metonymy for the wealth of description of Crusoe's attempts to reconstruct industrial and agricultural processes from first principles – description that partly comprises the 'realism' of *Robinson Crusoe* and that is a major source of the book's fascination. Gulliver's bread-making implies the triviality of such writing, and a respect in which its claim to realism insults the sophisticated reader's intelligence.

Even in respects in which there might seem to be a superficial congruence between *Crusoe* and the *Travels*, one comes to suspect that Swift may be parodying the striking of Defovian attitudes. Since it is a critical commonplace to cite *Crusoe* as an example of the congeries of attitudes towards trade and colonizing that define mercantile expansionism in the early modern period, readers are often surprised to find passages coming out strongly against, if not all forms of colonialism, then certainly the genocidal dimensions of the Spanish conquest of America. As we have noted, after Crusoe has discovered the cannibals practising their abominations on his island, he debates whether his loathing for their customs justifies his murdering them. In an early anticipation of the anthropological relativism that would follow Captain Cook's expeditions later in the century, Crusoe concludes that they are acting according to their own social codes, and that whatever he thinks of it, cannibalism is a practice that might make sense within an alternative cultural entity. This then leads him to excoriate Spanish colonial practice.[21] True, Crusoe does not continue to live up to the liberalism of these insights. As we have pointed out, the building of his 'castle' and 'bower' on the island apes an aristocratic English way of life, though this is also treated in the novel with an uncommon element of self-mockery. When Providence delivers him some subjects, he is only too willing to *subject* them, setting himself up as a governor supported by imperial authority. Again, though, Crusoe is really sporting with ideas of absolute feudal monarchy and religious toleration:

> My island was now peopled, and I thought myself very rich in subjects; and it was a merry reflection which I frequently made, how like a king I looked. First of all, the whole country was my own meer property; so that I had an undoubted right of dominion. 2dly, my people were perfectly subjected: I was absolute lord and lawgiver; they all owed their lives to me, and were ready to lay down their lives, if there had been occasion of it, for me. It was remarkable too, we had but three subjects, and they were of different religions. My man Friday was a pagan and a cannibal, and the Spaniard was a Papist: however, I allowed liberty of conscience throughout my dominions.[22]

With whatever degree of wry self-consciousness, this passage intimates that the English Crusoe is able to exercise a form of *tolerant* imperialism, which avoids the excesses of the Spanish colonizers of America.

At the end of *Gulliver's Travels*, there is a famous passage in which Gulliver explains why he has not claimed the lands he has discovered for the British flag (285–6). There are similarities between this passage and the one in Defoe's novel, concerning Crusoe's cultural relativism and condemnation of Spanish barbarity. If the passages are similar in content, they are nevertheless very different in tone. Swift's experience of Irish life imparted a testamentary authenticity to his attack on colonialism practised in the name of trade, which he may have considered to be absent in Defoe's case. Assuredly, Swift has in his sights Defoe's convenient assumption that such atrocities were only perpetrated by the *Spaniards*, with perhaps a sideswipe at Crusoe's evangelizing with respect to Friday:

> But this Description, I confess, doth by no means affect the *British* Nation, who may be an Example to the whole World for their Wisdom, Care and Justice in planting Colonies; their liberal Endowments for

the Advancement of Religion and Learning; their Choice of devout
and able Pastors to propagate *Christianity*. (286)

To the very end of *Gulliver's Travels*, the ideological investments of
Robinson Crusoe are thus put to the test of Swift's satire. Earlier, we
discussed Crusoe's discovery of the footprint as emblematic of the
difference between Haywoodian romance, the lifeblood of which is
coincidence, and the new form of the novel, with its commitment to
narrative, stories of singularity, and individuals who interest us for their
own sakes. A comparable emblem in *Gulliver's Travels* would be the
female Yahoo's impassioned embrace of Gulliver in book 4, chapter 8.
The ethical significance of this incident is paramount to Swift. In view
of it, Gulliver cannot wholly repudiate his affinity with the Yahoos,
because he is recognized by one of them as a desirable mate. The context of suppressed but continuous parody that we have been outlining
here has already led J. Paul Hunter to suspect that *Gulliver's Travels* is:

an accreting generic or class parody not only of travel narratives
per se but also of a larger developing class of first-person fictional
narratives that make extraordinary claims for the importance of the
contemporary, the knowableness through personal experience of
large cosmic patterns, the significance of the individual, and the
imperialistic possibilities of the human mind – a class parody, in
short, of what we now see as the novel and the assumptions that
enable it.[23]

Given the opportunity, Swift would have put paid to the novel's
progress. Despite Swift, by the close of the eighteenth century the
novel had gained a new status as a serious literary form capable of dealing with complex ethical issues. The major factor behind this sea change
was the demonstrable success of two powerful mid-century novelists,
Samuel Richardson and Henry Fielding. These will be the focus of
Chapter 4.

4
Teaching Readers to Read: Richardson and Fielding

The previous chapter plotted a triangulation between Defoe, Haywood and Swift in the 1720s, arguing that while the first two were involved in a market-driven competition to locate a successful fictional product, Jonathan Swift found one serendipitously, by writing against the grain of the early novel's emerging subject-matter and formal structures. In the 1740s, Samuel Richardson and Henry Fielding emerged as the individuals who would forward the fictional project. In the 1730s, however, it would have seemed far from inevitable that the novel as a genre had a future. Swift, as we have seen, did not intend *Gulliver's Travels* to be a contribution to it; if *Gulliver's Travels* did contribute to the project of prose fiction, it did so despite its author. Haywood did not write novels in the 1730s, and the most active literary forms were poetry, where Alexander Pope, James Thomson and Edward Young were the most powerful presences, and theatre, which was dominated by John Gay and Henry Fielding. The twentieth-century German dramatist Bertolt Brecht, in his writing about history plays, speaks of the need to represent history not as an inevitable process but as a series of turning points at which things might have turned out otherwise. To the historian of the novel, the late 1730s was just such a nodal point. We have already described an underlying process – 'novelization' – that we see as contributing to the onward development of prose fiction. Individuals have to embody that abstract process, however, and conditions have to favour their emergence.

Richardson saw a market opportunity in producing a livelier kind of conduct manual than had previously been attempted; while Fielding, after achieving considerable success as a playwright satirizing the government, had been put out of theatrical work by the Stage Licensing Act of 1737 and was looking for a new vocation. In publishing

Pamela (1740), Richardson was not merely or emptily pursuing a market; nor did he see himself primarily as a novelist furthering the project of fiction-writing. Rather, he was responding to a widely held perception that society was corrupted by degrees of immorality that established religious institutions were no longer capable of redressing. Church of England clergymen, it was widely considered, were no longer exercising an adequate pastoral duty of care. Widespread disappointment with the failure of the priesthood to be engagingly charismatic fuelled the rise of Methodism that began around this time.[1] John Wesley's movement or 'Connexion' had its origins in a 'Holy Club' established by a group of Oxford undergraduates in the 1720s; and it was in 1738 that the two Wesley brothers experienced a vivid spiritual metamorphosis – a conversion experience. By the 1740s, their movement was tightly organized into societies of members grouped into circuits and spearheading the activities of evangelical itinerant preachers. Emphasizing spiritual emancipation through personal faith in Christ, the Methodists were frequently banned from preaching by ecclesiastical authorities, and so took to the open air and to licensed meeting-houses, recruiting as ministers individuals who held other, often very ordinary jobs, and who preached in their spare time. For those such as Richardson who were too orthodox to countenance a popular and populist religious movement that had schismatic, not to say revolutionary, potential, the more appropriate response was to put the house in order from within. Richardson wrote his extended fictions because he believed that they could be instrumental in such a counter-reformatory project. Henry Fielding, meanwhile, found his vocation in opposing both the specific content of Richardson's programme for reviving virtuous conduct and the formal means through which he presented that programme. Importantly, though, he was just as convinced as Richardson that internal reform of a lazy, greedy, venal Church of England clergy was necessary, and that a newly responsible and serious use of fiction could help to bring it about. The second wave in the rise of the novel was fuelled by a crisis in religious observance, cotemporal with the rise of Methodism – which was, in its origins, a religious movement against the conservatism and corruption of the Church of England. This drew from Richardson a more detailed delineation of the workings of individual conscience than had been attempted by any previous writer.

Methodism's entanglement with the novel's story would be a lengthy one, in part because Methodism was the religious tendency within the Anglican Church that was most opposed to luxury and worldly pelf.

The increasing consumerism of an overfed and decadent society would be an important theme for a number of novelists later in the century. Despite this, Methodism continued to provide a target for satirically inclined novelists. Tobias Smollett's *Humphry Clinker* (1771), which we discuss more fully in Chapter 7, contains a treatment of the issue that is oddly disturbing. In the following passage, Jery Melford describes an open-air Methodist assembly being conducted by a footman, who turns out to be his uncle's newly acquired servant, Humphry Clinker himself. Whereas Melford 'could hardly keep [his] gravity on this ludicrous occasion', his uncle, Matthew Bramble, takes the incident far less lightly:

> 'What right has such a fellow as you to set up for a reformer?' 'Begging your honour's pardon, (replied Clinker) may not the new light of God's grace shine upon the poor and the ignorant in their humility, as well as upon the wealthy, and the philosopher in all his pride of human learning?' 'What you imagine to be the new light of grace, (said his master) I take to be a deceitful vapour, glimmering through a crack in your upper story – In a word, Mr. Clinker, I will have no light in my family but what pays the king's taxes, unless it be the light of reason, which you don't pretend to follow.'[2]

What offends Bramble is the affront to social rank presented by a servant's setting up as a spiritual director to gentlefolks. He offers Clinker the choice of being either a quack or a madman, a hypocrite or an 'enthusiast'. Given this choice, Clinker opts to think himself mad and to apply to Bramble for a cure. Bramble's vicious bullying of Clinker, his utter refusal to countenance the possibility that a mere footman could have a spiritual calling (despite the Gospels' insistence on the ordinary vocations of Jesus' followers), emphasizes the point that while he is an opponent of the contemporary itch for luxury, he is not an apostle of poverty or the simple way of life. At the point where religious matters intersect with issues of social status, the conservatism of Smollett's novel is beyond doubt.

Returning to Richardson: the fact that the novel genre did regain momentum after its decline in the 1730s was the result of a single unexpected commercial success, which did for the 1740s what John Gay's *The Beggar's Opera* (1728) had done a dozen years earlier, by creating an entirely new taste. Richardson's *Pamela; or, Virtue Rewarded* provoked a frenzied, uproarious reaction after its publication in November 1740, and was quickly followed by four further editions in 1741. Its author was a poorly educated, relatively obscure but prosperous London publisher and printer, already 50 years old, who had since his boyhood turned a penny by writing love-letters for his friends. Having established a reputation as a writer of conduct-books, Richardson was asked by fellow booksellers Charles Rivington and John Osborne to compile a set of 'familiar letters' that would offer advice on a range of everyday problems. Two of these, Letters 138 and 139, were devoted to instructing handsome servant girls on how to avoid the snares laid out for their virtue. It was these letters that provided the basis for *Pamela*. Interrupting the composition of *Letters Written to and for Particular Friends* (January 1741), Richardson produced *Pamela* in just three months, writing it in a white heat of creativity. As a commercial commodity, the novel was an instant success. The scope of the English Pamela cult is well captured by James Turner:

> A keen Pamela hunter in the 1740s could buy the novel in large or small format, with or without Francis Hayman's engravings and Richardson's sequel, plus *The Life of Pamela, The Celebrated Pamela, Pamela in High Life, Pamela; or Virtue Triumphant, Shamela Andrews, Pamela Censured, Joseph Andrews, Pamela; or the Fair Impostor, The True Anti-Pamela* and *Anti-Pamela; or Feign'd Innocence Detected* ... She could visit two Pamela waxworks, drop in on Joseph Highmore's studio to see his twelve Pamela paintings and buy the set of his engravings, then see David Garrick in *Pamela, a Comedy* ... The day would end in Vauxhall Gardens, sitting in front of Hayman's Pamela murals, cooling herself with the Pamela fan, and opening a magazine to read 'Remarks on Pamela, by a Prude'.[3]

There was no escaping Pamela even in church. In St Saviour's, Dr Benjamin Slocock praised the novel from the pulpit. In English villages where the novel was being read aloud to villagers, church bells were reportedly rung in celebration of Pamela's marriage.[4] A revealing personal response is that of Richardson's close friend, Aaron Hill – one of the most ubiquitous of the period's literati. In her recent biography of Hill, Christine Gerrard quotes from a letter that he sent to Richardson, which testifies to the sheer power that the novel exerted over its readers:

> If I lay the Book down, it comes after me. – When it has dwelt all Day long upon the Ear, It takes Possession, all Night, of the Fancy ... I am sometimes transform'd into plain Goodman ANDREWS, and

sometimes the good Woman, his Wife ... Now and-then, I am COLBRAND the *Swiss*: but, as *broad* as I *stride*, in that Character, I can never escape Mrs JEWKES: who often keeps me awake in the Night – Till the Ghost of Lady DAVERS, drawing open the Curtains, scares the *Scarer*, of me, and of PAMELA![5]

Pamela was amongst the earliest literary works to spawn this kind of 'soap opera' phenomenon, where the degree of emotional identification inspired between character and reader was so great as to blur the boundary between the fictional and the 'real' worlds.

Yet how could so many readers have taken to this seemingly saccharine story? A goody-two-shoes 15-year-old maidservant spends half the novel under siege from a bullying aristocrat identified only as Mr B. She is nevertheless capable of loving this despicable bully, and is rewarded for protecting her virtue by an introduction into polite society, marriage to Mr B., and social elevation. The novel's dialogue frequently appears so stylized and unnatural as to offer a formidable challenge to the reader's credulity. This is a typical exchange, from shortly before the wedding:

He saw the common-prayer-book lying in the window. 'I hope', said he, 'my lovely girl has been conning the lesson she is by-and-by to repeat. Have you not, Pamela?' and clasped his arms about me, and kissed me. 'Indeed, sir', said I, 'I have been reading over the solemn service!' 'And what thinks my fairest' (for so he called me) 'of it?' 'O sir,' said I, ''tis a very solemn, a very awful service; and, joined with the nearness of the great, though joyfully hoped-for solemnity, makes one tremble to reflect upon it!' 'No wonder', said he, 'it should affect my sweet Pamela: I have been looking into it this morning, and cannot but say, as you do, that I think it a solemn office. But this I tell my dear love', continued he, and again clasped me to him, 'there is not a tittle in it that I cannot joyfully subscribe to'. I kissed his hand; 'O my generous protector', said I, 'how gracious it is to strengthen thus the mind of your Pamela, which apprehends nothing so much as her own unworthiness!'[6]

Did it strike readers in the 1740s as convincing that people would actually speak like this, referring to themselves and each other in the third person and forming such perfectly subordinated clauses, voicing the while such morally unexceptionable sentiments about the marriage ceremony?

In *Before Novels*, J. Paul Hunter makes the important point that the average eighteenth-century reader both *valued* and *expected* didacticism in their literature.[7] Modern readers often respond to didacticism in eighteenth-century novels by refuting it on the literal level and arguing that it simply must be ironic. There is ample evidence, however, that many readers at the time responded every bit as sincerely to *Pamela* as Richardson could have hoped. In another address to the author, Aaron Hill informed Richardson of the reactions of a seven-year-old boy, Harry Campbell, who was then living with his family. As Hill read out Pamela's reflections by the pond, at the point when she contemplates suicide, this boy 'crept under his chair and sat with his head almost touching the book and his face bowed towards the fire, until he broke out into heart-heaving sobs'.[8] Pamela's plight was, it seems, drawing the sympathy of even the very youngest of literary consumers. Nevertheless, at least some contemporary readers responded quite as cynically as do many today, to the overt didacticism of Richardson's novel. In *The Reflector* (1750), Peter Shaw summarized this divergence of opinions thus:

> There are Swarms of Moral Romances. One, of late Date, divided the World into such opposite Judgments, that some extolled it to the Stars, whilst others treated it with Contempt. Whence arose, particularly among the Ladies, two different Parties, *Pamelists* and *Antipamelists* ... Some look upon this young Virgin as an Example for Ladies to follow; nay, there have been those, who did not scruple to recommend this Romance from the Pulpit. Others, on the contrary, discover in it, the Behaviour of an hypocritical, crafty Girl, in her Courtship; who understands the Art of bringing a Man to her Lure.[9]

As Shaw's overview illustrates, if *Pamela* was as much a cultural phenomenon as a literary text, the avid readers who made it so were deeply divided as to its instructive value and moral tendency. Yet how can a single textual matrix produce not merely different, but diametrically opposed, readerly uptakes? What generates the possibility of 'Pamelist' and 'Antipamelist' readings? This and other questions we shall now explore in greater detail.

Samuel Richardson, Pamela

Controversy was, we have suggested, central to Richardson's success with *Pamela*. Such controversy resulted partly from the author's positing of a language of the body that gives a supposedly 'natural' guarantee for the truth of the heroine's verbal statements. In the following passage, Pamela responds to Mr B.'s account of the arrangements he has made for looking after Pamela's parents:

> 'I have not words, sir', said I, (my eyes, I am sure, glistening with grateful joy) 'to express sufficiently my gratitude. Teach me, dear sir', and I pressed his hand to my lips, 'teach me some other language, if there be any, that abounds with more grateful terms, that I may not thus be choaked with meanings, for which I can find no utterance'.
>
> 'My charmer!' says he, 'your heart speaks at your eyes in a language that words *indeed* cannot utter. You most abound, when you seem most to want!' (390–1)

Pamela's eyes infallibly and incontrovertibly speak her heart. Although Pamela is not exactly strapped for a *verbal* answer here – she produces a lengthy, and grammatically sophisticated, compound-complex sentence – what she says asserts the inefficacy of language to express the fullness of feeling. Physiological symptoms are offered as an incontestable sign of equivalent emotional states: Pamela's tears represent both an expression of, and a guarantee *for*, the sincerity and moral virtue of her feelings. Anti-Pamelist works, such as Eliza Haywood's *Anti-Pamela; or, Feign'd Innocence Detected* (1741), were inspired by a cynical uptake on this aspect of *Pamela*. Haywood was typical of those readers who perceived that the physical and mental manifestations of Pamela's 'natural' virtue might well be feigned by women with very different motivations. Potentially, Pamela's 'language of the heart' offered a *license* for hypocrisy as much as an antidote *to* it. To Henry Fielding, for whom hypocrisy was the most potent moral scourge of the age, Richardson's naïve representation of virtue seemed practically to encourage this kind of moral duplicity.

Compared to Fielding, for whom hypocritical clergymen in search of the *dolce vita* form a prominent satiric target, Richardson is lenient in his representation of the clergy – as the example of Parson Williams attests. What is remarkable, however, is Richardson's perception that the novel could become a potent vehicle for ethical instruction, filling the gap left by a pulpit that was no longer satisfactorily exercising its function. Towards the end of the sequel volume to *Pamela* (commonly known as *Pamela II*), which was published in December 1741, Pamela is asked whether she is 'at all conversant' with novels, plays and romances or poets. Her reply is revealing:

> Not a great deal in the former: there were very few novels and
> romances that my lady would permit me to read; and those I did
> gave me no great pleasure; for either they dealt so much in the
> *marvelous* and *improbable*, or were so unnaturally *inflaming* to the
> *passions*, and so full of *love* and *intrigue*, that most of them seemed
> calculated to *fire* the *imagination*, rather than to *inform* the
> *judgment*. Titles and tournaments, breaking of spears in honour of a
> mistress, engaging with monsters, rambling in search of adventures,
> making unnatural difficulties, in order to shew the knight-errant's
> prowess in overcoming them, is all that is required to constitute the
> *hero* in such pieces.[10]

Pamela's distancing herself from 'novels' on the grounds that they lack
probability and, later, that they propagate *'first-sight love'*, prompts the
question of how exactly Richardson regarded his own literary productions. If they were not part of a discredited genre designated 'novel' or
'romance', what were they? For Richardson, we would contend, the
appropriate textual benchmarks were sermons and conduct manuals,
rather than the extended prose fictions that we now think of as novels.
In Richardson's hands, extended and repeated quotations from the
scriptures establish a reciprocity based on the recirculation of the scriptural in the fictional. In the first instance, Richardson's novels were
written to answer the question: what is it to live a truly Christian life?

Pamela invokes a powerful, Manichean sense of good and evil
('Manichean' refers to the view that the world is divided between the
powers of Light and Darkness, which we might refigure as good and
evil in the Christianized version). For the most part, Richardson's first
fictional outing portrays a simplified moral universe: Pamela good,
Mr B. bad; Mrs Jervis good, Mrs Jewkes bad; Bedfordshire good,
Lincolnshire bad. There are very few shades of grey here, very few
characters who exist where most 'real' people do, somewhere
in-between. But there is also an important twist. Under the influence of
Pamela's virtue, the bad are turned *into* the good. For the clergy,
assuredly, the power of the novel – the reason why it was read from the
pulpit – was that it offers an exemplary account of the efficacy of
Christianity. Richardson's novel was certainly far more pulpit-friendly
than Haywood's *Love in Excess*. In claiming that desire could not be
regulated by moral strictures, Haywood's text worked largely against
conventional morality. This is, perhaps, what Pamela has in mind when

she objects to '*first-sight love*'. In accordance with Biblical teaching, *Pamela* is a fable of how meekness and submission can triumph over strength and brute force. An example of this process in action is provided by the answers that Pamela makes to the quasi-legal articles that Mr B. has drawn up, in an attempt to make her his mistress. Anticipating the film *Indecent Proposal* (1993), B. offers Pamela £500 (then a phenomenal sum of money, more than most servants could conceivably earn in a lifetime) plus a list of other material possessions, not failing to blackmail her by suggesting that he will also rescue her poor-but-honest parents from their grinding poverty. He concludes by reminding her that she is in his power anyway – that he could always rape her and send her away empty-handed instead. Pamela's replies to this rake's bargain enshrine the idea that the soul is triumphant over the body:

> I know, sir, by woeful experience, that I am in your power: I know all the resistance I can make will be poor and weak, and perhaps stand me in little stead: I dread your *will* to ruin me is as great as your *power*; yet, sir, will I dare to tell you, that I will make no free-will offering of my virtue. All that I *can* do, poor as that *may* be, I *will* do, to preserve my honour: and then, if I cannot escape the violence of man, I can safely appeal to the great God my only refuge, with this consolation, that my will bore no part in the violation. (229–30)

It is an extraordinarily powerful response, asserting as it does the absolute centrality of freedom of the will. Mr B. might conquer Pamela's body, but he cannot conquer *her*: her irreducible core of self-hood, the freedom of her will to grant her body to him, or to *refuse* to grant it. To Pamela, the fact that Mr B. *wants* to do this to her is far more significant than the fact that he *can* do it. Pamela skilfully calls B.'s bluff with her response to his suggestion that he might marry her eventually if they get along well as whoremonger and mistress. As Pamela rightly points out, agreeing to that arrangement would in fact *disqualify* her from ever becoming his wife: 'What, sir, would the world say, were you to marry your harlot?' (231). Game, set and match to Pamela.

The contemporary reader would have followed this cat-and-mouse process, this tactical battle of the sexes, with gripped fascination. The titanic struggle between the angelic and the satanic powers is treated by Richardson with a new directness and immediacy. His detailed manner of representing the strategic thrust and parry between Mr B. and Pamela is what, above all else, places Richardson centrally in the novel's story. Famously, Richardson described his epistolary technique as 'writing, to the moment'. In the Author's Preface to his later novel, *Clarissa* (1747–48), he writes:

> 'Much more lively and affecting', says one of the principal characters [in *Clarissa*] must be the style of those who write in the height of a present distress, the mind tortured by the pangs of uncertainty (the events then hidden in the womb of fate), than the dry, narrative, unanimated style of a person relating difficulties and dangers surmounted, can be; the relater perfectly at ease; and if himself unmoved by his own story, not likely greatly to affect the reader.[11]

Richardson hoped that by using the epistolary or journal-based method, with a minimum of editorial intervention, he would be able to secure the advantages of giving his reader immediate and privileged access to the consciousness of his central character. This was a powerful, not to say provocative technique. There is something deliciously illicit about being permitted to read someone else's correspondence or private journal, in *having* this privileged access to another's inner self. In *Pamela*, the reader is party to the heroine's every thought and feeling, and to every distress and desire. We watch Pamela react to the crypto-lesbian advances of Mrs Jewkes. We feel her blushes as Mr B. exercises his seductive techniques. This level of emotional identification with the heroine is assisted by the novel's slow pace. Where *Love in Excess* had raced on from one plot element to the next, *Pamela* is daring and new partly *because* of its incredibly slow tempo. For some stretches of the discourse, it takes the reader almost as long to read it as it takes Pamela to live it. This approximation to real time underpins the empathy that the novel succeeds in creating. In *Pamela*, Richardson brought the real time of reading closer than it had ever been to the time dramatized in the novel itself.

If *Pamela* unfolds at leisure, providing verbatim transcripts of conversations with an obsessive concern for detail, this seeming form-lessness does not occlude a meticulously paced and planned narrative curve. As Mr B. discovers, the more Pamela resists, the more desirable she becomes. The value of her currency is raised, the more she keeps it out of circulation. And so Mr B.'s offers to Pamela become ever more generous. As this happens, so also the mysterious mechanism of love begins to take over. Before long, we learn that Pamela, like Belinda in

Pope's *The Rape of the Lock*, has 'An Earthly Lover lurking at her Heart'.[12] While Mr B. is realizing that he wants to *win* Pamela rather than rape her, so she is realizing that she *wants* to be won. In the event, Pamela is won via Mr B.'s reading of her letters. B. asks for and receives all of the correspondence that she has been sending home, and in it reads for himself the novel's account of his own viciousness and Pamela's virtue. He is, in other words, inscribed *in* the novel in the position of the reader *of* the novel. He becomes a reader, reading himself as a character. Through his reading of 'Pamela', Mr B. becomes exemplary of exactly the kind of morally reforming reading process that Richardson wanted his *real* readers to undertake.

In this part of Richardson's narrative, the erotics of the text become fascinating. Through some sado masochistic libidinal economy, Mr B. and Pamela become *helpers* rather than Manichean opponents, as they collude in the process of making meaning. At one particularly self-conscious moment, which again figures within the text the reader's own activity, the issue of the *interpretation* of the letters becomes crucial. Because, earlier in the story, Parson Williams had offered to marry Pamela as a way of easing her predicament, Williams has become the object of Mr B.'s jealousy – in narratological terms, his new opponent. What, though, are Pamela's real feelings towards Williams? Is he a genuine rival to Mr B.? How do we read the text at this point? The following passage is taken from the first edition of the novel, rather than the 1801 revised edition that is reproduced by the Penguin editor, Peter Sabor. Richardson clearly thought the passage too smart and racy for the Pamela he wanted to project, and he revised it greatly:

> 'I expect', continued he, 'that you will answer me directly, and plainly, to every question I shall ask you. In the first place, here are several love-letters between you and Williams.' – 'Love-letters? Sir', said I. – 'Well, call them what you will', said he, 'I don't entirely like them, I'll assure you …' 'Do you find, Sir, that I encouraged his proposals?' – 'Why', said he, 'you discourage his address in appearance; but no otherwise than all your cunning sex do to ours, to make us more eager in pursuing you'.
>
> 'Well, Sir', said I, 'that is your comment; but it does not appear so in the text'. – 'Smartly said!' says he: 'where the d — l gottest thou, at these years, all this knowledge?'[13]

This passage is highly revealing of Richardson's own conception of the reading process. For Richardson, *Pamela* is a text that means what it says, and that cannot be interpreted polysemically. This is Richardson's model of reading. Ideally, the reader (B.) should read the text (Pamela the character, and *Pamela* the novel) without irony or subversion. This process contrasts B.'s earlier reading of Pamela, where he had viewed her through the lens of his own cynicism. As Thomas Keymer has argued, this sceptical reading of Pamela anticipated, and provided the terms for, the later parodies of Richardson's text, not least Fielding's own.[14] Richardson himself, however, demanded a more transparent reading process, an interpretative procedure that was more conducive to the aims of the didactic novel. This moral model of reading did more than anything else to establish the novel as a respectable literary form, to distinguish the 'novel proper' from earlier forms like romance, that had fallen at the hurdle of ethical instruction.

As we have observed, in both Richardson's time and ours some readers have refused to read the author as he wanted to be read. Literary critics have drawn attention to the 'epistolarity' of Richardson's novels to make the point that, in these works, the referential function of meaning is displaced in favour of the activity of writing itself.[15] That is to say, rather than pointing beyond themselves to their import, the words and typographical devices used become features in and of themselves, especially in *Clarissa*. Modern readers who call attention to the strained 'epistolarity' of Richardson's writing often go on to claim that this feature undermines the novels' didactic authority. As Terry Castle puts the case in *Clarissa's Ciphers* (1982): 'The absence of authorial rhetoric and the shifting of authority to the reader makes the classic epistolary novel marvelously unfit, obviously, for didacticism of any kind.' Regarding Richardson's second novel, Castle further argues that 'the excruciating situation *Clarissa* dramatizes is that a rhetorical system is *not* "powerful" unless grounded in political power. Clarissa's "Story" everywhere lacks underlying authority. It is without social and material force.'[16] In *The English Novel: An Introduction*, Terry Eagleton puts the point in terms of the inherent tendency of language to evade the intentions of its employer:

> This master printer [Richardson] is out to master print, wrenching it into the service of a single meaning. Yet his writing is constantly in danger of exceeding his intentions and generating 'illicit' interpretations which he hastens to disown.[17]

In fact, Richardson fully understood how language can be manipulated against its intended meaning by those with illicit intentions: the entire plot of *Clarissa* depends upon it. He would not have thought, however, that it was not possible to read *Pamela* as Fielding read it – or to read Clarissa as complicit in her own rape – unless one *had* such intentions. In response to Terry Castle, he might have said that the significance of Clarissa's story is precisely that temporal political power – such as the patriarchal power of the Harlowe family and Lovelace – is temporary. Clarissa's rape is not a triumph of such power, but actually its overthrow, since what Lovelace wants above everything is her *consent* (this is an issue to which we shall return). To a great extent, the deconstructionist take on textual indeterminacy – that Richardson's language undermines its own desired meanings, securing not Clarissa's sacred virtue but rather her complicity in Lovelace's sex crimes – is not properly applicable to the novels of Richardson. Nevertheless, from the very outset there were readers who considered that Richardson's *achievements* were not simply identical to his *intentions*. Of these early sceptics, the most devastating was Henry Fielding.

To Fielding, Richardson's stories about women entailed a strange fetishization of female chastity and endless opportunities for hypocrisy. What should be made of all this endless talk about 'virtue'? How should one regard Richardson's puritanical notions of inner grace? Surely, thought Fielding, true religion does not consist in what people *believe* (or *say* that they believe), but in the charitable actions that they *perform*. Not what they *profess*, but what they *do*. For Fielding, looking into the heart and discerning its true motives was not as simple as Richardson had made it appear. What Fielding discerned in *Pamela* itself was a dangerous code of social mobility. From the outset, Pamela insists upon the equality in soul between a princess and a pauper, marshalling a whole lexicon of Biblical readings in her support:

> But, O sir! my *soul* is of equal importance with the soul of a princess, though in quality I am but upon a foot with the meanest slave. (197)

It is this insistence upon inner parity that makes Pamela the instrument by which the gentry will be reformed. At the heart of *Pamela* is the question: what *is* true gentility? An older aristocratic code of *droit de seigneur* that permits the rich and powerful to treat their servants like vassals comes under scrutiny as it is submitted to Pamela's searching simplicity. First Mr B. has to be converted to her view of true gentlemanliness, and then he has to become an evangelist for it. Whereas, in the first part of the novel, Mr B. has had to struggle to *avoid* becoming Pamela's husband, in the second half he has to struggle against his own clan to be *accepted* as such. He is forced to argue the case for his marriage against his own sister, Lady Davers, who refuses to accept it. Lady Davers presses home her objections by asking her brother to ' "Suppose … I had married my father's groom! what would you have said to that?" ' (440). B. replies that there is a gender-based difference in the situations. Whereas a man ennobles a lower born woman simply by dint of marrying her, a lady who marries beneath her status debases her whole family. This assertion of the sexual double standard, seemingly endorsed by the narrator, presents clear limits to the degree of radicalism implied in Richardson's social critique.

When, in the year following its publication, Fielding set about rewriting *Pamela*, he took the same set of narrative events (revolving around the social advancement of a servant girl) and showed that they might equally be motivated by hypocrisy, greed, and an illegitimate desire for social elevation. It was in 1741 that Fielding published the first of the anti-Pamelist texts: *An Apology for the Life of Mrs. Shamela Andrews. In which, the many notorious Falshoods and Misrepresentations of a Book called 'Pamela', are exposed and refuted; and all the matchless Arts of that young Politician, set in a true and just Light.* Shamela commences with Parson Tickletext (who is possibly based on Richardson's friend, Aaron Hill) writing to his fellow Parson Oliver about the moral sublimities of *Pamela*. Oliver replies that the true story is rather different from how it has appeared in Richardson's account:

> The true name of this Wench was SHAMELA, and not *Pamela*, as she stiles herself. Her Father had in his Youth the Misfortune to appear in no good light at the *Old-Baily*; he afterwards served in the capacity of a Drummer in one of the *Scotch* Regiments in the *Dutch* service; where being drummed out, he came over to *England*, and turned Informer against several Persons on the late Gin-Act; and becoming acquainted with an Hostler at an Inn, where a *Scotch* Gentleman's Horse stood, he hath at last by his Interest obtain'd a pretty snug Place in the *Custom-house*. Her mother sold Oranges in the Play-House; and whether she was married to her Father or no, I never could learn.[18]

As Ian Bell has argued, then: while *Shamela* was, to some extent, an 'unfair and partial misreading of *Pamela*', it also claimed to be revealing the '*real* meaning' of Richardson's text – a meaning that, in Fielding's view, Richardson had attempted to obscure beneath a surface sheen of virtue.[19] The carefully abridged story that follows Parson Oliver's revelations shows Shamela to be an artful scheming hussy. She is in cahoots with her parents and Nanny Jewkes to trick Squire Booby (Richardson's Mr B.) into marriage, while she conducts an affair with the well-hung Parson Williams, to whom she has mothered a bastard. The parody works by condensing and mocking Richardson's distinctive stylistic traits: his vocabulary; his grammatical structures; his use of verbatim conversations in 'writing, to the moment'; his heroine's moral *sententiae*; and his plot incidents. Hilarious as it is, though, *Shamela* is generated by a serious analysis. The agenda that fuelled this parody was so powerful that it went on to sustain an alternative blueprint for the novel, which would be expressed in Fielding's own fictions of the 1740s, *Joseph Andrews* (1742) and *Tom Jones* (1749).

Fielding's critique embraces both the form and the content of *Pamela*. To Fielding, writing to the moment was a sham – simply an excuse to write a titillating bodice-ripper and disguise it as serious didactic fiction. Do we really need an account of the lead-up to Pamela's loss of virginity on her wedding-night? And what about the narratology involved? An example: at one point in Richardson's novel, after recording endless banter between herself, Mrs Jewkes, and Nan, Pamela writes of going to her closet to scribble about this idle chit-chat. But when, the reader might ask, did you go to the closet to scribble *that* you scribbled? What exactly *is* the precise narrative instant of *Pamela*? The moment such questions arise, others quickly follow. As the more sceptical reader might well wonder: how is it that Pamela can write lengthy grammatical prose just after she has been sexually assaulted and actually lost consciousness? How, as Mr B. himself wonders, has she come by all her knowledge? How does a maidservant write at all, never mind write so well? This latter query touches on one of the key impulses behind the anti-Pamelist backlash – what Judith Frank has termed 'the scandal of Pamela's literacy'.[20] In Fielding's hands, 'writing, to the moment' is exposed as a confidence trick, perpetrated by Richardson upon the reading public. Readers like Fielding, who sought to reveal Richardson's sleights of text, did so mainly because they found its social tendency dangerous. By reading *Pamela*, servants might be encouraged to think that they could be elevated beyond their station, should they market their 'virtue' sufficiently astutely. In Richardson's time, sceptical readers were so not because the novel's 'epistolarity' signalled a crisis in *all* authority, in *all* attempts to regulate meaning (as Castle and Eagleton argue), but because they sensed in it a dangerous social radicalism.

Henry Fielding, Joseph Andrews

Published in 1742, the year after *Shamela*, *The History of the Adventures of Joseph Andrews and of his Friend Mr. Abraham Adams* is rooted in the same set of questions posed by the English religious reformation and the subsequent attempt to define a form of religious faith and practice that would prove widely acceptable, avoiding fanatical extremism. Fielding was fascinated by those who spoke the language of virtue, who had all the theological and moral technicalities at their disposal, but who acted in a fashion that did not square with, or flatly contradicted, their rhetoric. Conceptions of virtue based on an internalized inner light, that make faith a matter of profession, are derivable ultimately from extreme Protestantism, and lend themselves to hypocrisy. 'Virtue' in such theologies is defined negatively, as self-denial. Fielding's self-imposed task as a novelist was to put pleasure back into the representation of full-blooded living, and to afford the reader the delight of comedy rather than the duty of instruction. In the sexual realm, it seemed, the moral debate was far too exclusively dominated by the necessity of keeping a man out of a woman's bed. Fielding's 'latitudinarian' approach developed a more active conception of virtue, that was embodied in a red-blooded hero who was not especially good or moral in conventional terms. Fielding's heroes are all creatures of appetite to some degree: men of action, who never refuse invitations to eat or to fight – or, in Tom Jones' case, to other activities beginning with f. All are endowed with good humour, frankness, openness of countenance and Christian charity – presented by Fielding as the most overt and active of the virtues. However, such a valorization of robust masculinity contained the seeds of its own critique. Virtue here is siphoned back to a masculine ideal. Although Fielding could create a category of woman for whom virtue was not important, it remains important for his *virtuous* women. Fanny Goodwill and Sophia Western do not lose their virtue, but they are left in need of masculine protectors. Not armed with minds as quick-thinking and jurisprudential as Pamela's, they find themselves relatively defenceless.

Initially, *Joseph Andrews* reads like a sequel to the *Shamela* entertainment. Joseph is the brother of the super-virtuous Pamela and servant to Mr B[ooby]'s sister, Lady Booby. Joseph is every bit as virtuous as his sister, but sexual modesty in the male of the species releases different – comic – potentialities. When Lady Booby makes an attempt upon his virtue, assuming that no servant could possibly resist the advances of his mistress, he becomes *a* Joseph, alluding to the Biblical story of the

Joseph capable of refusing Potiphar's wife. In a man, such moral uprightness can seem risible and even compromising in gender terms. As Jill Campbell enquires: what is the 'meaning' of a 'male Pamela'?[21] Is he not a *real* man? The reader is amused both by Joseph's compromised, feminized virility, and by the clear indications that Lady Booby lacks those physical attributes that attract men to women. The following passage occurs during the second, longer conversation that takes place between Joseph and his employer. Here, Lady Booby is responding to Joseph's defence of his 'virtue', which takes her completely by surprize:

> 'Your Virtue! (said the Lady recovering after a Silence of two Minutes) I shall never survive it. Your Virtue! Intolerable Confidence! Have you the Assurance to pretend, that when a Lady demeans herself to throw aside the Rules of Decency, in order to honour you with the highest Favour in her Power, your Virtue should resist her Inclination? That when she had conquer'd her own Virtue, she should find an Obstruction in yours?' 'Madam,' said *Joseph*, 'I can't see why her having no Virtue should be a Reason against my having any. Or why, because I am a Man, or because I am poor, my Virtue must be subservient to her Pleasures.' 'I am out of patience', cries the Lady: 'Did ever Mortal hear of a Man's Virtue! ... And can a Boy, a Stripling, have the Confidence to talk of his Virtue?' 'Madam', says *Joseph*, 'that Boy is the Brother of *Pamela*, and would be ashamed, that the Chastity of his Family, which is preserved in her, should be stained in him'. (35)

Lady Booby is Joseph's (social) superior, but the nakedness of her desire for his body reverses that hierarchy, despite her desperate attempts to cling on to it. Unlike Mr B. with Pamela, Lady Booby does not have the option of physically coercing Joseph. Rather than seducing *him*, therefore, Lady Booby has to attempt to persuade Joseph to seduce *her*. Ironically, what acting in the more 'feminine' manner of Pamela enables Joseph to do here, is to prioritize his gender status – his masculinity – over his subordinate class position. Even while following Pamela's example constitutes Joseph's 'feminization' of himself – his refusal to perform the expected role of male aggressor – it also enables him to act with the greater 'Confidence' and 'Assurance' that so affronts Lady Booby.

Fortified by his sister's edifying letters, Joseph thus resists the frequent, hungry advances of his mistress, keeping himself pure for his childhood sweetheart, the milkmaid Fanny Goodwill. Compared to *Pamela*, a chamber-novel of confinement, *Joseph Andrews* is a 'road-movie' of a novel. Setting out in search of Fanny, Joseph finds the parson of his parish, Abraham Adams, whose name suggests him to be an innocent, a relic from a bygone era; a simple, pious Christian, who has a primitive purity of belief. Once all of the major characters are on the road, the novel is concerned with the incidents that befall them and with the parade of moral types. Orchestrated through implausible coincidences, the novel does not afford the truth-to-real-experience to which so many of Richardson's readers testified, but rather the kind of Providential patterning that one might find in a Shakespearean romantic comedy – as when Adams rescues a maiden in distress only to find that she is, in fact, Fanny Goodwill (125).

As this might suggest, narrative *shaping* is a central aspect of the reading experience of *Joseph Andrews*. Unlike Richardson, Fielding does not claim to be giving the reader an unmediated, direct account of a particular individual consciousness. The fictionality of the fiction, its crafted, designed, narrated texture, is at all times insisted upon as a product of conscious human endeavour. As creator, craftsman and moral commentator, the novelist does not conceal his presence from the reader. Richardson, as we have seen, was concerned to produce the closest possible identification between the reader and the protagonists in his texts. Fielding tries to create distance – what Bertolt Brecht would two centuries later call *Verfremdungseffekt*, sometimes translated as 'alienation'. Fielding uses the self-conscious narrator to create an ironic distance within which the reader's judgement can operate. The remarkable preface to *Joseph Andrews* refers to the work as a 'comic Epic-Poem in Prose' (3) – an intentionally, perhaps mischievously compact formulation, which signals both the novelty of Fielding's manner *and* its indebtedness to earlier forms of writing. Conscious of the weight of literary tradition operating behind the text, the informed reader of *Joseph Andrews* is invited to perceive allusions and references to the Bible, and also narrative and symbolic patterns from such precursors as Homer's *Odyssey* and Cervantes' *Don Quixote*. Joseph travels in search of an identity as does Odysseus. Like Don Quixote, Abraham Adams is an unworldly, imprudent, idealistic character, whose inability to see into others' motives further than they are willing to allow him serves to expose both his own naiveté and their compromised worldliness. Heavily imbrued with 'literariness', and invoking a classical tradition of storytelling in its deployment of the mock-epic, Fielding's writing interpellates a class of reader very different from that of Richardson's domestic dramas.

Ultimately, however, *Joseph Andrews* does not deliver the moral clarity that it promises. It is not Manichean. Writing about *Tom Jones*, the intellectual Elizabeth Carter (1717–1806), one of whose odes Richardson had filched and attributed to Clarissa, stated:

> Though nobody can admire Clarissa more than I do; yet with all our partiality, I am afraid, it must be confessed, that Fielding's book is the most natural representation of what passes in the world, and of the bizarreries which arise from the mixture of good and bad which makes up the composition of most folks.[22]

In *Joseph Andrews*, a perfect illustration of such 'bizarreries' is Parson Adams. That Adams is meant to be read as a sympathetic character is made clear in Fielding's Preface:

> It is designed a Character of perfect Simplicity; and as the goodness of his Heart will recommend him to the Good-natur'd; so I hope it will excuse me to the Gentlemen of his Cloth; for whom, while they are worthy of their sacred Order, no Man can possibly have a greater Respect. (9)

A classical scholar, caring nothing for fashion, Adams is a practising Christian of the kind that the novel shows to be an endangered species. His clear function is to contrast with those hypocrites such as Parson Trulliber who are a disgrace to the cloth that they wear. Despite this, Adams continually finds himself in situations where he is himself made to look like a hypocrite and where, were it not for the reader's privileged awareness of his true nature, we could not judge him otherwise. At one point in the novel, Adams, engaged in deep discussion with a Catholic priest in an inn, cries out that ' "if I had the greatest Sum in the World; ay, if I had ten Pounds about me, I would bestow it all to rescue any Christian from Distress" ' (221). Moments beforehand, this had been put to the test when the priest asked Adams for 18 pence to pay his bill, but Adams was unable to lend it because he found that all his money had been stolen. Adams' professions are sincerely meant, but his unworldly lack of prudence disables him from living up to them.

The complexity of human motivation referred to by Elizabeth Carter is exemplified by an incident in book 1, chapter 12. Joseph has been set upon by a pair of highwaymen and left naked in a ditch. What follows is recognizably an adaptation of the Parable of the Good Samaritan (Luke 10.30–37). In the scriptural source, the point of the parable is clear. Charity is exercised by a Samaritan who lacks the obligation either of nationality or of function (he is not a priest). Ideally, charity is other-regarding, transcending questions of self-interest. In Fielding's version, however, one after another of the travellers in the stagecoach refuses such charity to Joseph. The lady is a hypocrite whose professed modesty is betrayed by her uttering an oath and pre-ferring Joseph's nakedness to lending him a coat. Holding 'the Sticks of her Fan' before her eyes will afford her a good look at this nakedness. Judged by actions alone, the lawyer acts most charitably because he saves Joseph: but he does so through a concern for self-preservation and a craven fear of the law, rather than through benevolence. Yet self-interest is also the motive of the least charitable participant, the coach-man, who is the only one to show any feeling; 'a *little* moved', as he is, 'with Compassion at the poor Creature's Condition'. Joseph's modesty is such that he refuses to enter the carriage naked. How does the reader react to Joseph's own extraordinarily fastidious punctilio, a modesty that prevents him from saving his own life? At one level we are sup-posed to approve of this super-refinement; Joseph is concerned to avoid giving 'the least Offence to Decency'. Yet the narrator's reference at this point to the 'spotless Example of the amiable *Pamela*', which guides Joseph's behaviour, suggests that the aim here is less to exalt Joseph's modesty than to use it to poke fun at Richardson's concept of modesty. What, finally, do we make of the fact that it is the lowest and most unimportant individual, the Postillion, who gives Joseph his coat? At one level, this is simple Christianity: 'the last shall be first'. The Postillion's fate, however, is to be 'transported for robbing a Hen-roost' (46). Is this, then, the reward of charity? On the other hand, should there be no punishment for theft, if the thief is good-natured? As we shall see, Fielding's relatively complex analysis of such moral questions would be developed further in *Tom Jones*.

Samuel Richardson, Clarissa

Richardson's second novel, *Clarissa; or, The History of a Young Lady*, was published in three separate tranches spanning a year from December 1747 to December 1748. During this period, and for some time before it, Richardson discussed the work's progress with his close acquaintances and submitted drafts to what today might be called 'peer review'. Several of his expert readers – including Aaron Hill, Colley Cibber and Lady Bradshaigh – implored him to furnish a happy ending: if not to let Clarissa marry Lovelace, then at least to preserve her life. Richardson, however, refused the Hollywood-style closure demanded by romance. To Lady Bradshaigh he wrote on 26 October 1748:

> Religion never was at so low an Ebb as at present: And if my Work must be supposed of the Novel kind, I was willing to try if a Religious Novel would do good.

To Aaron Hill, on 7 November 1748, he wrote:

> I intend more than a Novel or Romance by this Piece; and that it is of the Tragic Kind ... But how have I suffered by this from the Cavils of some, from the Prayers of others, from the Intreaties of many more, to make what is called a Happy Ending![23]

Richardson's purpose, as he repeats in his letters of 1748, was to familiarize the reader with death. Intriguingly, in the letter to Hill just quoted, Richardson lists Henry Fielding as one of those who were demanding from him a happy ending. Since Fielding and Richardson are so often portrayed as mighty opposites, it is instructive to note that Fielding's response to *Clarissa* was nothing short of ecstatic. On 15 October 1748, well before its publication, Fielding wrote a rapturous account of his responses: '[Clarissa's] Letter to Lovelace is beyond any thing I have ever read. God forbid that the Man who reads this with dry Eyes should be alone with my Daughter when she hath no Assistance within Call.'[24] In his own novels, Fielding offered different solutions to the contemporary moral crisis because he was not impressed by the narrowly domestic, bourgeois scope of Richardson's investigation, by his method of 'writing, to the moment', or by his emphasis on the supposed 'virtue' of chastity. For all their differences, however, Fielding's response to *Clarissa*, as empathetic and involved as could be, proved him to be Richardson's ideal reader.

In the years that intervened between the publication of *Pamela* (1740) and *Clarissa* (1747–48), Richardson came to think that his earlier book suffered from crippling weaknesses. Mr B. is not a genuine rake. He does not take advantage of Pamela's various lapses in consciousness, despite the promptings of the much more effectively libertine Mrs Jewkes. Part of Richardson's project in producing *Clarissa* as what we might call an IMAX version of *Pamela* was, therefore, to provide a convincing rake who does not see unconsciousness as a significant objection to sexual conquest. Clarissa is raped while unconscious and under the influence of a sleeping potion. Such a fate testifies to the limitless villainy of Lovelace while it also safeguards Clarissa from any accusation of consent. Her decision, post-violation, not to support her own life, is in Richardson's way of thinking more of a moral triumph because no shred of culpability can attach to her. Equally important to Richardson was the need to take the rape victim up-market. Pamela's servant-girl status had been a source of considerable ideological ambivalence. On the one hand, as we have seen in the various anti-Pamelist texts, sceptical readers found subversive potential in the idea of a servant-girl climbing the social ladder. On the other hand, a comment made in the novel by Sir Simon Darnford, to the effect that Mr B. 'hurts no *family*' by his brutish treatment of Pamela, also points to a 'so what?' factor surrounding the earlier narrative, that weakened Richardson's social critique.[25] In the earlier novel, Richardson had not shown how the heroine's fate could pose any material problems to the rich and privileged. Higher status readers, such as the fictional Sir Simon, could simply dismiss the attempted seduction as an everyday story, remarkable only because Mr B. does not succeed. Clarissa's story, by contrast, strikes at the very heart of the ideology of the privileged '*family*'.

Clarissa concerns the rape of the daughter of a wealthy family with powerful connections; who, by dint of being the beneficiary of her grandfather's will, is also an independent legal personality. Richardson's rake is Robert Lovelace (which can be pronounced 'Loveless'), a young man of equal wealth and superior rank because his family is a venerable one. The story has tragic potential because it is acknowledged that Clarissa and Lovelace would be a perfect match if the latter could renounce his libertine ways, but they are star-crossed to the extent that James Harlowe, Clarissa's brother, has fought a duel with Lovelace and has faced the ignominy of accepting his life at the latter's hands. James' hatred prevents Lovelace from making legitimate advances towards Clarissa, but assists his illegitimate ones because Lovelace holds the threat of violence towards her brother over her, should she refuse to correspond with him. Lovelace has also been a suitor for her sister Arabella's hand but, contrary to custom, has discontinued his suit following Arabella's initial formal refusal of him. This courtship, Lovelace admits, has been a calculated ploy to gain admission to Clarissa's family. Lovelace's friend and chief confidante, Jack Belford, a former rake on the point of repentance as the story commences, tells Lovelace from the first that there is absolutely no purpose to his plan to seduce Clarissa. Since she is his ideal marriage partner – England affords no better – to ruin her would simply be counterproductive. As Clarissa herself asks after the rape: 'canst thou, Lovelace, be so mean – as to wish to make a wife of the creature thou hast insulted, dishonoured, and abused, as thou hast me? Was it necessary to humble Clarissa Harlowe down to the low level of thy baseness, before she could be a wife meet for thee?' (L267; 912). Earlier in the narrative, Clarissa is several times brought to recognize her sexual attraction to Lovelace by her friend, Anna Howe. The passionate rake is contrasted to the relatively emasculated and paternal nature of Anna's own inamorato, Hickman:

> I am so much accustomed ... to Hickman's whining, creeping, submissive courtship that I now expect nothing but whine and cringe from him ... Whereas Lovelace keeps up the ball ... and all his address and conversation is one continual game at racquet. (L128; 466)

Given the sheer repulsiveness of Solmes, the suitor produced for Clarissa by the Harlowe family, Lovelace is a magnetically erotic presence. For Clarissa, the possibility of reforming Lovelace is part of her initial attraction to him, though she also has to accept that this secret desire is evidence, even in such a paragon of virtue, of a foothold given to vanity.

In the book's first movement, leading up to Clarissa's absconding with Lovelace, things are so contrived as to block off every other avenue of escape for her. This initial movement demonstrates a serious breakdown in parenting. Clarissa's family operate an outdated political model of familial relations at a time when what has been called 'affective individualism' had promoted a more intimate, personal and emotional model. Anna Howe's letter to Clarissa of 9 March refers to her family in terms that would not be out of place in a diplomat's letter to his chief minister:

> Another would call your father a *tyrant* ... [your mother] is less to be pitied as she may be said ... to have long behaved unworthy of her birth and fine qualities, in yielding to *encroaching spirits* ... and this, for the sake of preserving a *temporary peace* to herself ... that has subjected her to an *arbitrariness* which grew and became established upon her patience – And now to give up the most deserving of her children, against her judgement, a sacrifice to the *ambition* and selfishness of the least deserving. (L27; 132–3. Italics ours)

Later, Clarissa's mother speaks of the family passing an 'act of oblivion' on her daughter's errant conduct if she will only agree to marry Solmes without more fuss. Operating like a monarch cementing a political alliance with a neighbouring potentate through the transfer of his daughter, Clarissa's father is under the inappropriate influence of his son James, like a non-constitutional, arbitrary monarch coming under the sway of a corrupt prime minister. Meanwhile, her mother is subdued to the point where she relinquishes the properly maternal role of protecting her daughter from the outrage of having a repulsive man pressed upon her. By offering to live single and to repudiate any marital interest in Lovelace, reverting to her father the real estate and income to which she is entitled under her grandfather's will (jealousy over which is a powerful motive for her siblings' cruelty to her), Clarissa removes any reasonable objection to her conduct. With refuge denied her by her uncles and by Anna Howe's mother, whose motive is to promote a model of obedience for her own much more wayward daughter, Clarissa has no way to escape the arranged and enforced marriage to Solmes other than to accept the protection of Lovelace's family.

Anna Howe is from the first a reader-between-the-lines of Clarissa's expressions with respect to Lovelace, and she is afforded amusement by her friend's very guarded phraseology:

> Love, though *so short a word*, has a *broad sound* with it. What then shall we call it? You have helped me to a phrase that has a *narrower sound* with it; but a pretty *broad* meaning nevertheless. *A conditional kind of liking!* – that's it ... (L37; 174)

The chess-game precision of Clarissa's language is gently ridiculed by her friend, as her own livelier but less subtle and nuanced intelligence attempts to flush Clarissa's feelings out into the open. Clarissa is adamant that whatever advantages Lovelace might possess in his *person* (her euphemism for his sexual magnetism), she could not love a man whose morals are defective. This mix of latent desire and overt morality sets up the conditions of Clarissa's confinement in Sinclair's brothel, and her rape while under the influence of a sleeping potion. Clarissa has, as had Pamela, 'An Earthly Lover lurking at her Heart'. Less than a week prior to the rape, Anna Howe writes to Clarissa under the pseudonym Laetitia Beaumont, informing her that the London house in which Lovelace has immured her is indeed a brothel. As Anna indicates:

> It was plain to me, indeed, to whom you communicated all that *you knew* of your own heart, though not all of it that *I found out*, that love had pretty early gained footing in it. (L229.1; 748)

Perhaps the single most brilliant stroke of plotting in the entire novel is the coming into Lovelace's hands of this key document (L229.1), and his masterly redaction of it that involves adding nothing at all but simply editing, so as to use only Anna's words and yet to withhold and distort the knowledge that it contains. Here, Lovelace's diabolical intelligence, and Clarissa's vulnerability even to words, even to the epistolary medium that is her natural terrain, is perfectly illustrated. As is demonstrated by Clarissa's excessive concern when Lovelace feigns the symptoms of serious illness in the brothel, this is a man for whom she both can and does care.

As we observed earlier in relation to *Pamela*, in recent decades a prominent strain in Richardson criticism has been the argument that the erotics of the text undermine the author's expressed intention to provide a heroine who is morally exemplary. Some critics go so far as to suggest that Clarissa is complicit in her own rape. Assuredly, the text can be read against the grain of Richardson's intentions, as we have already seen. Modern critics who read in this way, however, are usually disfiguring the novel in the interests of a post-modern theory of language (holding that it is endlessly interpretable) that may have had its moment in the sun. Should we really say more than that Clarissa, like Lear, 'does but imperfectly know [her]self'? Clarissa is unaware of how powerful her attraction to Lovelace really is. Nevertheless, the deeply ingrained intention of *Clarissa* is to depict the triumph of an unflinching, uncompromisingly militant Christianity. In the novel, Richardson takes on board the consequences of the view that death is the threshold to a happier state beyond the grave, and casts meekness and passivity as sources of indomitable strength. As he writes in the Postscript:

> And who that are in earnest in their profession of Christianity but will rather envy than regret the triumphant death of CLARISSA ...?
> (1498)

Clarissa's death wish is announced very early in the novel when, enduring her family's persecution, she regrets having survived an earlier illness. Richardson is extremely careful, however, to ensure that no coroner could bring in a suicide verdict on her death. She threatens to take her own life in self-defence when, shortly after the rape, Lovelace threatens to assault her a second time. Thereafter, the official medical diagnosis of her post-traumatic condition – one that resembles modern accounts of clinical depression and anorexia – is a 'broken heart'. Clarissa several times asserts that she will not die by an act of will, but neither does she 'strive officiously to keep alive', in John Betjeman's phrase. The falling-away of her flesh enables the triumphant emergence of her spirit, as she becomes a magnificent example of the Christian *ars moriendi* – ordering a coffin to be brought into her chamber, using it as a writing-desk, selecting herself the engravings that will be etched upon it, choosing her own legal executor, and writing a masterpiece of a will.

Where Fielding's concern is to expose hypocrisy, Richardson's interest is not in hypocrisy specifically, but in the integrity and fragmentation of the self. Even Anna Howe's self is fragmented to the extent that her 'lively' and 'spirited' personality causes her to treat her fiancé Hickman inauthentically, finding excuses to humiliate and abase him. Lovelace is not exactly a hypocrite, even if in Clarissa's letter to him, which he receives after her death, she quotes from her favourite Biblical book Job the text 'The triumphing of the wicked is short, and the joy of the hypocrite but for a moment' (L511; 1427). In his own opening letter, Lovelace complains that 'I pay for not being a sly sinner, a hypocrite: for being regardless of my reputation; for permitting slander to open its mouth against me' (L31; 142). His letters to Belford are frank about what he is and what he means to do, though because his vice is well attested in the community, it is necessary for him to win Clarissa's confidence and to plot with an ingenuity so fatiguing that from time to time even he wonders whether any sexual act can be worth such effort. Far more than sexual gratification, what motivates Lovelace is power – and, intermittently, a misogynistic spirit of revenge. Lovelace's most powerful fantasies about Clarissa project her total submission to him. He compares her sadistically to a caged bird, beating itself against the bars before 'finding its efforts ineffectual, quite tired and breathless, it lays itself down and pants at the bottom of the cage' (L170; 557). Clarissa's deeply ingrained purity represents nothing more to him than a particularly difficult challenge. Lovelace wants to bring this woman to the point where she will accept cohabitation with him, believing as he does that marriage can serve as a kind of puncture repair kit whenever he decides to do the decent thing. He joins all the members of her family, and indeed all the other characters in the story – friends and foes to Clarissa alike – in failing to listen properly to what she is saying. For Clarissa decides early in the novel, after it becomes clear that Lovelace will not leave her to her own devices in a place of safety, that she will never marry him – a deliberation from which she never swerves. This integrity, the unity of her selfhood, makes the explosive fragmentation of her self into a series of scattered, unfinished and erratic 'papers' a convincingly graphic account of post-violation trauma (L261). Setting these papers out on the physical page as sloping, cramped marginalia is Richardson's attempt to render in mimetic typography her fractured and disordered identity. As for Lovelace, his hollow victory is turned into defeat because Clarissa never consents. Lovelace's prize is Clarissa's *will*, and at all the significant points of decision, her will towards him is absent and he cannot triumph over it. 'My soul is above thee, man', she tells him repeatedly (L201; 646, L227; 734), and in the end he is forced to concur.

Significantly, Lovelace's debut in the novel is the letter that he writes to Belford on 13 March (L31), from which we discern that he sees himself not as a distinct self but as the head of a hellfire club of rakes, the leader of the pack. Their archaic use of the familiar 'thee' and 'thou', pronouns that had long since fallen out of use amongst most people, creates throughout an impression of bonding, but of an artificial and precarious kind. (When Clarissa herself adopts that 'Roman style' towards him post-rape, it is a measure of her contempt both for it and for him.) Lovelace's letters are constructed out of scraps of quotation from the poets, posturing self-interpellations, rhetorical questions, boasts and threats, anecdotes, pseudo-logical reasonings in self-exoneration, arguments designed to prove that black is white, and so on. What this adds up to is the construction of a character who is *homo rhetoricus* – a 'rhetorical' man, who has so many selves that he has no essential self or central core of being. His letters describe, in a dilletantish, unsettled style, a protean appearance that enables him to assume several convincing disguises, adding to the impression that he is, in himself, nothing. As Belford writes: 'such an air of levity runs through thy most serious letters; such a false bravery, endeavouring to carry off ludicrously the subjects that most affect thee; that those letters are generally the least fit to be seen which ought to be most to thy credit' (L339; 1077). All of Lovelace's virtues derive from the perverse and increasingly antiquated code of gentlemanly honour that it is one of the novel's major purposes to expose, by bringing it up against the Christian virtues that are embodied in the heroine. Clarissa's cousin Morden, the character who will be Lovelace's nemesis, defines the essential quality of libertinism as the refusal to observe 'the noble rule of doing to others what he would have done to himself' (L173.1; 563). However Lovelace might dress up his libertinism in the trappings of politeness – he repudiates, for example, crude anti-Catholicism and irreligion – it remains an anti-Christian creed opposed to the central teachings of Christ as expressed in the Gospels. To offset what we initially read as his 'charm',

Richardson never allows us to forget that he is capable of the most appalling acts of cruelty. From his plans to drown the rake Belton's mistress and her children and to ambush and rape the Howes, mother *and* daughter, to his devising of a parallel universe for Clarissa, Lovelace lives up to the billing that Anna Howe gives him – that of being satanic (L316; 1014).

After the rape, as Clarissa wastes away, Lovelace's parallel trajectory shows a hardening of his spiritual arteries. At a series of public appearances, the known rapist acts like a celebrity at a ball, and impersonates a tradesman, ridiculing the honest Smith family with whom Clarissa finds protection and in whose simple house she dies. Perhaps the most extraordinary of Lovelace's performances is his meeting with Hickman, reported in Letter 346, in which Lovelace dances verbal rings around his 'straight man':

HICKMAN: You will acknowledge, I suppose, that you promised Miss Harlowe marriage, and all that?

LOVELACE: Well sir, and I suppose what you have to charge me with is that I was desirous to have *all that* without marriage?

Lovelace picks up on Hickman's embarrassed and weak expression 'and all that', to turn it into an indecency and to retaliate upon him with another question. He brings Hickman to the brink of violence by manufacturing resentments, only to pirouette away from them, refusing to explain how his defloration of Clarissa was effected. The climax to the interview is masterly in its macabre perversion. Lovelace claims that he blames Clarissa for not being entirely truthful. Upon Hickman's enquiring how Clarissa Harlowe, a name that is a by-word for integrity, can be accused of untruth, Lovelace leads him through a tissue of riddles to the claim that she has another lover, 'a misshapen, meagre varlet; more like a skeleton than a man!' Astonished, Hickman speculates that he must be 'Some Jew, or miserly citizen ... Some East-India governor ... But, I fancy ... we must surely have heard of him.' To which Lovelace replies:

Heard of him! Ay, sir, we have all heard of him – but none of us care to be intimate with him – except this lady – and that, as I told you, in spite to me – His name, in short, is DEATH! – DEATH, sir, stamping, and speaking loud, and full in his ear; which made him jump half a yard high. (L346; 1097)

The interview gives a vivid sense of Lovelace's real but arid intelligence. Emphasizing the difficulty in knowing how to take him, Hickman's nonplussed reaction underlines Lovelace's peculiarly plastic personality – a selfhood that dismantles the unity of Clarissa's being but that, in the process, also proves self-corroding.

Despite the novel's length, unprecedented in English fiction, Richardson's art in *Clarissa* could be called 'minimalist'. His stories are organised by nodal events and occurrences rather than by what in traditional terms one would call plot. In the opening phase, interviews first with Solmes and then with her family become such nodes. Later, her reaction to her father's curse and ardent desire to be reunited to her family create a prevailing atmosphere of hope, the exploitation of which enables Lovelace to visit events upon her such as the impostures of 'Captain Tomlinson'. As an artist, Richardson's interest lies in the imposition of constraints that threaten to give the discourse nowhere to go, and from which, Houdini-like, he escapes by introducing unexpected turns of the screw. In the manner of earlier periodical essays such as Addison's *Spectator* papers, the texture of individual letters is highly varied and the use of other genres such as poems, plays and religious meditations creates an interest in the typographical variations of the pages. Readers can hardly fail to notice that the two shortest letters are those announcing Clarissa's rape (L257) and her death (L479). It is a measure of Richardson's artistry that he follows the latter, not with the sentimental release for which Clarissa's death offers an opportunity, but with a letter from one of the minor rakes in Lovelace's circle, Mowbray, from whom we have never heard before and will never hear again. The callous insensitivity with which this pale imitation Lovelace expresses himself ('I never heard of such a woman in my life. What great matters has she suffered, that grief should kill her thus?' (L480; 1359)) is more eloquent even than the set-piece tearfest that follows, in Belford's account of the heroine's last moments upon earth.

Henry Fielding, Tom Jones

Published on 28 February 1749, Fielding's *The History of Tom Jones* was conceived, written and read in conscious opposition to *Clarissa*.

In the summer after its first publication, Richardson asked Aaron Hill's daughters, Astrea and Minerva, to read it and to give him their honest opinion. They proved to be careful and discriminating readers:

> The whole Piece consists of an inventive Race of Disappointments and Recoveries. It excites Curiosity, and holds it watchful. It has just and pointed satire ... Its *Events* reward sincerity, and punish and expose Hypocrisy; shew Pity and Benevolence in amiable Lights, and Avarice and Brutality in very despicable ones. In every Part it has Humanity for its Intention. In too many, it *seems* wantoner than it was meant to be. It has bold shocking Pictures; and (I fear) not unresembling ones, in high Life, and in low.

Tom Jones, they conclude, deserves to please 'if stript of what the Author thought himself most sure to *please by*'. Richardson was furious. His reply to the girls of 4 August 1749 reproved them for enjoying a novel with 'a very bad Tendency', and in a tub-thumping excoriation of their reactions to it, he only let slip as an afterthought that he had not himself read it.[26]

As the Hill girls discerned, *Tom Jones* considers the question of virtue, and the ways in which it can be mystified by hypocrites, under a different set of initial assumptions to those expressed in *Clarissa*. As Fielding writes in book 15, chapter 1:

> There are a set of religious, or rather moral writers, who teach that virtue is the certain road to happiness, and vice to misery, in this world. A very wholesome and comfortable doctrine, and to which we have but one objection, namely, that it is not true.[27]

To what extent, we might ask, does the denouement of Fielding's *Tom Jones* sustain this characteristically witty and Fieldingesque formulation? The novel's detective-fiction element, the solution to the riddle of how the infant Jones came to be in Allworthy's bed, which is the search for his true identity, seems to issue in the opposite conclusion. For is Tom not virtuous, and does not his road lead to happiness, as surely as his wicked stepbrother Blifil's leads to misery? Everything depends upon how virtue is to be defined, and the need to define virtue was precisely what fuelled Fielding's career as a novelist in opposition to Richardson. Elaborating on the same tactic as in *Joseph Andrews*, in *Tom Jones*

Fielding sets up a parallel situation to that obtaining in the rival *Clarissa*, developing his novel to vastly outgrow the plot similarities. Both novels explore the ideologies that sustain political and familial authority. What is the basis of authority, and how should it be wielded? How is truly *moral* conduct defined, and how is it authorized? If morality derives its authority from religion, what kind of religion produces the most serviceable morality and what kind, conversely, is most open to abuse? And how does an artist represent such issues? In what tone should he do so? Using what devices of representation?

Sophia Western is placed, in the novel, in a situation analogous to that of Clarissa Harlowe. Like Clarissa, Sophia concedes that she will never marry where her guardians cannot sanction her choice – she concedes to them the power of veto. She cannot, however, concede to them the positive power to make her choice against her own inclination. Like Clarissa, she is involved with a man who is considered unsuitable and whose behaviour towards her compromises her own estimation of that man's suitability. Like Clarissa, the threat of incarceration pushes her into flight and precipitates her into a vicious world in which she is entirely out of her depth. Clarissa's man, though, is unambiguously vicious, as we know from reading his own letters where this is self-confessed. Some ambiguity still attaches to the question of how far he might be reformed by the love of a good woman, and some attaches to the question of how far Clarissa's feelings are engaged by him, however vicious he is. In *Tom Jones*, however, vice and virtue are far more ambiguous categories. A keystone of Fielding's ideology is that people and events do not present themselves in monochrome. Even if Fielding is unable to sustain such a complex, grey-area analysis of human conduct across his entire range of characters, he certainly does so in the case of his central protagonist.

Throughout his oeuvre, and especially powerfully in *Tom Jones*, Fielding wrestled with the perception that in the grip of religious tendencies that stressed the individual rather than the community, faith rather than works, there were so-called Christians who did not practice what they preached. Hypocrisy, Fielding feared, had become endemic in the clerical profession and in society at large. At the other end of the behavioural spectrum were those ultra-charitable individuals such as Abraham Adams and Squire Allworthy, who were easy meat for the hypocrites. The hypocrite has an uncanny ability to arrange the world in ways that seem entirely plausible to the idealist. Hypocrites can *talk* the world into a shape that will convince individuals who are not naturally suspicious and who cannot easily conceive that such villainy exists.

Allworthy and Blifil fit easily enough into the categories of the virtuous and the vicious: indeed, they structure those categories by embodying their absolute limits. For the majority of the characters who populate *Tom Jones*, though, the world is a vale of soul-making, and upon which side of the great divide they fall is determined partially by circumstance. Black George and Nightingale are clear examples of characters who would be virtuous if the world would only help them along a little. In the introduction to book 7, the narrator himself makes this point with respect to George Seagrim's theft of 500 pounds from Jones, further reflecting that 'we, who are admitted behind the scenes of this great theatre of nature ... can censure the action, without conceiving any absolute detestation of the person, whom perhaps nature may not have designed to act an ill part in all her dramas' (301). What determines Fielding's narratorial position of interventionist omniscient narrator is the conviction that only by constructing an author-God who can know the entire story of an agent's motivation, who can judge the calibre of hearts, can it be determined whether that agent is or is not virtuous. The Richardsonian epistolary method confined what could be known to what people could write about themselves and others – to a universe of pure discourse, of words alone. For Fielding, everything about this assumption was to be distrusted. Sincerity in pure language is not to be found because there is no way to break through its boundaries to the realm of action that would underpin it. It is telling that, whereas Pamela's letters underwrite for Mr B. her authenticity of character and create the conditions for their loving relationship, Tom Jones' letter proposing marriage to Lady Bellaston is what comes close to ruining any possibility of a match with Sophia – the further irony being that the letter is a complete sham.

Fielding's technique of 'retrospective motivation' is vitally important in enacting this epistemological position. Fielding suppresses important information that would help to explain events (especially coincidences), but then supplies it many pages later. In this way, he capitalizes on an atmosphere of the 'wonderful' or the 'marvellous' that he later brings within a realistic convention – except that it is never quite that. A good example occurs in book 15, chapter 5. Just as the wicked Lord Fellamar is about to rape Sophia Western, Squire Western enters, accompanied by his parson. Drunk, as usual, he fails to notice that Sophia is 'disordered, pale, breathless', and her neckerchief awry. Despite the parson's request to 'animadvert that you are in the house of a great lady', Western commits a second, verbal rape upon his daughter by assaulting her in his unintelligible Mummerset (stage rustic accent) and demanding that she marry the scheming hypocrite, Blifil:

> 'I'll forgee her if she wull ha un. If wot ha un, Sophy, I'll forgee thee all. Why dost unt speak? Shat ha un? Damn me, shat ha un? Why dost unt answer? Was ever such a stubborn tuoad?' (708)

Squire Western seems to overlook altogether the presence of Lord Fellamar, whose understanding of what Western has just said is no better than the reader's, but who imagines that the Squire has been pressing Fellamar's own suit with Sophia:

> 'Though I have not the honour, sir, of being personally known to you; yet as I find, I have the happiness to have my proposals accepted, let me intercede, sir, in behalf of the young lady, that she may not be more solicited at this time.'
> 'You intercede, sir!' said the squire, 'why, who the devil are you?'
> 'Sir, I am Lord Fellamar', answered he, 'and am the happy man, whom I hope you have done the honour of accepting for a son-in-law'.
> 'You are a son of a bitch', replied the squire, 'for all your laced coat. You my son in law, and be damned to you!' (710)

Western is a Jacobite Tory, whose hatred of Whig peers such as Fellamar could not be more intense. At the beginning of the next chapter, Fielding writes:

> Though the reader in many histories is obliged to digest much more unaccountable appearances than this of Mr. Western, without any satisfaction at all; yet, as we dearly love to oblige him whenever it is in our power, we shall proceed to shew by what method the squire discovered where his daughter was. (712)

Fielding refers us back to book 14, chapter 3, and to a train of circumstances that led up to Western's interposition. While Western's arrival is rendered explicable, however, it is not rendered *natural*. He is still a *deus ex machina*, an agent of Providence sent to rescue his daughter from harm. *Tom Jones* is articulated through a patterning of such Providential concatenations of circumstance. Rather than concealing the artifice of the artist-God behind the screen, of posing as a mere editor of correspondence (as does Richardson), Fielding takes every opportunity of highlighting this artifice. Not only does Fielding deploy an intrusive narrator but, as in the introduction to book 16, he deploys a metalanguage that addresses the legitimacy of so doing. Coincidental meetings such as those that take place in the Inn at Upton are not defended on the grounds that in life they happen, so much as on the grounds that they are necessary evidences of a universe contrived by a deity just as the discourse that renders them in the novel is contrived by its author.

At the formal level, Fielding's ideological differences from Richardson are displayed in the 'interchapters' that introduce each new Book in the narrator's characteristic voice. The first of these discourses allies the author with professional writers. He is not, he says, 'a gentleman who gives a private or eleemosynary [relating to an inn or tavern] treat' – implicitly contrasting himself with Richardson and his inner circle of carefully selected readers – but 'one who keeps a public ordinary' and who caters for an anonymous clientele of paying customers: the book-buying public. The author, Fielding's metaphor continues, is a cook whose basic meat is 'human nature'. 'What else', he asks rhetorically, 'is the subject of all the romances, novels, plays and poems, with which the stalls abound?'. *Tom Jones*, however, wishes to define itself against previous and rival attempts at prose fiction on the grounds both of the quality of its 'meat' – its fidelity to lived experience – and the 'author's skill in well dressing it up' (52). This discussion hints at a tension between the egalitarian and the elitist that will develop as the essays proceed. By the introductory chapter to book 2, the narrator has already abandoned the subservient culinary posture of the opening interchapter, and is now styling himself 'the founder of a new province of writing' who is 'at liberty to make what laws I please therein' (88). Readers are no longer the demanding inn guests who get what they pay for, but are 'subjects' bound to believe in and to comply with the writer's laws. He is, though, prepared to enter into a contract to secure mutual pleasure and benefit, being not a *jure divino* tyrant, but rather a constitutional monarch. Given the broader setting of the book against the background of the 1745/46 Jacobite rebellion (when the Young Pretender, Prince Charles Edward Stuart, invaded Britain in an attempt to restore his exiled father to the throne) and the opposite sides taken on this national question by Squire Western and his sister, and by Jones and Partridge, this metaphor for the nature of creative authority is highly charged. For Fielding, the desideratum of creative freedom for both reader and writer exists in constant tension with the need to put distance between himself and less able practitioners and consumers of his craft.

In the introductions to books 2 and 3, Fielding asserts the right to move through narrative time at whatever pace suits him, concentrating on nodal points of interest and leaving it to the reader to fill in the gaps at will. Again, the implicit contrast is with the exhaustive, moment-by-moment chronicling of fictional time that his rival, Richardson, had attempted. By book 5, Fielding is justifying his own introductory essays on the grounds that he can make whatever rules he wishes for his new species of writing. Serio-comic in tone, this introduction itself sponsors the serio-comic in all art, with a mock genuflection to pantomime as a cultural form that is quintessentially serio-comic. In pantomime, however, the contrast that is actually operative is between the 'duller' and the 'dullest', rather than the serious and the comic, the implication being that any reader who could enjoy pantomime could not be qualified to enjoy *Tom Jones* (202). Book 8 continues the narrator's concern with creative genius and freedom from such rules as are prescribed by critics, a theme that is developed further in book 9. Rules of a very general kind, however, do apply to the novelistic 'historian'. He must stick to what is possible, which rules out a great deal of what happens in classical epic, and contrasts with the kinds of farfetched events that are the stock in trade of 'romances'. He must also stick to what is probable. Now even in real life, which it is the business of the 'historian' to record, some extraordinary things happen, and so he must sometimes fall into the 'marvellous' (though this is still distinguishable from the *incredible*). Nevertheless, the historian of private events (and here Fielding means the author of *Tom Jones*) has to eschew even those amazing things that actually happen, and that sometimes make their way into 'true' histories. He must, that is, follow even more stringent tenets of plausibility than does life itself. Finally, there must be 'conservation of character': characters must only do what it is in their nature to do. The kinds of final-act conversion that comedy is habituated to staging are absurd and unnatural (435–9).

Thus the narrator, who had begun his work in such an egalitarian spirit, purveying fare to consumers for a fair price, becomes more prescriptive and elitist as the essays proceed. In book 6, he admonishes the reader who has the temerity to disagree with his strictures on love, stating that 'you have, I assure you, already read more than you have understood' (253). Such readers are advised to stop wasting their time. Clearly, not everyone's money is desirable; some patrons are very much more welcome than others at the table of the text. In book 10, the distinction between a professional literary critic and the ordinary reader seems to be elided as Fielding warns readers not to condemn anything that happens in the book just because they do not immediately comprehend its relevance:

> This work may, indeed, be considered as a great creation of our own; and for a little reptile of a critic to presume to find fault with any of its parts, without knowing the manner in which the whole is connected, and before he comes to the final catastrophe, is a most presumptuous absurdity. (467)

Earlier, in book 9, the narrator has been telling us that the function of his introductory essays is to make his kind of narrative literally inimitable. They are a kind of thumbprint, ensuring that Fielding's work will be impossible for hacks to reproduce. 'Whereas to the composition of novels and romances, nothing is necessary but paper, pens and ink, with the manual capacity of using them', to write a work such as *Tom Jones* requires 'genius' – further to be distinguished into invention and judgement. These faculties are 'gifts of nature which we bring with us into the world'. 'Invention' is a creative faculty, but it is the ability to get to the heart of matters, not to invent wild and fantastical events (436–7). Learning, defined as knowledge of history and of previous literary achievements, is essential to the writer of serious fiction, as is wide experience of the world. In what he has to say about plagiarism in book 12, Fielding allies himself unashamedly with ancient writers, from whom he will deem it an honour to appropriate; whereas stealing from his contemporaries, who are very poorly provided and have nothing worth stealing, can be deemed a crime.

When Fielding borrows the device from epic of the invocation to the Muses, to serve as introduction to book 13, the faultlines in his narratorial stance become yet more evident to the reader. Invoking the 'love of fame' enables him to assimilate himself to the august lineage of those who have written for reputation – Milton prominent amongst them – and to express the hope that 'when the little parlour in which I sit at this instant, shall be reduced to a worse furnished box, I shall be read, with honour, by those who never knew nor saw me, and whom I shall neither know nor see' (607). His second inspiration, however, is a 'much plumper dame', described entirely in Dutch terminology; namely, the spirit of profit. The literary effects of this 'inspiration' are deleterious. The profit-motive is responsible for saccharine poetic compliments, for destroying the distinction between comedy and tragedy, for imparting tedium to history, for quack and hack writing; and it is for money that 'Monsieur Romance performs his surprising tricks of dexterity'. If Fielding asks this goddess to 'keep back thy inspiration', he nevertheless invites her to 'hold forth thy tempting rewards'. Fielding wants his novel to succeed with the book-buying public, to bring him physical comforts and material rewards, but not by sacrificing standards of literary quality. Prompted to write, then, by the twin impulses of fame and profit, Fielding implores the assistance of Genius, Humanity, Learning and Experience. 'Genius' here is an attribute that enables the writer to 'remove that mist which dims the intellects of mortals, and causes them to adore men for their art' (608). Genius, it appears, is a natural capacity to see through the pretences that human beings adopt to mask their true motives. It is an antidote to hypocrisy, and the writers who possessed it in the literary tradition with which Fielding wishes to be allied are Aristophanes, Lucian, Cervantes, Rabelais, Molière, Shakespeare, Swift and Marivaux.

In chapter 5 of book 12, an incident occurs that offers a more *narrative* dramatization of Fielding's differences with Richardson over the ideology of representation. Tom and Partridge have encountered a puppet show performing only the serious part of the play, *The Provoked Husband*. This play was a huge success on the English stage when it was premiered in 1728, being a completion and revision, by Colley Cibber, of an earlier unfinished play by Sir John Vanbrugh called *A Journey to London*. The narrator, speaking presumably for Tom's apprehension of the show (though articulating thoughts that Tom himself could not be presumed to have in just this form), tells us that 'it was indeed a very grave and solemn entertainment, without any low wit or humour, or jests; or, to do it no more than justice, without anything which could provoke a laugh' (567). Such 'grave matron[s]' as were rhapsodizing over *Clarissa* are highly pleased with this performance, leading the puppet-master to elaborate his view that the throwing out of comedic material such as Punch and Joan [Judy] from puppet shows has made them rational entertainments calculated to improve morals. Other bystanders get on the puppet-master's bandwagon, excoriating all that is 'low'. An exciseman recalls the first night of *The Provoked Husband* in the theatre, and what he recalls is precisely the comic material that made the audience rock with laughter: 'but the gentlemen in our gallery could not bear anything so low, and they damned it' (568). Here, then, is the Rabelaisian, populist Fielding, lamenting the loss of entertainments that amused the people, desperately sorry to see the spirit of didacticism infecting vernacular forms of grass-roots comedy. Fielding would have seen the vogue for Richardsonian didacticism as contributing to a tendency that destroys any clear distinction between the comic and the serious and actually promotes the hypocrisy that it apparently exposes.

Tom Jones is in many ways a novel of mixed messages. To an extent, its interrogation of contemporary sexual morality is challenging. Tom is not moral or virtuous by the exacting standards of his age, but his sexual generosity and occasional pugnacity are represented as *natural* impulses incapable of harming anyone. Tom never ruins any decent woman. All those with whom he consorts are covered by some kind of insurance policy: Molly Seagrim is already involved with the philosopher, Square; Lady Bellaston is a predatory serial harasser of young men. When Tom is required to express his opinions about sexual conduct, he does so to Nightingale in the most conventional of terms, painting a sentimental vignette of the distress Nightingale will cause if he abandons Mrs Miller's daughter (679–80). In *Tom Jones*, the reader is asked to endorse the lessons about prudence that the protagonist must internalize if he is to be a fit consort for Sophia, but he is not asked to face the consequences of the sexual double standard. The reader is asked to entertain, for much of the discourse, the possibility of a love-match between a wellborn heroine and a foundling without birth or rank, but is not finally asked to endorse that. When the riddle of Tom's identity is solved, he turns out to be from the wrong side of the blanket, but a member of the Allworthy clan. Whatever its pretensions to progressivism in its disposition towards the reader, *Tom Jones* is a conservative book judging by its outcomes. Whatever challenges are issued by the politics of its form – the narratorial interventions demanding the privilege of setting its own rules in accordance with the 'genius' of its inventor – those formal interpositions also become more muted and conservative as the novel progresses. Beginning by asserting the credentials of the professional author writing in an entirely new form for an anonymous book-buying public, *Tom Jones* complicates that model by its gentlemanly homage to the ancients, its increasingly *de haut en bas* (from on high) attitude to the reader, and its elitism. The narrator's sponsorship of the 'low' and the purely comedic is aimed primarily at the *bourgeois* didacticism of those who supported the po-faced Richardson. It does not, however, eschew didacticism of its own inimitable brand.

5

Renewing the Novel:
Novelty, Originality and
New Directions

As we saw in Chapter 4, during the 1740s Richardson and Fielding advanced both the art and the standing of prose fiction, each initiating a new line of novelistic development. Both authors would go on to publish one further novel in the early 1750s, Fielding with *Amelia* (1751) and Richardson with *Sir Charles Grandison* (1753–54). Right up to the end of the century, both authors would also continue to be honoured as the progenitors of modern prose fiction. But what about other novelists at this time, who found themselves writing in the wake of Richardson and Fielding? The fate of the novel in the second half of the eighteenth century has proved a perennial thorn in the side of literary histories of the early novel, particularly those that are concerned with tracing the 'origins' of the genre. Typically, the development of the novel post-Fielding receives only limited attention in such histories – a trend that was inaugurated by Ian Watt's influential account, which concludes with just a brief, inconclusive discussion of Laurence Sterne. Implicit in this approach to the fiction of the second half of the century is the idea that, after Fielding, the future of the novel was essentially secured – that authors now knew precisely how to write a novel (or, like Sterne, how to parody the novel genre), and that a market of novel-readers was now firmly established. The true state of affairs was rather more complex. Despite Richardson and Fielding's rival masterworks of the 1740s, during the 1750s the future direction and even the survival of the novel were again uncertain. In financial terms, novel-writing remained far from secure as a profession. As James Raven has shown, while the general trend from the early 1740s was towards an increase in the number of new novels published, it is not until the 1780s that we see a *sustained* (year-on-year) increase in the output of new novels – an increase that was itself part of a broader expansion in print publication.[1]

Accompanying this economic insecurity was an artistic dilemma. Whereas, in the early decades of the century, 'the novel' was partly forged through local competition – through commercial rivalries and artistic contestation over the means and the legitimacy of the new imaginative prose – in generic terms the new fiction produced during the 1750s and 1760s had to deal principally with what was *already established* – with the legacy of powerful precursors, rather than with fresh challenges from new artistic rivals. For aspiring novelists at this time, a key question was: how to respond to the Richardson–Fielding duopoly? What should a novelist now take from, and in what ways could s/he depart from, the newly minted templates for the genre? As this burden of the immediate past revealed, even as the new species of writing had secured to itself a degree of moral authority that could not be claimed by such earlier works as *Love in Excess* or *Moll Flanders*, the very *new*ness of the species – the novel's very claim to *novelty* – had also left it with a problematic, if not oxymoronic identity, as a discrete literary genre that was nevertheless defined by a continual process of renewal.

For contemporary aspirants in the field of prose fiction, the advances of the 1740s thus constituted something of a mixed blessing. In this and the following chapter, we explore the generic aftermath of Richardson and Fielding, in novels that played out variations upon these new literary models, and that can be viewed as mediating between imitation and invention. In particular, we examine texts that participated in the creation of new *sub*-species of the novel – the 'novel of circulation', the 'quixotic' novel and the sentimental novel – along with more radical departures (the Gothic novel) and works that to some extent represent 'one-offs', such as Sterne's *Tristram Shandy* (1759–67). To begin with, we consider John Cleland's *Memoirs of a Woman of Pleasure* (1748–49), popularly known today as *Fanny Hill*. Sexually frank and verbally inventive, Cleland's text constitutes an intriguing response to the dual claims of Richardsonian and Fieldingesque fiction. Following Cleland, we move on to Francis Coventry's *Pompey the Little* (1751), which inaugurated a new novelistic sub-genre: the 'spy-novel', or 'novel of circulation'. Coventry's experimental work offered a variation upon the Fieldingesque novel specifically, its non-human protagonist enabling a more distanced form of social satire than had been provided by *Joseph Andrews* or *Tom Jones*. Another variation upon the Fielding prototype was the 'quixotic' novel, which played more insistently than had Fielding on its relation to Cervantes' *Don Quixote*. Our primary example here is Charlotte's Lennox's *The Female Quixote* (1752), a work which Fielding himself praised as superior to *Don*

Quixote in certain respects, and which offers the most fully developed representation of a key contemporary image: that of a young woman led astray by reading too many French romances. To the extent that it constitutes the most Richardsonian of the mid-century 'quixotic' novels, *The Female Quixote* adds a further nuance to our sense that, from the 1740s, the novel developed along the twin tracks set in motion by Richardson and Fielding. During the 1760s, a more decisive departure from these lines also appeared in the form of the Gothic novel. Resisting both of the contending forms of contemporary realistic (and anti-romantic) novel, the Gothic drew on a modern sense of the medieval past in order to give freer rein to the writer's imagination. In the concluding section of this chapter, we analyse Horace Walpole's *The Castle of Otranto* (1764), a notably 'theatrical' take on Gothic which, as the first novel of its kind, staged a significant disruption of the novel genre's recent development. As well as highlighting what a range of writers took from Richardson and Fielding, then, we shall be addressing how authors negotiated the differences *between* these generic models, and the various ways in which a new generation of novelists consciously digressed from the big-hitters of the 1740s.

What was the cultural context for novelistic innovation during these decades? The textual experimentalism of novelists at this time possessed lively counterparts in the other arts. Partly as a result of the restrictions imposed by the Stage Licensing Act, the early 1750s experienced what Walpole himself described as a 'new madness' for 'Oratorys' – 'Oratorys' being lectures, usually comic in mode, written and performed by playwrights, actors and writers such as Samuel Foote, Charles Macklin and Christopher Smart.[2] As Lance Bertelsen has argued in relation to these and other works of the 1750s (notably Fielding's posthumously published travelogue, *A Journal of a Voyage to Lisbon* (1755)), at this historical moment changes in the cultural order, and in notions of cultural value, afforded new validity to a variety of experimental, self-reflexive, indeed *novel* cultural forms.[3] During the following decade, a further manifestation of such modern energies appeared in the form of George Alexander Stevens' *Lecture on Heads*, which was first performed at the Little Haymarket Theatre in 1764. Presented with the aid of 50 papier-mâché 'heads', the *Lecture* combined satire on social character types with displays of facetious learning, such as a mock-erudite dissertation on sneezing and snuff-taking. In the realm of aesthetic theory, such artistic innovation was authorized by new ideas about the creative process itself, which were articulated formally in contemporary treatises on originality and genius. The first and most famous of such works was

Edward Young's *Conjectures on Original Composition* (1759). By the end of the 1750s, Young's ideas about original writing were not themselves entirely innovative. While, in the treatise itself, Young declared that 'it seems an original subject to me, who have seen nothing hitherto written on it', James Boswell recorded Samuel Johnson's surprise at finding the author 'receive as novelties what Mr. Johnson thought very common thoughts'.[4] A more sympathetic reader was Samuel Richardson. Not only had Richardson acted as close adviser to Young during the writing of the work but, as its subtitle declared, Young's text was specifically addressed to 'the Author of *Sir Charles Grandison*'. To a considerable extent, in fact, the *Conjectures* constituted an amplification of Richardson's own claims to originality. In an important passage that also ratifies Richardson's moral claims as a writer, Young singled out his friend for particular praise:

> A friend of mine has obeyed that injunction [to aspire to write as brilliantly as possible]; he has relied on himself, and with a genius, as well moral as original (to speak in bold terms), has cast out evil spirits; has made a convert to virtue of a species of composition, once most its foe. As the first Christian emperors expelled demons, and dedicated their temples to the living God.[5]

In this passage, Young added to the raft of contemporary testaments to Richardson's reformation of prose fiction. So powerful was Richardson's gift of genius, Young suggested, that it had enabled him to act as a kind of secular exorcist, casting out the cultural evils of romance and the early eighteenth-century novel. As this eulogy to his reforming friend also attests, Young's ideas about originality were themselves closely associated with the 'new species of writing' that Richardson had helped to invent during the previous decade.

The burden of Young's treatise lay in differentiating 'original' from imitative composition. Speaking of the moderns' relationship to ancients such as Homer, Young urged writers to imitate 'not the composition, but the man'. That is to say, contemporary authors should endeavour not to mimic the *writings* of their predecessors, but rather to write *as* they did, *originally*. As Young continued: 'Let us build our compositions with the spirit, and in the taste, of the ancients; but not with their materials.' It was in this sense that Young endorsed Richardson as a truly original author who had created something entirely new – something that had, in Young's terms, risen 'spontaneously from the vital root of genius' (as against Fielding's more self-consciously learned and allusive relationship to his literary forebears).[6] From the rarefied perspective of the *Conjectures* itself, most of the novels that we shall be analysing in this chapter would probably be deemed to be more imitative than original (in Young's Cartesian terms, the products more of manual industry than of mental inspiration). Even so, the *Conjectures* remains pertinent insofar as it throws into relief the burden that the new valuation of originality placed upon novelists at this time. For, if the burgeoning genre of the novel was partly defined by its very 'novelty', how was the new novel writer to proceed? Should such a writer now imitate Richardson, or Fielding, or perhaps both? Or, *à la* Young, should s/he imitate not the compositions, but the men, doing as those writers themselves claimed to have done by creating ever more, and ever newer, species of novelistic writing?

Such considerations, we would argue, became particularly pressing during the 1750s and 1760s, not least on account of the appearance of review journals, *The Monthly Review* (founded 1749) and *The Critical Review* (founded 1756), whose writers frequently lamented the paucity of invention in the new prose fictional products that they were forced to review. While the newly minute scrutiny to which prose fiction was being subjected may itself have heightened the sense that originality *was* a problem in the novel at this time, the reviewers' laments were far from entirely unfounded. As Thomas Keymer has shown, much minor fiction of the 1750s was written very much in the wake of, if not in imitation of, the novels of Fielding – particularly in comic expansions upon the games with readers, and with the broader contexts of novelistic reception, contained in Fielding's (supposedly) inimitable 'interchapters'.[7] In the novel market, the issue of originality would be further foregrounded by the many stylistic imitations of Laurence Sterne that mushroomed during the 1760s. To some extent, the imitative discourse that developed around Sterne's works replayed the buzz of literary activity that had been sparked by Richardson's *Pamela*, two decades earlier. As with the post-*Pamela* productions, much of this Sterneiana was critical of the original author himself, not least in response to Sterne's sexual humour. At the same time, other works appeared simply to borrow the author's distinctive style, or rather the most valued part of it: the 'pathetic' manner of the stories of Le Fever and Maria, in *Tristram Shandy*, and of *A Sentimental Journey* (1768), Sterne's second and final novel.

What were the implications of such material, with regard to the nature of literary creativity? Could only Sterne himself be original in his own manner? Or was Sterne's style *inherently* original, regardless of

who adopted it? We shall address Sterne's own 'originality' in Chapter 6.
In what follows, we explore some of the most significant new directions
taken by the novel from the late 1740s onwards. Set against the achievements of Richardson and Fielding, some of these variably experimental
works can certainly look like regressive steps in the history of the genre.
In terms, for instance, of one of the core characteristics that we would
now attribute to and expect of a novel – the realization of individual
consciousness – a number of these works could be said to lack *either*
Richardson's 'characters of nature' *or* Fielding's 'characters of manners'
(the phrases are Johnson's).[8] And yet, partly for this very reason, these
works reveal the particular challenges faced by novelists writing at mid-
century: in the shadow of Richardson and Fielding, in an insecure marketplace, and in a genre that demanded novelty and innovation. It is to
these new, mid-century voices that we now turn.

John Cleland, Memoirs of a Woman of Pleasure

Published in two volumes in November 1748 and February 1749, John
Cleland's *Memoirs of a Woman of Pleasure* intersected the publication of
Clarissa (whose final instalment appeared in December 1748), and pre-
ceded *Tom Jones* by just a fortnight. Of the three works, the *Memoirs*
undoubtedly occupies the most problematic position in the history of
the British novel, providing a particular embarrassment to any account
that centres upon the moral reformation of prose fiction in the post-
Pamela era. As a detailed portrayal of the sex life of a teenage prostitute
named Fanny Hill, which James Boswell was probably not alone in
finding 'most licentious and inflaming', this situation could perhaps
hardly be otherwise.[9] The *Memoirs'* relationship to the works of
Richardson and Fielding involves far more, though, than a simple coincidence of publishing history. While an earlier version may have circu-
lated in manuscript during the 1730s, in its final form Cleland's novel
represented a further contribution to the *Pamela/Shamela* controversy
that had animated literary culture during the early 1740s. At the levels
of language and style, the *Memoirs'* alignment with *Shamela* is most
clearly signalled by Cleland's adoption of the parodic term 'vartue', and
by Fanny's account of her sexual reunion with her true love, Charles, in
which a shift from past to present tense extends Fielding's joke about
the suspect immediacy of Pamela's epistolary retrospection: 'I see! I feel!
the delicious velvet tip! – he enters might and main with – oh! – my pen
drops from me here in the ecstasy now present to my faithful memory!'.[10]

More broadly, the sexual frankness of the novel, which scholars of the sexual literature of the period have viewed as part of an Enlightenment project to liberate sexual pleasure from its moral and religious shackles, also represents a response to Richardson's reduction of 'virtue' to a woman's sexual status; to the intactness (or otherwise) of the hymen. As Bradford Mudge puts it, Cleland's novel 'refuses to make an ethical state (virtuous or corrupt) contingent upon a bodily condition (virginal or experienced) ... Cleland's target is Richardson's fetish: the male adulation of female chastity'.[11] It would be wrong, though, to view the *Memoirs* as merely an elaboration upon Fielding's critique of *Pamela*. Just as the 'artless' (45) Fanny is not the mercenary, self-serving creature that Shamela is, so Cleland's reaction against Richardson did not involve a *wholesale* rejection of bourgeois norms and ideals. Indeed, in a 'tail-piece of morality' that is only partly parodic, Cleland's heroine ultimately emerges as a *champion* of 'VIRTUE' – albeit a version of virtue that is now happily untethered from the Richardsonian 'fetish' of female chastity (223).

Cast in the form of two letters to an unnamed female correspondent, *Memoirs of a Woman of Pleasure* comprises Fanny's first-person account of what she now looks back on as the 'scandalous stages', or 'loose part', of her life (39). The tale that Fanny has to tell is the by-then familiar one of an innocent country girl who, having been orphaned (and thus lacking familial protection), sets off to London to make her fortune, but is instead ensnared by the forces of vice that prevail in the metropolis. In Fanny's case, the vices in question are predominantly sexual ones. Fanny is not in the capital a full twenty-four hours before the bawd, Mrs Brown, persuades her to take up a place in her house of ill repute (the naïve Fanny assuming that she is to be a serving girl, rather than a sex worker). The story that follows proceeds by sexual gradations, as Fanny is incrementally initiated into the arts of whoring. At Mrs Brown's establishment, Fanny is initially broken in by Phoebe Ayres. Under the guise of female companionship, and in the tradition of the 'whore dialogue', Phoebe first ignites in Fanny the flames of sexual passion, the 'inflammable principle of pleasure' (60). Following some further lesbian dalliances, Fanny comes to want more than what she now terms 'this foolery from woman to woman' (71), although not before she has been revolted by the first man to whom Mrs Brown offers her: the elderly Mr Crofts, who possesses a 'yellow cadaverous hue' and 'breath like a jakes' (i.e. a toilet), and whom Fanny further maligns in a series of animal images, as when he looks 'goats and monkeys' (with grotesque bestial desire) at her (53–4).[12] Like the later episode

involving Mr Norbert (in which Fanny fakes her virginity), this
encounter with Crofts foregrounds the process whereby the high
moral value placed upon chastity leads to a corresponding *economic*
value, so that Mrs Brown can seek to secure a 'good market' for the
profitable 'commodity' of Fanny's maidenhead (47, 51). Significantly,
having evaded the advances of Crofts (who agrees terms for, but fails
to take her virginity), Fanny's first actual act of heterosexual intercourse takes place beyond the sphere of prostitution. It is her first and
only true love, Charles, who, having rescued her from the clutches of
Mrs Brown, teaches Fanny the distinction between 'mere lust' and 'true
love' (79). When Charles disappears, though, the once-more defenceless heroine becomes the kept mistress of Mr H–, a manly aristocrat
whom Fanny contrasts to the bulk of modern 'pretty' gentlemen (101),
but who cheats on her with Hannah, a Shamela-like maidservant.
Having been discovered in the act of avenging this slight, which
she does by seducing the well-hung servant, Will, Fanny is forced
to leave Mr H–, and she ends volume 1 taking a place in another
bawdy-house, this time the more up-market establishment of Mrs Cole.

It is at Mrs Cole's that the 'woman of pleasure' first participates
actively in prostitution; moving, as she puts it, 'from a private devotee
to pleasure into a public one' (130). Importantly, rather than triggering
a free-fall from grace, Fanny's arrival at Cole's establishment provides
her with a safe and secure environment, and with a surrogate for the
family she has lost. Developing a mother–daughter bond with Cole,
who turns out to be an exceptionally considerate bawd, Fanny now
embraces the opportunity to experiment freely with her sexual desires.
Indeed, the second volume of Cleland's text provides a kind of novelized guidebook to the sexual practices of the age. Like Phoebe's lesbian
disposition in volume 1, many of the practices depicted in this erotic
A–Z are ostensibly positioned as aberrations, 'arbitrary tastes for which
there is no accounting' (49). In the *Memoirs*, though, such deviant
appetites are largely indulged, not only by the text itself (for the
reader's pornographic pleasure), but also by the narrator and the other
characters. Rather than being scorned for his perversity, for instance,
the Puritan-like flagellant, Mr Barvile, is commiserated with as someone who labours 'under the tyranny of a cruel taste' (180). As Fanny
reports, Mrs Cole herself 'rather compassionated than blamed those
unhappy persons who are under a subjection they cannot shake off to
those arbitrary tastes that rule their appetites of pleasure with an unaccountable control' (181). Such, we surmise, is also the novel's attitude
to most of the other overpowering 'tastes' that Fanny encounters (even

as this interest in eccentric sexual 'tastes' sabotages the more rarefied contemporary interest in establishing general standards of *aesthetic* 'taste'). Notoriously, the only sexual practice that comes in for severe condemnation in the novel is sodomy. Where other opportunities arise, however, Fanny is happy to experiment to the full; until, being once more persuaded that 'the pleasures of the mind were superior to those of the body' (211), and now financially independent, she is finally reunited with Charles, with whom she settles down to a state of domestic bliss.

As even this brief overview might suggest, the *Memoirs* is an unusual and, in certain respects, conflicted novel. The work's radical bent is most starkly revealed in its conclusion, where Fanny goes unpunished for her immersion in prostitution. As Peter Wagner observes, Fanny's prosperous fate can be viewed as a 'mocking parody of Defoe's and Hogarth's warning moralism' – a parody, in particular, of Hogarth's graphic morality tale, *A Harlot's Progress* (1732), in which the harlot, Moll Hackabout, is arrested, jailed, and dies, diseased.[13] Unlike Richardson's *Clarissa*, Cleland's is not a work of the 'Tragic Kind'. If Fanny's happy ending represents a radical subversion of contemporary moralism regarding prostitution, though, this comic conclusion is driven by a somewhat less radical emphasis upon romantic love. At various points in his narrative, Cleland downgrades experiences of sexual pleasure that fail to rise above the physical. Although, during intercourse with Mr H–, all of Fanny's 'animal spirits' might rush 'mechanically' to her 'center of attraction' (thereby naturalizing the body as sexual rather than, as in Richardson, ethical), the pleasure that this gives the narrator is nevertheless 'a pleasure merely animal', which remains categorically inferior to the 'mutual love-passion' that she had earlier shared with Charles (101). The novel's manifesto regarding pleasure – that love provides the foundation for true sexual satisfaction – is strongly reasserted towards the end of the *Memoirs*, as Fanny apostrophizes love as 'the Attic salt of enjoyment ... it is undoubtedly love alone that refines, ennobles, and exalts it' (220). This eulogy to love notwithstanding, the reader is liable to end the novel feeling that, taken as a whole, the *Memoirs* is indeed fixated upon sex. Particularly in the second volume, what Cleland often appears to be envisioning is a (hetero)sexual utopia; a realm of infinitely sustainable, constantly varied acts of ecstatic intercourse, in which a succession of supremely well-endowed men and nubile female beauties share in ever-more climactic pleasures. The 'things' that Fanny's letters describe in 'minute detail' (120), then, are primarily *sexual* 'things'. As a general rule, whatever has no bearing upon the world, and the industry, of sexual pleasure is simply bracketed out of Cleland's text.

What relationship, we might ask, does Cleland's portrayal of Fanny's sexual adventures bear to the realities of prostitution in eighteenth-century Britain? One way of approaching this issue is by comparing the novel to another work published in the same year: *Satan's Harvest Home; or, The Present State of Whorecraft, Adultery, Fornication, Procuring, Pimping, Sodomy, and the Game at Flatts* (1749). As its title indicates, this text constituted a wide-ranging attack upon the sexual vices of the age. In the section on 'whorecraft', the author considered the 'vast Body of *Courtezans*' who were plying their trade on the streets of London. Like *Memoirs of a Woman of Pleasure*, *Satan's Harvest Home* envisages the capital as a place of sexual experience, whose inhabitants are skilled at preying upon the innocence of country girls. At the same time, though, there are also significant differences between the situation described in *Satan's Harvest Home* and that depicted in Cleland's work, which can help us to pinpoint more precisely what was distinctive about the *Memoirs*. Consider, for instance, the following passage from *Satan's Harvest Home*, which addresses the consequences of the rise in the number of prostitutes operating in London:

> The greatest Evil that attends this Vice, or could befal Mankind, is the Propagation of that infectious Disease call'd the *French Pox*, which in two Centuries, has made such incredible Havock all over *Europe*. In these Kingdoms, it so seldom fails to attend Whoring, now-a-days mistaken for Gallantry and Politeness, that a hale robust Constitution is esteem'd a Mark of Ungentility and Ill-breeding, and a healthy young Fellow is look'd upon with the same View, as if he had spent his Life in a Cottage. Our Gentlemen of the Army, whose unsettled Way of Life makes it inconvenient for them to marry, are hereby very much weaken'd and enervated, and render'd unfit to undergo such Hardships, as are necessary for defending and sup-porting the Honour of their Country ... our Gentry in general, seem to distinguish themselves by an ill state of Health; in all Probability, the Effect of this pernicious Distemper. Nothing being more common, than to hear People of Quality complain of *rude vulgar Health*, and curse their *Porterly Constitutions*.[14]

In essence, this passage presents a sexualized version of mid-eighteenth-century concerns about the health of the nation. Here, venereal disease is blamed for the ill health that other writers would attribute to 'the vapours', 'the spleen', or to the national hypochondria that had come to be known as 'the English malady'. The nationalistic aspect of the discussion is manifest in the reference to 'the *French Pox*', as venereal disease (more specifically, syphilis) was commonly known. This foreign sexual distemper, it is here argued, was enervating the British male, rendering the country incapable of defending itself against its enemies (such as France itself). For the author of *Satan's Harvest Home*, then, the 'present state of whorecraft' was intimately linked to a state of national debility, to the simultaneously moral and physical decline of the British people.

Cleland's own depiction of 'whorecraft' presents a striking contrast to such anxieties. Far from spreading venereal disease far and wide, Fanny and her colleagues entirely avoid sexual infection. In Cleland's text, in fact, Fanny is more likely to improve than to impair the health of her clients. Before his fatal journey to Bath, for instance, Mr Norbert – the consumptive maiden-hunter – experiences an improvement in his health, as he keeps Fanny as his beloved mistress (179). More generally, and more significantly, the *Memoirs* also embraces the apparently modish error highlighted by *Satan's Harvest Home*, of mistaking 'Whoring' for 'Gallantry and Politeness'. As Cleland confirms on a number of occasions, Mrs Cole is a *refined* bawd, who deals only with 'customers of distinction' (125). In this concern with the quality of her clientele, Cole resembles another fictional bawd from earlier in the period, who had been described in *The London Bawd* (1711). Emphasizing the gentility of her house, this earlier bawd had claimed that, as 'none but Persons of Quality' could be admitted there, 'the Ladies Honours are thereby secur'd'.[15] In Cleland's text, similarly, 'Whoring' is allowed to remain honourable if it is done with the right sort of people – that is, with 'Persons of Quality', or upper-class men.

Just what kind of 'refinement' is it that Cleland accords to Mrs Cole's brothel? Consider Fanny's early account of her new workplace:

> In short, this was the safest, politest, and, at the same time, the most thorough house of accommodation in town, everything being conducted so that decency made no intrenchment upon the most libertine pleasures, in the practice of which, too, the choice familiars of the house had found the secret so rare and difficult of reconciling even all the refinements of taste and delicacy with the most gross and determinate gratifications of sensuality. (132)

In Fanny's view, Mrs Cole and her circle have perfected an ordinarily elusive combination of refinement and sexual satisfaction. Significantly,

Fanny emphasizes that the 'libertine pleasures' of the house – the excesses of sensual indulgence – are not tempered by any regard to the dictates of 'decency', or conventional (ethico-sexual) restraints. Rather, what has been forged here is a form of what we might call 'polite libertinism'. Instead of denying or restraining their sexual urges, the company have found a way to *genteelize* their sexual practices. The most sustained demonstration of this refined libertinism in action is provided early in volume 2, during a group sex scene that is punningly referred to as 'the country dances' (150). Following Emily's turn in these 'dances', Fanny returns to her theme of the refinement of the occasion:

> As soon as he had disengaged, the charming Emily got up, and we crowded round her with congratulations and other officious little services; for it is to be noted that, though all modesty and reserve were banished the transaction of these pleasures, good manners and politeness were inviolably observed: here was no gross ribaldry, no offensive or rude behaviour, or ungenerous reproaches to the girls for their compliance with the humours and desires of the men. (157)

In this scene, a moral, or *ethically* based notion of female 'modesty and reserve' is displaced by an *interpersonal* model of decorous behaviour. While 'decency' is again not allowed to dull the enjoyment of sexual pleasure, no lewd words are spoken, and the women continue to receive the respect of the men. As Fanny suggests, then, in a situation in which conventional codes of *sexual* conduct have been entirely transgressed, the niceties of *social* conduct remain firmly in place, and might even be said to be encouraged by the party's transgression of notions of sexual morality which, Fanny elsewhere suggests, are grounded in vulgar prejudices.

To interpret the text only in this manner would, certainly, be to take the *Memoirs* too much on its own terms. For modern readers in particular, there are further considerations that seriously compromise this idealized vision of polite prostitution, not the least of which are the palpable inequalities of gender and class that underpin it. In promulgating her philosophy of pleasure, Fanny herself promotes the 'talent of pleasing' over all 'titles, dignities, honours' – an argument that sounds very much like a parodic, sexualized version of Pamela's 'levelling' promotion of virtue over hereditary status (117). As in the real world of prostitution, however, in the *Memoirs* it is principally disempowered, low-born women who sell their services to high-born men. Such inequality permeates even the most romanticized of sexual occasions.

During the 'country dances', for instance, the women operate under what Cleland terms a 'doctrine of passive obedience and nonresistance' to the sexual tastes of the men (134). While Fanny might very well be at liberty to 'refuse' the men (150), it is also clear that the power of choice ultimately lies with the men themselves – that it is in the men's gift to *allow* the women this option of refusal. In other ways, also, the novel reveals the strain involved in idealizing Mrs Cole's sexual academy as a locus of refinement. Describing Harriet's congress with a young baronet, for instance, Fanny states that 'All her air and motions breathed only unreserved, unlimited complaisance, without the least mixture of impudence or prostitution' (152). In part, what Fanny is trying to do here is to remove all taint of monetary transaction from the sexual transaction between the pair. Clearly, though, this praise of Harriet's selfless generosity involves the rather dubious proposition that what we are viewing here is a form of prostitution *without* 'prostitution'. As Randolph Trumbach has argued, then, in comparison with the real world of prostitution what Cleland constructs in the *Memoirs*' second volume is in many respects a 'domesticated fantasy' – an idealized image of 'whorecraft' that takes place in a safe, controlled environment, and that largely lacks the complications of pregnancy, disease, drunkenness and criminality.[16]

To allow that Cleland's representation of sexual behaviour is in many ways unrealistic is not to suggest that his text lacks significance for the development of the novel at mid-century. Intriguingly, one of the key means by which Cleland endeavours to maintain the reader's interest in Fanny's serial sexual adventures is by having her seek after new pleasures. Having tired of Mr Norbert, the under-performing maiden-hunter, for instance, Fanny embarks upon a 'novel' adventure in which she is 'treated like a common street-plyer' by a young sailor (177). Similarly, the narrator's willingness to submit to the prickly attentions of the flagellant, Barvile, is explained by a correspondingly unaccountable impulse on her own part: 'a sudden caprice, a gust of fancy for trying a new experiment' (181). Fanny's own desire for sexual novelty and experimentation, then, plays an important role in enabling Cleland to vary the sexual feast of his narrative, thereby maintaining the engaging 'novelty' of the *Memoirs* itself. Alongside this pursuit of new sexual diversions, Fanny is also instrumental in educating the reader in the particular kind of reader response required by the *Memoirs* – what we might call the aesthetic art of pornographic spectatorship. During a number of sex scenes to which she is only an observer, Fanny directs and (through this direction) validates the reader's own curious gaze.

Besides simply *looking*, though, Fanny is herself aroused by what she observes. During the novel's first scene of heterosexual intercourse, which sees Mrs Brown engaging with a Herculean horse-grenadier, Fanny attests to the pleasure of voyeurism, as watching the scene makes 'every vein' in her body 'circulate liquid fires' (62–3). Here and elsewhere, as Fanny and others peep through crevices onto explicitly sexual prospects, the thrill of access to private (female) space, which had generated some of the less purely moral interest in Richardson's *Pamela*, is taken a considerable stage further. The visual pleasures enjoyed by Fanny and her fellows *within* the narrative are not, of course, fully identical to the voyeuristic pleasures offered to the reader *of* Cleland's novel. Neither should we ignore the gender bias implicit in the text's pornographic designs upon the reader (although the sexual attractions of *men* are by no means simply overlooked in the work – witness Fanny's description of her first night with Charles). Importantly, though, the assumption that a correspondence exists, between the voyeurism represented *in* the text and the textual voyeurism of the reader, continues to operate until the very end of the work; when, during her passionate reunion with Charles, Fanny keeps 'the curtains undrawn', once more inviting the reader to gaze upon the private space of sexual pleasure (217). As a number of recent critics have argued, this voyeuristic model of sexual–textual response also informs the novel's much-noted scene of male sodomy. For while, in Fanny's and Mrs Cole's view, the 'taste' for sodomy is a sexual aberration too far, what Fanny's narrative report of the episode offers to the *reader* of the novel is a fairly full description of same-sex penetration between two men – a description that was probably responsible for the warrant that was served on the author, printer and publisher of the *Memoirs* in November 1749.

Further to these proffered pleasures of narrative novelty and affective voyeurism, there is also one other important way in which Cleland set about securing his readers' interest in his novel. As the *Memoirs* reveals, with regard to verbal (as opposed to graphic) texts the *ennui* that pornography is liable to induce is a matter not just of running out of sexual positions to describe, but of running out of language with which to describe them. The need to vary the sexual idiom of the novel is addressed directly in Fanny's letters. At she commences her account, Cleland's narrator is fairly optimistic about her ability to recapture in writing the excitement of her scandalous past. Acknowledging that her letters will violate the 'laws of decency', Fanny nevertheless endeavours to convey her sexual history 'with the same liberty that I led it' (39). Her exclamation – 'Truth! stark naked truth' – quibbles nicely upon two meanings: a veracious (historical or realistic) narrative, and the sexual subject matter *of* that narrative. By the time of her second letter, however, Fanny is more aware of some of the difficulties involved in the writing of sexual memoirs. As she notes, to describe yet more sexual adventures using the same 'images' and 'figures' would simply dull the interest of the reader (129). Broadly speaking, we would argue, Fanny's dilemma of representation was the same problem that had faced the author himself. Cleland's solution to this problem was to lace the *Memoirs* with inventive euphemisms, so that, in this novel, pubic hair becomes 'the downy sprig-moss'; the female pudendum, the 'soft laboratory of love'; and a baronet's penis, 'the master-member of the revels' – a kind of phallic 'master of ceremonies' (153–4). In depicting the sexual panorama of his age, in fact, Cleland drew upon a wide range of available idioms. During the course of the *Memoirs*, the reader is regaled with *nautical* terms (during Fanny's encounter with the sailor); *botanical* imagery (as when Dick's penis is described as 'the genuine sensitive plant' (198)); *musical* metaphors (as at the end of the novel, when Fanny and Charles play 'over again the same opera, with the same delightful harmony and concert' (221)); *mechanical* imagery (as when the phallic 'engine' is 'well wound up' (205)); traditional *poetic* imagery, of liquid, fire and liquid fires; *religious* figures (as when the baronet sends into Harriet his 'soul, distilled in liquid sweets' (154)); *military* metaphors (because, as Fanny suggests, 'it is in love as it is in war, where the longest weapon carries it' (199)); and even terms imported from the discourse of *taste*, or aesthetic appreciation – as when Will's gigantic penis is described as 'an object of terror and delight' (as something both sublime and beautiful, or a member that is simultaneously 'Gothic' and picturesque (109)). Coupled with the novel variety of 'adventures' depicted within the narrative (126), this *linguistic* variegation was designed to diversify the novel sufficiently to maintain the reader's interest in its succession of sex scenes. Ultimately, it could be argued, the novel concludes as much due to verbal as to sexual exhaustion. Yet if, finally, the *Memoirs* runs out of new words to convey the pleasures of the flesh, this very *striving* for verbal ingenuity remains one of the work's most distinctive contributions to the discourse of the novel.

Francis Coventry, Pompey the Little

One of the more peculiar sub-species of the novel to have emerged during the second half of the eighteenth century was the 'spy-novel', or 'novel of circulation'. Typically, such novels feature as their central character an animal or inanimate object, whose adventures are narrated (sometimes by the animal or object itself) as it passes through the hands of various owners. Among the better-known examples of such works are Charles Johnstone's *Chrysal; or, The Adventures of a Guinea* (1760–65) and Tobias Smollett's *The History and Adventures of an Atom* (1769). In an assortment of other works, it was also possible for contemporary readers to follow the fortunes of items of clothing (a waistcoat or petticoat; an Irish smock; a golden-headed cane); vehicles (a post-chaise; a sedan-chair; a hackney coach); creatures (mouse, cat, flea, fly and louse); and other units of currency (a bank note; a rupee; a silver penny). In these formally baggy works, the central figure acts as a 'spy' upon various sectors and levels of society, its non-human status allowing it an unusual degree of access to a broad spectrum of characters and, within this, to various scenes of *private* life, into which the novels enable their readers to peep. Along with its variety of protagonists, this spy-centred sub-genre of the novel also incorporated other variations of tone and emphasis. Viewing such works as a subspecies of the 'amatory novel', in his broad study of eighteenth-century erotic literature, Peter Wagner notes that many of these works possess a bawdy impulse, a bias towards erotic and scandalous subject matter.[17] Recently, scholars have become particularly interested in the works that feature currency, and have debated whether these fictions illustrated the individual alienation produced by a commercial society (and a commercial print culture), or whether, by personalizing money itself, they may have helped readers to come to terms with life *in* such a society.[18] Our own discussion returns to what can be viewed as the first fully fledged British circulation novel: Francis Coventry's *The History of Pompey the Little; or, The Life and Adventures of a Lap-Dog* (1751). While Coventry's experimental narrative may lack the erotic and economic interest of some of the later examples of circulation fiction, it is especially revealing of the ways in which this new generic variation both drew upon, and deviated from, the Fieldingesque novel of social 'adventures'.

In terms of artistic technique, *Pompey the Little* offers a good illustration of what Wayne Booth has described as Fielding's pervasive influence upon the kind of narrator employed in the new fiction published during the 1750s. As Booth observes:

Fielding's narrator was immediately imitated by almost everyone. The result was that, whereas most novels in previous decades had used the self-conscious narrator only incidentally, most novels in the fifties indulged in a great amount of intrusive play. Novelists were aware that something had happened to the role of the narrator, and that they must somehow abandon the 'old style' and take up with the new.[19]

As Booth indicates, for novelists writing in the immediate wake of Fielding's elaboration upon the narratorial voice it was difficult, if not impossible, simply to revert to the stable, unobtrusive, or effaced narrator that had characterized much previous fiction. In *Pompey the Little*, the 'new', Fieldingesque narrator makes his presence felt in various allusions to the reader, such as jokes upon the reader's hope that the work may be nearly over (and regarding the reader falling asleep), or when he warns the reader – 'my gentle Friend, whoever thou art' – against making particular 'Applications' of the characters sketched in the novel to real people (which is itself an adaptation, into the novel, of a Swiftian satiric technique). At a more basic level, such narrative self-consciousness also permeates the novel's chapter-headings: 'Containing what the Reader will know, if he reads it'; 'A prodigious short Chapter'; and 'A Dissertation upon *Nothing*' (the latter being a somewhat hackneyed joke regarding the *substance* of nothing, which had recent precedents in works by, among others, Rochester, Swift and Fielding himself).[20] If, like many of his contemporaries, Coventry drew heavily upon the narrative self-awareness of Fielding's new province of fiction, though, he was by no means backward in acknowledging the debt. In an effusive Dedication that he added to the third edition of the novel (1752), the apprentice writer was happy to attest that Fielding did 'unquestionably stand foremost in this species of composition' (Fielding's novels being 'master-pieces and complete models in their kind'), and criticized those readers who expressed contempt for the genre – who were, as he put it, 'much too wise to be amused' by a novel (xli–xliii). As this Dedication shows, even within a few years of the publication of *Joseph Andrews* and *Tom Jones*, Fielding was being canonized as the premier native exponent of a form of writing that, largely due to his own work, now had strong claims to cultural importance.

If Coventry was influenced by Fielding, then, he hardly sought to hide his hero's light under a bushel. Besides his imitation of the Fieldingesque narrative voice, Coventry also adopted the bathetic, mock-heroic style that was one of the tonal keynotes of the 'comic Epic-Poem in Prose'. Nowhere is this better seen than in the novel's opening chapter – entitled '*A Panegyric upon Dogs, together with some*

Observations on modern Novels and Romances' – which begins with the
bold assertion that 'VARIOUS and wonderful, in all Ages, have been
the Actions of Dogs ...'. The following (edited) extract gives a flavour
of the chapter's pseudo-learned, mock-heroic humour:

> IF we look back into ancient History, we shall find the wisest and
> most celebrated Nations of Antiquity, as it were, contending with
> one another, which should pay the greatest Honour to Dogs. ... and
> if we descend to later Times, we shall not want Examples in our own
> Days and Nation, of great Men's devoting themselves to Dogs. ... as
> no Exception can reasonably be taken against the Dignity of my Hero,
> much less can I expect any will arise against the Nature of this Work,
> which one of my Cotemporaries [*sic*] declares to be an *Epic Poem in
> Prose*; and I cannot help promising myself some Encouragement, in
> this *Life-writing Age* especially, where no Character is thought
> too inconsiderable to engage the public Notice, or too abandoned to
> be set up as a Pattern of Imitation. The lowest and most con-
> temptible Vagrants, Parish-Girls, Chamber-Maids, Pick-Pockets, and
> Highwaymen, find Historians to record their Praises, and Readers to
> wonder at their Exploits: Star-Gazers, superannuated Strumpets,
> quarrelling Lovers, all think themselves authorized to appeal to the
> Publick, and to *write Apologies* for their Lives. Even the Prisons and
> Stews are ransacked to find Materials for Novels and Romances. ...
> when such Multitudes of Lives are daily offered to the Publick, writ-
> ten *by the Saddest Dogs*, or *of the saddest Dogs* of the Times, it may be
> considered as some little Merit to have chosen a Subject worthy the
> Dignity of History; and in this single View I may be allowed to
> paragon myself with the incomparable Writer of the Life of *Cicero*, in
> that I have deserted the beaten Track of Biographers, and chosen a
> Subject worthy the attention of polite and classical Readers. (1–6)

As the comic repetition of the word 'dogs' in this chapter testifies,
Coventry's novel is not only self-conscious, but also often self-ironizing
and self-deflating. As with Fielding's own use of the mock-heroic, however, this tongue-in-cheek defence of the narration of a dog's life and
adventures provides a means of mocking subjects who are deemed to be
even *less* worthy of attention than the hero of the current work. Some
of Coventry's targets here are, in fact, Fielding's own. The novel about
a chamber-maid, for instance, is *Pamela* itself; and Coventry also appropriates from the opening of *Joseph Andrews* Fielding's mockery of Colley
Cibber's autobiographical *Apology* (1740) and of Conyers Middleton,

author of a biography of Cicero (1741). To these now decade-old targets, Coventry adds new offenders of his own, including recent novels such as *The History of Charlotte Summers, the Fortunate Parish Girl* (1750). Intriguingly, a passage that initially appeared in this chapter, but which Coventry deleted for the third edition, contained further hits at the 'memoirs of a lady of quality' (Lady Vane), which had appeared in Smollett's *Peregrine Pickle* (1751), and at Cleland's *Memoirs of a Woman of Pleasure* (whose heroine, Fanny Hill, is herself referenced later in *Pompey*, as one of the female acquaintances of Williams, a student at Cambridge (181–2)). In effect, what Coventry was doing here was updating Fielding's satiric audit of the debased products of contemporary culture – 'debased' in the double sense of both addressing low or unworthy subject-matter, and of being written without recourse to the historical knowledge and verbal resources of the properly educated writer. Indeed, for all the irony involved in this chapter's introduction of its heroic subject, Coventry's comic display of learning about canines was at least partly aimed at the very 'polite and classical' readers who, in theory at least, would refuse to go near tales of such 'low' exploits as those of vagrants, pick-pockets and highwaymen.

In the main body of *Pompey*, Coventry's central narrative conceit – the circulation of a Bologna lap-dog – provides a flexible vehicle for satire upon a range of social affectations. As the narrator observes, Fortune has destined Pompey to 'a great Variety of Adventures' (17). In tracing these adventures, the novel itself takes in a variety of character types, occupations, and social classes: Methodists, scholars, and professional writers; fashionable aristocrats, low-born workers, and the aspiring bourgeoisie. Throughout the novel, though, it is to scenes of high life that Pompey continually returns. This is the case even when he ends up in prison, where he is joined by two Lords – self-styled 'Men of Fashion' who, believing that they are not bound by the legal and moral codes that apply to the rest of society, are actually dissipated rakes (80). Like Gay's *The Beggar's Opera*, one of the lessons of Coventry's satire is that the fashionable world of the upper classes is far from hermetically sealed from the lives of criminals and the lower orders – a point that is nicely verbalized in the phrase 'a Mob of Quality' (151). Within the narrative itself, the association of civility and criminality is perhaps most fully realized when a Frenchified gentleman (Jeremy Griskin) is revealed to be a malefactor, recently returned from transportation to Jamaica. As the self-enamoured Griskin himself observes: 'Having been a pick-pocket, a sharper, a slave, and a highwayman, I am now the peculiar favourite of all the ladies at *Bath*' (94). That scenes of high life should provide the dominant arena of Pompey's circulation is, though, entirely apposite. As the example of Belinda in Pope's *The Rape of the Lock* attests, during this period lap-dogs were most commonly associated with upper-class ladies, for whom they represented an accoutrement of conspicuous fashionability. Indeed, it might very well be argued that, even in this canine-centred spy-novel, Coventry courted a kind of representational realism. For, as well as passing mainly through the hands of ladies and gentlemen, during the course of the narrative Pompey is not admitted anywhere to which, in real life, a lap-dog could not *plausibly* gain access.

If Pompey spends most of his days among upper-class ladies and gentlemen, however, it is this very social milieu that bears the brunt of Coventry's satire. What were the perceived failings of eighteenth-century high society, that Coventry sought to expose in his novel? Above all, we would suggest, the novel presents the social world of the privileged as a superficial milieu, which is uninterested in enquiring beyond the surface of things. This fixation upon outward appearance is revealed by the vanity of the English gentleman, Hillario (whose primary concern is his clothing, and whose principal talent is a 'most accomplished Way of talking Nonsense' (13–14)), and by the novel's satire upon fashionable occasions of social display, such as 'drums' (parties organized by upper-class ladies). As Coventry reveals, this was also an elitist culture, which imagined itself as an exclusive club, inaccessible to the majority. The elite's desire to demarcate those in the club from those beyond the pale is most clearly articulated when the vainglorious Count Tag, an ageing suitor to the respectable Aurora, sets about explaining the meaning of the phrase '*people one knows*':

> '*O mon dieu!*' cries the *Count*, 'your lordship surely can't ask such a question. The people one knows, my lord, are the people who are in the round of assemblies and public diversions, people who have the *scavoir vivre*, the *ton de bonne compaigne*, as the French call it – in short, people who frize their hair in the newest fashion, and have their cloaths made at *Paris*.'
>
> 'AND are these the only people worth one's regard in life?' said his lordship.
>
> 'ABSOLUTELY, my lord!' cries the *Count*, 'I have no manner of idea or conception of any body else.' (130)

The very use here of the phrase 'people one knows' places Tag in the camp of Fielding's Lady Booby (and of her mimic, Mrs Slipslop), whose appellations for her social inferiors had provided the negative counterpart to Tag's self-descriptors: '*strange Persons, People one does not know, the Creature, Wretches, Beasts, Brutes*'.[21] As the Count's theatrical defence of his own haughtiness reveals, such fashionable aloofness was partly a matter of *style*, which leant heavily upon a modish idiom of Frenchified keywords (an accumulation of effete lingo that Tag's noble respondent terms 'contemptible jargon'). This fashionable idiom recalls the then-current idea that a gentleman was characterized by a quality of *je ne sais quoi* ('I know not what') – a certain indefinable *something*, that marked 'the Quality' off from the rest of the race. For Coventry himself, the particular irony of this process of social demarcation lay in the fact that the truly defining characteristics of the *beau monde* were its triviality and modishness. As the narrator states early in the novel: 'the fashionable Part of the World are glad of any fresh Topic of Conversation, that will not much fatigue their Understandings; and the Arrival of a new Fop, the Sight of a new Chariot, or the Appearance of a new Fashion, are all Articles of the highest Importance to them' (14). This critique of the fashionable turn for novelty also extends to the novel's satire of the Methodist movement. Mocking Lady Harridan's late conversion to the evangelical cause, Coventry presents a pitiless portrait of the movement's female followers: 'battered and super-annuated jades of pleasure, who being grown sick of themselves, and weary of the world, were now fled to methodism, merely as the newest sort of folly, that had lately been invented' (65). As Coventry insinuates, a religiously motivated retreat from the giddy round of pleasures did not necessarily represent the polar opposite to an unthinking immersion *in* such trivial pursuits – the warmth with which these former ladies of fashion threw themselves into their new enthusiastic vocation might involve (at best) a sublimation and (at worst) a simple redirection of their former passions. As the novel's broad critique of the taste for new things also shows, despite the relative new-ness of their own medium, writers of novels at this time did not necessarily welcome *other* new forms of cultural practice, and were indeed far from fully embracing the contemporary passion for 'novelty' itself.

What role, we should ask, does Pompey himself play in Coventry's satiric rendering of fashionable culture? Periodically, Pompey not only observes his owners, but becomes intimately entangled in their lives, going so far as to attempt to emulate them. As the novel reveals, given its close association with its owner, the lap-dog was liable to be drawn into the social and amorous commerce between upper-class men and women. By praising Pompey, for instance, Hillario is able to convey

'indirect Compliments to his Mistress', and to secure access to the
apartments of Lady Tempest, on the pretext of visiting Pompey himself
(9, 20). As in the opening chapter, the narrative's continual return to
the subject of dogs itself plays an important role in undermining the
pretensions of the characters it sketches. As Coventry bathetically notes
towards the end of a lengthy account of the life and marriage of Lady
Tempest, 'What gives her a Place in this History' is not any outstanding
personal quality or noteworthy achievement but rather 'her Fondness
for Dogs' (26). These early scenes also see Coventry parodying fashionable society through comic analogies between the courting habits of
canines and humans. At the same time that an Italian nobleman
engages in an amorous intrigue with a courtesan, for instance, the
nobleman's lap-dog (Pompey's father) begins 'an Affair of Gallantry
with a Favourite little Bitch named *Phyllis*, at that Time the Darling of
this *Fille de Joye*' (7). In time, and in more mock-heroic fashion,
Pompey himself starts aping the manners and lifestyle of his owners.
In chapter 6, in which (as the jocular chapter heading puts it) 'Our Hero
becomes a Dog of the Town, and shines in High-Life', Pompey is ush-
ered by Lady Tempest into experiencing 'all the Joys and Vanities' that
the town has to offer. The particular irony of Pompey's newly acquired
gentility is that it exposes the only *imperfectly* refined and accomplished
nature of this 'refined and accomplished Age'. As the narrator informs
us, having become a 'Dog of the Town', and now 'perfectly well-bred',
Pompey naturally 'gave himself up to Intrigue, and had seldom less
than two or three Amours on his Hands at a time with *Bitches of the
highest Fashion*'. The genteel 'breeding' of the English upper classes, it
seems, is indistinguishable from the physical 'breeding' of beasts. What
Coventry positions here as the *ill*-breeding of Pompey also extends to
his attitude towards the members of other social classes. Like his well-
to-do owners, the lap-dog, as a canine 'of Quality', quickly assumes an
air of superiority over dogs of 'inferior Station' (30–1). At such
moments, Coventry's diminutive mutt becomes not just the medium
but also the butt of the novel's satiric critique of high society.

In the 'novel of circulation', then, the central figure is as much a
satiric device as he (or 'it') is a fully fleshed out, novelistic character.
As Liz Bellamy notes, perhaps the key difference between the works of
Fielding and Smollett on the one hand, and that of Coventry on the
other, is that the central actor of *Pompey the Little* lacks *volition* – the
ability to make his own decisions, and thus to partake in the formation
of his own destiny.[22] Coventry's use of a non-human protagonist
produces an essentially *passive* hero, whose behaviour we can only

minimally evaluate in moral terms. Beyond Pompey himself, in the reading it is increasingly noticeable that what the novel describes is largely a *succession* of characters, who bear little if any social relationship to one another. This problem bears upon Bellamy's broader argument that the 'novel of circulation' portrays society as 'a series of atomised and alienated individuals': 'The characters of the novel of circulation are almost invariably selfish and self seeking, the products of a fragmented society unrestrained by effective ethical codes.'[23] If Bellamy's argument is largely correct in terms of Coventry's characters, it nevertheless misrepresents the tone of a novel like *Pompey the Little*, which partakes of a more tempered form of satire than her description would imply. As John Cleland noted in a laudatory account of the work in *The Monthly Review* for February 1751, although Coventry 'laughs at the world', he does so 'without doing it the honour to be angry with it. His lashes, however smart, carry with them rather the marks of a benevolent correction, than of the spleen of misanthropy.'[24] As Cleland intimated, *Pompey the Little* does not ultimately reduce men to beasts. In terms of the recent satiric tradition to which Coventry alludes in the novel, a stark contrast to the parodic fashioning of Pompey as a 'Dog of the Town' would be Swift's destabilizing account of the relationships between the human (but increasingly unstable) Gulliver, the bestial (but clinically rational) Houynhnms, and the liminal Yahoos, in book 4 of *Gulliver's Travels*. The necessary qualifications to Bellamy's argument, with regard to *Pompey* specifically, are also highlighted by its failure to take into account the role of less disreputable or (socially and morally) unmoored characters, the most notable examples of whom are Theodosia, Aurora and Aurora's honourable suitor. Despite their romantic monikers and their dalliance in resorts of fashionable pleasure, Theodosia and Aurora are presented by Coventry as properly refined ladies. While these women might 'laugh at some Follies of their Acquaintance' at Bath (that 'great Rendezvous of Pleasure'), they do so reasonably, 'without Severity, or Ill-nature'. As Coventry also observes, Theodosia is a woman of 'good Sense', rather than a mere 'Slave to Pleasure' (116–17). As the inclusion of such characters attests, if *most* of the individuals in Coventry's novel are selfish and self-seeking, even in this benighted social and moral landscape there also are exceptional individuals, who can be held up as having successfully integrated the polite social forms and ethical codes of the period.

If the society depicted by Coventry is not *entirely* fragmented, though, the novel itself remains largely a tissue of fragments, or satiric vignettes. Like *Memoirs of a Woman of Pleasure*, when compared with

Fielding's novels, *Pompey the Little* is lacking in *design*, in the kind of organizing vision that might provide the text with a more consequential, ethical and narrative structure. Coventry must surely have been aware of this weakness. In the novel's Dedication to Fielding, the author himself declares that 'Few books of this kind have ever been written with a spirit equal to *Joseph Andrews*, and no story that I know of, was ever invented with more happiness, or conducted with more art and management than that of *Tom Jones*' (xliv). Clearly, the crafted 'art and management' of Fielding's novelistic blockbuster would not be easily emulated. It was, perhaps, the futility of attempting to match the authorial artistry of Fielding's recently published 'master-piece' that set Coventry himself on a different path. In the final analysis, *Pompey the Little* is most revealing as an example of a mid-eighteenth-century text carrying the techniques that Fielding had introduced into the novel into new kinds of narrative territory, thereby adding a novel twist to the 'comic Epic-Poem in Prose'. Original to the extent that it employed a non-human protagonist, Coventry's work inaugurated an intriguing sub-species of the novel which, in dispensing with the advances that had recently been made in psychological insight and narrative architectonics, veered the genre towards the path of impressionistic social satire.

Charlotte Lennox, The Female Quixote

In the preceding paragraph, we referred to techniques that Fielding had 'introduced' into the genre of the novel. In certain respects, it is more accurate to say that he had *re*-introduced such techniques into the genre, or that he introduced certain techniques for the first time into the *eighteenth-century, British* novel. For, in instigating his new province of fiction, Fielding had himself drawn upon the past – most notably, in terms of prose literature, upon Cervantes' *Don Quixote*. As the title-page to *Joseph Andrews* openly avowed, Fielding's first novel was written 'in imitation of the manner of Cervantes'. Following Fielding, the 'manner of Cervantes' would continue to exert a considerable shaping influence upon the development of the British novel during the important first phase of its consolidation as a serious cultural force. What was this foreign text that played such an important role in the making of the novel? Originally published in Spain at the beginning of the seventeenth century (in 1604/05 and 1614/15), *Don Quixote* relates the story of a bookish gentleman who reads so many chivalric romances that he loses his wits, starts to believe that he is himself a romantic hero (or 'knight errant'), and goes out into the world in search of noble adventures. In his heroic acts, Quixote is guided by his love for Dulcinea del Toboso, his idealized (and imaginary) vision of a romantic mistress. Inevitably, because the deluded Quixote interprets the real world *through* romance conventions, his actions are absurdly misguided. Most famously, perhaps, when confronted by a windmill, what Quixote sees is a giant, which he sets about attacking. In another famous episode that exemplifies the text's interest in the clash between chivalric codes of conduct and the laws of the state, Cervantes' knight of the woeful countenance liberates a group of galley slaves (chain-ganged criminals). As this episode demonstrates, his noble intentions notwithstanding, Quixote is a social menace, whose adventures often cause harm to both himself and others (not least to his squire, the earthy Sancho Panza). Framing these narrative adventures, *Don Quixote* also displays a sophisticated metafictional self-consciousness about its status as a work of artistic representation. This important aspect of Cervantes' comedy comes to the fore in part 2, in which Don Quixote and Sancho Panza are themselves informed that the history of their adventures in part 1 has now been published. Ironically, this printed embodiment of their exploits only serves to confirm Don Quixote in his romantic delusions. As nobody else has accompanied them on their travels, Quixote reasons, the author of this history must certainly be some enchanter, who possesses magical access to their deeds. Later, Quixote and Sancho also hear about a *false* continuation of their history, also recently published. Overhearing a stranger relate that this fraudulent sequel describes the knight falling out of love with Dulcinea, Don Quixote forcefully declares the falsity of this report, which casts doubt upon his possession of the core knightly virtue of *constancy*. In this episode, Cervantes presents his readers with the spectacle of a fictional character declaiming against the misrepresentation of himself in a fictional text, which is criticized for being unfaithful to the life of the *real* Don Quixote. As this layering of textual ironies suggests, any novel written in 'imitation' of the Cervantic manner was likely to make great comic play of the relationship, and the disparity, between the worlds of fiction and reality.

While many novels written after *Joseph Andrews* display this Cervantic inheritance to some degree, a more specific sub-species of 'quixotic novel' also developed at this time, the foremost examples of which are Charlotte Lennox's *The Female Quixote; or, The Adventures of Arabella* (1752), Tobias Smollett's *The Life and Adventures of Sir Launcelot Greaves* (1760–61), and Richard Graves' *The Spiritual Quixote; or,*

The Summer's Ramble of Mr. Geoffry Wildgoose (1773). Here, we focus
on *The Female Quixote*, the work that made Lennox's name as a writer
of merit, and that can be regarded as having initiated this novelistic sub-
species. With its feminized take on the Quixote myth, Lennox's novel
lacks some of the textual effects that attest to Cervantes' influence upon
other works of this period. It was from *Don Quixote*, for instance, that
Fielding and Smollett drew the license to incorporate into their works
the kinds of 'low' material, incidents, and idioms that represented the
'impolite other' of Richardsonian fiction. *The Female Quixote*, certainly,
exercises more verbal and textual discretion than either the quotidian
comedy of these authors, or the extreme self-referentiality of Sterne's
Tristram Shandy. For critics steeped in the Augustan comic tradition,
this is precisely the problem with the work. In his book-length study of
Cervantes' presence in eighteenth-century England, for instance,
Ronald Paulson devalues Lennox's achievement largely on account of
his sense that she was a writer 'from the camp of Richardson' (whose
Pamela he calls a 'prototype of the solemn Quixote'), rather than from
the camp of the ironic Fielding, and his amiable Parson Adams.[25]
In other respects, though, Lennox's recasting of Dulcinea *as* Quixote
involved an especially apposite reworking of Cervantes' model. For, by
contrast to the situation that subsisted in early seventeenth-century
Spain, in eighteenth-century Britain the reading of romances was identified almost entirely with women. Emulating Cervantes' tale of 'the
bad Effects of a whimsical study' (as her opening chapter-heading
puts it), *The Female Quixote* thus portrayed romance-reading as the
modern woman's quixotism.

It is the novel's treatment of the French romance tradition that lies
at the heart of the modern critical debate over *The Female Quixote*.
In what follows, we present the novel as a double-edged discourse,
which allows of two main kinds of reading that focus respectively on
genre and gender. The more immediate reading is the 'anti-romance'
reading, which concerns the relationship between fiction and history.
From this perspective, Lennox's novel represents a substantial contribution to a contemporary anti-romance discourse. Significantly, a number
of important contributions to this discourse had appeared during the
early 1750s, immediately prior to *The Female Quixote*, as the publication of *Clarissa* and *Tom Jones*, along with growing nationalistic sentiment, strengthened the case for the novel and gave renewed impetus to
the project of differentiating it from the more suspect fictionality of
romance. Along with *An Essay on the New Species of Writing* (1751),
which extolled Fielding's success in heroically vanquishing the romance

and driving it from English shores (and which is sometimes attributed to Francis Coventry), these years also saw the publication of Samuel Johnson's famous discussion of the topic in issue number 4 of his periodical, *The Rambler* (which was published on 31 March 1750). What, precisely, was the relationship between this context of ideas, and Lennox's tale of a quixotic lady whose head is turned by reading too many of these apparently outmoded and unrealistic narratives? By fleshing out the more formal critiques mounted in essays, pamphlets, and novelistic prefaces, we would suggest, Lennox's novel both particularized, and elaborated upon, the contemporary reaction against romance. From the outset, Lennox is at pains to render Arabella's acquisition of her romantic folly psychologically plausible. Notably, the heroine's quixotism is partly inherited from her father, a 'grave and melancholy' man who, sickened by the machiavellian quality of court life, has retired to a country 'Castle'.[26] It is in this provincial retreat that Arabella comes under the sway of romances. As Lennox explains: 'The surprising Adventures with which they were filled, proved a most pleasing Entertainment to a young Lady, who was wholly secluded from the World', so that Arabella's mind now takes a 'romantic Turn'. Far from enjoying the works simply as a form of imaginative escapism, however, the unworldly Arabella embraces the narratives as 'real Pictures of Life' (7). It is this belief then – that romances are veracious histories, rather than extravagant fictions – that constitutes Arabella's quixotic error.

What follows in the novel is, in essence, a comic enlargement upon this error, which shows how, like Don Quixote, Arabella reads the world itself through assumptions and expectations garnered from her books. As with Cervantes' own mock-hero, Arabella's emulation of her romance models can be rather pedantic, narrowly focused upon recalling textual *precedents* for particular occasions and modes of conduct. As Lennox cannily demonstrates via the disjunction between Arabella's romance models and her actual reality, French romance is heavily dependent upon a restricted register of language and plot conventions, which revolve almost entirely around love. With great comic precision, Lennox parodies the stilted, arcane, and genre-specific phraseology of romance discourse, in which a typical declaration of love interest becomes an assertion that a lady 'does not hate' her suitor, and love itself becomes merely the sum of its associated keywords, 'such as Wounds, Darts, Fires, Languishings, Dyings, Torture, Rack, Jealousy, and a few more of no Signification, but upon this Subject' (149). No less stereotypical than its inflated idiom is the plot of romance.

The rules of the genre – which manage to be at once convoluted and formulaic – are nicely mocked at the end of book 3:

> For by the Laws of Romance, when a Lady has once given her Lover that Permission [to love her], she may lawfully allow him to talk to her upon the Subject of his Passion, accept all his Gallantries, and claim an absolute Empire over all his Actions; reserving to herself the Right of fixing the Time when she may own her Affection: And when that important Step is taken, and his Constancy put to a few Years more Trial; when he has killed all his Rivals, and rescued her from a Thousand Dangers; she at last condescends to reward him with her Hand; and all her Adventures are at an End for the future. (137–8)

In the language of Lennox's own age, what we have here is a delicious satiric 'receipt' (recipe) for a romance. Underpinning this passage is the assumption that, in order to satirize the genre, one need do little more than offer a succinct *précis* of its usual course of events. As Lennox would seem to argue here, then: when boiled down to its essential constituents, and judged by the new fictional standards of the 1750s, the French romance tradition is self-evidently absurd.

As she plays them out in her own (mid-eighteenth century) life, Arabella's romantic notions are revealed to be not only absurd, but also improper and dangerous. As Charlotte (her prospective sister-in-law) points out, by contrast to Arabella's qualms about a lady allowing her suitor to 'press her Hand, write to her, and talk to her of Love', in eighteenth-century British society it is Arabella's willingness to visit an unrelated, bed-ridden man that is unseemly (185). The heroine's misprision of her prospective father-in-law as a potential lover can also be read as offering a grave threat to proper notions of rank and social priority. By the end of the novel, moreover, Arabella's romance-motivated behaviour poses a serious threat to her personal well-being, as she moves from the security of her rural home to the public spaces of Bath and London. The most thoroughgoing critique of romance is outlined in the long penultimate chapter, in which a clergyman Doctor performs what Glanville refers to as the 'Miracle' of persuading Arabella to give up her quixotic belief in the reality of the romance world (382). As the Doctor realizes, the 'cure' of Arabella hinges upon persuading her that romances are not true histories, but merely narrative fictions. In effect, Arabella's romance-tinted spectacles have produced a category error, a confusion between material and historical reality, and the products of fancy. It is in the novel's own interest, *as* a novel, to correct this error, endangering as it does the more 'realistic' view of life to which the genre had tied itself, in order to establish itself as a serious form of writing in contradistinction to romance.

As Catherine Gallagher has argued of Lennox's novel, then, 'the Quixote's cure begins not with the renunciation but with the acknowledgement of fiction' – with persuading Arabella that the events she has read about in her romances are not factually true.[27] From Arabella herself, the Doctor's insistence upon the fictionality of romance draws a potentially tricky question regarding the value of *any* kind of fiction. What the Doctor also argues, therefore, is that not *all* fiction need be tarred with the brush of romance. Asserting that 'The only Excellence of Falshood ... is its Resemblance to Truth', the Doctor offers as the primary exhibit in his defence of fiction the works of Richardson: 'An admirable Writer of our Time, [who] has found the Way to convey the most solid Instructions, the noblest Sentiments, and the most exalted Piety, in the pleasing Dress of a Novel, and, to use the Words of the greatest Genius in the present Age [Samuel Johnson], "Has taught the Passions to move at the Command of Virtue" ' (377–8). By welding his novels to virtue, the Doctor suggests, Richardson had succeeded in producing fictions that, while not *historically* true, were, more usefully, ethically and emotionally *truthful*. As this twin appeal to Richardson and to a *deeper* fictional truthfulness indicates, in order to bring *The Female Quixote* to a resolution Arabella has to be persuaded that romances are not only fiction but, also, *bad* fiction.

The climax to the undeceiving of Arabella arrives as the Doctor proceeds to condemn the encouragement of bloodshed in romance fiction – an encouragement for which Arabella has herself previously been criticized by characters such as Sir Charles (her uncle and the father of her suitor, Glanville), Charlotte (Glanville's modish sister), and even Lucy, her own maid-servant. Perhaps more significant, however, is what the Doctor goes on to say regarding the moral effects of romance-reading:

> It is impossible to read these Tales without lessening part of that Humility, which by preserving in us a Sense of our Alliance with all human nature, keeps us awake to Tenderness and Sympathy, or without impairing that Compassion which is implanted in us as an Incentive to Acts of Kindness. If there be any preserved by natural Softness, or early Education from learning Pride and Cruelty, they are yet in danger of being betrayed to the Vanity of Beauty, and taught the Arts of Intrigue. (381)

Reading romances, it would seem, encourages haughty self-glorification. What is particularly interesting here is that, even as the Doctor commences in inclusive terms, discussing natural virtues that we *all* possess, it soon becomes clear that his real concern is with the effect of romance-reading upon *female* readers – the readers who would be most strongly identified with the qualities of 'Tenderness' and 'Sympathy', but who might also be most susceptible, the Doctor implies, to the failings of vanity and artfulness. At the conclusion of Lennox's novel, then, romances are presented as dangerous partly because they encourage women away from a proper (benevolent and decorous) femininity. By absorbing themselves in the affairs of romance heroines, female readers are seduced into the vices and follies to which, on account of their sex, unprotected women are presumed to be naturally prone. The re-feminization of Arabella herself is dramatically confirmed in the short concluding chapter as, finally persuaded by the Doctor's arguments, the now undeceived heroine is successfully returned to the social and epistemological fold of marriage and real life.

This leads us nicely into the second main critical approach to the novel, which focuses less upon romance *per se* than upon gender – or, more precisely, upon the relationship between women as represented in French romances and eighteenth-century constructions of femininity. As critics have increasingly wondered: did Lennox write this nearly 400-page novel simply as a contribution to the contemporary discourse that sought to discredit romance fiction? Is the anti-romance reading an entirely adequate account of the work that the novel does? Even if the novel was *principally* designed to mock romances, are there not aspects of the work that appear to *exceed* or *escape* this intention? In its penultimate chapter, certainly, Lennox reinforced the anti-romance rhetoric of contemporary cultural criticism. In the figure of the Doctor, moreover, Lennox portrayed what has long been recognized to be a distinctly Johnsonian figure. Along with the more obvious satire upon the pernicious effects of reading romances, though, Lennox can also be seen to have drawn upon the romance genre in more productive and searching ways. To follow this line of enquiry, it is necessary to consider what Arabella *herself* gains from her reading, in the 350 or so pages that *precede* the Doctor's miracle cure.

To a significant degree, we would argue, Arabella's quixotic behaviour enables her to disrupt, and thereby to contest, prevailing ideas about what constituted proper conduct in a lady. Although driven by the erroneous belief that she has the power to command ailing lovers to live, for instance, Arabella's willingness to visit bed-ridden men is motivated by an *ethical* concern for the well-being of others, which is set against the social scruples of the more superficial Charlotte – scruples that would prevent a polite woman from attending, and tending to, a sick man. Although such behaviour often appears absurd to her peers, Arabella appropriates for herself the power to stipulate the terms of her relationships with men. Such is the case even in situations in which she would be expected to remain entirely submissive, such as in her dealings with Glanville's father, who at one point she asks to leave her presence, so that she may mourn the death of her father (63). Throughout the novel, in fact, we observe Arabella challenging others' ideas of what 'seemly' behaviour in a woman actually entails. While Lennox's novel certainly participated in the contemporary attack upon romance fiction, then, Lennox also used Arabella's investment in this now maligned genre in order to reflect upon some of the less empowering constraints that had been placed upon women – and upon novelistic *representations* of female roles – by the middle of the eighteenth century. Inevitably, such reflection also encompassed the behaviour of men. Arabella's romantic vision of the correct relationship between men and women is pointedly revealed during the long episode involving Sir George, a fortune-hunter who is well-versed in the language of romance. As Arabella easily perceives from his relation of his history as Prince Viridomer, George is rather an amorous opportunist than a true, *constant*, romantic hero. If he has captured the idiom of romances, George has yet failed to appreciate the gendered power structure, the emphasis upon constancy *to women*, that comprises one of their principal attractions for Arabella. We do not wish here to argue that Lennox thus sought to recuperate romance itself. Rather, what this line of interpretation contends is that certain of the elements of that tradition of writing, most notably the centrality that it accorded to women, gain renewed appeal in an age in which women were increasingly being tutored in restrictively 'feminine' codes of conduct. In her romantic quixotism, what Arabella is able to experience is an alternative world in which women might refuse to comply with their domestication, the rendering of themselves into sweet, submissive, sentimental creatures.

What the narrative model of romance provides for Arabella, then, is a way of imagining – and of fashioning for herself – the significant social experience that her situation lacks, but that her education and her other qualities demand. As Wendy Motooka has argued, Arabella's quixotism might also be read as her 'feminism – her desire to be a noteworthy, fully participating member of society, on a par with men'.[28] While the notion of Arabella as a feminist certainly requires some qualification,

Motooka's argument does foreground an important way in which Lennox's novel can be said to have involved a productive appropriation – rather than simply an outright rejection – of the world of romance. Set beside the broad split between private femininity and public masculinity that we have observed in the novels of Richardson and Fielding, Arabella emerges as exceptional insofar as she is a *lady* who has *adventures* – a woman, that is, who assumes for herself a public significance. This of course begs the question of what role a real, mid-eighteenth-century Arabella would have been expected to play in the contemporary social order. As Amanda Vickery has argued, for women in particular the expanding leisure culture of the period opened up new possibilities for public, social pleasure. However, as Vickery's detailed account of the lives of genteel ladies also reveals, the day-to-day experience of such a life was likely to remain dominated by the imperatives of 'obedience', 'fortitude', 'resignation', 'prudent economy' and domestic 'duty'.[29]

In Lennox's novel, the sedate quality of ladies' lives is highlighted by the Countess at Bath, who tries to persuade Arabella that proper ladies do not have 'Adventures', but that 'the History of a Woman of Honour' comprises merely 'few and natural Incidents' (327). The implied opposition here, between female adventures and female honour, is, though, less secure than the Countess implies. For, notwithstanding all her adventures, Arabella herself remains morally innocent, retaining throughout the novel what Glanville calls 'the Goodness of her Heart' (309). Crucially, it is in her moral purity that Arabella becomes the normative standard for the novel's satiric attack, not upon romances, but upon contemporary society. As Lennox insists, the elite culture of the time cannot provide the *kind* of public participation that Arabella desires. The likely disparity between the virtuous integrity of Lennox's heroine and the lives of the fashionable is suggested early in the novel, as Arabella converses with Miss Groves:

> The young Lady, tho' perfectly versed in the Modes of Town-Breeding, and *nothing-meaning* Ceremony, was at a Loss how to make proper Returns to the Civilities of *Arabella*: The native Elegance and Simplicity of her Manners were accompanied with so much real Benevolence of Heart, such insinuating Tenderness, and Graces so irresistible, that she was quite oppressed with them; and, having spent most of her Time between her Toilet and Quadrille, was so little qualified for partaking a Conversation so refined as *Arabella*'s, that her Discourse appeared quite tedious to her, since it was neither upon Fashions, Assemblies, Cards, or Scandal. (68)

What we see in this passage is that Arabella's social and ethical virtues – her elegance, simplicity, benevolence, tenderness and graces – are underpinned by the very rural seclusion that has caused her to resort to the reading of romances. By contrast, the world inhabited by Miss Groves is one of gossip, scandal and other fashionable frivolities – which, as Arabella notes later of the similarly facile lives of the ladies at Bath, involves little more than a whiling away of time in untaxing, 'trifling Amusements' (279). Despite the fact that Miss Groves has been a 'celebrated Beauty' both in town and at court (74), in social and moral terms she is clearly no match for Arabella's uncomplicated, country refinement. By contrasting Arabella with a character like Groves, *The Female Quixote* thus demonstrated that the contemporary sphere which might have appeared to present Arabella with opportunities to exercise a significant social presence was, in reality, a frivolous culture of merely superficial gentility – a culture that was, in effect, all entertainment and no instruction.

It is in the final books of the novel that Arabella makes her own entrance into this public arena. What happens when Arabella appears within this evidently less than ideal scenario? This is Lennox's description of her heroine's entrance into the fashionable Assembly Rooms at Bath, on the occasion of a society ball:

> It is not to be doubted but much Mirth was treasur'd up for her Appearance; and the occasional Humourist had already prepared his accustom'd Jest, when the Sight of the devoted fair One repell'd his Vivacity, and the design'd Ridicule of the whole Assembly.
> Scarce had the first tumultuous Whisper escap'd the Lips of each Individual, when they found themselves aw'd to Respect by that irresistable [*sic*] Charm in the Person of *Arabella*, which commanded Reverence and Love from all who beheld her. (272)

In a nicely ironic twist, what Lennox shows here is that, even in the competitive social environment of the Assembly Rooms, Arabella's virtue still shines through. As her beauty and charm disarm the pre-prepared jests of the assembled company, what we see is that Arabella's presence functions to cleanse this environment of its impolite displays of wit. For all her romantic fancies (and she is *dressed* here as the romantic heroine, Julia), Arabella is thus presented as a peculiarly moral presence in this fashionable world. In such episodes, Lennox clearly depends upon an identification of virtue and beauty – of ethics and aesthetics – that had been theorized earlier in the century by philosophers of the

'moral sense' school, such as Francis Hutcheson. As we also see during
the scenes at Bath, Arabella's motive in enquiring after *other* peoples'
'adventures' is not to indulge in idle tittle-tattle, or in more corrosive
forms of social gossip, but rather to discover histories that she might
admire, esteem and be instructed by (274). In Arabella's own view,
fashionable gossip-mongering is but an 'ill-natur'd Pleasure' (277).
Contrary to the Johnsonian Doctor's claim that romances teach women
the 'Arts of Intrigue', then, what Arabella brings to these centres of
eighteenth-century pleasure is the ethical agency – and the true, *natural*
gentility – that they are deemed to be lacking. As we have argued,
Arabella's *actual* behaviour is not being promoted as desirable in itself,
as a direct model for the emulation of real women. Rather, through her
narrative of Arabella's adventures, Lennox pointed up the lack of
either public roles, or public role *models*, for an intelligent, educated,
eighteenth-century lady. In the final analysis, the female quixote's odd
humour thus generates a significant pay-off in the novel: for Arabella
(in the form of public adventures), for the author (in terms of social
satire), and for the reader, whose enjoyment of the narrative is liable to
derive at least partly from the *frisson* of indecorum and disorder that
Arabella's adventures continually evoke.

Horace Walpole, The Castle of Otranto

> He beheld his child dashed to pieces, and almost buried under an
> enormous helmet, an hundred times more large than any casque ever
> made for human being, and shaded with a proportionable quantity
> of black feathers.[30]

This image, of a piece of deadly but impossibly enormous armoury, can
be regarded as the moment when the Gothic novel truly begins. While
the 'shrieks, horror, and surprise' (18) of those around him have prepared Manfred to face some kind of horror, the supernatural intervention of the gigantic helmet marks the moment at which *The Castle of
Otranto: A Gothic Story* casts itself adrift of the new standards of novelistic plausibility, thereby initiating an alternative mode of prose fictional
writing. First published in late December 1764, Walpole's novel wil-
fully embraced the repertoire of romantic excesses – giants, knights,
castles, and a host of other unnatural expedients – that Samuel Johnson
had happily reported having been excised from the new 'comedy of
romance', at the beginning of the previous decade.[31]

If, for Johnson, this new species of writing was 'to be conducted nearly by the rules of comic poetry', then the Gothic novel's radical departure from these rules owed more to the eighteenth-century rediscovery of the *sublime*, the key classical statement on which was the ancient Greek treatise, *Peri Hupsous (On the Sublime)*, which was traditionally ascribed to Longinus. The key *modern* discussion of the topic, published seven years before Walpole's novel, was Edmund Burke's highly influential *A Philosophical Enquiry into the Origin of our Ideas of the Sublime and Beautiful* (1757). Put succinctly, Burke's argument was that the sublime and the beautiful constitute the primary categories of aesthetic experience. Whereas the beautiful is essentially a social category, characterized by what is bounded and limited and subject to specific *form* (as in small, smooth and delicate objects), the sublime is a representation of experience capable of instilling fear by bringing one into the presence of death and threats to one's self-preservation. As Burke outlines early in the *Enquiry*:

> Whatever is fitted in any sort to excite the ideas of pain, and danger, that is to say, whatever is in any sort terrible, or is conversant about terrible objects, or operates in a manner analogous to terror, is a source of the *sublime*; that is, it is productive of the strongest emotion which the mind is capable of feeling. ... But as pain is stronger in its operation than pleasure, so death is in general a much more affecting idea than pain; because there are very few pains, however exquisite, which are not preferred to death; nay, what generally makes pain itself, if I may say so, more painful, is, that it is considered as an emissary of this king of terrors. When danger or pain press too nearly, they are incapable of giving any delight, and are simply terrible; but at certain distances, and with certain modifications, they may be, and they are delightful, as we every day experience.[32]

Here we can see the philosophical justification for the Gothic novel. From a safe vantage point, such novels enable readers to experience delightful pains and dangers, enabling vicarious access to obscurity, darkness, and incarceration, the supernatural and the terrible. Transcending social categories, these phenomena connect with elemental realms of power, will and desire, of incest and family romance. If Edward Young's treatise on 'originality' provided a forceful statement of the need for authorial creativity (the invention of the literary *producer*), then Burke's treatise on the sublime might be regarded as a primer in *affect*, in responses engendered in aesthetic *consumers* – not least the consumers of sublime, Gothic horror.

Touching base with other testaments to a contemporary taste for literary primitivism and antiquarianism – the 'Ossian' poems of James Macpherson, Thomas Percy's *Reliques of Ancient English Poetry* (1765) – Horace Walpole's intervention into the field of prose fiction put a supernatural spin on Henry Fielding's authorial procedure: making the novel new, by making it old. In the preface to the first edition, Walpole slyly presented *Otranto* as a translation, by one William Marshall, of a medieval Italian text by 'Onuphrio Muralto', which itself described events set in the distant past. It was only in the preface to the second edition that Walpole came clean about his own authorship of the work. For his contemporaries, this admission completely altered the meaning of the text, rendering it far more unsettling than it had been on its initial appearance. As a writer for *The Monthly Review* put it, so long as the work was assumed to be a translation of a much older text, 'we could readily excuse its preposterous phenomena, and consider them as sacrifices to a gross and unenlightened age'. Once revealed as a 'modern performance', however, it became 'more than strange, that an Author, of a refined and polished genius, should be an advocate for re-establishing the barbarous superstitions of Gothic devilism!'.[33] Evidently, this reviewer was not convinced by the second preface to the novel, in which Walpole presented a theoretical justification for his authorial practice that was grounded in the relationship between older and contemporary forms of 'romance' (i.e. between medieval romance and the modern novel). As Walpole argued:

> It was an attempt to blend the two kinds of romance, the ancient and the modern. In the former all was imagination and improbability: in the latter, nature is always intended to be, and sometimes has been, copied with success. Invention has not been wanting; but the great resources of fancy have been dammed up, by a strict adherence to common life. But if in the latter species Nature has cramped imagination, she did but take her revenge, having been totally excluded from old romances. The actions, sentiments, conversations, of the heroes and heroines of ancient days were as unnatural as the machines employed to put them in motion.
>
> The author of the following pages thought it possible to reconcile the two kinds. Desirous of leaving the powers of fancy at liberty to expatiate through the boundless realms of invention, and thence of creating more interesting situations, he wished to conduct the

mortal agents in his drama according to the rules of probability; in short, to make them think, speak and act, as it might be supposed mere men and women would do in extraordinary positions. (9–10)

Via this hybrid admixture of old and new, Walpole went on to claim, he had created a 'new species of romance' (14). Walpole's desire to liberate imagination from the shackles of the contemporary novel offers a telling contrast to the authorial aesthetic of Richardson, who had denied to himself the realms of creative fancy as he 'laboured hard', as he put it, to 'rein in' his invention.[34] In hindsight, the first preface to *Otranto* can also be read as mocking the modern over-valuation of realism; as when 'Marshall', a supposed mid-eighteenth-century scholar, claims that 'the groundwork of the story is founded on truth', impressed as he is by the circumstantial detail in the work's descriptions of the interior of Manfred's castle (8). By charting a middle way between the extremes of romance and the novel, Walpole's project in *Otranto* thus comprised an attempt, in the new era of prose fiction, to re-authorize the more *un*-realistic and *extra*-ordinary inventions of authorial fancy.

Importantly, though, Walpole's own new species of writing did not entail a *completely* free play of imagination. Rather, the remit of 'proba bility' is narrowed here to the requirements of *psychological* probability; so that, in *Otranto*, characters should ideally respond in recognizably human ways to external events that are themselves implausible and marvellous. In practice, Walpole's realization of this relationship between character and environment is only partially successful. Not surprisingly, perhaps, the characters' 'natural' reaction to the 'extraordinary' is invariably to be terrified, which hardly conduces to the portrayal of psychological subtlety. Even the most complex character, Manfred, is primarily motivated, in sub-Macbethian fashion, by his paranoia regarding the implications of an ancient prophecy. The novel's evocation of *terror* – what Marshall, in the first preface, calls the 'principal engine' of the work (6) – is in fact intimately related to the character of Manfred, not only in the obvious sense that the novel's supernatural agents of vengeance operate to relieve him of his ill-gotten eminency, but also in the sense that, in his treatment of others, the monomaniacal tyrant is himself a *source* of fear (a quality that is both materialized and symbolized by his Gothic castle). *Otranto* is, though, by no means a work of unmitigated terror. Throughout the novel, the fear experienced by the characters is leavened by *pathos*. As Emma Clery has argued, 'Walpole's innovation was to bring together wonder and compassion, broadening the parameters of sympathy to include experience of the miraculous and the terrible, and artfully extending the limits of what could be felt by the reader as "real".[35] Within the novel, a notable occasion for the exercise of pity is the moment of Matilda's demise – a verbal tableau that is also a lengthily drawn-out death scene. Disturbing the elevated emotionalism of terror and pathos (both of which depend upon heightened displays of feeling) is a third representational mode: the *comic*. In his second preface, Walpole defended the buffoonery of his lower class characters via a patriotic appeal to the model of Shakespeare, whose intermingling of comic and tragic elements had been criticized by the eminent French writer, Voltaire. The novel's comic impulse goes deeper, though, than mere buffoonery. For, as modern readers tend to discern fairly quickly, *The Castle of Otranto* is also pervaded by a wry self-consciousness about the very romantic and supernatural repertoire that it was reintroducing into the genre of the novel.

Unusually for a 'Gothic' novel, the supernatural is often presented by Walpole both theatrically and with a sense of amusement; so that, echoing Manfred, the reader is often liable to find himself asking, 'What new absurdity is this?' (33). As James Watt observes, the consequence of Walpole's dilettantish detachment from the world that he describes in the narrative is that *The Castle of Otranto* 'constantly hovers on the verge of bathos'.[36] Walpole's appreciation of the impossibility of any simple *return* to supernatural fiction (and the modern sense that belief in the supernatural is lamentably *primitive*) is highlighted by the novel's association of superstition with the vulgarity of the populace. In the text, this superior stance is mainly adopted in bad faith, as particular characters endeavour to rationalize, downplay, or simply deny the reality that, as they are aware, the supernatural possesses in the world of the narrative itself. These very moments, however, also remind the reader that what they are reading is a textual *throwback*, rather than a work which, as *The Monthly Review* charged, actually sought to re-establish 'barbarous superstitions'. Even as it disturbed the canons of neo-classical propriety, *The Castle of Otranto* recaptured such superstitions, and an associated register of extreme passions, for the aesthetic enjoyment of readers living in a self-consciously civilized and enlightened age. In the service of the sublime, we might say, Walpole's novel enforced an unbridgeable gap between the reader and the 'Gothic' world of the narrative – a gap that was simultaneously temporal, epistemological and generic.

For all that such phantasms exist in the world depicted *within* the novel, then, *The Castle of Otranto* does not simply reinstate a belief system that might allow of the possibility of *actual* giants, walking pictures or speaking skeletons. Instead, Walpole's novel refers such effects to the realm of the *imagination*. Intriguingly, part of the novel's appeal to imaginative invention inheres, not in extravagant shock tactics, but in moments that see a conscious failure or withholding of description. An important device here is the 'inexpressibility topos', the authorial reference to things or emotions that lie beyond the compass of words. As the narrator advises concerning Jerome's discovery of the 'mark of a bloody arrow' on Theodore's shoulder, for instance: 'The passions that ensued must be conceived; they cannot be painted' (57). While a writer's use of this topos (commonplace or motif) is always liable to arouse a suspicion that he is simply incapable of describing what he claims to be indescribable, such verbal impasses, which are also characteristic of the contemporary sentimental novel, are entirely fitting in a work that was designed to arouse the reader's *own* capacity for Gothic emotionalism. Also critical to the Gothic reader response is an *obscurity* of representation. As Burke had argued, 'to make anything very terrible' required this 'obscurity', an uneasy uncertainty about the precise nature of the danger at hand.[37] A notable element in *Otranto*'s own discourse of darkness is its network of secret and subterranean passages, which would become a staple of the Gothic novel but which, significantly, Walpole himself does not describe in any *precise* detail. A useful contemporaneous correlative here is the Italian printmaker, Giovanni Battista Piranesi's famous series of etchings entitled *Carceri* (Prisons), especially as he adapted them for a second edition. In their earlier state (1749–50), Piranesi's act of imaginative creativity involved fictional, yet distinctly realized images of institutions of justice, that drew upon his interest in ancient Rome. In the revised series of 1761, however, the etchings became darker and more disciplinary, the figures and their surroundings less clearly differentiated, and the overall effect more foreboding, with the relative obscurity evidently more in tune with the possibilities for the creative engagement of the viewer's *own* imagination. (In both editions, we might note, one of the key etchings is 'The Gothic Arch', which depicts a vast complex of (sometimes implausibly) interconnected archways, conceived on a massive scale; an oppressive yet oblique setting for human incarceration.) With their perceptible movement towards *less* distinct and precise representation, Piranesi's etchings provide a fitting visual analogue for the ominous *mise en scène* of the contemporary Gothic novel.

As modern psychoanalytic approaches to the genre have shown, the symbolic imagery of the Gothic novel figures forth the dark, powerful, subconscious recesses of the mind. In a reaction against the kinds of psychoanalytical readings that have long dominated studies of the Gothic, however, recent critics have begun to offer more historically grounded accounts of the genre. With regard to *The Castle of Otranto* specifically, such readings tend to focus on the significance of class and property in the familial tragedy that the novel relates, and on its political and ideological investments. In a recent example of this approach, Markman Ellis reads the novel in relation to Walpole's political beliefs, and to particular political events during the 1760s (most notably those involving the libertarian agitator, John Wilkes).[38] One of the key difficulties faced by such readings is the novel's ending. For political readings of the work, the theme of usurpation, and of a rightful return to legitimate succession, is ultimately grounded in a nostalgic vision of an original English constitution – that of the *Witenagemote*, the balanced political assembly of the Anglo-Saxons, which Walpole certainly took some interest in, and which could be regarded as having been ruptured by the imposition of the 'Norman yoke' (following the Norman conquest of England in 1066). As in Shakespearean tragedy, however, the ending of *Otranto* falls far short of evoking confidence in the *new* regime, despite its re-establishment of rightful succession. While the reign is now legitimate, and seems unlikely to revert to the overbearing tyranny of Manfred, the grief-stricken melancholy of Theodore would not seem to offer a very solid basis upon which to construct a brave new *Witenagemote*. Indeed, as both Ellis and Clery acknowledge – while, from a historicist perspective, psychoanalytical criticism is compromised by its abstraction of particular textual motifs into a symbolic system of 'Gothic' archetypes, it is not finally clear that *The Castle of Otranto* itself allows of any *decisive*, historical-allegorical reading.

What happens to the Gothic novel after *The Castle of Otranto*? There was, in fact, a notable gap between the publication of Walpole's text and the next significant work of Gothic fiction, Clara Reeve's *The Champion of Virtue: A Gothic Story* (1777) – republished the following year in its revised and more familiar form as *The Old English Baron* (1778). As Clery observes, 'The concept of a modern mode of "Gothic story" was seemingly immobilised by the reputation of *Otranto* as a one-off novelty or caprice.'[39] For Reeve herself, a further problem was that Walpole's supernatural machinery seemed too extravagant, straying too far beyond the limits of probability – a charge to which Walpole responded by attacking Reeve for the dullness of her own, more restrained performance. Before the end of the eighteenth century, the Gothic novel would mutate into the far-flung Orientalism of

William Beckford's *Vathek* (1786), the 'explained' supernatural of Ann Radcliffe's novels, and the sexual and religious excesses of Matthew Lewis' *The Monk* (1798). Given the historical parameters of our study, we do not here follow the Gothic line any further. Yet it is instructive to remember where the line began, and in what climate. For all its primitive, medieval and romantic leanings, the Gothic novel owes its origins to a period of novelistic 'novelty' and cultural innovation.

6

The Sympathetic Strain: Sterne and Sentimental Fiction

Laurence Sterne, Tristram Shandy

> Who has not *Tristram Shandy* read?
> Is any mortal so ill bred?[1]

In the final weeks of 1759, the first two volumes of a new fictional work were published in York, at the author's own expense. Entitled *The Life and Opinions of Tristram Shandy, Gentleman,* the book was the first piece of extended prose fiction by Laurence Sterne, a middle-aged clergyman who, having tired of his involvement in local, political and ecclesiastical affairs, had cast his gaze towards the prospect of literary fame. From such humble beginnings emerged the cultural phenomenon of the 1760s. Given its origins in provincial obscurity, the hubbub that Sterne's book managed to create among the fashionable literary culture of London was truly remarkable. As with *Pamela* during the 1740s, the publication of *Tristram Shandy* provoked a mini-industry of printed responses, both imitative and antagonistic, along with assorted other testaments to its permeation of contemporary culture: a *Tristram Shandy* card game; *Tristram Shandy* china ware; a *Tristram Shandy* race horse. As Boswell's enraptured response above vividly conveys, to have failed to peruse Sterne's book during the early months of 1760 could have made one appear unfashionably 'ill bred'. And yet, from the very beginning, responses to *Tristram Shandy* were rarely untinged by concerns about the work's moral moorings. Soon enough, in fact, both Sterne and his book would themselves come to seem 'ill bred'. Whereas *Pamela* had clearly been *designed* to promote ethical conduct, even if Richardson's critics

164

often chose to read against the grain of the author's intentions, Sterne's textual game of prurient double-meanings rendered the ethical import of his own writing far more problematic, not least to readers who were concerned to establish their *own* possession of good breeding.

Such unease about the impropriety of *Tristram Shandy* would become widespread as awareness grew of Sterne's status as a man of the cloth. Beyond its immediate social splash and the wave of uneasy responses that followed, however, Sterne's text offered the keenest interrogation of novelistic form and prose fictional technique in the post-Richardson and Fielding era. At what remained a precarious moment in its early history – and in the midst (as we have seen) of various kinds of novelistic experimentation – it was Sterne's work pre-eminently that was responsible for revitalizing the genre. Positioning his text both within and outside of the main line of novelistic development, Sterne achieved commercial success by extending earlier experiments in fictional form, and by insistently 'novelizing' other kinds of writing (such as satire and travel literature). This is not to say that early readers of *Tristram Shandy* only or always perceived it as a contribution to the fledgling genre. As an early review published in the *London Magazine* reveals, admiration of the work's opening volumes coexisted with bafflement regarding their generic identity: 'Oh rare Tristram Shandy! – Thou very sensible – humorous – pathetick – humane – unaccountable! – what shall we call thee? – Rabelais, Cervantes, What?'. To this reviewer, Sterne's work appeared impossible to place within the contemporary cultural landscape, and seemed to have perhaps more in common with *earlier* milestones of prose fiction, such as Rabelais' *Gargantua and Pantagruel* (1532–52) and Cervantes' *Don Quixote*. From the outset, though, other reviewers also registered links to more recent prose productions. In Tobias Smollett's *Critical Review*, Sterne's characters were praised as 'excellent imitations of certain characters in a modern truly Cervantic performance': namely, Smollett's own *Peregrine Pickle* (1751). Writing in *The Monthly Review*, William Kenrick praised Sterne (or 'Mr. Tristram Shandy') rather more decisively, as 'a writer infinitely more ingenious and entertaining than any other of the present race of novelists'. As Kenrick also noted, Sterne's work enacted a significant change of novelistic focus, from the narration of 'Lives and *Adventures*' to the relation of a 'Life and *Opinions*'. As Kenrick's review demonstrates, while Sterne's book clearly disturbed the set of readerly expectations that now attached to the genre, such generic subversion by no means precluded responses that located the work in relation to the period's 'new species' of prose fiction.[2]

Sterne's text is not, it might be argued, actually presented to us *as* a novel. Its immediate generic form is rather that of a first-person autobiography, albeit one that appears to have been written by a whimsical, erratic, and disorganized life-writer, who is incapable of sticking to the point and giving us a satisfactory account of his personal history. To Tristram Shandy, explaining himself to the public entails trawling through the key episodes in his family's history, many of which took place before he was even conceived (in both senses), let alone actually born. On one level, certainly, Sterne's text reads as much like a comic pseudo-autobiography as a novel. In recent decades, moreover, literary scholars have tended to emphasize the *satiric* and (mock-) learned aspects of the work, delving ever deeper into the archives in order to unearth the mass of allusions, borrowings, and other materials out of which Sterne pieced together his heterogeneous medley of a narrative. While *Tristram Shandy* can indeed be read both as pseudo-autobiography and satire, though, it is important not to downplay too greatly its novelistic qualities. As Thomas Keymer has recently demonstrated in *Sterne, the Moderns, and the Novel* (2002), Sterne's text was richly responsive to the prose fictional productions of the 1740s and 1750s. All the same, if we do choose to read *Tristram Shandy* as a novel, then we need to regard it as a *satiric* novel, and as a novelistic satire *upon* the genre, as it had developed during the preceding decades. A key narratorial strategy in the work, which both aligns it with and differentiates it from the novels of Fielding, involves self-conscious, and frequently flamboyant reflections upon the very art of life-writing. Claiming to have reconciled 'progressive' and 'digressive' (linear and lateral) modes of narration, Tristram, the novel's author-by-proxy, describes the organizational 'machinery' of his work as being 'of a species by itself'.[3] As well as echoing his predecessors' claims to novelistic novelty, Tristram here anticipates Walpole's assertion that, in *The Castle of Otranto*, he was creating a 'new species of romance'. In Sterne's own hands, though, this declaration of singularity constitutes not a direct statement of either generic alignment or textual uniqueness, but rather a wry reflection upon the genre's investment in originality. Through Tristram's exaggerated claims for his work, Sterne foregrounded the paradoxical nature of a genre that appeared to require continual renewal, not least via repeated assertions of difference from what had come before.

Throughout *Tristram Shandy*, Sterne's showboating narrator stages comic coups that play upon the art, and the ironies, of narrative representation and printed form – as when he declares himself to be in three places at once, or threatens to tear the following page out of his book (out of every single *copy* of the printed work?). As these narratorial flourishes might suggest, central to any interpretation of the hyper-self-consciousness of *Tristram Shandy* is the narrator himself. A character in his own right, Tristram asks to be regarded as a literary genius even as he reserves the license to wear a 'fool's cap', his 'hare-brain'd' writing veering between tricksy ingenuity and artistic incompetence (1:6, 11; 3:28, 175). As the reader continually needs to ask then: to what degree is Tristram actually in control of his text? In one of the novel's most noted episodes, Tristram's father, Walter, and his Uncle Toby make painfully slow progress down a flight of stairs, while Tristram struggles to work out how to get them to the bottom, so that he can continue his narrative:

> IS it not a shame to make two chapters of what passed in going down one pair of stairs? For we are got no farther yet than to the first landing, and there are fifteen more steps down to the bottom; and for aught I know, as my father and my uncle *Toby* are in a talking humour, there may be as many chapters as steps;   let that be as it will, Sir, I can no more help it than my destiny: – A sudden impulse comes across me – drop the curtain, *Shandy* – I drop it – Strike a line here across the paper – I strike it – and hey for a new chapter!
>
> The duce of any other rule have I to govern myself by in this affair – and if I had one   as I do all things out of rule – I would twist it and tear it to pieces, and throw it into the fire when I had done – Am I warm? I am, and the cause demands it – a pretty story! is a man to follow rules – or rules to follow him? (4:10, 231)

Extending the use of disruptive narrative devices that we have seen at work in the fiction of the 1740s and 1750s, Tristram is here significantly more intrusive than Fielding's narrators had been. Engaged in a multi-layered play of chapters and steps, life and art, mimesis and diegesis (narrated action and narrative telling), Sterne creates comedy out of the sheer *modernity* of the novel, its lack of clear formal rules and established, historical precedents. Beneath these flashes of metafictional merriment, however, lies narratorial anxiety, as Tristram finds himself caught between his dual roles as an autobiographer, bound by fidelity to his family history, and as a modern creative writer, who demands the freedom to intervene in the telling of that history and, theatrically, to 'drop the curtain' over it at moments of mimetic crisis. Frustrated with the constraints placed upon him by the principal characters in his history, Tristram thus concludes here by striking a chord with the narrator of *Tom Jones*, who had similarly appropriated to himself the authority to write by his *own* rules, rather than following those established by other people.[4]

Set beside the authoritative interventions of Fielding's narrators, though, it is also apparent that, rather than establishing his own rules, Tristram himself is not really following any rules at all. Part of Tristram's difficulty as an author is precisely what many modern readers find most engaging about the novel; namely, the narrator's psychological self-consciousness. Tristram's 'objective' work as a family historian, that is to say, is continually being defeated by the subjective workings of his mind, as his absorption in his self engenders disarray within his text. Viewed in this light, Sterne's novel can appear to be as much a parodic elaboration upon Richardson's minute psychological portraiture, as it is upon Fieldingesque techniques of *narrative* self-consciousness. Taking this further, we might say that the latter of these elements is predicated on the former – that the self-reflexive narrative playfulness of *Tristram Shandy* is a consequence of Tristram being so wrapped up in his self that he is unable to set either his life or his text in sufficient order. The narrator's response to generic expectations exposes further this lack of authorial and psychological self-discipline. Rather than carving out an appropriate space for his rebellion against his literary forebears, Tristram simply interrupts his narrative history mid-flow, for no other reason than that he experiences a 'sudden impulse', or whimsical desire, to do so.

How should we assess this miniature rebellion against formal and generic constraints? Revealingly, by the end of the passage Tristram has become heatedly impassioned – a lack of narratorial composure that is highlighted by his confusion of abstract 'rules' (or artistic principles) and material 'rules' (measuring devices). By contrast, Sterne might seem here to be the detached puppet-master of the situation, coolly manipulating his authorial surrogate and creating comedy from Tristram's narrative dilemmas. To suggest that we need to maintain a distinction between Sterne and Tristram is not necessarily to argue (as have some critics) that the author adopted an entirely detached, satiric attitude to his narrator, mocking him as a latter-day version of the Hack persona of Swift's *A Tale of a Tub* (1704). Rather, we would argue that it is *through* his representation of Tristram's authorial difficulties that Sterne reveals both the possibilities, and the limitations, entailed by the contemporary commitment to novelty and originality. When, for instance, Tristram offers his famous paradox – that, having narrated only up to the first day of his life after a year of writing, he has 'three hundred and sixty-four days more life to write just now, than when I first set out' – the narrator indicates that 'the very novelty of it alone' renders the observation worthy of the reader's attention (4:13, 234). Within the narrative fiction, the fact that Tristram runs into this novel predicament can be partly accounted for by failures of composition – of selection and organization – that point up his inadequacies as a writer. While Sterne implicitly distinguishes his own performance from such artlessness, however, in producing this paradox of the ever-receding text he also claimed the authorial cachet available to such ingenious displays of narrative wit. In this manner, Sterne wrought a comic twist upon the arguments of Edward Young, who had suggested that, in writing, 'All eminence, and distinction, lies out of the beaten road; excursion and deviation are necessary to find it ... '. In *Tristram Shandy*, we might say, Sterne directs Tristram *too far* off the beaten road, in order both to exploit, and to critique, the modern illusion of *absolutely* original creative activity.[5]

Alongside this narrator-centred play with the act of writing itself, one of the most distinctive features of *Tristram Shandy* is its manipulation of ideas and vocabulary drawn from a range of discourses – the languages of legal and medical texts, philosophical treatises and scientific works, religious tracts and critical commentaries. In a number of instances, such material is introduced wholesale into Tristram's narrative. A useful summary of the novel's interpolations is provided by Michael Rosenblum:

> The main road of *Tristram Shandy* is the language of the autobio graphical narrative, but in the interpolation we switch to the language and conventions of the sermon (Volume II), the legal contract (the marriage articles of Volume I), the theological deliberation (the Doctors of the Sorbonne in Volume I), the curse (Volume III), the mock-romance (The Tale of Slawkenbergius in Volume IV or The Fragment on Whiskers in Volume V), the educational handbook (the *Tristrapaedia* of Volume V), the personal history (Trim's tale of the Fair Beguine in Volume VIII), or the travel book (Volume VII).

As Rosenblum indicates, in constructing *Tristram Shandy* Sterne included both genuine (pre-existing) documents, such as Ernulphus' Excommunicatio and his own sermon on 'the Abuses of Conscience' (which had already been published separately in 1750), and also spurious (i.e. *new*) documents of his own creation, such as the bawdy Slawkenbergius's Tale in volume 4. This *compilation* of a range of textual material involved a more varied and recurrent form of interpolative practice than the kinds of interpolated *stories* that had been occasionally included in the novels of Fielding and Smollett (such as the history of Leonora, in book 2 of *Joseph Andrews*). Intriguingly, Rosenblum himself sees in Sterne's inclusion of such material a form of 'realism', to the extent that 'Realism in the eighteenth-century novel' can be taken to mean 'quite simply the representation of such contemporary forms as the sermon, the guide-book, and the neo-classical oration, in the same way that realism in the modern novel would mean representing such characteristic modern forms as the commercial or the telephone conversation'.[6] This, assuredly, is a rather different notion of verisimilitude than we are accustomed to encountering in critical discussions of the 'realistic' novel (such as Ian Watt's focus upon the verbal *manner* of novelistic representation). Indeed, beyond its inclusion of other texts and part-texts, *Tristram Shandy* is characterized by a more fully incorporated play with learned jargon and ways of thinking that is usually discussed in terms not of realism but of Sterne's art of 'learned wit'. Drawing upon philosophical and encyclopaedic works such as John Locke's *Essay Concerning Human Understanding* (1690) and Ephraim Chambers' *Cyclopædia* (1728), Sterne's play of learned wit in *Tristram Shandy* emulated such previous exemplars of the tradition as François Rabelais and Robert Burton (whose *Anatomy of Melancholy* (1621) he also drew upon for textual material, particularly in the novel's later volumes). Comparison of *Tristram Shandy* with texts from this tradition can help us to pinpoint more precisely the relationship in which Sterne's text stands to both the satiric mode and the novel genre.

During the eighteenth century itself, this parodic play with learned discourses occupied an especially prominent role in satiric texts produced by the Scriblerians – the powerful group of writers that included Alexander Pope, Jonathan Swift, John Arbuthnot and John Gay. As a number of eighteenth-century readers noted, the Scriblerian satire that appears to have had the most direct influence upon *Tristram Shandy* was *Memoirs of the Extraordinary Life, Works, and Discoveries of Martinus Scriblerus*, a prose work of long gestation that was first published in 1741. Both the affinities and the differences between the *Memoirs* and *Tristram Shandy* can be revealed by comparing the depiction of Walter Shandy with that of Martinus Scriblerus' father, Cornelius. This is how Cornelius Scriblerus is characterized in the *Memoirs*:

He never had cohabitation with his spouse, but he ponder'd on the Rules of the Ancients, for the generation of Children of Wit.

He ordered his diet according to the prescription of Galen, confining himself and his wife for almost the whole first year to Goat's Milk and Honey. ... His Wife miscarried; but as the Abortion proved only a female Foetus, he comforted himself, that, had it arrived to perfection, it would not have answer'd his account; his heart being wholly fixed upon the learned Sex. However he disdained not to treasure up the Embryo in a Vial, among the curiosities of his family. ... He had already chalked out all possible schemes for the improvement of a male child; yet was so far prepar'd for the worst that could happen, that before the nine months were expired, he had composed two Treatises of Education; the one he called *A Daughter's Mirrour*, and the other *A Son's Monitor*.[7]

In the character of Cornelius, the Scriblerians directed their satire at the scientific *virtuoso*, whose learning is presented as combining two kinds of intellectual failure: speculative abstraction, and trifling experimentation. Attempting to live out the knowledge that he has acquired from books, Cornelius believes that, if he can ensure that his child is born according to the conditions laid down by ancient authorities, he will be able to create a perfect male heir, by bringing him up in accordance with his own system of education. As Cornelius' treasuring up of an embryo as a 'curiosity' reveals, much of what he regards as scientific endeavour actually lacks *any* real use or purpose, and may be regarded rather as a perversion of the natural life processes upon which he is endeavouring to improve. As his wholly dispassionate response to his wife's miscarriage suggests, Cornelius is *only* interested in the success of his learned endeavours. This lack of natural feeling is further highlighted later in the *Memoirs*, as Cornelius and his wife argue about the education of their son. In words that reinforce the disjunction between Cornelius' detached, pseudo-scientific schemes and the flesh-and-blood reality of the subject of his experimentation, Mrs Scriblerus finds herself forced to plead with Cornelius to spare their only descendant: 'We have but one child, and cannot afford to throw him away upon experiments'.[8]

While, by contrast to Cornelius Scriblerus, Walter Shandy collects not monstrous curiosities but only books of mad learning, aspects of the Scriblerians' anti-virtuoso satire can also be said to inform Sterne's representation of Tristram's father. To begin with, Cornelius' sacrifice of his son to his experiments is echoed by Walter's sacrificing of his brother's feelings to his hypothesis of Christian names, during their disputes concerning Tristram's aunt Dinah. In response to Toby's distressed plea for him to let the issue alone, Walter offers the blunt question, 'What is the character of a family to an hypothesis? ... Nay, if you come to that – what is the life of a family' (1:21, 56). Significantly, the one practical experiment that Walter *is* extremely interested in is the Caesarean operation that he wishes he could have performed upon his wife, despite the fact that, at the time, such operations always resulted in the mother's death. For all his comparative lack of (pseudo-) scientific experimentation, Walter's project of educating his son also parallels that of Cornelius, as each father attempts to test out upon his offspring his own hobby-horsical theories. As Tristram relates in the novel, Walter is 'systematical, and, like all systematick reasoners, he would move both heaven and earth, and twist and torture every thing in nature to support his hypothesis' (1:19, 45). As an object of satire, Walter's philosophical speculations and systems are all shown to be ultimately self-defeating. In volume 5, for instance, Walter becomes so absorbed in writing the *Tristra-pædia* – an educational treatise for his son – that Tristram himself is, as he puts it, 'neglected and abandoned to my mother' for three of his most important formative years. (This moment, it might be noted, also shows the extent to which Tristram has inherited Walter's Cornelius-like disregard for women.) Just as Tristram, the adult author, is thrown 'so many volumes back' as he writes slower than he lives, the early part of the *Tristra-pædia* is thus 'rendered entirely useless', as the young Tristram grows up before the relevant parts of the work are completed (5:16, 309; 4:13, 234).

Like Cornelius Scriblerus, then, Walter is finally unable to force the world to fit in with his hypotheses. While his assorted theories concerning generation, noses, names and education are exposed for all their comic absurdity, however, Walter himself is by no means merely an object of ridicule. Fleshed out over the course of a longer prose fiction than the *Memoirs*, Walter also becomes a far more sympathetic figure. In the moments of self-recrimination that succeed his disputes with his brother, Toby, for instance, Walter gains an extra dimension of self-awareness that the more straightforwardly satiric Cornelius is never able to achieve. Indeed, one of the distinguishing characteristics of *Tristram Shandy* is that, even as it utilizes much of the language and many of the techniques of earlier eighteenth-century satiric discourse, except in a few instances (such as the satire of John Burton as Dr Slop) Sterne's work seems far less geared towards satiric *attack*. During the eighteenth century, this aspect of Sterne's writing was picked up on by admiring readers such as his black correspondent, Ignatius Sancho, who observed that whereas Swift had excelled in 'grave-faced irony', Sterne 'lashes his whips with jolly laughter'.[9] For Sancho, certainly, Sterne's satire seemed to be as much about good-humoured mockery – about producing a comedy that might actually serve to *defuse* conflicts – as it was about reproducing the more barbed, corrective satire of the early eighteenth century. Sterne's rather different use of learned discourse in particular can be seen in the passages of *Tristram* that concern laughter itself. Refuting the idea that his work is directed at any specific targets, for instance, Tristram contends that,

> If 'tis wrote against any thing, – 'tis wrote, an' please your worships, against the spleen; in order, by a more frequent and a more convulsive elevation and depression of the diaphragm, and the succussations of the intercostal and abdominal muscles in laughter, to drive the *gall* and other *bitter juices* from the gall bladder, liver and sweet-bread of his majesty's subjects, with all the inimicitious passions which belong to them, down into their duodenums. (4:22, 247)

As in his subsequent description of the beneficial effects of 'True *Shandeism*' (4:32, 278), Sterne here no doubt mocks the medical terminology in which Tristram, following contemporary scientific practice, wraps his description of laughter's bodily motion. If such language is partly parodic, though, in *Tristram Shandy* it is also expressive, not only describing but also enacting the text's intended effect upon the reader, in an anatomical flourish that reveals an exuberant delight in language itself. In a work in which few if any characters, including the animals, entirely avoid physical ailments and impairments, such language provides an especially appropriate means of describing laughter – the principal bulwark against gall, bile, jaundice and the spleen.

In its later volumes, *Tristram Shandy* becomes less overtly satiric and mock-learned, the most notable development being the elaboration of a discourse of moral sympathy that had been glimpsed earlier in the novel, during such episodes as Uncle's Toby's conciliatory treatment of a fly and Trim's tearful reading of Yorick's sermon. Traditionally, the novel's increasing investment in such affecting scenes has been linked to contemporary criticism of the work. It is important to recall here that *Tristram Shandy* was originally written and published in serial form (in five instalments spaced over nine years), a crucial consequence of which being that Sterne was able to engage in a textual dialogue with his critics, to alter the style of his work *as* he wrote it and to come up with more that was *novel*, as the critics complained that he grew dull. During the 1760s, the reviewers waged something of a critical campaign to persuade Sterne to write more decorous and instructive narratives, that might help in the social project of reforming the nation's morals. The foremost campaigner in this line was Ralph Griffiths, proprietor of *The Monthly Review*. This is from Griffiths' review of volumes 7 and 8 of *Tristram Shandy*:

> Give up your Long Noses, your Quedlinbergs, and your Andoüillets. – Dr. Slop, indeed, is a *great* character: but, try your strength another way. One of our gentlemen once remarked, in *print*, Mr. Shandy – that he thought your excellence lay in the PATHETIC. I think so too. In my opinion, the little story of Le Fevre has done you more honour than every thing else you have wrote, except your Sermons. Suppose you were to strike out a new plan? Give us none but amiable or worthy, or exemplary characters; or, if you will, to enliven the drama, throw in the *innocently humorous*. ... In fine, Mr. Shandy, do, for surely you can, excite our passions to *laudable* purposes – awake our affections, engage our hearts – arouze, transport, refine, improve us. Let morality, let the cultivation of virtue be your aim – let wit, humour, elegance and pathos be the means; and the grateful applause of mankind will be your reward.

For Griffiths, as for many at this time, merely entertaining readers was not enough. Ideally, indeed, contemporary readers should not have *been* entertained by the kind of impolite comedy in which Sterne had already indulged – in jokes about long noses and genital deficiency, hot chestnuts falling into men's laps, and crevices in chimney-pieces that cause ageing bachelors to exclaim, 'Right end of a woman!' (2:7, 83). What especially perturbed Griffiths about Sterne's predilection towards such material was the apparent waste of talent that it involved, from the pen of a writer who was particularly gifted at drawing virtuous examples that might be emulated by readers, via engaging scenes of refined pathos. In the same review, indeed, Griffiths accorded Sterne's pathetic style the highest possible compliment, in his appraisal of the author's description of the Widow Wadman's concupiscent eye: 'Never was any thing more beautifully simple, more natural, more *touching*! ... *Richardson* – the delicate, the circumstantial RICHARDSON himself, never produced any thing equal to the amours of Uncle Toby and the Widow Wadman!'.[10]

Griffiths' review is often regarded as the catalyst for Sterne's second novel, *A Sentimental Journey*. Whether or not Sterne responded to

Griffiths quite so specifically, the presence of more 'sentimental' narratives in the later volumes of *Tristram Shandy* suggests that the author was already feeling under pressure to conform more fully to the new standards of improving discourse and literary decorum. In *Tristram Shandy* itself, however, such appeals to sentiment afforded as many problems as they did solutions. Consider for instance the conclusion to the tale of lieutenant Le Fevre (comically renamed 'Le Fever') in volume 6, which Griffiths singled out for praise as one of the principal beauties of Sterne's text:

> The blood and spirits of *Le Fever*, which were waxing cold and slow within him, and were retreating to their last citadel, the heart, – rallied back, – the film forsook his eyes for a moment, – he looked up wistfully in my uncle *Toby*'s face, – then cast a look upon his boy, – and that *ligament*, fine as it was, – was never broken. –
>
> Nature instantly ebb'd again, – the film returned to its place, – the pulse fluttered – stopp'd – went on – throb'd – stopp'd again – moved – stopp'd – shall I go on? – No. (6:10, 353–4)

Here, at the end of his quintessentially affecting tale, Sterne reveals the discursive or textual status of the sentimental narrative, its existence as a mode of *writing*, rather than as a simple, unmediated or mimetic expression of *feeling*. As Tristram foregrounds his own role in the production of the story, the sentimental narrative becomes as much an object for the reader's scrutiny, as an occasion for the exercise of moral sympathy. Within *Tristram Shandy*, in fact, the sentimental mode continually struggles to attain to a privileged space, which would separate it from the other kinds of writing that are variously mocked and subverted elsewhere in the work. Further evidence of this *detachment* from pathos is provided by the story of the mad peasant girl, Maria, in volume 9. Having asked Maria what resemblance she perceives between himself and her goat, Tristram addresses the reader who might be concerned that he is mocking this unfortunate girl:

> I do intreat the candid reader to believe me, that it was from the humblest conviction of what a *Beast* man is, – that I ask'd the question; and that I would not have let fallen an unseasonable pleasantry in the venerable presence of Misery, to be entitled to all the wit that ever Rabelais scatter'd – and yet I own my heart smote me, and that I so smarted at the very idea of it, that I swore I would set up for Wisdom and utter grave sentences the rest of my days – and never – never

attempt again to commit mirth with man, woman, or child, the longest day I had to live. (9:24, 529–30)

Through this narratorial address to his readers, Sterne tackled the contradictory impulses that had come to motivate his text. On the one hand, in the presence of Maria – a personification of 'Misery' and the very emblem of sentimental 'virtue in distress' – Tristram distances himself from the more bawdy, Rabelaisian elements of his work. And yet, even this scene of overt, narratorial and authorial repentance is not entirely unproblematic. Within the passage itself, a discordant note is immediately sounded by the incongruous construction, 'to commit mirth' (*fornication* being something that, verbally speaking, one is more likely to 'commit'). Furthermore, as Griffiths would himself lament in his review of volume 9, any degree of pathos that Tristram does manage to achieve in this episode is effectively deflated at the end of the chapter, as Tristram turns abruptly from Maria to exclaim 'What an excellent inn at Moulins!' (9:24, 530). Perhaps the main obstacle to the moral credibility of the episode, however, is that it appears in a volume of *Tristram* that is primarily concerned with the comic climax to the Widow Wadman's campaign to discover precisely where Uncle Toby received his war wound. While Sterne *did* partly rein in his satiric impulses in the later volumes of the work, then, his bawdy wit and his pathetic style would remain uneasy bedfellows to the very end of the novel. In the heterogeneous world of *Tristram Shandy*, the sentimental mode would always struggle to become more than a stylization, simply one more *kind* of textual discourse.

Sarah Scott, Millenium Hall

If *Tristram Shandy* staged a movement, however incomplete, towards a discourse of sentiment that was directed more at the heart-strings, than at the satiric *hauteur*, of its readers, then this movement brought it more fully into line with the direction that novelistic discourse as a whole was taking at this time. The increasingly dominant trend in novel-writing was towards novels of sensibility, usually written by women, and directed – as Smollett's Jery Melford would note – towards the 'propagation of virtue'.[11] Behind the genre's increasing promotion of ethical improvement lay the influence of Richardson. Under the sway of *Pamela* and *Clarissa*, the impulse to bring fictional writing into line with the new moral imperatives can be seen in novels as diverse as

Fielding's *Amelia* and Eliza Haywood's *The History of Miss Betsy Thoughtless* (1751). The kind of didacticism that, in one view, forms the stock-in-trade of the latter, would surely have astonished any contemporary reader familiar with the amatory prose that Haywood had written a generation earlier, during the 1720s. In a by-now well-known formulation, Terry Eagleton describes Richardson's own fiction as enacting a 'bourgeois "feminization of discourse" ' – a process that is often seen as driving the mainstream of moral fiction published during the succeeding decades.[12] It is important, though, to resist the temptation to think of the majority of novels published during these decades as an unindividuated lump, produced within the broad terms of 'sensibility' or 'feminization', or even as a straightforwardly *bourgeois* mode of discourse. A pertinent case in point is Sarah Scott's *A Description of Millenium Hall* (1762). Certainly, in announcing its intention to 'excite in the READER proper Sentiments of Humanity, and lead the Mind to the Love of VIRTUE', the title-page to *Millenium Hall* located the work immediately within the terms of the improving agenda that critics would increasingly seek to impress upon Sterne during the same decade. With its portrayal of rational and practical, noble and *high*-bourgeois paragons of virtue, however, Scott's novel also inflected this agenda in a manner that, for modern readers, might seem to give the work a problematically conservative bias (in terms of social class) but, at the same time, a degree of proto-feminist force.

Millenium Hall can be regarded as the fullest literary expression of the social manifesto of the 'Bluestocking' movement, which originated in intellectual gatherings held in London during the 1750s by a group of gentrified and professional women led by Frances Boscawen, Elizabeth Vesey and Elizabeth Montagu ('Queen of the Bluestockings' and Scott's sister). These gatherings formed the hub of a large wheel: extended networks of women engaged in wide-ranging philanthropic, social and cultural activities, from rescuing fallen women, through establishing houses of industry for the poor and the disabled, to publishing works by subscription for deserving authors. In her novel, Scott depicts several projects similar to those that the Bluestockings sponsored in real life. Notably, the ladies' estate, around which the novel revolves, incorporates a secluded 'asylum', in which people with severe physical afflictions can live in comfort, away from the cruel gaze of the social world. For the day-to-day running of the Hall, the ladies also employ a number of physically impaired workers, who are unable to gain employment elsewhere. As the housekeeper (who herself has an impaired hand) tells the narrator: 'the cook cannot walk without crutches, the kitchen maid has but one eye, the dairy maid is almost stone-deaf, and the house maid has but one hand'. While he initially finds the whole idea whimsical, the narrator ultimately decides that this employment of unfortunate women actually represents a noble 'refinement of charity'.[13] Within the novel, Millenium Hall is offered as an alternative to and a solution for various forms of cultural dispossession and social marginalization. If *Millenium Hall* can thus be said to envision a utopian, philanthropic community, this is a utopia of an unusually cloistered kind, which is itself secluded away from the rest of society. And yet, because the novel portrays a predominantly *female* utopia, it also offers a particularly acute analysis of the social evils from which contemporary women might have wished to seek refuge, such as the stigmas of being an 'old maid' (an ageing spinster) or a 'toad-eater' (a woman who was well born, but who lived in reduced financial circumstances, and who was thus forced to seek employment as the paid companion to an imperious, and possibly unpleasant rich lady – the misery of which situation had previously been powerfully evoked in Sarah Fielding's novel, *The Adventures of David Simple* (1744 and 1753)). In approaching the work as a species of 'utopia', therefore, the questions that we need to ask of Scott's novel are: what does Millenium Hall actually stand for, and what social issues or problems was Scott addressing through her representation of its female community? How does the community at Millenium Hall actually work? And to what extent did Scott seek to present this utopian vision as a feasible programme or blueprint for an alternative social reality?

We can begin by considering the qualities that are embodied in the six central female characters who make up the core community of Millenium Hall. Early in the novel, Scott describes the young Louisa Mancel in the following manner:

> Thus her understanding opened in a surprizing degree, and while the beauty and graces of her person, and her great progress in genteel accomplishments, charmed every eye, the nice discernment, and uncommon strength of reason which appeared in her conversation, astonished every judicious observer; but her most admirable qualities were her humility and modesty; which, notwithstanding her great internal and external excellencies, rendered her diffident, mild, bashful, and tractable; her heart seemed as free from defects, as her understanding was from the follies, which in a degree are incident to almost every other person. (91)

In this description of the teenage Louisa, we can already observe the distinctive combination of qualities that Scott wished to attribute to her leading ladies. As Scott indicates, Louisa possesses the ideal characteristics of the eighteenth-century proper lady, being not only graceful and beautiful, but also reserved, humble, and (as is emphasized elsewhere) pious. While Louisa's 'most admirable qualities' may be her 'humility and modesty', though, she also possesses other qualities that were not always either attributed, or even allowed, to that part of the population which could still be referred to as the 'fair sex'. Particularly noteworthy from a modern perspective is Scott's emphasis upon Louisa's *intellectual* capacity, her 'uncommon strength of reason'. During the eighteenth century, even those who were prepared to allow that a woman might possess the intellectual strength to cope with the education that Louisa receives, often retained a sense that such accomplishments in the realm of learning would inevitably compromise a woman's more characteristically *feminine* qualities. At a time when intellectual knowledge could still be described as 'manly learning' – and in which, as for Cornelius Scriblerus, men might be defined as 'the learned Sex' – learned ladies were often viewed as unfeminine, indeed as peculiarly masculinized (Mrs Selwyn, in Frances Burney's *Evelina* (1778), is one example of such). The most striking aspect of Scott's representation of Louisa, then, is that she is allowed to possess *all* of her qualities – her social graces, her moral virtues *and* her intellectual fibre – at the same time. Secured to a feminine sensibility, Louisa's rationality thus provides an alternative to the more *masculine* exercise of 'reason', which is criticized elsewhere in the novel as aggressively Procrustean (72).

This female capacity for reason is especially crucial to the novel's promotion of social *duty* – of acting for the greater good in accordance with ethical precepts, rather than acting merely in one's own interests. The importance of social responsibility is highlighted by Miss Melvyn's concern to provide a good example by marrying Mr Morgan; a decision that involves her in a rigorous exercise of self-scrutiny, as she endeavours to ensure that she is directed by a principled sense of public duty, rather than by her own, emotional inclination. A further example of such socially directed virtue is the consistently generous attitude that Miss Trentham adopts towards those who have treated her badly in the past. Throughout the novel, in fact, the reader is regaled with examples of the reasoning and Stoic-like self-control of the Millenium Hall ladies. This conferral upon women of qualities that had traditionally been associated with men is all the more intriguing given that, in the world portrayed within the novel, men themselves appear to have completely mislaid these attributes. In the final analysis, even the most virtuous men are shown to lack sufficient control over their passions. The behaviour of Sir Edward Lambton – who, believing himself crossed in his love for Louisa Mancel, goes off in a rage to fight in Germany, where he dies – is only the most extreme example of such weakness. That even the previously solid Mr Alworth fails in this regard, switching his affections from the virtuous Harriot Trentham to the society girl, Miss Melman, only confirms the comprehensive instability of Scott's male characters, their inability to emulate either the self-command or the self-sacrifice that is exercised by the ladies of the Hall.

By securing the faculty of reason for the leaders of her female utopia, Scott ensured that these women were fit to govern a landed estate and, more particularly, that they could plausibly take up their positions as the agents of the various charitable enterprises to which their male visitors are introduced during the novel. As Dorice Elliott notes in a discussion of the novel's relationship to contemporary philanthropic projects, despite the fact that the *official* ideology of such enterprises was grounded in what were regarded as feminine virtues, the institutions themselves were 'usually organized, supervised, and managed by men'. Among the most notable institutions established during this period were the Foundling Hospital, which was set up in 1739 for the care of orphans and abandoned children; the Lock Hospital, which treated women for venereal disease; the Magdalen Asylum, for the relief of penitent prostitutes; and the Female Orphan Asylum. As Elliott nicely argues, in *Millenium Hall* Scott portrays women *themselves* as the founders and managers of such enterprises, rather than as merely the distressed victims treated within them, under the watchful eye of *male* philanthropists.[14]

If *Millenium Hall* projects a radical reversal of a traditional scheme of polarized gender attributes, though, it is as much a *social* milieu – the world of fashionable London – which represents the anti-utopian 'reality' against which Scott pits Millenium Hall itself. In the novel, this world is depicted in the series of 'inset narratives' that relate the ladies' lives prior to their arrival at the Hall. As depicted in these narratives-within, the courtly and fashionable culture of the period, while not necessarily or inherently vicious, constitutes a social arena that tends towards the superficial in both ethics and social behaviour, and that is also ideally suited to the deceptions of social disguise, the duplicitous masking of less than virtuous inclinations. Significantly, this is a culture that lacks any true sense of *community*, of mutual goodwill and concern for the moral well-being of others. As a number of the inset narratives pointedly reveal, the fashionable world is a dangerous place for any *truly* innocent lady, who is liable to be insufficiently suspicious of the motivations of her male suitors. The threat of the predatory (as opposed to the protective) male is highlighted both by Mr Hintman's base designs upon Louisa Mancel, and by the early history of Lady Mary Jones, whose projected 'adventure' to Scotland, for the purpose of marrying Mr Lenman (who is, it transpires, already married), is only narrowly averted (176). As in *The Female Quixote*, Lady Mary's experience provides a stark reminder of the dangers that involvement in clandestine 'adventures' posed for eighteenth-century women. It was not only metropolitan men, however, that respectable women had to contend with. Equally problematic in Scott's novel are women who have assimilated the values of this fashionable culture. Conscious of the superior merit and attractions of her stepdaughter, for instance, the second Lady Melvyn adopts a competitive attitude towards the youthful Miss Melvyn. Alongside such socially divisive schemers, another female type who Scott presents as subverting the communal potential of fashionable assembly is the *coquette*. As epitomized by Miss Melman, the coquette is concerned only with exercising her flirtatious arts in public, and seems to possess little real existence beyond the sphere of her social performances. Indeed, as Scott's novel intimates, insofar as she lacks any significant degree of *interiority* – of reflective self-consciousness or ethical substance – the coquette occupies a space at the very heart of the public culture of fashionable London.

For all the surface attractions of its round of assemblies, balls, and social visits, then, Mrs Maynard's inset narratives offer a series of modern parables regarding the hazards of this metropolitan and courtly culture. Importantly, rather than as a mere retreat or escape from this hazardous metropolitan environment, Scott's heroines construct their new community precisely in *opposition* to the values of that environment. Eschewing the showiness of social display, the ladies of Millenium Hall opt for a plain simplicity of appearance, rejecting what are referred to early in the novel as the 'trumpery ornaments' of fashion (61). The question of what a true society or community of people actually comprises is a subject of open debate during the visitors' time at the Hall. In a discussion with Mr Lamont, for instance, Mrs Mancel emphasizes the difference between a mere 'croud' of people and a truly social location or situation. Against Lamont's intimations that the ladies' moral gravity has been achieved only at the expense of pleasure, Mancel argues that the ladies wish to 'change noise for real mirth, flutter for settled chearfulness, affected wit for rational conversation' (111–12).

Later in the novel, similarly, the moral progress of the initially
light-headed Lady Mary Jones is exemplified by her rejection of fashionable 'dissipation' and 'tumultuous pleasures' for the more discreet
and modest environment of Millenium Hall itself (191). The ladies'
Cornwall retreat is, then, a place of 'solidity', rather than of what was
known in the period as the *bon ton* – the easy, but potentially frivolous,
vivaciousness of town life. Significantly, in one of the rare instances in
which the Millenium community does allow a townish pleasure to take
place within its environs – in this case, a 'rustic ball' – it turns out to be
so restrained and well-ordered as actually to be praised by the narrator
for its 'decorum' (162). As such, the Millenium ball provides a striking
contrast to the representation of masquerade entertainments in other
contemporary novels, in which such occasions generally pose a serious
threat to female virtue.

Scott's novel, then, is evidently suspicious of the social (and readerly)
attractions of performance, intrigue and adventure. As Betty Schellenberg
observes, *Millenium Hall* constructs 'a gendered dichotomy of duty,
self-control, and happiness on the one hand, and desire, self-indulgence,
and misery on the other'.[15] To what extent, though, did Scott envision
Millenium Hall as a feasible model for a different kind of community?
Within the novel itself, the burden of this question lies with the reactions of the male visitors to the Hall. The responses of Lamont, in
particular, provide a guide to the persuasive force of the ladies.
Throughout the novel, Lamont's objections to aspects of the community are consistently answered to his satisfaction, so that his doubts
about the project gradually drift away. To a great extent, in fact,
Lamont provides a foil to the women's scheme. While the narrator himself is favourably predisposed towards the ladies' community – it is he,
after all, who labels it *as* utopian, by calling it Millenium Hall in the first
place – Lamont is a refugee from the very social milieu whose values the
ladies are rejecting. Enabled by a generous father to 'partake of every
fashionable amusement', we are told, Lamont's natural exuberance had
led him into 'all the dissipation which the gay world affords', where-
upon 'that vivacity, which, properly qualified, might have become true
wit, degenerated into pertness and impertinence'. In the figure of
Lamont, then, fashionable society is shown both to appeal to those of a
vain and showy disposition, and to recast actual talents or capacities in
its own, immoral and irreligious image. Nevertheless, while 'Fashion,
not reason, has been the guide of all his thoughts and actions', Lamont
has fortunately remained 'good-natured, and not unentertaining …
where he does not desire to shine' (55). Under the good influence of

the Hall ladies, Lamont is thus brought to reassess his metropolitan way of life, and is perhaps well on his way to reformation when, towards the end of the novel, the narrator is surprised to discover him reading the New Testament. In many ways, of course, this turnabout is highly serendipitous, involving as it does both a separation of Lamont from his usual sphere of life, and a residence in the kind of utopian community upon which the domestic tourist was not often likely to stumble. Nevertheless, the apparent religious conversion of Lamont clearly provides one of the most significant means by which Scott sought to validate the communal virtue of Millenium Hall. If even the initially sceptical and slightly frivolous Lamont can be persuaded into religion by sheer force of the ladies' example, then the prospects for the community exerting further influence might seem to be good.

Significantly, as it is filtered through the lens of the narrator, the novel also moves from portraying the Hall as an Arcadian, exotic or other-worldly place, to a plausible, material one. In the early pages, the Ladies' estate is described in terms that seem to highlight its *un*reality, its difference from the everyday world. Following a reflection upon the 'rural simplicity' of a group of female hay-makers, for instance, the narrator expresses his wish to see more of what he terms both an 'earthly paradise' and a 'fairy land' (57–8). By the novel's end, though, the estate has come back down to earth, and the ladies' lives appear to the narrator to be far more capable of imitation. In terms of fiction published during the middle decades of the eighteenth century, an instructive contrast here is provided by Samuel Johnson's account of the 'Happy Valley', in his philosophical oriental tale, *Rasselas* (1759). As described by Johnson, the 'Happy Valley' is quite clearly a fictional place, which is rather symbolic of a state of mind than descriptive of somewhere that could actually exist in the real world of its readers. By contrast, Scott's far more verisimilar Hall pointedly retains many of the features of the landed estate and of a recognizable social structure. Along with the cultivation of their respective accomplishments, the ladies are involved in all the practical details – including, importantly, the financial arrangements – of their utopian community. To this extent, what Scott projects in her novel is a plausible philanthropic community, which is not only constructed within the terms of the cultural ideology of femininity, but which is run by women themselves.

In other respects, though, the cultural project that the novel describes also contains the seeds of its own limitations. One key problem here is the required *independence* of the women. Within the novel, the institution of marriage is positioned as requiring women to suppress any prior personal ambitions, to submit themselves wholly to pleasing, and promoting the interests of, their husbands. Early in the novel, for instance, we hear that the first Lady Melvyn did all that she could to make the rather unaccomplished Sir Charles appear to better effect in society (not surprisingly, his daughter will act in the same manner upon her own marriage). Given that the selfless impulses of virtuous married women are presented by Scott as being quite *properly* directed towards aiding their husbands, though, it can only be by remaining (or becoming) unmarried that such benevolent dispositions can be directed towards the good of a broader community. Beyond this necessity of singledom (at least, in *hetero*sexual terms), the novel also leaves unanswered the question of what happens beyond the moment in which the work is itself set. Does the male visitors' return to the world, now under the influence of Millenium Hall, constitute a testament to the likely success of the community beyond its own confines? Or, less optimistically, will the ladies' own influence always be restricted to this *local* community, with the novel's conclusion marking the moment at which men are required to take this vision out into a wider, more public sphere? Again, the key question here is whether a broad *feminization* of values (i.e. a promotion of values identified *as feminine*) necessarily leads to the social and cultural empowerment of actual women. At the end of Scott's novel, certainly, the virtuous ladies of Millenium Hall appear destined to remain on their Cornish estate. While the ladies' private sphere may have expanded into a whole community, the women themselves do not seem free to go forth into the world and further disseminate their ideas. In part, this is because to do so would compromise the very values that inform their project, not least what the narrator calls 'that modesty which has induced them to conceal their virtues in retirement' (53). It is not entirely to deny the novel's radical, proto-feminist potential to observe that, in the final analysis, the communal virtue of Millenium Hall remains tethered to a relatively *private* model of female agency.

Laurence Sterne, A Sentimental Journey *and* *Henry Mackenzie*, The Man of Feeling

In *Millenium Hall*, as we have seen, Scott depicted a form of *rational* sensibility that was manifested in practical, philanthropic endeavour. In a number of respects, this representation of female enterprise renders Scott's novel somewhat unrepresentative of the novels of sensibility that were being produced at this time. Rarely would the snares to virtue be so successfully neutered as they are in the environs of Millenium Hall. Rather, as in Scott's inset narratives, the sentimental novel tended to focus upon the *distress* of its virtuous subjects. As John Mullan observes regarding Frances Sheridan, whose *Memoirs of Miss Sidney Bidulph* (1762) was dedicated to her advisor, Richardson: 'the influence of Richardson is marked, in the novels of the 1750s and 1760s, not simply by the habitual apotheosis of sensibility, but by the association of sensibility with a virtue under threat. It is a virtue which has to be *in extremis*'.[16] In its turn, this fictional endangering of virtue points to a further key factor in the contemporary appeal of the sentimental novel: its incitement to readerly compassion. In a famous remark, Samuel Johnson is recorded having spoken to the author of *Miss Sidney Bidulph* thus: 'I know not, Madam, that you have a right, upon moral principles, to make your readers suffer so much'.[17] For all that it incorporates a compliment, Johnson's remark is also suggestive of a broader movement in the direction of prose fiction during this period – what we might call the development of the novel of 'sentiment' into the 'sentimental' novel. Gradually, the kinds of moral precepts that were to have been gleaned through the example of Pamela's or Clarissa's virtuous conduct in extreme circumstances would become secondary to the production of sentimental *affect*, of a primarily *emotional* response in the reader. As readers are increasingly encouraged to 'suffer' along with fictional individuals, that is, the imagined threat to these characters' virtue becomes less securely tied to a lesson in ethical principles, and more an occasion for the reader's luxuriance in the very *spectacle* of suffering.

Particularly revealing of this 'sentimental' stage in the development of the novel are those fictions that centred not upon *female* virtue '*in extremis*', but upon *men* of feeling. Such works had been germane to the discourse of sensibility from the outset – from Sarah Fielding's *David Simple*, to Richardson's *Sir Charles Grandison*, Henry Brooke's *The Fool of Quality* (1765–70), Oliver Goldsmith's *The Vicar of Wakefield* (1766), and *Sir George Ellison* (1766), Sarah Scott's narrative of the prehistory of the narrator of *Millenium Hall*, which would be suggestively re-titled *The Man of Real Sensibility* for a condensed version of 1774. Here, we focus upon two short works that, in different ways, have come to epitomize the 'sentimental' novel: Sterne's *A Sentimental Journey through France and Italy* (1768) and Henry Mackenzie's *The Man of Feeling* (1771). While, in both novels, a heightened capacity for 'feeling' becomes almost an end in itself, for the same reason both works can also be read as offering critiques of the contemporary valorization of affective sensibility. Central to both novels is a new model of sentimental masculinity. Throughout this period, men were being urged to take on board what were regarded as the more 'feminine' values of modesty, delicacy, and sympathy, in an attempt to soften conventional constructions of masculine conduct. By absorbing the values of this more feminine sensibility, it was thought, men would come to reject traditional forms of roguish and aristocratic behaviour – activities such as hunting, duelling, gambling, excessive drinking, speaking obscenities and, of course, preying upon women. As partly 'feminized' men, Yorick and Harley can thus be situated within what Markman Ellis has termed a 'gendered transformation of manners', which gradually took place over the course of the eighteenth century.[18] At the same time, though, both novels also query the nature and value of the 'man of feeling', his social location and, more specifically, his relationship to a modernizing, commercial society. As these novels ask: where does the man of feeling fit into the world? What is his social status or prestige? how can he best put his moral virtues to use? Or, to recast these questions in more problematic terms: how valuable *is* this new male sensitivity? What are its *limitations*? And what are the *obstacles* that the man of feeling is likely to come up against, in his endeavour to lead a moral life?

One way of beginning to answer these questions is to consider the kind of social world that the novels envisage. One of the great ironies of the 'sentimental' novel is that, in the main, it actually offers an extremely suspicious and pessimistic vision of contemporary society, reinscribing a Hobbesian landscape in which the vicious and self-interested many continually impose upon the good and virtuous few. Likening life to a 'race' in his *Human Nature* (1640), Thomas Hobbes had argued that this race had 'no other goal, nor no other garland, but being foremost'. Even the sympathetic faculty of 'pity', Hobbes had suggested, was driven by a prior concern for one's *own* well-being, rather than by a pure concern for the well-being of others.[19] In the sentimental novel, it is just this kind of competitive, unfriendly, and *un*sympathetic environment that characters of true feeling tend to find themselves moving in. The striking *exceptionality* of the sentimental subject, and of altruistic benevolence, in these novels is well discussed in John Mullan's important study, *Sentiment and Sociability* (1988). As Mullan argues:

> The novel of sentiment in the eighteenth century, committed as it might be to the celebration of fellow-feeling, elaborates pathos from

exactly the disconnection of special experiences of sympathy from dominant patterns of social relationship ... much of what is called 'sentimental' fiction actually depicts benevolence as a limited and exceptional propensity.[20]

An exemplary illustration of this *unsentimental* vision of social relations is provided by *The Man of Feeling*. From the outset, Mackenzie's novel asserts the moral desideratum of remaining uncorrupted by the world. Within the society depicted in the novel, however, there appears to be no real place where a man such as Harley might live at all. As Mackenzie pointedly registers, Harley is both a man of 'extreme sensibility' and a mere 'child in the drama of the world'.[21] It is this very unworldliness of character that allows him to be so easily fooled by appearances, and by the deceptions of others. During his time in London, for instance, Harley mistakes a former footman and pimp for a gentleman, and is taken in by a pair of sharpers, who gamble him out of his money. In this lack of practical, worldly *nous*, Harley can be regarded as a sentimental-ized version of Fielding's Parson Adams. Mackenzie's depiction of the imposition of the knowing upon the innocent and virtuous also recalls more recent novels, such as Goldsmith's *The Vicar of Wakefield*. In one of the most famous scenes in Goldsmith's novel, Dr Primrose's son, Moses, is persuaded to waste part of the family's fortune on 'a groce of green spectacles', which turn out to be largely worthless. Soon after-wards, Primrose is himself duped out of a horse by the sharper, Mr Jenkinson.[22] A particular foible of Harley's (the man of feeling's own, hobbled hobby-horse) is his misplaced pride in his skill at phys-iognomy (reading a person's character from the features of their face) – an art that turns out to be almost entirely untrustworthy. In one of the key episodes in Mackenzie's novel – Harley's encounter with the pros-titute, Emily Atkins – the man of feeling does in fact appear to read cor-rectly the situation with which he is confronted. Given that he is prone to believe *any* tale of distress, however, it is fair to say that even an appropriate exercise of sympathy, and a successful act of charity, can ultimately be achieved by Harley only through luck, rather than judgement.

While Harley stands out as a caring and morally innocent character, then, Mackenzie's novel is evidently aware of the practical limitations of 'feeling' alone. The alienation of sympathetic feeling from the modern metropolitan environment is more fully thematized towards the end of the text, as Harley approaches his death. In this passage, the narrator, Charles, records Harley's deathbed speech, in which the man of feeling reflects back upon his life:

> He had by this time clasped my hand, and found it wet by a tear
> which had just fallen upon it. – His eye began to moisten too – we
> sat for some time silent – At last, with an attempt to a look of more
> composure, 'There are some remembrances' (said Harley) 'which
> rise involuntarily on my heart, and make me almost wish to live.
> I have been blessed with a few friends, who redeem my opinion of
> mankind. I recollect, with the tenderest emotion, the scenes of pleas-
> ure I have passed among them; but we shall meet again, my friend,
> never to be separated. There are some feelings which perhaps are too
> tender to be suffered by the world. The world is in general selfish,
> interested, and unthinking, and throws the imputation of romance
> or melancholy on every temper more susceptible than its own. I can-
> not think but in those regions which I contemplate, if there is any
> thing of mortality left about us, that these feelings will subsist; – they
> are called, – perhaps they are – weaknesses here; – but there may be
> some better modifications of them in heaven, which may deserve the
> name of virtues.' (95)

At the beginning of this scene, we have what is often referred to as a
sentimental *tableau*. Rather than the busy action of novelistic adventure, what we find ourselves reading about here are pauses, gestures,
emotions and silences. This tableau scene nicely exemplifies what Ann
Jessie Van Sant has termed the 'miniaturization of experience' that
occurs in sentimental novels.[23] Instead of a flow of tears, Mackenzie
describes first a single tear, and then the merest suggestion of a possible
tear to come, as an eye *begins* to moisten. During sentimental set-pieces
of this kind, narrative time is in effect slowed down, so that each small
action is allowed to convey the fullest possible meaning (a technique
that, as we saw earlier, had been problematized at the conclusion of
Sterne's tale of lieutenant Le Fevre). With the solemnity of his
deathbed scene thus established, we proceed to Harley's more measured and composed account of himself. As this sentimental self-diagnosis
demonstrates, while the man of feeling believes in the reality of human
virtue, as it appears within his own small circle of acquaintance, he is
by now only too aware that the world more generally is a 'selfish,
interested, and unthinking' place. Notwithstanding the support of his
own sentimental coterie, then, it is clear that Harley's extremity of
sensibility cannot survive in eighteenth-century society – that he is
unrealistically 'susceptible' of emotion and fancy; that his feelings will

always be 'too tender' for the world; and that, in this life at least, his 'virtues' can only ever be regarded as 'weaknesses'.

While, in his exceptional capacity for feeling, Harley is presented as something of an exemplary figure, then, his example does not provide any kind of practical model for living the moral life. The novel's ambivalence about the *value* of this model of sentimental masculinity is further registered in its very final paragraph, as the narrator recalls his now-departed friend:

> I sometimes visit his grave; I sit in the hollow of the tree. It is worth a thousand homilies! every nobler feeling rises within me! every beat of my heart awakens a virtue! – but it will make you hate the world – No: there is such an air of gentleness around, that I can hate nothing; but, as to the world – I pity the men of it. (98)

This, assuredly, is a somewhat equivocal eulogy to the man of feeling. To begin with, it is suggested that Harley's grave – and, by implication, his life – affords an exemplary text of pious, moral instruction, which has inspired the narrator's own sense of virtue. While the narrator may temper his hatred of the world with pity for its inhabitants, however, there clearly remains a significant downside to this scene of mortal contemplation and awakening virtue. As the graveyard location here suggests, virtues such as Harley's can exist only *away from* the scene of significant human activity. In taking moral inspiration from Harley, the narrator thus renders himself a man who, like Harley, is not *of* the world in any real, practical sense. Indeed, it is only from this position of detached retreat that the narrator is able to speak of 'the world' beyond, as though any reflections he might make upon that world bore no relation to himself.

As in *The Vicar of Wakefield*, then, in Mackenzie's novel the principal obstacles to living a moral life are the ways of the world as it already exists. In comparison with Goldsmith's novel, *The Man of Feeling* actually offers an even more extreme vision of the distresses of a sensitive man in an unsentimental society. In an essay on the novel genre that he wrote for his periodical, *The Lounger*, during the 1780s, Mackenzie would go on to mount an explicit critique of an 'enthusiasm' of sentiment that was not fully grounded in, and guided by, a prior moral 'principle'.[24] Read in the context of this essay, *The Man of Feeling* can appear more critical than we might initially assume, both of Harley's own 'romantic enthusiasm', and of the kind of benevolent 'humanity' that is possessed by Miss Walton – which, as the narrator records, consists in 'a feeling, not a principle' (65, 13). And yet, as Harley's deathbed speech itself demonstrates, Mackenzie's novel also sounds a lament for the unhappy fate of men such as Harley. Ultimately, we might say, *The Man of Feeling* falls into a kind of ideological impasse, at once wanting to promote the value of 'feeling' against a coldly competitive, commercial society, and yet unable to envisage how someone possessing this affective moral capacity might actually survive in the real world.

As *The Man of Feeling* testifies, then, writers of 'sentimental' novels were themselves wary of any outright celebration of 'feeling'. More specifically, the sub-genre of the 'man of feeling' novel can be viewed as offering narrative explorations, or *thinkings through*, of the meaning, and the viability, of the new, sentimental male. If these novels problematized even as they helped to construct this feminized masculinity, though, then they also approached the problem of modern masculinity in a number of different ways. The variation *within* the 'man of feeling' novel can be illustrated by setting Mackenzie's novel beside *A Sentimental Journey*. Sterne's second novel traces the journey that its protagonist, Yorick, makes around France, observing the successes and failures of his attempt to improve his manners through contact with French refinement. In much the same way that *The Castle of Otranto* can seem proleptically parodic of the Gothic novels that would follow in its wake, *A Sentimental Journey* often reads like a satire in advance of the more lachrymose emotionalism on display in Mackenzie's work. A revealing contrast to the melancholic finale of *The Man of Feeling* is provided by a graveyard scene that occurs early in Sterne's text. The scene follows Yorick's reconciliation with a monk (whom he had initially snubbed), which is achieved via a sentimental exchange of snuff-boxes. Upon returning to France, Yorick learns that the monk, Father Lorenzo, has died, and decides to visit his grave. At Lorenzo's graveside, Yorick relates, 'I burst into a flood of tears – but I am as weak as a woman; and I beg the world not to smile, but pity me'.[25] As in *The Man of Feeling*, to a certain degree the feminization of the man of feeling here represents a laudable sign of his refined sensibility. Yorick's open confession of his feminine 'weakness' is especially striking in the context of contemporary anxieties regarding the moral fibre of the British male. In his influential jeremiad (political sermon), *An Estimate of the Manners and Principles of the Times* (1757–58), John Brown had positioned the period's sponsorship of male pity as part of a movement towards a general effeminacy that posed a threat to the nation's safety. Relating 'Effeminacy' to 'Cowardice', Brown argued that '*Pity* is generally strong in *Women*: And hence Pity, or Humanity, is the natural Growth of an *effeminate Nation*: That is, of a Nation which *resembles Women*'.[26] For Brown, the new emphasis upon the sentimental virtue of 'Pity' epitomized the pernicious downside of the 'gendered transformation of manners', the spread of 'feminine' standards of behaviour throughout society. On one level, Yorick's blubbering behaviour at the monk's graveside would seem to confirm Brown's fears about the erosion of a strong-minded, British masculinity. In other respects, though, this scene also signals a more positive apprehension of social relations than was common in the sentimental novel. By contrast to the narrator of *The Man of Feeling*, who concludes by pitying the world for its lack of feeling, in his own graveyard reflection Yorick uses the occasion of his seemingly effeminate weakness in order to ask the world to pity *him*. Whereas Mackenzie's narrator assumes a certain monopoly upon virtue, then, the implication of Yorick's own statement is that the world *itself* possesses the capacity for pity – a capacity that, during his travels, Yorick will attempt to draw out. One of the basic contrasts between *A Sentimental Journey* and *The Man of Feeling*, in fact, lies in the very different visions that they project of society at large. Significantly, unlike Harley or Goldsmith's Dr Primrose, Yorick *doesn't* find himself being duped by a succession of worldly sharpers. Rather, Sterne's text seeks specifically, if often wryly, to oppose this conception of the world as a 'hostile kind' of place (16). This is not to say that Sterne himself was unaware of the potential limits to sensibility's reach. A letter written to Dr John Eustace in February 1768, for instance, sees the author complaining quite explicitly that 'There is so little true feeling in the *herd* of the *world*'.[27] This late sense of personal disenchantment notwithstanding, the social vision of Sterne's own 'sentimental' novel can be justly regarded as far less pessimistic than that of *The Man of Feeling*.

If *A Sentimental Journey* offers a comparatively upbeat assessment of the possibilities for benevolent feeling in the world at large, though, at a more local level it also raises difficulties regarding the very operation of moral sympathy. As Adam Smith had shown in *The Theory of Moral Sentiments* (1759), the act of sympathy was more properly viewed as involving an 'imaginary change of situation' with another, than a genuine sharing in that other's actual feelings.[28] In Sterne's hands, the centrality of the *imagination* to the exercise of sympathy, and the inaccessibility of the other that Smith's theory implied, prompts a playful dramatization of sympathy in action. In order to exercise his sympathetic faculties, of course, the aspiring benevolist needed to discover suitable recipients for his attentions. A quixotic traveller 'in quest of melancholy adventures' (107), Yorick himself is determined to discern distress wherever he can, often based upon little evidence other than that provided by his imagination. Despite only a brief acquaintance, for instance, Sterne's narrator decides that Madame de L*** must be a widow, and thus in need of his sympathetic companionship. By contrast, Yorick's self-conscious uncertainty in the face of beggars, who stage sentimental performances before him in order to earn their alms, indicates his unease with more immediate opportunities for philanthropic engagement. The darker, and potentially solipsistic or self-indulgent side of the sentimental *search* for distress is also revealed during the chapter entitled 'The Captive', in which Yorick imagines a prisoner who has been locked away for 30 years. Here, the sympathetic imagination becomes almost sadistic, and indeed masochistic, as Yorick fancifully shuts the prisoner in his cell and darkens the 'little light' that shines upon him, with the narrator suffering all the while he paints this (*fictional*) picture to himself (70–1). As these episodes reveal, then, for all its comparative optimism and lightness of verbal touch, Sterne's text itself bore witness to the limitations of a sympathetic faculty that was insufficiently moored not just in moral principles, but in the material realm of real objects and situations.

Accompanying such testaments to the vexed relationships between sympathy, imagination and distress are the difficulties that Yorick runs into on account of his passions. The novel's delicate interlacing of decorous sensibility and sexual desire is nicely illustrated by a passage that readers often find initially opaque. In this scene, which takes place in his hotel room, Yorick is seated on the bed with Madame de R***'s *fille de chambre*, or chambermaid. Having fastened a loose buckle on one of the *fille de chambre*'s shoes, Yorick lifts her other foot in order to check that both shoes are now well buckled. This is what happens next:

> in doing it too suddenly – it unavoidably threw the fair *fille de chambre* off her center – and then –

THE CONQUEST

YES – and then – Ye whose clay-cold heads and luke-warm hearts can argue down or mask your passions – tell me, what trespass is it that man should have them? or how his spirit stands answerable, to the father of spirits, but for his conduct under them?

If nature has so wove her web of kindness, that some threads of love and desire are entangled with the piece – must the whole web be rent in drawing them out? – Whip me such stoics, great governor of nature! said I to myself – Wherever thy providence shall place me for the trials of my virtue – whatever is my danger – whatever is my situation – let me feel the movements which rise out of it, and which belong to me as a man – and if I govern them as a good one – I will trust the issues to thy justice, for thou hast made us – and not we ourselves. (90)

As its exclamatory energy might suggest, in this passage Yorick hits upon a very heated way of defending his moral virtue. We can employ Roland Barthes' notion of *jouissance* here to elucidate the different levels at which Yorick's language is working at this point in the novel. In *The Pleasure of the Text* (1975), Barthes distinguishes between the level of *representation* – what is actually being said or described in a narrative – and the level of *figuration* – what is happening in terms of the medium of representation itself (in essence, this is a narratological reworking of the Saussurean linguistic distinction between signified and signifier). With this in mind, we can posit that while, at the level of representation, Yorick is defending his self-control in the face of sexual temptation, at the level of figuration (or language itself) the text has become an erotic site, what Barthes calls the 'text of bliss'.[29] In effect, Yorick's sexual excitement becomes displaced here into his very act of writing. While, on one level, Yorick may indeed act with decorum towards the *fille de chambre*, his word choices – the qualified but suggestive chapter title, 'The Conquest' (which is designed momentarily to lead the reader into assuming a *rakish* 'conquest'); the plea to be allowed to feel the rising 'movements' that belong to the narrator, as a man; the reference to the possible 'issues' of the encounter; and even, it might be suggested, the passing allusion to whipping – slyly encourage the reader to consider how the text might also be operating on other levels than the chaste one for which Yorick himself argues. Ironically, this more suspicious reading of the passage is later supported at the level of representation itself, when the master of the hotel observes that the *fille de chambre* actually spent two hours in Yorick's hotel room. In a process which calls into question his reliability as a narrator, Yorick's defence of natural sexual drives, and of his conduct under them, is thus qualified by both the excited language in which he makes this defence, and by an alternative reconstruction of events that the narrative makes available to the reader, which sees Yorick spending the best part of two hours tumbling on his bed with a young girl, or tumbling a young girl on his bed.

As Janet Todd has suggested, then, more than merely a man of feeling, Yorick is a 'connoisseur of feeling' (with 'feeling' here having a broader reach than purely *moral* sensations).[30] Indeed, whereas innocent men of feeling such as Primrose and Harley are presented as being too naïve for the world, and thus too easily taken in by others, Yorick has more often been read as possessing the opposite fault, of being simply too *knowing* to be properly virtuous. Ironically, it is precisely his apparent *lack* of naivety that has caused many readers to suspect both Yorick's virtue, and the moral tendency of the text in which he appears. It is important, therefore, to emphasize that the narrator's complexities and failings are part of Sterne's *own* interest in the novel. In essence, we would argue, what Sterne explored in *A Sentimental Journey* was whether it was possible for a man to possess a heightened capacity for 'feeling', while also being fully aware of the 'ways of the world'. To return to the terms of Mackenzie's *The Man of Feeling*, this would be a man who was possessed of 'extreme sensibility', but who was not, like Harley, a mere 'child in the drama of the world'. Read in the light of the contemporary 'man of feeling' novel, then, we can say that, in *A Sentimental Journey*, Sterne sought to construct a character who might attempt to act in ways appropriate to moral innocence, even as he fully interacted in the world of (adult, and sexual) experience. Even this, though, is not the entire story with regard to Sterne's own 'man of feeling'. For, at the same time that it depicts this more knowing, indeed canny 'innocent' in the world, Sterne's narrative also stages an *internalization* of experience, which reveals the limitations to the self-comprehension of the modern, psychological subject. Like Tristram Shandy, and perhaps even more so, Yorick cannot always firmly establish the divisions between the real and the imagined, the outside world and internal sensations. By contrast to *The Man of Feeling*, in which the obstacles to virtue are located in the external social world, in *A Sentimental Journey* the moral uncertainties and impediments to sympathetic engagement thus lie largely within the man of feeling *himself*.

Mary Wollstonecraft, Mary, A Fiction

To complete the story of sentimental fiction, it is necessary to look forward to the end of the period covered by our study. In the final decades of the eighteenth century, one of the keenest critics of the culture of sensibility was Mary Wollstonecraft. In a number of writings,

Wollstonecraft sought to expose the foundation of 'sensibility' in a construction of femininity that cast women as delicate, instinctive, charming and mentally weak. Consider this excerpt from the introduction to what is now Wollstonecraft's best-known work, *A Vindication of the Rights of Woman* (1792):

> My own sex, I hope, will excuse me, if I treat them like rational creatures, instead of flattering their *fascinating graces*, and viewing them as if they were in a state of perpetual childhood, unable to stand alone. ... I wish to persuade women to endeavour to acquire strength, both of mind and body, and to convince them that the soft phrases, susceptibility of heart, delicacy of sentiment, and refinement of taste, are almost synonymous with epithets of weakness, and that those beings who are only the objects of pity and that kind of love, which has been termed its sister, will soon become objects of contempt.
>
> Dismissing then those pretty feminine phrases, which the men condescendingly use to soften our slavish dependence, and despising that weak elegancy of mind, exquisite sensibility, and sweet docility of manners, supposed to be the sexual characteristics of the weaker vessel, I wish to shew that elegance is inferior to virtue, that the first object of laudable ambition is to obtain a character as a human being, regardless of the distinction of sex; and that secondary views should be brought to this simple touchstone.[31]

Here, certainly, Wollstonecraft tackled the characterization of women as possessors of both exquisite sensibility *and* elegant refinement. As this excerpt also shows, while Wollstonecraft wished to question the influence of the contemporary construction of the sentimental woman, this was for entirely different reasons than John Brown had had in mind. What Wollstonecraft sought in the *Vindication* was to *denaturalize* the association of women with the virtues of sensibility; in effect, to undo the very project that Richardson and his followers had been involved in pursuing. Because it was associated with states of mental and bodily weakness, Wollstonecraft suggested, the ideal of female delicacy had caused women to become not only the possessors of pity, but also *objects* of pity in their own right. Insisting upon the primacy of reason and the consequent need for female education, Wollstonecraft thus envisioned a society in which women might possess not a separate realm of delicate, 'feminine' virtues, but the same abilities that had been allowed to, and appropriated by, eighteenth-century men.

In relation to our novelistic case studies in this chapter, Wollstonecraft's *Vindication* can be viewed as pushing further Scott and the Bluestockings' nascent attempt to reclaim for women the 'masculine' realm of reason. An awareness of Wollstonecraft's treatise on woman also renders especially intriguing her own first foray into the realm of fiction: *Mary, A Fiction* (1788). Providing not just a critique of sensibility but a kind of late flourishing of sentimental discourse itself, Wollstonecraft's novel investigates the value and the social consequences of sensibility in a manner that is far less clear-cut than the *Vindication* might lead us to expect. As it pushes the sentimental novel to its very limits, however, *Mary* also marks the moment at which sentimental discourse begins to collapse in upon itself. In the very process of producing her sentimental heroine – a *woman* of feeling to match Mackenzie's Harley – Wollstonecraft exposes yet further the practical *limitations* of sensibility, and of the assumptions regarding society, morality and gender that underpinned it. Through an intensification of sentimental concerns and fictional techniques, Wollstonecraft's short novel, which at times reads like a condensed abstract for a longer fictional work, thus reveals the pressure that had come to bear upon the discourse of sympathy by the end of the period with which we are dealing.

In the novel's early chapters, Wollstonecraft sets up a contrast between the leisured life of idle frivolity that occupies Mary's mother, Eliza, and the 'artless' world of both Mary herself, and the tale that narrates her.[32] Possessing only the 'few superficial accomplishments' required of women in polite society, Eliza divides her day between the sofa and the card table, whiling away her time with her two dogs, to which she lisps out 'the prettiest French expressions of ecstatic fondness' (5, 6). What Eliza precisely *lacks*, it would seem, is the capacity for any sort of moral engagement with the world in which she lives; a sense of the *duties* incumbent upon her privileged social position, and a degree of reflection upon her own mortality. Significantly, of all her valueless amusements, Eliza's reading of sentimental novels is singled out for particular mockery. Wollstonecraft's attitude towards such works is made clear when, having described Eliza's novels (which are full of 'delicate struggles' and 'uncommonly pretty turns of thought'), the narrator suggests that she could easily reproduce such writing in *Mary* itself:

> If my readers would excuse the sportiveness of fancy, and give me credit for genius, I would go on and tell them such tales as would force the sweet tears of sensibility to flow in copious showers down beautiful cheeks, to the discomposure of rouge, etc. etc. Nay,

I would make it so interesting, that the fair peruser should beg the hair-dresser to settle the curls himself, and not interrupt her. (6)

Mocking the presumed effect that such stereotypically 'sentimental' writing would have upon her readers, Wollstonecraft here touches base with a contemporary satiric discourse *against* the sentimental novel (to which we shall return in our conclusion) – though with the notable twist that, in this instance, the female reader of such lachrymose fare is being satirized by a *female* writer, rather than by a male one. Far from helping to inculcate the principles of religion and virtue, Wollstonecraft insinuated, the sentimental novel had now become part of the *problem* – simply another fashionable commodity, which neither demanded nor was treated with any more seriousness by its readers than the fixing of hair, playing at cards, or indulging of lap-dogs.

If the sentimental novel might thus appear to have lost its (moral) way, though, it was not simply the case that Wollstonecraft wished to jettison the 'sentimental project' in its entirety. Indeed, the *continuities* between Wollstonecraft's text and the concerns of sensibility are strongly evidenced throughout the narrative account of Mary's life, which occupies the remainder of the novel. Crucially, Wollstonecraft stresses the fact that, by contrast to her mother, Mary herself possesses not only 'thinking powers' (3), but also many of the more familiar attributes of the figure of feeling. Mary's self-education itself consists more of a course in imaginative fancy than a training in what would have been regarded as 'reason' during the period. As we soon learn, moreover, 'compassion' is the 'governing propensity' of Mary's heart. The young girl's exceptional capacity for feeling is attested as the narrator describes her response to her mother's neglect:

Her sensibility prompted her to search for an object to love; on earth it was not to be found: her mother had often disappointed her, and the apparent partiality she shewed to her brother gave her exquisite pain – produced a kind of habitual melancholy, led her into a fondness for reading tales of woe, and made her almost realize the fictitious distress. (8)

Capable of feeling 'exquisite pain' of her own, Mary is able to imagine herself in, or *into*, the distressing situations of others. For all that she shares with her mother this immersion in 'tales of woe', it is important to register the important *differences* between Mary and Eliza, who is presented as lacking the mental powers required to *think* herself into the situations of those she reads about. Mary's own capacity for compassion is cemented by the suicide of a girl who lives in her neighbourhood during her childhood, which so strongly impresses itself upon her imagination that 'every night of her life the bleeding corpse presented itself to her when she first began to slumber' (8). With its melancholy, indeed Gothic tenor, this formative experience can be contrasted to a sentimental moment from the second volume of *Tristram Shandy*, during which Tristram suggests that he owes 'one half of my philanthropy' to the 'accidental impression' that was made upon him by his Uncle Toby's literal unwillingness to hurt a fly, which had buzzed about him one dinner time.[33] With her account of the impression that the young girl's suicide has upon Mary, Wollstonecraft presented her own readers with the *tragic* version of Tristram Shandy's more whimsical education in moral feeling.

While she is capable of exercising rational control over her 'appetites and whims' (12), then, Mary nevertheless exhibits some of the more typical characteristics of the later eighteenth-century woman of feeling. In other ways too, *Mary* reproduces ideas and motifs that were common to the sentimental novels of the period: the entwining of 'feeling' with bodily illness and mental affliction; jibes against the dirt and moral bankruptcy of London; the inadequacy of words to any true expression of emotion; the *fragmentation* of sentimental narrative (as in Mary's journal entries); and the notion that whereas worldly happiness can only ever be imperfect, in heaven it will be possible to '*feel* in what happiness consists' (34). If the use of such conventions indicates that *Mary* shares many of the positive ideals of sensibility, however, Wollstonecraft also pushes further the novelistic probing of sympathy's local operation and practical utility that we saw at work in the 'man of feeling' novel. As the narrative continually shows, if Mary is able to feel intensely, she is also *vulnerable* to an intensity of feeling. Like Harley, Mary is ultimately unable to find a proper role in life, a suitable social location for her benevolence. More keenly than Mackenzie, though, Wollstonecraft also reveals the *self-regarding* nature of moral feeling, the potential for self-indulgent luxuriance contained in what Mary terms the 'luxury of doing good' (11). Consider, for example, the 'rhapsody' upon sensibility that Mary produces towards the end of the novel:

> Sensibility is the most exquisite feeling of which the human soul is susceptible: when it pervades us, we feel happy; and could it last unmixed, we might form some conjecture of the bliss of those paradisiacal days, when the obedient passions were under the dominion of reason, and the impulses of the heart did not need correction.

It is this quickness, this delicacy of feeling, which enables us to relish the sublime touches of the poet, and the painter ... Softened by tenderness; the soul is disposed to be virtuous. Is any sensual gratification to be compared to that of feeling the eyes moistened after having comforted the unfortunate?

Sensibility is indeed the foundation of all our happiness; but these raptures are unknown to the depraved sensualist, who is only moved by what strikes his gross senses; the delicate embellishments of nature escape his notice; as do the gentle and interesting affections. (43)

From this passage, we can easily discern the reason why writers such as Wollstonecraft continued to be drawn to the ideals of sensibility even in the latter decades of the century. Despite the reservations that had been expressed earlier in *Mary*, regarding the fashionability of sentimental writing, the discourse of sensibility still afforded a powerful language for describing the opposite ethical position to a life of selfish passions and unrefined excesses (the life of the 'depraved sensualist', in Mary's somewhat overblown characterization). What is also revealed by Mary's 'rhapsody', however, is the ethical difficulty that arises from the fact that sensibility is as much a pleasure to be enjoyed by the privileged figure of feeling, as it is a source of virtue, an impetus to social philanthropy. While sensibility might indeed direct one to comfort the 'unfortunate', it could also be experienced as desirable *in itself*, insofar as it is sensibility, as Mary describes it, that provides the greatest happiness that is possible upon earth, that enables the privileged to enjoy the productions of genius and taste, and that enables the sentimental elect to signify that they actually *possess* moral virtue. Within the novel, the unflattering implications of the sentimentalist's thirst for 'melancholy pleasure' (50) are further registered when Mary is faced with the ingratitude of one of the destitute figures whom she has attempted to help. As her dispirited reaction to this ingratitude suggests, for all that Mary's benevolence 'knows no bounds', and that the 'distress of others' carries her sympathetically 'out of herself' (11), she nevertheless needs to have the value of her sensibility *confirmed*, by those upon whom she exercises her benevolence.

What Mary refers to as the 'raptures' of sensibility, then, are evidently as much to do with her own happiness, and with reinforcing her sense of her own moral worth, as they are with improving the less advantageous conditions in which others are forced to live. Ultimately, even this pleasure (which, as we have seen, is intimately linked to her capacity for melancholy) cannot prevent Mary from ending the novel longing for the death that will put her beyond the realm of worldly misery. Rather than offering a straightforward critique of sensibility, however, this problematization of sensibility can be regarded as an *extension* of the methods of previous sentimental novelists, such as Goldsmith and Mackenzie. Although, from the very outset, *Mary* is positioned in opposition to the sentimental sub-genre of the novel, neither this early critique, nor the novel's broader exploration of the limitations of sensibility, constituted a wholesale rejection of eighteenth-century sentimentalism. What the reader observes in *Mary* is, rather, the *strain* under which the discourse of sympathy was functioning by this point in the period. Like Wollstonecraft's novel, which ends abruptly and inconclusively, sentimentalism apparently now had nowhere left to go. During the 1790s, in the aftermath of the French Revolution, this strain upon the discourse – a discourse of emotional excesses – would become finally insupportable.

7
Narrating the Nation: Leisure, Luxury and Politeness

By the second half of the eighteenth century, the novel had established itself as one of the most important media for examining contemporary social developments and cultural concerns. In this chapter, we move back from the cusp of Revolution to consider the visions of Britain that were offered in two novels published during the 1770s: Tobias Smollett's *Humphry Clinker* (1771) and Frances Burney's *Evelina* (1778). Working both the comic and the sentimental seams of the genre's development, these novels constituted perhaps the most successful attempts that had thus far been made to synthesize the panoramic social vision of Fielding with a Richardsonian attendance to the minutiae of personal feeling and individual situation. Following the lead of scholars such as John Brewer and Roy Porter, who have tracked the transformation of British culture between the English Restoration and the French Revolution, we focus here particularly upon the novels' portrayal of a leisure culture of pleasure gardens, assembly rooms, spa towns and sociable pastimes – all part of a new 'entertainment industry' that included the novel itself.[1] Through the observations of their central characters, Smollett and Burney's novels recreate in vivid detail the contemporary experience of this commercialized culture of pleasure and politeness. In the process, the novels also dramatize contemporary debates over the direction that the country was taking. While many people would certainly have concurred with William Blackstone's recent description of the English as a 'polite and commercial people', the nation's growing prosperity, its claims to politeness and, especially, the relationship *between* politeness and commerce, were also sources of considerable unease. In effect, the nation possessed a double vision of itself: a progressive perspective, which viewed it as refined and prosperous, and a more conservative perspective, which viewed its commercial success as being driven by private passions and avaricious self-interest. As cultural commentators were now asking, then: was Britain a polite or a luxurious nation?

During the 1770s, the state of the nation's manners and morals came under renewed scrutiny in the light of the public scandals and outlandish modes of dress and behaviour which seemed to typify the decade. A notable brouhaha with literary associations followed the posthumous publication, in 1774, of Philip Dormer Stanhope, the fourth Earl of Chesterfield's *Letters to his Son*. Designed initially to tutor his illegitimate son in the social art of refined self-presentation, upon their publication the *Letters* were widely interpreted as recommending courtly forms of polite conduct only as a means of self-serving and as a mask for immorality. Today, the best-known put-down of the *Letters* is Johnson's remark that, rather than true politeness, they taught 'the morals of a whore, and the manners of a dancing-master'. In her private journal, Frances Burney outlined similar reservations, writing that Chesterfield's epistles were 'written with a tendency to make his son a man wholly unprincipled; inculcating immorality; countenancing all *Gentlemanlike* vices; *advising* deceit; and *exhorting* to Inconstancy'.[2] As Diana Donald observes, the formal, courtly code of politeness promoted in the *Letters* was already something of an anachronism by the 1770s; the polite ideal now entailed more natural and sincere behaviour, manners modified by the new moral imperatives of sensibility.[3] Nevertheless, Chesterfield's apparent countenancing of sexual immorality and emphasis on the importance of outward show did not seem altogether out of tune with the times. Among other testaments to aristocratic ill-breeding, the 1770s witnessed the affectations and indiscretions of Georgiana, Duchess of Devonshire; the trial of the Duchess of Kingston (Elizabeth Chudleigh) for bigamy; and the excesses of male 'macaronis' (a new breed of socially disruptive, aristocratic man about town).[4] The decade also saw a trend towards extravagance in women's dress – most notably, a new vogue for elaborate headdress – which was soon being reflected in novels, plays and satiric prints. In Oliver Goldsmith's 'laughing comedy', *She Stoops to Conquer* (1773), for instance, Mrs Hardcastle, who has never been to London, models her hairstyle on fashion prints included in a magazine sent up from the capital.[5] In *Humphry Clinker*, even the servant, Win Jenkins, has her hair 'cut and pippered, and singed, and bolstered, and buckled, in the newest fashion', by a French *frisseur* (or 'freezer', as she misconstrues this foreign term).[6] As Evelina discovers in Burney's novel, before going out in the capital it was necessary to '*Londonize*' oneself, to alter one's appearance in line with prevailing metropolitan fashions.[7] To adopt such fashions was to stake one's claim to genteel sophistication – an act of particular importance to the *nouveau riche*, seeking to claim their place in polite society. As *Humphry Clinker* and *Evelina* both testify, however, neither the fashionable obsession with public display, nor the imitative behaviour of upstart *parvenus*, were truly compatible with contemporary ideals of polite conduct.

Of central importance to Smollett and Burney's engagement with these contemporary social developments was the epistolary style of their novels. During the 1760s, the novel in letters had become one of the most popular forms within the marketplace for fiction. Traditionally in literary criticism, the epistolary format is viewed as providing readers of novels with privileged access to characters' most private selves, an idea that is not discouraged by such comments as Pamela's assertion that, in writing her letters, she 'wrote' her 'heart'.[8] As *Humphry Clinker* and *Evelina* demonstrate, however, as well as for exhibiting a character's innermost feelings, the letter format is very well suited to capturing the *social* moment, as characters recreate their recent experiences for close and trusted correspondents. In Smollett and Burney's novels, as indeed in Richardson's own, the idea that letters offer *unmediated* access to a character's true feelings itself needs to be qualified by an awareness both of *why* they are writing, and of who they are writing to, and thus *for*. If we can partly agree with Gerald Newman's claim that Evelina represents 'the very personification of Sincerity', then the reader's sense of this heartfelt frankness needs to be tempered by Julia Epstein's reminder that even Evelina screens some of her feelings and enthusiasms from the main recipient of her letters: her guardian, the Reverend Mr Villars.[9] Another way of putting this is to say that, if these novels offer access to their characters' private thoughts and feelings, they also record written forms of social *conversation*. As Lord Chesterfield himself put it, letters should ideally be regarded as 'familiar conversations, between absent friends'.[10] Indeed, while reading the letters in these epistolary fictions can sometimes feel like peering into other people's personal diaries, they also offer a pleasure akin to that of social *gossip*. For William Hazlitt, writing in the following century, *Humphry Clinker* could be regarded as 'the most pleasant gossiping novel that was ever written'.[11] If the characters in these novels are *themselves* involved in a form of social gossip, then as readers we might well be regarded as eavesdropping on their conversations. It is to these sociable, epistolary conversations that we now turn.

Tobias Smollett, Humphry Clinker

In his final, and most sophisticated work of prose fiction, Smollett crafted what we might call a novel of 'domestic tourism'. In the form of letters sent by the members of a small family group, *The Expedition of Humphry Clinker* (1771) offers its readers a vicarious experience of a realistically delineated, country-wide journey. From their country seat in Monmouthshire, Matthew and Tabitha Bramble, accompanied by their nephew and niece Jery and Lydia Melford, and attended by their servant, Winifred Jenkins, travel to Bristol, Bath and London. Near Marlborough, they acquire another servant, the eponymous Humphry Clinker, who joins their entourage, and who later turns out to be Matthew Bramble's son. From London, they move northwards along the east coast of England, via Harrogate, Scarborough and York, and then across the border, passing through Edinburgh and the west of Scotland. They head homewards along the west coast of the country, via Dumfries, Carlisle, Derbyshire and the Peak District, failing finally to make it back to Wales due to a coach accident, which puts them under the protection of Bramble's old College friend, Charles Dennison, and provokes a series of coincidences that tie up the loose ends of Smollett's rambling plot. During the course of their travels, Bramble and his party interact with a varied array of characters, some of whom are fictionalized versions of real people. One of the earliest figures to be encountered, for instance, is James Quin, the most famous actor from the pre-Garrick generation; and Smollett himself also makes an appearance in his own novel, casting himself as a generous-minded, financially independent author. By stark contrast, a country doctor called Grieve turns out to be the eponymous hero of one of Smollett's earlier novels, *Ferdinand Count Fathom* (1753). Somewhat disturbingly, from the reader's viewpoint, purely fictional characters, and people who actually exist, are thus treated in the novel as though they all occupy the same plane of existence. In this manner, Smollett teases the boundary between the imagined world of *Humphry Clinker* and the real, extra-fictional world to which it refers, and which it often describes in sharply realized detail.

    In terms of both national identity and the novel genre, the central travelling party whose journey the reader follows during *Humphry Clinker* is carefully constructed by Smollett. To a certain degree, the period's sense of Welshness is displayed in Matthew Bramble's hot-headed, passionate, crusty, old-fashioned, and independently minded character. At the same time, the early letters of Bramble's nephew, the more ironic (and to some extent 'Anglicized') Jery, paint an increasingly complex picture of Matthew's character. As these letters gradually reveal, Bramble's bloodymindedness masks a deeply charitable impulse, a heartfelt concern for others. If he 'affects misanthropy', this is only in order to 'conceal the sensibility of a heart, which is tender, even to a degree of weakness' (28). Where Jery had initially been put off by Bramble's ostensibly 'unpleasant' manner (8), he is soon describing his uncle as a (Celtic) variation upon the man of feeling; as a delicate, sentimental being, somewhat akin to the hero of Mackenzie's *The Man of Feeling*, which was published in the same year as *Humphry Clinker*. As Jery goes on to record, Bramble possesses 'nerves of uncommon sensibility', and is 'as tender as a man without a skin' (65, 49). As his own letters to Dr Lewis powerfully attest, the sentimental Bramble is also a stringent satirist of English culture, who continually exposes the current corruption and degeneration of the nation in which he had himself formerly lived, before his retreat back to the rural simplicity of Wales. Binding together these contrasting facets of his personality – his sensibility and his spleen – is Bramble's ill-health, which not only enables him to be sensitive to people and interests other than his own, but which also causes him to be over-sensitive (or, over-sensit*ized*) to the world around him. At the centre of Smollett's novel, then, is a principal protagonist whose identifying 'humour' combines the characteristics of the satirist, the sentimentalist, and the valetudinarian, and who is thus both ideally suited to taking the temper of the times, and incapable of giving us an entirely impartial diagnosis of the nation's ills.

In his depiction of his central female characters, Smollett goes somewhat further in combining elements from the dominant strains of the novel's recent development. While Lydia, like her fellow travellers, is herself an observer of people and places, she also carries the burden of a Richardsonian storyline. In conducting a romantic liaison with the mysterious itinerant, Wilson, against the wishes of her family, Lydia stands somewhere *between* Richardson's heroines, being somewhat less subservient than Pamela, but not quite so subversive as Clarissa. Tabitha and Win, by contrast, are Fieldingesque in cast, and build upon the comic pairing of Lady Booby and Mrs Slipslop. Like Booby and Slipslop in *Joseph Andrews*, Tabitha and Win support much of the more farcical comedy of Smollett's novel. In Tabitha's case, this comedy derives mainly from her frantic efforts to avoid the status of an old maid, which lead the increasingly desperate Tabitha to set her cap at nearly every man that she lays her eyes on. In Win's case, a good deal of the humour arises from the erratic orthography (spelling errors) and malapropisms (ludicrous mis-uses of words) that characterize her epistolary correspondence. In Win's hands, for instance, such polysyllabic words and foreign phrases as 'metamorphosed' and '*valet de chambre*' are absurdly transformed into 'matthewmurphy'd' and 'wally de shamble' (337, 219). In his rendition of Win's mis-writings, Smollett develops Fielding's representation of Mrs Slipslop's trouble with 'hard Words', along with her more elementary mis-speakings, such as her mistaking of '*Ironing*' for 'Irony', and the revealing slip, 'I am not *Meat* for a Footman I hope' (our italics).[12] Four years after the publication of *Humphry Clinker*, this register of verbal slips would achieve its most famous representation in the form of Mrs Malaprop, in Richard Brinsley Sheridan's comic play, *The Rivals* (1775). Malaprop herself, we might note, is a relatively well-to-do lady, somewhat akin to Tabitha Bramble (whose own letters are by no means immune to absurd slips of the pen). In the novels of Fielding and Smollett, however, such vulgar errors are associated not simply with women but, more particularly, with *lower class* women, registering both a lack of formal education and, in the case of Slipslop in particular, an affectation of linguistic prowess that reflects broader, *social* aspirations.

For a Scotsman such as Smollett, such verbal blunders almost certainly possessed further resonance in terms of contemporary constructions of British national identity. In particular, many of Smollett's countrymen had become sensitive about their use of dialect words ('Scotticisms') and, more broadly, about what was perceived to be their mispronunciation of the English language – to the extent that the Irish-born elocutionist, Thomas Sheridan (father of the playwright), had given highly popular public lectures in Edinburgh during the early 1760s, that were geared towards helping Scotsmen to achieve the prescribed forms of 'polite' (that is to say, courtly, English) pronunciation. This sensitivity about *linguistic* differences between the English and the Scots formed one element within a broader concern that the political union of the two nations had not been entirely successful. Britain in its modern form had only been created in 1707, by an Act of Union that subsumed the Scottish Parliament into the English, and that was negotiated in an atmosphere of mutual suspicion, sometimes even hatred. 'Britain', we might say, was an imposed political identity, and one that took a long time to root itself in the imaginations of the people who lived in the geographical area that it encompassed. In one view, the Scots can be said to have prospered in the decades following the Act, especially after the massacring of the Jacobite armies at Culloden in 1746 neutralized the Highland threat and rendered London more hospitable to Scots.

As they began to penetrate the English political, trading, military and colonial establishment, however, the third quarter of the century also witnessed a nationalistic English backlash against the Scots, a reaction which intensified during the early 1760s, when the Earl of Bute became the first Scottish prime minister in Britain. This backlash against Scottish ascendancy is nicely captured by Linda Colley's account of some of its livelier expressions. As Colley observes:

> English insecurity in the face of this new Scottish leverage helps to explain the obsession in so much written and visual polemic at this time with Scottish sexual potency. The most extreme expression of this was the claim that Lord Bute was bedding George III's mother, the Princess Dowager. In one ribald print after another, the elegant and almost certainly entirely innocent Scottish minister was shown flaunting his long legs (of which he was intensely proud) before the swooning princess, or mounted provocatively on a broomstick, or with a set of rampant bagpipes placed as suggestively close to his body as the artist could conceivably devise. ... This was not an attack on immorality in high places. The accusation that one Scottish minister was penetrating the mother of the King of England was symbolic shorthand for the real anxiety: namely, that large numbers of Scots were penetrating England itself, compromising its identity, winning access to its riches and cutting out English men. As the princess was made to say in one splendidly filthy cartoon, her hand located firmly under Lord Bute's kilt: 'A man of great parts is sure greatly to rise.' And just how far were Scotsmen going to rise?[13]

As Colley's overview indicates, the immediate backdrop to the writing of *Humphry Clinker* was an unprecedented wave of Scotophobia in England. Already, in the 1760s, a Welsh traveller to Scotland, Thomas Pennant, had been struck by the Scots' resentment at the unflattering way in which they were being portrayed in England. In response, Pennant's *Tour in Scotland*, which was published in the same year as Smollett's novel, aimed (as he later recalled) to 'conciliate the affections of the two nations'.[14] While Smollett's novelistic representation of this somewhat un-united kingdom is far from straightforward, we would argue that, broadly speaking, Smollett wrote *Humphry Clinker* with a purpose in mind similar to that of Pennant. As Matthew Bramble observes in the novel's opening volume: 'it is a reproach upon me, as a British freeholder, to have lived so long without making an excursion to the other side of the Tweed' (66). As Smollett's novel seems centrally concerned to ask, then: what kind of nation-state *is* Britain? And what does it mean to *be* a 'Briton'?

As Bramble and his party move around the country, the most remarkable individuals that they encounter are themselves representatives of the country's Celtic margins. In the book's early stages, these eccentric characters might seem designed as much to reinforce contemporary prejudices as to 'conciliate' the different nationalities within Britain. Sir Ulic Mackilligut, for instance, is a novelistic adaptation of the blundering stage Irishman, whose native brogue is rendered phonetically, and who is first encountered in ludicrous attire, taking lessons in deportment from a dancing-master. Similarly, the first Scotsman to whom we are introduced is the fraudulent and hypocritical Micklewhimmen. The second of the novel's significant Scotsmen, Lieutenant Lismahago, presents more of a challenge to interpretation. Lismahago is a thing of shreds and patches, an absurd, unfashionable, harlequin Don Quixote, whose pride and argumentative vigour are at odds with his actual, impoverished circumstances. At the same time, Lismahago also represents the well-educated but conservative Scotsman, and is, like Bramble, a kind of counter-cultural figure, a freethinker in religious matters who opposes contemporary trends towards luxury and conspicuous consumption. During their conversations together, the outlandish Lismahago and the prickly Bramble frequently find themselves in disagreement. While they might differ in many of their opinions, however, their gradual recognition that they also have much in common – a more fundamental sense of shared values – offers something of a model of national *rapprochement*, an allegory for how Scots and (Anglo-) Cambrians might enter into amicable relations with one another through a mutual recognition that, in the final analysis, they were on the same side. Significantly, as the travellers move closer to Scotland, the extent of English Scotophobia itself becomes a topic of the epistolary conversation. As Jery observes, for instance: 'From Doncaster northwards, all the windows of all the inns are scrawled with doggrel rhimes, in abuse of the Scotch nation; and what surprized me very much, I did not perceive one line written in the way of recrimination' (197). If the English possessed a predilection for verbally abusing their neighbours, those south of the border could also be extremely uninformed about northern Britain. In the novel itself, this is perhaps best illustrated by Tabitha's belief that (as Jery puts it) 'we could not go to Scotland but by sea'. As Jery asserts in response to this lamentable apprehension of domestic geography: 'the South Britons in general are woefully ignorant in this particular. What, between want of curiosity, and traditional sarcasms, the effect of ancient animosity, the people at the other end of the island know as little of Scotland as of Japan' (213–14).

Smollett's novel, we would contend, is itself partly designed to rectify this ignorance, by *showing* Scotland to the south. By familiarizing southern readers with northern Britain, the novel sought to move the country's *internal*-national relations from a position of antagonistic alienation to one of understanding and mutual respect. This project is significantly advanced from the end of the novel's second volume, as the party passes into Scotland itself. Lismahago's Scottishness gains in status, for instance, when the travellers arrive in Edinburgh – a city that, despite its denizens' penchant for emptying their chamber pots on the heads of passers-by, is home to several men of genius, and the cradle of the Scottish Enlightenment. As the group go on to discover, in fact, Scotland was itself far from possessing a *single*, uniform national identity. Having moved on from Lowlands Edinburgh to the Scottish Highlands, the travellers are enchanted by the region's romantic, sublime, and picturesque scenery, and by the warmth of the locals' hospitality. At the high-point of this novelistic homage to Caledonia, the group experiences the area around Loch Lomond as a positive Arcadia. If this Arcadia is located suspiciously close to Smollett's own birthplace, it also possesses the important function of both anticipating and facilitating the party's climactic movement to the estate run by the Dennisons. Through a nuanced but in many respects appealing depiction of the Scottish nation, *Humphry Clinker* thus endeavoured to disarm contemporary Scotophobic prejudices, and to effect a reconciliation between the constituent nations of Britain that was grounded in an informed appreciation of Scotland's own, natural and cultural diversity.

If Scotland and the Scots occupy an unusually prominent place in Smollett's novel, what kind of nation was England itself? One of the particular pleasures of reading *Humphry Clinker* is the opportunity that it provides for encountering contrasting perspectives upon English society. In particular, as Bramble and his party make their way around the country, a broad split emerges in the characters' evaluations of key contemporary sites of leisure and entertainment, such as the spas, assembly rooms and pleasure gardens of Bristol, Bath, London, York, and Harrogate. To the young and inexperienced Lydia Melford, for instance, the city of Bath constitutes 'an earthly paradise' – 'a new world', where 'All is gaycty, good-humour, and diversion' (39) – and London similarly affords a sociable setting that leaves her reeling in 'a maze of admiration' (91). For Lydia, the contemporary world of fashionable entertainment is an arena of extraordinary delights, in which the eyes, the ears and the palate are able to feast upon the finest and most spectacular images, music, and sumptuous repasts. To a great extent, though, Lydia's wide-eyed amazement at the pleasures available to her at the English cultural hotspots is out of tune with the general tenor of Smollett's text. For, as critics have often noted, one of the tonal keynotes of *Humphry Clinker* involves an attack upon the invidious progress of luxury and conspicuous consumption. If luxury represents a 'taste for superfluous things', as one observer of eighteenth-century England put it, then conspicuous consumption might be defined more narrowly, as the social display *of* those things.[15] The critique of contemporary luxury formed an important conservative strand in eighteenth-century social thought, which had at its root the belief that the more the country prospered commercially, the greater the risk of social and moral corruption. As articulated in the novel by Lieutenant Lismahago, this model of national development envisioned a movement from virtuous simplicity to luxurious degeneration, as the leisured individuals of an increasingly wealthy society attempted to civilize themselves by cultivating the social arts and, in the process, over-indulged themselves in their newfound prosperity. Significantly, in *Humphry Clinker* the problem of modern luxury is associated with the state of *English* society specifically. In this account, moreover, it is the very milieu of social pleasure that so appeals to Lydia Melford which affords the most visible symptoms of a contemporary national malaise.

Early in *Humphry Clinker*, this anti-luxury discourse is powerfully voiced by Matthew Bramble. In Bramble's own eyes, Bath represents not a paradisiacal 'new world', but a more hellish vision of anarchic disorder. A complaint about the lack of planning that seems to have gone into the physical construction of the city, for instance, leads to the expression of broader anxieties regarding the apparent threat to the organization of society itself:

> All these absurdities arise from the general tide of luxury, which hath overspread the nation, and swept away all, even the very dregs of the people. Every upstart of fortune, harnessed in the trappings of the mode, presents himself at Bath, as in the very focus of observation ... Knowing no other criterion of greatness, but the ostentation of wealth, they discharge their affluence without taste or conduct, through every channel of the most absurd extravagance; and all of them hurry to Bath, because here, without any further qualification, they can mingle with the princes and nobles of the land. ... Such is the composition of what is called the fashionable

company at Bath; where a very inconsiderable proportion of genteel people are lost in a mob of impudent plebeians, who have neither understanding nor judgment, nor the least idea of propriety and decorum; and seem to enjoy nothing so much as an opportunity of insulting their betters. (36–7)

The central problem identified here by Bramble is the upward mobility, and public presence, of people who, in his view, are not truly genteel – who lack the secure sense of social rank that comes with being born into privilege. At the heart of this problem is the new commercial wealth of the nation, which might enable even the very 'dregs' of society, as the patrician Bramble puts it, to participate in amusements that had previously been restricted to those of high birth. As his reference to the 'ostentation of wealth' suggests, Bramble is particularly taxed by the problem of conspicuous consumption, the social display of new money, which Bramble himself regards as vulgar, and as inimical to any true exercise of gentility. During the party's time at Bath, an alternative viewpoint is offered by Bramble's nephew, Jery. In a discussion with Bramble and the actor, Quin, Jery argues that 'those plebeians who discovered such eagerness to imitate the dress and equipage of their superiors, would likewise, in time, adopt their maxims and their manners, be polished by their conversation, and refined by their example' (51). From this more optimistic, progressive perspective, the desire of the lower and middle ranks of society to emulate their superiors could be regarded as a valuable impulse towards a broader, social improvement. Unfortunately for Jery, the social experiment that the trio conduct in Bath, by observing the behaviour of the company at one of the city's Assembly Rooms, reveals not an arena of refined manners, of sophistication and social regard for others, but rather a realm of rude self-serving, in which there is 'nothing but justling, scrambling, pulling, snatching, struggling, scolding, and screaming' (52). Significantly, as the party later learn, the main disputants in this scene of social disorder come not from 'the purlieus of Puddle-dock' – an area of London associated with crime and prostitution – but from 'the courtly neighbourhood of St. James's palace' (53). In this essentially conservative account of the cultural enfranchisement of the lower and middling sorts, then, the confusion of classes highlighted by Bramble threatens to dilute – and perhaps even erase – the gentility of those who are indeed of high rank, but who are now becoming, as he puts it, 'lost in a mob of impudent plebeians'.

As David Weed usefully observes, Bramble's anxiety regarding the corrosive effects of commerce and the increasing intermingling between classes upon the 'body politic' – upon what we might call the health of the nation – is literalized in the novel in grotesque images of physical decay and of the *literal* consumption of bodies.[16] During his time at Bath, for instance, Bramble discovers that the supposedly medicinal water drunk at the Pump-room is not completely distinct from the water in which the ill and diseased bathe; and also that the water that he drinks at Abbey-green has been filtered through the ground of a cemetery, upon which the private bath there was built. As Bramble reflects with considerable disgust, therefore: 'as we drink the decoction of living bodies at the Pump-room, we swallow the strainings of rotten bones and carcasses at the private bath' (46). In London, similarly, Bramble discovers that even the capital's much-praised water is

> impregnated with all the filth of London and Westminster – Human excrement is the least offensive part of the concrete, which is composed of all the drugs, minerals, and poisons, used in mechanics and manufacture, enriched with the putrefying carcases of beasts and men; and mixed with the scourings of all the wash-tubs, kennels, and common sewers, within the bills of mortality. (120)

In these somewhat splenetic accounts, we observe not only an unmasking of the polite pretensions of fashionable locations, such as the bathing spaces of Bath, but also some of the less positive consequences of contemporary urban expansion. As Bramble suggests, if London was often promoted as a refined arena of leisure, pleasure, and politeness, it was also an 'overgrown monster', and for that reason also a national 'centre of infection' (87, 118). Given his personal sensitivities, Bramble finds himself struggling to cope with the mass of human material – both the sheer number of bodies, and the inevitable increase in waste matter – that resulted from this commercially driven urban growth. In his critique of the unhygienic, ramshackle organization of the key centres of English civil society, Bramble thus exposes the filthy underside to what the historian Peter Borsay has termed the 'urban renaissance' that took place in England during the eighteenth century.[17]

In the large urban environments that the company visit during their national tour, then, Bramble finds himself confronted with the pressures that were being placed upon both the hierarchical status quo, and the state of the nation's health. The health that appeared to be at risk here was not only physical, though, but also moral. As Bramble comes to realize, the national virtues upon which England prided itself – such as what Squire Burdock refers to as the '*old English hospitality*' (164) – were not necessarily possessed by contemporary Englishmen themselves (within the novel it is rather the *Scots* who display this national characteristic of hospitality). At the same time, Bramble himself begins to long for a mode of living that is the very opposite to what he has encountered in London – for what, in contrast to the 'adulterate enjoyments' of the capital, he terms 'the genuine pleasures of a country retreat' (118). This is the further purpose of the party's journey northwards. For it is in the final volume of the novel that Smollett produces a vision of an alternative social space, away from the bustle and disorder of urban conglomerations, which might offer a model for restoring the integrity of the English nation. This space is the humble estate managed by the Dennisons. Smollett's account of the Dennisons' unostentatious life of 'rural felicity' (320) bears significant affinities to the life of Mr Wilson and his wife, which Fielding had eulogized in the interpolated story of Wilson's life, in book 3 of *Joseph Andrews*. Like Mr Wilson, Charles Dennison has retreated from the busy world maligned by Matthew Bramble, in order to cultivate his own estate as an independent, landed gentleman. The *meaning* of the independence that Dennison achieves on his estate – and the opposition that it implied to the world of commerce – is usefully summarized by Susan Jacobsen:

> For Smollett, the logic was obvious: commerce depended on individual self-interest and social and economic competition without regard to either one's neighbour or to the nation's well-being. Hence, commerce posed both an individual and a national threat. The solution, Smollett maintained, was for the landed gentry to determine political policy; unlike either the court aristocracy or the men of commerce, country gentlemen like Bramble were entirely independent, had no self-interested motives, and could not be swayed by bribery or influence.

As Jacobsen's analysis suggests, a figure such as Charles Dennison could be viewed as being free from corruption due to the security of his estate, which is susceptible neither to the ebbs and flows of commerce, nor to the pressures of courtly or political interest. As Jacobsen also goes on to argue, though, this apparently laudable vision of gentrified freedom from corruption does not necessarily lead us to an optimistic reading of the novel. Rather, as Jacobsen herself puts it: 'Despite its *de rigueur* happy marriages, the novel's ending is ultimately pessimistic and nostalgic. The gentry cannot stop "the tide of luxury"; they can only remove themselves from it.'[18] Jacobsen's interpretation tallies nicely with Michael McKeon's account of 'conservative ideology', which we referred to in Chapter 1. Read in this light, what we have in the final volume of *Humphry Clinker* is Smollett looking back longingly to the seventeenth-century culture of landed gentlemen, but also discovering that, in the wake of the country's recent commercial progress, it is rather more difficult to conceive how such gentlemen might now exert the significant cultural influence that Smollett wishes to attach to them. To put it another way, we can regard *Humphry Clinker* as offering a broader, more socially engaged investigation of the problematic that Mackenzie was tackling in *The Man of Feeling*: namely, what role could the truly virtuous man play in contemporary British society? As this line of interpretation suggests, then: if Smollett's novel achieves some degree of success in envisioning a process of *national* reconciliation, between the English and their Celtic neighbours, it nevertheless fails finally to conceptualize a *cultural* space that might provide a buffer against the contemporary progress of commerce and of its ethically corrosive consequence, luxury.

This is, of course, to assume that Jacobsen's understanding of Smollett's ideological project in the novel – and of the ultimate failure of that project – is correct in the first place. Finally, therefore, it is worth pausing to assess the traditional critical emphasis upon Smollett's critique of luxury in *Humphry Clinker*. An exploratory attempt to rethink this reading comes from the hand of Aileen Douglas, in her book on *Smollett and the Body* (1995). As Douglas suggests:

> Bramble's implication in the processes of luxury – the nature of his illness, his consumption of texts, and the generous gifts to his womenfolk – works to dissolve the gender differences on which critiques of luxury (including Bramble's own) depend. Traditionally, luxury was seen as driven by women ... such a view is supported by important incidents in *Humphry Clinker*, but the novel does not leave the typology of luxury intact.[19]

What Douglas points to here as the gendered implications of the attack on luxury can be seen in the contrast between Mrs Dennison – who occupies a similar role to Mrs Wilson, in *Joseph Andrews* – and Mrs Baynard – whose excessive investment in conspicuous wealth ruins the Baynard estate. While this attack on English luxury is certainly made in the text, though, *Humphry Clinker* is not – or, not merely – a treatise concerning luxury. Rather, even as it offers an extended meditation upon the pernicious tendency of an excessive thirst for commercial wealth and higher social status, Smollett's novel also displays the genre's characteristic *dialogism* – as, during his conversations with Lismahago, Bramble himself *contests* the lieutenant's overview of the progress of luxury. To Aileen Douglas' assessment of factors that qualify the anti-luxury theme in the novel, we might also add the nature of Bramble's 'humour', which we noted earlier; the fact that, as the character is himself aware, what Bramble presents in his letters is a partly splenetic and occasionally misanthropic view of English society. This jaundiced perspective, it might be argued, should be taken no more at face value – as an accurate, objective account of the real social world – than should the similar anti-luxury diatribe that is launched by 'The Misanthropist', in chapter 21 of Mackenzie's *The Man of Feeling*. Just as Mackenzie's novel contains a narrative framework of material and editorial interventions that qualifies the misanthropist's worldview, so *Humphry Clinker*, the literary *locus classicus* of anti-luxury discourse, itself allows for a reading that would downplay its ostensible investment in a rigidly conservative, social and cultural critique.

Frances Burney, Evelina

Notwithstanding the qualifications that the novel makes to his attack upon the luxury of the times, *Humphry Clinker* remains dominated by the male, patrician voice of Matthew Bramble. By stark contrast, Frances Burney's literary debut, *Evelina; or, The History of a Young Lady's Entrance into the World* (1778), offers the reader a snapshot of 1770s Britain from the perspective of a 17-year-old girl, as she experiences the world of urban London for the very first time.[20] While it is far less wide-ranging, geographically speaking, than Smollett's novel, *Evelina* offers an alternative exploration of many of the same issues that we have been examining in relation to *Humphry Clinker*, and is particularly notable for the lively assurance with which it brings to life the public leisure culture of the capital. Importantly, it is Evelina herself who, through her letters to her guardian, the Reverend Mr Villars, and her friend, Maria Mirvan, provides the dominant voice in the novel. Despite his reclusiveness and his tendency towards moralizing, Villars is a model of virtuous guardianship, a clear contrast to vicious sexual schemers such as Mr Hintman, Louisa Mancel's guardian in Scott's *Millenium Hall*. Significantly, though, Evelina is not accompanied by Villars either to London or to Bristol (where most of the action of the novel's third and final volume takes place). As a consequence, Evelina gains space to develop her own feelings, ideas, and opinions – an opportunity that is largely denied to Maria by her father, Captain Mirvan, who on one occasion publicly rebukes his daughter for presuming 'to have a taste of your own before my face' (121). In public, Evelina herself is usually forced to maintain a decorous feminine reserve, which reveals little of what is going on under the surface. In her private (and frequently journal-like) letters, by contrast, Evelina's maturing personality is vividly conveyed, as she gradually develops a deeper understanding of the world of manners and misdemeanours into which the novel casts her.

The significance of the centrality that the novel accords to Evelina's own voice is highlighted by comparison with the sceptical framing of the opinions of Lydia Melford, in *Humphry Clinker*. In Smollett's novel, Lydia is first introduced to us through the unflattering evaluations of her brother, Jery, who asserts that she is 'quite ignorant of the world', and her uncle, Matthew Bramble, who observes that she has 'a languishing eye, and reads romances'. The novel's subversion of Lydia's youthful female voice is perhaps most clearly seen in relation to her enthusiasm for some of the key sites of the contemporary leisure culture. To Lydia, for instance, Ranelagh Gardens – the most exclusive of London's pleasure gardens – appears 'like the inchanted palace of a genie'. Attending a musical performance in the Gardens by the Italian castrato, Tenducci, Lydia relates that his voice 'warbled so divinely, that, while I listened, I really thought myself in paradise'. As we have seen, Lydia's elation at Ranelagh reflects her more general disposition towards London, in which she finds herself lost in a 'maze of admiration'. However, Lydia's enjoyment of the capital's pleasures is qualified in the novel both by her later, more cautious assessment of the centres of leisure through which the travelling party has passed, and by the dominance of Matthew Bramble's alternative perspective upon these 'genteel' spaces and social pursuits. Ultimately, Lydia's enthusiasm for the pleasures of London is positioned as the response of an immature girl making her first entrance into the world; the effect of a fancy which is easily taken in by, if not overpowered by, all that glisters in fashionable society.[21]

In Burney's novel, Evelina's introduction to London society is itself partly designed to prevent her from developing romanticized notions of 'the world'. As Maria's grandmother, Lady Howard, explains: 'When young people are too rigidly sequestered from it, their lively and romantic imaginations paint it to them as a paradise of which they have been beguiled; but when they are shewn it properly, and in due time, they see it such as it really is, equally shared by pain and pleasure, hope and disappointment' (18). Accordingly, Evelina's own initial account of London's pleasures is more sober and mixed than Lydia Melford's. In her first letter from London, Evelina expresses disappointment with the capital's houses and streets, with The Mall in St James' Park, and with 'the *Palace*' (i.e. Buckingham House). At other moments, though, Evelina also expresses Lydia-like entrancement at some of the key locations for the experience of refined pleasure. Her account of Ranelagh, in particular, seems almost to respond to Lydia's. To Evelina herself, Ranelagh is 'a charming place, and the brilliancy of the lights, on my first entrance, made me almost think I was in some enchanted castle, or fairy palace, for all looked like magic to me' (41). A further verbal echo of Lydia's remarks on Ranelagh occurs as Evelina describes an evening spent at the opera: 'I could have thought myself in paradise, but for the continual talking of the company around me' (42). Here, certainly, Evelina's enjoyment of the paradisiacal scene is a *little* more qualified than Lydia's had been. More significant, however, is the fact that Burney's novel contains no equivalent of Matthew Bramble, who might steamroller over Evelina's account of her perceptions and pleasures. As a consequence, and for all its heroine's own reservations, *Evelina* paints a more favourable picture of the fashionable leisure culture than had Smollett. In Burney's novel, 'polite' society is allowed to retain more of its polite lustre.

Evelina's perspective, then, possesses a level of authority in Burney's novel far beyond that allowed to Lydia in *Humphry Clinker*. If Burney's novel accords refined locations like Ranelagh more in the way of genuine allure, though, the capital's genteel entertainments also throw into stark relief numerous deviations from prescribed modes of polite conduct. Like the inset narratives in *Millenium Hall*, *Evelina* delineates many of the dangers that fashionable social gatherings might pose to a 'young, artless, and inexperienced' woman, particularly one who is unmarried and who, though possibly of only a moderate fortune, is nonetheless possessed of 'conspicuous beauty' (8). Such occasions, we should recall, were designed not only to encourage refined sociability, but also to facilitate encounters with suitable prospective partners, within the eighteenth-century marriage market. As Amanda Vickery notes, central to the idea of the 'genteel' lady was the ability to be 'self-possessed in social encounters': to exhibit ease, self-control, and seeming self-sufficiency.[22] Judged by this standard, Evelina's first performances in the fashionable whirl are not entirely successful, marked as they are by interpersonal uncertainty and visible embarrassment. Her first

London ball, for instance, quickly exposes Evelina's 'confusion' about how she should be acting in polite company (34). In the reflective mode of her letters, Evelina already discerns that it is principally in the outward forms of social behaviour that she differs from the other participants at this gathering: 'These people in high life have too much presence of mind, I believe, to *seem* disconcerted, or out of humour, however they may feel' (35). Such is politeness' split between the public (social) and private (inner) selves – a split which leads to a high dividend being placed upon the *appearance* of self-composure. At this early point in her experience of 'the world', Evelina is not sufficiently possessed of this social 'presence of mind', and is vulnerable even to an accusation of 'ill manners' from a snuff-taking fop (36). During a subsequent evening spent at a ridotto (a private social gathering involving dancing and music), the heroine is brought into further difficulties as she endeavours to shake off the attentions of Sir Clement Willoughby – an endeavour which ends in tears, before she is rescued by the 'politeness' of Lord Orville, who removes Willoughby from her presence (52). As the distressed debutante is forced to confess after these two fraught occasions, then: 'I am too inexperienced and ignorant to conduct myself with propriety in this town, where every thing is new to me, and many things are unaccountable and perplexing' (53).

As these early social outings reveal, polite society is populated by various kinds of gentleman, but very few who behave towards women in a manner truly polite. Foremost among the novel's males is Lord Orville. In Evelina's eyes, Orville's 'manners are so elegant, so gentle, so unassuming, that they at once engage esteem, and diffuse complacence'. Notably, Orville is 'most assiduously attentive to please and to serve all who are in his company' – 'the art of pleasing in company' being a long-standing definition of social politeness (80). Orville's willingness to serve others, we might note, is a quality that is shared by Evelina herself; who, as Lady Howard observes, possesses a kind of innate politeness, 'a natural desire of obliging, joined to a deportment infinitely engaging' (22). To a certain degree, Orville can be regarded as a feminized man, whose traditional repertoire of aristocratic virtues is softened by the period's new sense of a desirable, masculine 'delicacy'. If he is partly feminized, though, Orville nevertheless avoids the whimsicality of Yorick, the weakness of Harley and the spleen of Bramble. Rather, in Orville we are offered a model of the new, polite gentleman, an exemplar of 'true politeness' (329) who doesn't play cards and who endeavours to act according to reason, rather than simply following the fashions of the moment. As such, Orville provides the standard by which all of the other men in this fashionable social sphere are to be judged.

Unfortunately for Evelina, as depicted in Burney's novel the London social scene is dominated by fops, libertines and rakes in gentlemen's clothing. Within this world, male harassment is often masked as 'gallantry', an otherwise acceptable form of polite courtship, but one which high-born yet morally disreputable men seek to exploit to their own (sexual) ends. Instead of putting the heroine at her ease, one of the principal aims of the men within this milieu seems to be precisely to discompose ladies like Evelina. As this might suggest, as much as her own social inexperience, it is the impertinence and manipulation of such men that causes Evelina's embarrassments and faux pas, drawing her unwillingly into 'adventures' of the kind that Arabella had actively sought out in *The Female Quixote*. A minor irritant to Evelina is the fop, Lovel, who can be regarded as a generic descendant of Tinsel, the superficial wit from Lennox's novel. Affecting worldliness through a smattering of French phrases, Lovel is always keen (in a popular contemporary tag) to *see and be seen*. At the theatre, for instance, Lovel watches the audience, rather than the actors; although, as his subsequent comments reveal, his ignorance of the play is at least partly affected, designed to give him an air of gentlemanly nonchalance. For an early slight, when she had refused to dance with, and indeed laughed at him, Lovel becomes mischievous, if not malicious, in his behaviour towards Evelina (as when he tells Orville's sister, Lady Louisa Larpent, that Evelina is a '*toad-eater*' (327)). More domineering than this social pest is the libertine Lord Merton, who on various occasions both speaks licentiously to Evelina, and stares at her. The latter is a form of ill manners that, earlier in the decade, had led to the notorious 'Vauxhall Affray' – an episode that was catalyzed by a group of macaronis attempting to 'stare' a young lady 'out of countenance' in Vauxhall Gardens.[23] Merton is, in fact, on the brink of marriage to Orville's sister, Louisa, a woman who takes no interest in Evelina, but who has an inflated sense of herself as a creature of refined feeling ('I am *nerve* all over!', as she announces at one point (317)). Despite this prior attachment, Merton continues to be forward with Evelina in Bristol, exhibiting a 'freedom of gallantry' that greatly discomposes her (347). Even more problematic for Evelina is the elegant but wily Sir Willoughby, an ingratiating figure who wheedles his way into others' company, and who is adept at manipulating Evelina into situations in which they will be alone together, so that he can declare his passion for her, throw himself at her feet, or make great play of soliciting her forgiveness for previous impositions of the same kind. As Barbara Zonitch nicely observes, the form of 'protection' that Willoughby intermittently offers Evelina is not very different from the 'mode of abuse' that she suffers at the hands of other men in the novel.[24] Willoughby's behaviour epitomizes the kind of superficially polished but privately unprincipled conduct that appeared to have been sanctioned in Lord Chesterfield's *Letters*. Rather than endeavouring to act like a true gentleman, Willoughby is actually playing a *game* of politeness, paying lip-service to 'honour' in order to further his sexual ambitions. For all his talk of love and adoration, Willoughby has no intention of actually *marrying* Evelina. As he confesses in a heated exchange with Orville, even if he were to marry, it would not be to a girl of such 'obscure birth', whose 'only dowry is her beauty' (385). Rather, Willoughby's efforts are aimed at procuring Evelina for his mistress. In his unbecoming conduct, Willoughby thus bears out the Reverend Villars' early observation to Lady Howard, that Evelina has 'too little wealth to be sought with propriety by men of the fashionable world' (19).

Judged by the standards of true politeness, then, the conduct that Evelina experiences at the hands of most of the men in fashionable society can be regarded as entirely improper. If Evelina suffers partly on account of her uncertain origins, however, her 'obscure birth' itself renders her a troubling presence in high society – as is indicated when Lovel experiences difficulty in finding out 'who' Evelina is (39). In the language of Fielding's Lady Booby, to the social elite it is unclear whether Evelina is a person one knows, or a person one does not know. For much of the novel, Evelina's high-born acquaintances in London know her only as Miss Anville (a mocked-up surname that is a near-anagram of her first name). As Evelina is herself aware, until her tearful reconciliation with her father it is unclear just what name she *can* claim as her own. It is this uncertainty over the heroine's origins and status that enables Burney to investigate at length not just upper tip-top society but, also, middle-order aspirations to become part of this exalted social stratum. Here, we move from the impolite manners of the nominally 'genteel' to an emulative imitation of elite behaviour. During her first trip to London, Evelina's experience of shopping in the capital produces a wry account of the activities of its tradesmen. Rather than at the split between public and private selves, the novel's satiric gaze here is directed at these individuals' overbearing and exaggerated attendance to 'ceremony'. Just as the male mercers (dealers in fine fabrics) all take 'care, by bowing and smirking, to be noticed', so the milliners (vendors of accessories to female clothing) are mainly 'finical' and 'affected' men, who appear to know more about women's dress than women themselves do (29–30). The tradesman's proper attendance to public propriety, it seems, has now degenerated into absurdly effeminized male behaviour. In Evelina's more personal contact with the trading classes, by contrast, such mimicking of the behaviour of the upper orders will highlight rather the *vulgarity*, than the effeminacy, of those doing the mimicking.

At the heart of Evelina's experience of the middling orders are the Branghtons, who are connected to the heroine through her grand-mother, Madame Duval. By contrast to *Humphry Clinker*, in which such social *parvenus* are often treated as an unindividuated mob, *Evelina* fleshes out in detail the lives of this aspirational trading family. As Evelina discovers only too keenly, the Branghtons are largely strangers to good manners. Upon first being introduced to the family, Evelina is mortified to find her grandmother filling Mr Branghton in on 'all the most secret and cruel particulars' of her situation (77). The vulgar materialism of the family's mindset is also indicated, in the novel's first volume, by their suggestion that Madame Duval should attempt to claim Evelina's inheritance from her father (Evelina being, to her grandmother, little more than a meal-ticket). During her second trip to London, in volume 2, Evelina is located in Holborn and, when visiting the Branghtons, at Snow-Hill: two insalubrious areas of the city, with associations of business and trade. Among other occasions, the family's bad manners and lack of moral centre are revealed as they enjoy both the relation of a violent prank that Captain Mirvan and Sir Willoughby have played upon Madame Duval, *and* Willoughby's discomfort as he attempts to deny his involvement in the episode. To Evelina, the 'elegant politeness', 'flattering attention', and 'high-bred delicacy' of Lord Orville now begin to feel to like a distant, 'romantic illusion' (192). In their place, she suffers instead the more vulgar 'gallantry' of Mr Smith, the Branghtons' lodger (199); the lovelorn attentions of Monsieur Du Bois, her grandmother's French companion; and the prospect of being married off to the boorish Young (Tom) Branghton. She is also forced to endure the family's presumptuous behaviour towards Lord Orville, when they use Evelina's name in order to commandeer his coach; along with some of the less securely refined locations of leisured amusement, such as the pleasure gardens at Marylebone, where she is lost in a crowd of 'bold and unfeeling' men, and waylaid by a couple of prostitutes (260). During her second stay in London, then, Evelina is even more put upon than before, being exposed to rougher company than she is accustomed to, and forced to bear both the excessive familiarities of the

Branghton circle, and the mortification of being seen *with* them, by members of the more fashionable company that she had mixed with during her first visit to the capital.

In the unremittingly vulgar picture that it paints of the Branghtons, their environs and their acquaintances, Burney's novel can be aligned with Diana Donald's argument regarding the graphic satire produced during this decade, that 'social aspiration and the "genteel mania" ' were 'the key themes of 1770s caricatures to a far greater extent than satire on the aristocracy itself'.[25] In Evelina's own, somewhat self-justifying words, it is not their station in life *per se*, but their '*pretensions*' to greater refinement than they actually possess, that is the source of her problem with the Branghtons (195). The arts of politeness, she intimates, can only be convincingly carried off by the truly high-born. Confronted by the low-bred gallantry of Mr Smith, Evelina even looks back favourably on the 'compliments' and 'fine speeches' of Sir Willoughby, whose language, if it is 'too flowery', is nevertheless 'always that of a gentleman' (199). To a large extent, *Evelina* shares its heroine's patronizing take on the cultural ambitions of the middle classes. The novel's comedy of class condescension is perhaps nowhere better seen than in the exposure of Mr Smith's lack of polite taste, as he attempts – badly – to interpret a painting on display in the Picture Rooms at Vauxhall Gardens (226–7). As this trip to Vauxhall also reveals, so strong is Evelina's own prejudice against the unrefined upstarts with whom she is now associated, that she is ashamed to be seen with them even by Willoughby, notwithstanding his continuing harassment of her. Significantly, though, Evelina's second stint in the capital also serves to distinguish further the opportunistic Willoughby from the courteous Lord Orville. Whereas the only *strategically* 'polite' Willoughby exploits the change in Evelina's circumstances to treat her with even less respect than he had previously, Orville's conduct remains laudably constant, despite this apparent plunge down the social scale.

While Evelina's time with the Branghtons exposes the vulgar manners of the middling orders, Burney's novel also incorporates a satiric discourse about alien mannerisms adopted from abroad – more specifically, from France. By this time, satire against the overly Frenchified Briton, which fed into the genre's increasing nationalism, had become something of a staple in the eighteenth-century novel. In *Joseph Andrews*, for instance, Fielding had contrasted the 'pretty' (but also muscular and manly) Joseph to the effete gentleman, Beau Didapper, who is both impertinent and immoral in his conduct towards Fanny Goodwill, and excessively concerned about his appearance. At the conclusion of the interpolated 'History of Leonora', we are also informed that the mercenary and self-preening Bellarmine finally 'returned to *Paris*, to the great delight of the *French*, and the honour of the *English* Nation'.[26] The depiction of both of these characters is informed by anti-Gallic sentiments that would become increasingly pervasive in the decades that followed the publication of *Joseph Andrews*. Increasingly, both the sense of English/British national identity, and the idea of a proper British *masculinity*, would be constructed in opposition to the perceived effeminacy of the French; and, more specifically, to the Frenchification of male aristocrats, young English travellers who often appeared to return from the continent transformed into vain, fashionable beaus.[27] In *Humphry Clinker*, one of Clinker's own functions – carried through in his rivalry with the Frenchified fop, Dutton, for the attentions of Win – is to reinforce the sense that British identity is created out of contrast with and enmity towards all things French. Employing a food-based contrast typical of such satire, Jery Melford posits that while Clinker is like a solid English pudding, Dutton resembles a frothy, insubstantial 'syllabub'.[28] This comedy of national stereotypes is continued in *Evelina*. A lively example of nationally inflected anti-fop satire occurs towards the end of Burney's novel, as the Gallophobic Captain Mirvan tells Lovel that he is about to see someone who looks like his twin brother, only to present him with a monkey, fully dressed in fashionable clothes, whom he calls 'Monsieur *Grinagain*' (443–4). If this satire upon Lovel as a Frenchified fop fitted easily into the novel genre's nationalistic discourse, however, Burney also infused her own play of national comedy with a gendered component that complicates our interpretation of its role in her novel. For, over the course of *Evelina*, Captain Mirvan's aggressive Gallophobia is most keenly directed not at Frenchified fops but, rather, at Evelina's grandmother, Madame Duval.

In a letter that she wrote to her prospective publisher, Thomas Lowndes, in 1776, Burney commented on Mirvan and Duval thus: 'The characters of the Sea Captain, and *would be* French woman, are intended to draw out each the other; and the ignorance of the former, in regard to modern customs, and fashionable modes, assists in marking their absurdity and extravagance.'[29] As Burney here attests, both of these characters are to be regarded as satirically compromised by the antagonistic relationship that develops between them. Mirvan, certainly, is a far from straightforward mouthpiece for contemporary anti-Gallic prejudice. 'Surly, vulgar, and disagreeable', as Evelina describes him (42), Mirvan is an unreconstructed seaman, whose conduct is characterized by brutish violence and vulgar speech (his profane oaths and sea-terms being the polar opposite of polite conversation). As Evelina notes of his response to a puppet-show in French and Italian, Mirvan also possesses a 'fixed and most prejudiced hatred of whatever is not English' (54). Mirvan's antagonist, Madame Duval, matches his strident Anglophilia in her shrill Anglophobia. In Duval's own eyes, 'no nation under the sun can beat the English for ill-politeness' (56). However, as Evelina observes in a comment that was added to the 1779 edition of the novel, 'nothing can be more strangely absurd, than to hear politeness recommended in language so repugnant to it as that of Madame Duval' (74). Duval is, in fact, something of an impolite oxymoron, being both Frenchified, and low-born; as Villars notes early in the novel, prior to heading off to France with Mr Evelyn (Evelina's grandfather), Duval had been 'a waiting-girl at a tavern' (14). During her second trip to London, which is forced upon her by Duval, Evelina is frequently mortified by her grandmother's behaviour. As she uncomfortably recalls, when Duval attempts to dance a minuet at a Hampstead ball, she proceeds 'in a style so uncommon; her age, her showy dress, and an unusual quantity of *rouge*, drew upon her the eyes, and, I fear, the derision of the whole company'. Here, as elsewhere, Evelina is highly attuned to the undesirability of a woman's making a public 'exhibition' of herself, rendering herself the focus of others' critical gaze and sharp tongues (248). If Duval is perfectly capable of rendering *herself* a ridiculous public spectacle, though, her abrasive encounters with Captain Mirvan move beyond mere social shaming, carrying a threat of harm which disturbs the otherwise urbane tone of Burney's novel.

From the outset, Mirvan and Duval are trading insults, in verbal altercations that only confirm their shared lack of polite polish. During a second visit to Ranelagh, which leaves Evelina embarrassed by the pair's 'continual wrangling and ill-breeding', Mirvan articulates more brazenly his previously expressed anti-Gallicism, during a conversation upon the benefits of travel to Paris: 'What, I suppose you'd have me learn to cut capers? – and dress like a monkey? And palaver in French gibberish? ...' (65, 67). Thereafter, the animosity between the pair shifts from verbal insults to physical violence – a shift that inevitably favours the sea-hardened Captain. In response to Mirvan's 'extacy' of joy upon her muddy fall at Ranelagh – a fall to which he may well have contributed – Duval spits in the Captain's face (72). Rather than apologizing for his extreme ill manners, however, Mirvan proceeds to lay hands upon Duval, shaking her violently. Nor is this the only time that

Mirvan physically abuses her. An elaborate trick organized by the Captain (and abetted by Willoughby) sees Duval being roughly handled, violently shaken once more, and tied up in a ditch. Burney provides a telling description of the alteration in Duval's appearance following this ditch-trick:

> So forlorn, so miserable a figure, I never before saw. Her head-dress had fallen off; her linen was torn; her negligee had not a pin left in it; her petticoats she was obliged to hold on; and her shoes were perpetually slipping off. She was covered with dirt, weeds, and filth, and her face was really horrible, for the pomatum and powder from her head, and the dust from the road, were quite *pasted* on her skin by her tears, which, with her *rouge*, made so frightful a mixture, that she hardly looked human. (165–6)

In satiric terms, Mirvan's '*sport*' (168) against Duval entails both an unmasking and a metamorphosis. As her female accoutrements come off, Duval is gradually stripped of her 'artificial' feminine identity – an effect that is compounded by the mess that is made of her Frenchified cosmetics. Ultimately, though, the effect of Mirvan's inhumane trick is not only to de-feminize Duval but, also, to de-humanize her. Recast as monstrous, Duval is transformed here into a grotesque hybrid, a frightful mixture of dirt, weeds, filth and dust, pomatum, powder, and rouge.

Upon the success of his trick, Mirvan's characteristic response is to revel in Duval's humiliation. For the reader of *Evelina*, however, the extremity of Duval's dressing down is liable to be far more unsettling. As the episode reveals, while Madame Duval might be a vulgar, affected upstart, Mirvan is something much worse: an intimidating, misogynistic bully. As Margaret Anne Doody observes, Mirvan 'regards physical assault on a woman under the guise of jest as a sublime source of social pleasure'.[30] Mirvan is not, in fact, the only male in the novel to take pleasure from the physical maltreatment of women. An extension of the Captain's heartlessness occurs in volume 3, in the form of a footrace between 2 old women (who are both over 80) that is organized purely for the gambling entertainment of the company at Bristol. During this episode, Evelina again finds herself powerless to act upon the 'pity' that she feels for the subjects of the sport (345); here, as elsewhere, it is the men who dictate the terms of the company's activities. In perhaps the novel's most shocking moment, Evelina is prevented from going to the aid of one of the women (who has fallen), by Merton's cry of 'No foul play! no foul play!' (346). Merton, it seems, views the footrace with absolute dispassion, as a wager like any other. Merton is not, though, the only participant in this wager. As with Mirvan's homosocial bonding with Willoughby via the ditching of Duval, the reader's sense of the cruelty of the footrace is liable to be heightened by the fact that this is a *communal* (male) venture, rather than the aberrant behaviour of an unsociable individual. Indeed, as Kristina Straub observes, insofar as he objects to the footrace only because it involves gambling, even the otherwise compassionate Lord Orville is implicated in this collective act of leisured cruelty.[31]

With the Mirvan–Duval conflict and the women's footrace, Burney reworked the kind of grotesque, Cervantic comedy that Fielding had introduced into the British novel, in a manner that highlighted the *problem* of uncivilized, masculine violence. Within her novelistic exploration of the world of polite manners, and in what critics have often classed as a 'novel of manners' (by analogy with dramatic 'comedies of manners'), these episodes stand out as being of another order, as almost purposely unpalatable. Like *The Female Quixote*, *Evelina* does ultimately conclude with the comic resolution of marriage – what Straub dubs its 'fairy-tale' ending.[32] It would be wrong, though, to forget either the difficulty with which this resolution is achieved, or the social tensions that lie just beneath the surface of the novel's sophisticated comedy. To the modern reader, the sub-generic designation 'novel of manners' is itself liable to suggest something rather twee, a narrative stroll along the promenade of etiquette. As Zonitch argues, however, in Burney's hands at least 'the novel of manners is more than just a textbook for distinguishing proper from rude behavior'. Rather, as Zonitch argues more broadly, 'a preoccupation with manners suggests not social stability but a volatile instability … the concern with manners and standards of behavior at this historical juncture bespeaks a contemporary anxiety about the possibility of turbulent and unruly desires erupting at the social surface'.[33] For all their differences of tone and style, in a broad sense Burney's novel shares with *Humphry Clinker* this anxiety about the social eruption of uncivilized impulses. If, as in Smollett, much of this anxiety concerns the intrusion into cultural life of unruly upstarts, what *Evelina* also offers is a more particular sense of the vulnerability of women within the existing social and cultural order. Even as things already stand, *Evelina* suggests, women are susceptible to a range of social impositions, powerless to prevent acts of male aggression that are often masked as polite overtures but which, on occasion, are only too physically real.

8
Conclusion: Making the Novel, Reading the Novel

Working as we have been on a book about the making of the novel as a literary genre, we were eager to read the most recent high-profile account of the novel in English: Terry Eagleton's *The English Novel: An Introduction*. Given the probable wide dissemination of this book and its likely influence on popular understanding of the topic, we have to register our disappointment with Eagleton's approach. In Eagleton's study, the early history of the novel is represented by Defoe and Swift, Richardson and Fielding, and Sterne; which is to say, by a handful of male writers from a canon that is only slightly less circumscribed than that constructed by Ian Watt nearly half a century ago. There is no room here, it would seem, for early century amatory fiction, for non-Shandean sentimentalism or the Gothic, or for less well-known spin-offs and sub-genres, such as the novel of circulation or women's utopian fiction. In Eagleton's account, moreover, there are no notable women novelists before Jane Austen. In a brief preface, Eagleton offers, as an excuse for confining his study 'so high-mindedly to the literary canon', 'the need to discuss authors whom students are at present most likely to encounter in their work'.[1] In reality, many eighteenth-century novelists who escape Eagleton's purview, and particularly many women novelists, are now regularly taught in universities, as important authors in their own right. In order both to reflect and to foster this trend, our own approach has been not simply to consider such works as the amatory novels of Manley and Haywood, but to examine them as part of the same literary history as the prose fictions of Defoe and Swift. There is more at stake here than a simple desire to expand or to vary a restricted, old-fashioned canon. At this stage in the day, we would argue, it is untenable to discuss the early British novel without taking into account both the contemporaries of the old canonical novelists, and the variations that were worked upon the genre even during the eighteenth century itself. That this should be the case is largely due to the substantial amount of scholarly and critical work that has been done on the eighteenth-century novel during the last 20–30 years – a body of work that, symptomatically, Eagleton largely ignores. As Eagleton's study sadly demonstrates, any discussion that fails to engage with this body of work must operate in an interpretative void, where our understanding of this key period in the formation of the British novel remains locked in the past, rather than continually developing, deepening, becoming more nuanced.

Our aim in this study has been to put forward a new reading of the eighteenth-century novel, which gives due attention both to the formal characteristics of the genre, and to the broader, social and cultural factors that played a part in its formation. Through detailed readings of key texts, we have thus offered our own 'narrative' of the novel's early history. In constructing our account, we have posed a series of questions. When does the story of the British novel in fact begin? What were the key factors that facilitated the appearance of this newest of literary genres? How important to its progress were formal and ideological differences between its early practitioners? And how did the genre manage to secure its place within the cultural landscape of eighteenth-century Britain? The preceding chapters have, we hope, gone some way towards providing answers to such questions. As we argued in Chapter 1, the novel did not arise in a void, but was itself the starkest manifestation of a broader process of 'novelization', which also saw older literary genres – poetry and drama – paying keener attention to the familiar material of contemporary life. In tracing the making of the novel genre itself, we have given special emphasis to artistic and commercial competition between authors (such as Haywood and Defoe); to rearguard reactions against the fledgling genre (as with Swift's anti-novelism); to experimental efforts that were made to revitalize a flagging genre, in the middle decades of the eighteenth century; to newly dominant strains, most notably the sentimental; and to the novel's increasing role as a forum for examining the life of the nation. In the story that we have been telling, canonical, non-canonical, and only-very-recently canonical novels have appeared cheek-by-jowl, and women writers have played as important a role as male ones. Throughout our study, we have also sought to maintain a dialogue with the many scholars who have come before us in the field of eighteenth-century fiction, participating in the post-Wattian debate over the emergence, early development, and cultural consolidation of the genre.

The features of style, ideology, influence and voice that we have explored in a range of eighteenth-century novels also need to be understood in the context of the changing material and cultural conditions in which these novels were written and read – conditions that, again, Eagleton largely effaces. In this concluding chapter, we want to turn to a number of aspects of contemporary print culture which affected the ways in which novels were both produced and consumed during the period that we have been surveying. This was a time of enormous change within British print culture. As Terry Belanger observes, by stark contrast to the situation that pertained a century earlier, before the lapsing of the Licensing Act in 1695, by the 1790s England had become a 'well-developed print society'.[2] In this expansion of the print trade into a fully fledged commercial industry, novels played an increasingly significant – if often uncertain – part. As we have already observed, the century by no means witnessed a *steady* increase in novelistic production. As James Raven has shown, while the publication of new novels stood at a higher level after 1740, there remained considerable variation within this increased output, with for instance a dip in the late 1750s and a sharp increase in 1771–72 (what *The Critical Review* called a 'prolific scribblerian year'). Such variations partly reflected broader economic conditions, as during the bad commercial years of the late 1770s.[3] The financial remuneration that novelists received for their works was also unevenly spread. While a very few authors, such as Richardson and Walpole, could print their works themselves, most novelists had to rely upon others to reimburse them for their intellectual labour, by purchasing the copyrights to their texts. At a time when publishers often preferred to reissue proven bestsellers than to pay for freshly minted works, much depended on a writer's reputation. For the majority of authors, certainly, a career in the emerging 'profession' of imaginative writing was something that had to be painfully eked out, with many novelists receiving just a handful of guineas for their works. There were, nevertheless, some spectacular successes, not least among the authors whom we have analysed in this study. As we noted in Chapter 3, whether as novel or anti-novel, the copyright to *Gulliver's Travels* brought Swift £200 – a considerable sum at a time when a middle-class family could live comfortably on £50 a year. Subsequent to his apparent astonishment at being offered £200 for *Joseph Andrews* (he was actually paid £183, 11 shillings for the copyright to the work), Fielding went on to earn £600 from *Tom Jones* and £800 from *Amelia*, both enormous sums at the time, and both supplemented by further payments from Fielding's famously generous publisher, Andrew Millar. Having himself paid for the printing of the initial York edition of the first instalment of *Tristram Shandy*, with money lent to him by a local acquaintance, Sterne reaped £450 from James Dodsley for the copyright to the same instalment, along with £380 for the copyright to volumes 3 and 4. For the remaining three instalments, the author retained his copyright, amassing his financial return through copies sold on commission by the publishers Thomas Becket and Peter Dehondt, who also sold *A Sentimental Journey* (which, like Sterne's sermons, was published initially by the subscription method of advance payment). Also during the third quarter of the century, Johnson received £125 for *Rasselas*, Goldsmith took £60 for *The Vicar of Wakefield*, and Smollett gained £210 from the copyright to *Humphry Clinker*. Writers like Fielding, Johnson, and Smollett were, though, established names in the literary marketplace. Although Francis Coventry received £30 from Robert Dodsley merely for the *alterations* required for the third edition of *Pompey the Little* (in the process assigning ownership of the work to Dodsley), this was after the novel had already proven its commercial worth; the unproven author had no doubt received much less for his initial manuscript. *Evelina* brought the young and unknown Frances Burney just £20 (later supplemented by a further £10 from her publisher, Thomas Lowndes). For her follow-up novel, *Cecilia* (1782), however, the now-lauded authoress received £250, this time from Thomas Payne and Thomas Cadell. During the following decade, Burney made £1000 from the copyright to *Camilla* (1796), along with a comparable sum from the subscribers to the first edition; while Ann Radcliffe is believed to have garnered the princessly sums of £500 and £800 respectively from her Gothic novels, *The Mysteries of Udolpho* (1794) and *The Italian* (1797).[4] Such, then, were the possible rewards available to authors whose previous novels had proved popular, or who had already made a literary name for themselves through other kinds of writing.

Allied to the establishment of the profession of novel-writing was the campaign to secure the legitimacy of the upstart genre. As we have seen, efforts to legitimize the novel, which gained impetus during the 1740s, frequently focused upon the shortcomings of romance fiction. Famously (or perhaps notoriously), in his preface to *Joseph Andrews*, Fielding accepted the term 'romance' while arguing for a comic form that, though non-metrical, one could 'refer' to Homer's lost comic epic, the *Margites*. One of Fielding's aims, however, was precisely to banish the kind of writing contained in 'those voluminous Works commonly called *Romances*, namely, *Clelia, Cleopatra, Astræa, Cassandra*, the *Grand Cyrus*, and innumerable others which contain, as I apprehend, very little Instruction or Entertainment'.[5] By the middle of the century, the novel's claim to cultural importance was being promoted both in writing about the genre and within novels themselves. In a review of Smollett's *Peregrine Pickle* that John Cleland contributed to *The Monthly Review*, for instance, the English 'biographical' novel – that is, the story that bases itself upon the life of a particular individual – is said to be a deeply pondered and rational response to 'the flood of novels, tales, romances, and other monsters of the imagination, which have been either wretchedly translated, or even more unhappily imitated, from the French, whose literary levity we have not been ashamed to adopt, and encourage the propagation of so depraved a taste'.[6] As Cleland's review signals, the defence of new novelistic writing and the dismissal of romance were increasingly politicized in terms of developing nationalistic tensions between England and France. Novelists also began to use a character's willingness to adopt a 'romance' idiom as a verbal marker for their insincerity, if not outright immorality. In Frances Sheridan's *Memoirs of Miss Sidney Bidulph* (1761), for instance, Miss Price exposes the unworthiness of Mr Ware, a man who plots her ruin, by commenting that 'He fell at my feet, begged my pardon, and talked all that sort of stuff which I have read in romances'.[7] The scepticism about 'romance' language on display here also pointed up the greater authenticity of Sheridan's own writing – appropriately enough in a novel bold enough to represent a mastectomy as a central incident. That such anti-romance discourse continued even into the final quarter of the century should serve to remind us that the novel's journey to respectability remained a long and faltering one. Complaining, in her preface to *Evelina*, that 'In the republic of letters, there is no member of such inferior rank, or who is so much disdained by his brethren of the quill, as the humble Novelist', Burney would still feel it necessary to warn her readers against 'the gentle expectation of being transported to the fantastic regions of Romance, where Fiction is coloured by all the gay tints of luxurious Imagination, where Reason is an outcast, and where the sublimity of the *Marvellous*, rejects all aid from sober Probability'.[8] Increasingly, however, outright *opposition* to the novel – the 'anti-novel discourse' in its sharpest form – was in decline, as the various efforts made to legitimize the new imaginative fiction gradually began to take hold.

How did readers set about acquiring copies of the latest novels? One of the most significant new organs for the dissemination of prose fiction was the circulating library. During the second half of the century, such libraries mushroomed not only in London, but also in provincial centres such as Bath and Newcastle – to the extent that, as

Roy Porter notes, 'By 1800 there were 122 circulating libraries in London, 268 in the provinces'.[9] For an annual subscription fee (of perhaps half a guinea to a guinea), these libraries gave readers access to a constant supply of books, at a very small fee per text. Novels were, in fact, only one of many kinds of literature made available to subscribers, by no means all, or even the majority of whom were women. However, as we shall see, the novel and its female readers figured especially strongly in the symbolic representation of circulating libraries. These institutions might even be viewed as having encouraged the proliferation of new novels: in his essay on the genre that appeared in *The Lounger*, for instance, Henry Mackenzie maligned the 'common herd of novels' being produced by the 1780s as 'the wretched offspring of circulating libraries'.[10] Nevertheless, at a time when novels were comparatively more expensive than they are today (rising from an average of around 1–2 shillings per volume in the first half of the century, to 2–3 shillings in the second half), the circulating libraries provided an important means of access to the genre for consumers of fiction who were unable to afford the cover price of the texts themselves.

If novel-*writing* was becoming an increasingly respectable employment, how were readers *themselves* represented during this period? As we have seen, in the early pages of *Humphry Clinker*, Matthew Bramble describes his niece, Lydia, as a 'good-natured simpleton', who possesses 'a languishing eye, and reads romances'.[11] If romances are again the target here, such slurs against the reading public frequently encompassed the novel as well. The idea that prose fiction was consumed mainly by simple-minded female readers became well-established during the second half of the eighteenth century, and is most famously dramatized in *The Rivals*. Sheridan's play tells us a good deal about popular perceptions of novel-reading during the later eighteenth century: about who read novels, what kinds of novels they read, where these works might be acquired, and about the imagined *effects* of novel-reading. In this scene from the beginning of Act 1, scene 2, the character Lydia Languish is 'sitting on a sopha with a book in her hand' at her aunt's house in Bath, when her maid Lucy enters to report the outcome of her investigations among the local libraries:

> LUCY.   Indeed, Ma'am, I transferr'd half the town in search of it: – I don't believe there's a circulating library in Bath I ha'n't been at.
> LYD.   And could not you get '*The Reward of Constancy?*'
> LUCY.   No, indeed, Ma'am.

LYD.   Nor '*The Fatal Connection?*'
LUCY.   No, indeed, Ma'am.
LYD.   Nor '*The Mistakes of the Heart*'?
LUCY.   Ma'am, as ill-luck would have it, Mr. Bull said Miss Sukey Saunter had just fetch'd it away.
LYD.   Heigh-ho! – Did you inquire for '*The Delicate Distress*'? –
LUCY.   – Or '*The Memoirs of Lady Woodford*?' Yes indeed, Ma'am. – I ask'd every where for it; and I might have brought it from Mr. Frederick's, but Lady Slattern Lounger, who had just sent it home, had so soiled and dog's-ear'd it, it wa'n't fit for a christian to read.
LYD.   Heigh-ho! – Yes, I always know when Lady Slattern has been before me. – She has a most observing thumb; and I believe cherishes her nails for the convenience of making marginal notes. – Well, child, what *have* you brought me?
LUCY.   Oh! Here Ma'am.
        [*Taking books from under her cloke, and from her pockets.*]
        This is '*The Gordian Knot*', – and this '*Peregrine Pickle*'. Here are '*The Tears of Sensibility*' and '*Humphrey Clinker*'. This is '*The Memoirs of a Lady of Quality, written by herself*', – and here the second volume of '*The Sentimental Journey*'.
LYD.   Heigh-ho! – What are those books by the glass?
LUCY.   The great one is only '*The whole Duty of Man*' – where I press a few blonds [pieces of lace], Ma'am.[12]

With one important exception, all of the books mentioned in this passage are contemporary works of prose fiction, particularly sentimental fiction. By contrast to this light, affective literature, Lucy's reference to *The Whole Duty of Man* points to the more useful and instructive kind of text which, in theory, a young lady like Lydia *should* have been reading. A well-known handbook of popular piety, *The Whole Duty of Man* had been frequently reprinted since its first publication in 1659. Given that this religious work is the *only* mentioned text that is unlikely to be read by Lydia, by the end of the above passage Lucy's allusion to the 'christian' reader has become highly ironic. At this moment, Sheridan's play partly recalls an episode from Fielding's *Shamela* during which Shamela lists her 'few Books', which include not only religious texts (including *The Whole Duty of Man* itself), but also plays, a volume of Manley's *The New Atalantis*, and the pornographic text *Venus in the Cloyster; or, The Nun in her Smock*, which had been published in 1724 by the notorious Edmund Curll.[13] In *The Rivals*, however, it is not a lower class go-getter but a young society lady who is presented as both symbolizing and embodying the debased tastes of the reading public. Sheridan's play more generally, we might note, offers up a comic critique of fashionable society – of the same social grouping that Smollett had attacked in *Humphry Clinker*. In a development of considerable irony, though, in Sheridan's hands *Humphry Clinker* itself becomes a symptom of this society – a *part* of Lydia's store of reading, rather than a moral corrective *to* it.

In this scene from *The Rivals*, then, novels occupy the same position that romances had occupied both in Matthew Bramble's criticism of his romance-reading niece and, in a more complex way, in Charlotte Lennox's *The Female Quixote*. For many observers, indeed, romances and novels – particularly sentimental novels – were as bad as each other, insofar as they were both deemed to pander to a primarily female readership with emotionally engaging tales of thwarted love or virtue in distress. From this perspective, the modern novel had simply replaced, rather than profitably displaced, the earlier romance tradition, so that novels were, in effect, merely modern romances. Sheridan's play, though, also affords a more complex picture of the contemporary prose garden. As we might ask, for instance: is not the passage we have quoted from *The Rivals* itself testament to the broad process of 'novelization' that we have been outlining? What we have here, after all, is a scene in a play which, in addressing the proliferation of prose fictions and the reasons for their popularity, both evinces its own interest in contemporary cultural life, and recalls the similar concerns of a number of recent *novelists*. Even as he draws upon contemporary anti-novel (and anti-novel-*reading*) discourse, in fact, Sheridan might very well be regarded as sending that discourse up. Later in the same scene, for instance, Lydia endeavours to hide her disreputable texts from Sir Anthony Absolute and Mrs Malaprop (also mentioned now are Smollett's *Roderick Random* and Mackenzie's *The Man of Feeling*). In place of these prose fictions, Lydia displays, as her properly edifying reading, works by the bluestocking, Hester Chapone, James Fordyce's sermons, and Chesterfield's *Letters*. Fordyce's are the same sermons, we might notice, that the geeky Mr Collins attempts to read to the Bennett children in Jane Austen's *Pride and Prejudice* (1813); while Chesterfield's *Letters*, as we have seen, were hardly regarded as unequivocally 'improving' literature at this time, certainly not on a moral par with bluestocking writing. Sheridan's scepticism about anti-novelistic moralizing is further suggested by the famous passage in which Sir Anthony Absolute launches a full-scale verbal assault upon the source of

Lydia's novels: the circulating libraries. As Sir Anthony opines: 'a circulating library in a town is, as an ever-green tree, of diabolical knowledge! – It blossoms through the year! – And depend on it, Mrs. Malaprop, that they who are so fond of handling the leaves, will long for the fruit at last'.[14] Here, the playwright's subversion of anti-novel discourse is revealed in the comic slippage between the physical act of reading and its moral consequences, as turning the pages (leaves) of the kind of 'feeling' fiction that absorbs Lydia engenders an illicit longing for forbidden (sexual) fruit. Even as Lydia exemplifies the archetype of the languishing female reader, then, Sheridan's play also goads the anti-novel discourse, mocking the heavy-handed proscriptions of those who opposed the novel on exaggerated ethical grounds.

A comparable ambivalence about the growth of the novel-reading public also informed more sober forms of cultural commentary at this time. An important new filter for the reception of books, for instance, was provided by the founding at mid-century of two dedicated review journals, *The Monthly Review* (1749) and *The Critical Review* (1756). These journals endeavoured to provide their readers with an account of each newly published text. This development involved more, though, than simply an increase in the amount of information now available to literary consumers. As Frank Donoghue notes, the reviewers also sought to 'create hierarchies of taste and mould habits of reading that they hoped would influence the book purchases of individuals and circulating libraries'.[15] Not satisfied with providing merely descriptive accounts of new works, the reviewers fashioned a role for themselves as cultural authorities, as shapers of the national taste. This project did not entirely favour the novel. As Joseph Bartolomeo observes, the journals' pages are peppered with complaints about 'the burden of reading novels'.[16] In part, such complaints reflected a sense that, viewed from the plane of high culture, the novel was still not a respectable literary form. For one disgruntled critic writing in *The Critical Review* in 1756, the novel-reading community, which supported 'the circulating libraries of this learned metropolis', consisted mainly of 'idle templars, raw prentices, and green girls'.[17] Reviewers throwing up their arms in exasperation at second-rate examples of the genre did not, of course, necessarily imply criticism of the acknowledged masters of the craft, such as Richardson and Fielding. Indeed, it was another established novelist, Tobias Smollett, who had founded *The Critical Review* in the first place. Soon enough, though, novelists themselves began to mock the reviewers' claims to refined cultural discrimination, most notably in *Tristram Shandy*'s jibes at the aggressive analyses of these so-called 'gentleman' critics, but also in novels such as Richard Graves' *The Spiritual Quixote* (1773), a prefatory 'postscript' to which depicts the reviewers as a 'sett of *censorious Christians*' who 'will not suffer a man to nod in his elbow-chair, without giving him a jog; nor to talk non-sense, without contradicting or ridiculing him'.[18] A more complex response occurs in Burney's *Evelina*, in a prefatory address 'To the Authors of the Monthly and Critical Reviews'. Appealing for the 'patronage' and 'protection' of 'those who publicly profess themselves Inspectors of all literary performances', the self-cast 'Magistrates of the press, and Censors for the Public', Burney's address might well be regarded as querying the reviewers' authority even as it curries their favour, through an exaggerated show of sycophantic self-abasement by a mere novelist at the court of the critics.[19] More broadly, what these self-conscious novelistic reactions to the reviewers highlight is that the new critical journals formed an important part of the context not only of the reception, but also of the *production* of new novels during the second half of the eighteenth century.

To speak collectively of 'novels' or of 'the novel' at this time is itself, though, somewhat misleading. What, readers might reasonably have asked, was the essential nature of this modern genre? As we have seen, as soon as it ever threatened to settle into a single, clearly identifiable form of writing, the novel was prone to diversification, to re-channelling itself in new directions. Certainly, a particular kind of template or definition of the genre does achieve prominence during these years, in contrast again to romance fiction. A notable formulation here is that provided by Clara Reeve, in *The Progress of Romance* (1785):

> The Romance is an heroic fable, which treats of fabulous persons and things. – The Novel is a picture of real life and manners, and of the times in which it is written. The Romance in lofty and elevated language, describes what never happened nor is likely to happen. – The Novel gives a familiar relation of such things, as pass every day before our eyes, such as may happen to our friend, or to ourselves; and the perfection of it, is to represent every scene, in so easy and natural a manner, and to make them appear so probable, as to deceive us into a persuasion (at least while we are reading) that all is real, until we are affected by the joys or distresses, of the persons in the story, as if they were our own.[20]

Notwithstanding the fact that she was seeking to *recuperate* romance, Reeve's overview of the differences between the romance and the novel recalls that outlined in Congreve's preface to *Incognita*, which we considered in Chapter 2. In its description of the novel genre itself, Reeve's account also tallies with J. Paul Hunter's list of the predominant 'characteristics' of the genre (as discussed in Chapter 1). Indeed, for all the variety of novels and novelistic sub-genres that are available to modern book-purchasers, this basic sense of what a 'novel' entails has survived to the present day. During the later eighteenth century, though, this characterization was already being complicated, to a greater or lesser degree, by the sub-types and more distinctly deviant variations upon the genre that we have noted, such as circulation fiction, oriental and utopian works, and the Gothic novel. Even by the end of the period with which we are dealing in this study, 'the novel' could no longer be easily regarded as just *one* species of prose-fictional writing.

Broadly speaking, the two *kinds* of novel that produced most unease among cultural commentators were the sentimental and the Gothic. As Markman Ellis has shown in persuasive detail, during the 1780s the ongoing 'critical resistance to sentimental fictions' was 'revived and revised in a more sophisticated and more literary manner', in journal essays that developed a debate concerning the 'moral tendency' of the novel.[21] For the sentimental novel, though, it is equally possible to produce evidence of considerable contemporary approval. Consider for example this extract from a letter that Robert Burns, the well-known Scots poet, wrote to an acquaintance in 1783:

> In the matter of books, indeed, I am very profuse. – My favorite authors are of the sentim¹ kind, such as Shenstone, particularly his Elegies, Thomson, Man of feeling, a book I prize next to the Bible, Man of the World, Sterne, especially his Sentimental journey, M°pherson's Ossian, &c. these are the glorious models after which I endeavour to form my conduct, and 'tis incongruous, 'tis absurd to suppose that the man whose mind glows with sentiments lighted up at their sacred flame – the man whose heart distends with benevolence to all the human race – he 'who can soar above this little scene of things' – can he descend to mind the pault[r]y conccerns [*sic*] about which the terrae-filial race fret, and fume, and vex themselves?[22]

In this extract, Burns describes the ideal process by which sentimental writing – presented here as an exemplary discourse – might both generate a feeling of benevolence in the reader, and provide a means of imaginative escape from the business, and the busy-ness, of the

workaday world. In the quoted passage itself, this literature's enlivening
of its reader's sensibilities does not, perhaps, lead to a social *exercise* of
benevolence, to any actual *works* of charity. Nevertheless, for Burns, the
feeling literature of sensibility *is* moral – is, indeed, the *most* moral of
modern discourses. And, as his description of *The Man of Feeling* as a
book that he prizes 'next to the Bible' indicates, the sentimental *novel*
is located at the very centre of this privileged discourse (also included
here, along with *The Man of Feeling* and *A Sentimental Journey*, is one
of Mackenzie's later novels, *The Man of the World* (1773)). Here, then,
we can observe one route by which novels might come to be held in
extremely high estimation in the later decades of the eighteenth
century. With Burns' epistolary reflections, we have moved a considerable distance from public slurs upon the novel as a form of fashionable
fodder dished up for a frivolous female readership.

Insofar as their very success depended upon readers' sympathetic
identification with characters depicted in situations of emotional distress, sentimental novels could be regarded as distilling or crystallizing
a key characteristic of the genre more generally – the process by which,
as Clara Reeve put it, 'we are affected by the joys or distresses, of the
persons in the story, as if they were our own'. Gothic novels, however,
lay at a further remove from what (with appropriately Gothic 'scare'
quotes) we might call Reeve's 'mainstream' model of 'realistic' fiction.
As we saw in our discussion of Walpole's *The Castle of Otranto*, Gothic
writing was at least partly founded on a desire to escape the drawing-
room proprieties of Richardsonian fiction, to probe the wellsprings of
the human imagination by re-legitimizing tales of suspense and the
uncanny which might root into the human psyche at a deeper level than
that of conventional morality. Inevitably, given these aims and impulses,
respectability did not come easy to Gothic. A pointed critique of Gothic
fiction was provided by a review of Burney's *Camilla*, which appeared
in the recently founded review journal, *The British Critic*, in 1796:

> To astonish by the marvellous, and appal by the terrific, have lately
> been the favourite designs of many writers of novels; who, in pursuit
> of those effects, have frequently appeared to desert, and sometimes
> have really transgressed the bounds of nature and possibility. We can-
> not approve of these extravagances. The artful conduct of an inter-
> esting plot, and the dramatic delineation of character, are certainly
> the features that give most dignity to this species of fiction; these are
> found in great perfection in those English novels which are admitted
> as models; those of Richardson, Fielding, and Smollett: and their

merits cannot be rivalled by any thing imported from the regions of fairy tale.[23]

As this review confirms, eighteenth-century Gothicism partly involved a return to the very 'romance' conventions against which the novel was now being defined. The *British Critic*'s critique here formed part of a rearguard action, an attempt to fortify the mainline of English 'realist' fiction against the encroachments of the Gothic imagination. By 1796, this was perhaps a case of shutting the stable door after the night-mare had bolted. As Thomas Mathias facetiously remarked, the 'spawn' of Walpole's 'Otranto Ghosts' were now to be had 'in every novel shop'.[24] The Gothic novel would not be stopped in its tracks, although, as we might also note, to speak of even the 'Gothic novel' in this unitary way is to downplay the formal variety and authorial contestation that existed within this sub-generic deviation from the 'model' eighteenth-century novel.

By the end of the 1780s, and certainly by the end of the century, then, we witness a situation in which 'the novel' is already significantly fractured, into a mainstream model of realistic fiction, and variations that troubled or more strongly resisted this formulation. Already under way here is the process of generic specialization that, today, has become the proliferation of novelistic niche-markets, which we noted at the outset of our study in relation to the modern categories of science fiction. Alongside this splintering of 'the novel' (and of the novel-reading public), though, it is also important to register the concurrent forma-tion of a privileged, higher brow canon of eighteenth-century novels – of what *The British Critic* termed 'those English novels which are admitted as models'. In the early nineteenth century, the process of canon-formation would be further encouraged by the publication of large-scale collections of novels, most notably Anna Barbauld's 50-volume *The British Novelists* (1810) and Walter Scott's 10-volume *Ballantyne's Novelist's Library* (1821–24). In the opinion of Claudia Johnson, Barbauld's collection – which *includes* the Gothic novels of Walpole, Reeve, and Radcliffe – constitutes 'the first novelistic canon'.[25] In her prefatory essay 'On the Origin and Progress of Novel-Writing', Barbauld provides a succinct, if overly simplified account of the cultural consoli-dation of the British novel during the middle decades of the eighteenth century:

The first author amongst us who distinguished himself by natural painting, was that truly original genius De Foe. His *Robinson Crusoe* is to this day an *unique* in its kind, and he has made it very interesting without applying to the common resource of love. At length, in the reign of George the Second, Richardson, Fielding, and Smollet [*sic*], appeared in quick succession; and their success raised such a demand for this kind of entertainment, that it has ever since been furnished from the press, rather as a regular and necessary supply, than as an occasional gratification.[26]

In Barbauld's historical assessment, the successive successes of Richardson, Fielding and Smollett meant that, by the third quarter of the eighteenth century, the novel genre had become securely embedded within the cultural life of the nation. Regularly supplied, and constantly in demand, from this point onwards novels would be permanently in vogue.

What Barbauld also testifies to here, of course, is the *commercial* success story that the novel represented. In conclusion, we should like to turn to one final contemporary reading of the novel's early progress, which elucidates further the relationships between fashionability, canon-formation and commercial success. Our quotation is from a review by James Noorthouck of an anonymous novel entitled *The Labyrinths of Life*, which appeared in *The Monthly Review* for July, 1791. Here, Noorthouck offers his own account of the making of the British novel:

> Two of the earliest fabricators of this species of goods, the modern novel, in our country, were Daniel Defoe, and Mrs. Haywood; the success of *Pamela* may be said to have brought it into fashion; and the progress has not been less rapid than the extension of the use of tea, to which a novel is almost as general an attendant, as the bread and butter, especially in a morning. While we are on this subject, it is also to be noted, that nothing is more common than to find hair-powder lodged between the leaves of a novel; which evinces the corresponding attention paid to the inside as well as the outside of a modern head. Richardson, Fielding, Smollett, and Sterne, were the Wedgwoods of their days; and the imitators that have since started up in the same line, exceed all power of calculation![27]

As in Wollstonecraft's *Mary* and Sheridan's *The Rivals*, novels are positioned here among the accoutrements of the fashionable – as objects which exist in the same cultural space (and, perhaps, on the same material level) as tea, bread and butter, and hair powder. That novels are said to form the diversions of a morning hints at the perceived lack of attention required to understand such works; and Noorthouck's allusion to the proliferation of novels might also be taken to imply that, as well as being easy to read, novels are easy to *write*, at least in the hands of uninspired 'imitators'. Evidently, then, Noorthouck is somewhat ambivalent about the value of the genre, and about the recent eruption in its output. At the same time, though, Noorthouck's review presents a narrative of the novel's early history that the modern reader is liable to find strangely familiar. Already in the early 1790s, there has emerged a recognizably modern, 'mainstream' canon of the eighteenth-century novel – incorporating Defoe, Richardson, Fielding, Smollett and Sterne – that would not have much troubled Ian Watt, or indeed some of the scholars who have followed in his wake. Noorthouck's significant addition to the 'big five' male writers is, of course, Eliza Haywood, who would later be airbrushed out of the picture (she is even omitted from Anna Barbauld's comparatively female-friendly collection of British novelists, though Barbauld does at least allow that Haywood's later novels are 'by no means void of merit').[28] Absent from Noorthouck's account is any mention of the Gothic novel, or of the other novelistic sidings that we have reintegrated into our own story of the making of the genre. And yet, for all its omissions and its critique of the genre's contemporary fashionability, what Noorthouck's review strongly conveys is the extent to which the 'new species of writing' had now managed to establish itself in Britain. Of particular resonance here are the entrepreneurial terms in which Noorthouck accounts for this process, not least in his casting of Richardson, Fielding, Smollett and Sterne as 'the Wedgwoods of their days'. Noorthouck's commercial idiom was, we would finally suggest, more than merely figurative. Whatever the novel's ascendancy might have said about the moral state of contemporary British society, by the end of the eighteenth century this innovative but frequently maligned genre was rightly being viewed as one of the most successful products to have been manufactured within Britain's new, commercial economy.

Notes

Preface

1 D.H. Lawrence, 'Why the Novel Matters'. First published posthumously in *Phoenix* (1936); reproduced here from D.J. Enright and Ernst de Chickera, eds, *English Critical Texts* (London: Oxford University Press, 1962), pp. 286–92 (p. 289).

Chapter 1   Introduction: Modelling the Novel

1 For definitions of these sub-categories, see *The Encyclopaedia of Science Fiction*, ed. John Clute and Peter Nichols (London: Orbit, 1993). See under the entry 'Terminology'.

2 Isobel Grundy, 'Restoration and Eighteenth Century', in *The Oxford Illustrated History of English Literature*, ed. Pat Rogers (Oxford: Oxford University Press, 1987), pp. 214–73 (p. 253).

3 Margaret Anne Doody, *The True Story of the Novel* (New Brunswick, NJ: Rutgers University Press, 1996), p. 16.

4 Ian Watt, *The Rise of the Novel: Studies in Defoe, Richardson, and Fielding* (London: Chatto & Windus, 1957), p. 15.

5 Watt, *The Rise of the Novel*, p. 25.

6 John Richetti, *Popular Fiction Before Richardson: Narrative Patterns, 1700–1739* (Oxford: Clarendon Press, 1969; repr. 1992), pp. 2, 3, 4.

7 J.C.D. Clark, *English Society 1688–1832: Ideology, Social Structure and Political Practice during the Ancien Regime* (Cambridge: Cambridge University Press, 1985).

8 Daniel Defoe, *The Life and Adventures of Robinson Crusoe*, ed. Angus Ross (Harmondsworth: Penguin, 1965), p. 28.

9 William B. Warner, *Licensing Entertainment: The Elevation of Novel Reading in Britain, 1684–1750* (Berkeley, CA: University of California Press, 1998), pp. 32–3.

10 Lincoln B. Faller, *Crime and Defoe: A New Kind of Writing* (Cambridge: Cambridge University Press, 1993), pp. 37ff.

11 Ian Watt, 'Flat-Footed and Fly-Blown: The Realities of Realism', *Eighteenth-Century Fiction*, 12:2–3 (January–April, 2000), 147–66 (p. 157). Watt's lecture, from which this article is derived, was first delivered in 1978.

12 Lennard J. Davis, *Factual Fictions: The Origins of the English Novel* (New York: Columbia University Press, 1983).

13 Laurie Langbauer, *Women and Romance: The Consolations of Gender in the English Novel* (Ithaca, NY: Cornell University Press, 1990), p. 29.

14 Deborah Ross, *The Excellence of Falsehood: Romance, Realism, and Women's Contribution to the Novel* (Lexington, KY: University Press of Kentucky, 1991).

15 Michael McKeon, *The Origins of the English Novel, 1600–1740* (Baltimore, MD: Johns Hopkins University Press, 1987).

16 Lennard J. Davis, 'Dialectics on the Loose: The History of the Novel in Infinite Regress', *The Eighteenth Century*, 30:3 (Autumn, 1989), 43–50 (p. 47).

17 Jane Spencer, *The Rise of the Woman Novelist: From Aphra Behn to Jane Austen* (Oxford: Blackwell, 1986), p. 20 and *passim.*

18 Nancy Armstrong, *Desire and Domestic Fiction: A Political History of the Novel* (New York: Oxford University Press, 1987).

19 Kathryn Shevelow, *Women and Print Culture: The Construction of Femininity in the Early Periodical* (London: Routledge, 1989).

20 J. Paul Hunter, *Before Novels: The Cultural Contexts of Eighteenth-Century English Fiction* (New York: Norton, 1990), xix, p. 81, and *passim.*

21 Warner, *Licensing Entertainment*, pp. 116, 123, and *passim.*

22 Robert Mayer, *History and the Early English Novel: Matters of Fact from Bacon to Defoe* (Cambridge: Cambridge University Press, 1997), p. 154.

23 J.A. Downie, 'The Making of the English Novel', *Eighteenth-Century Fiction*, 9 (1996–97), 249–66.

24 Homer Obed Brown, *Institutions of the English Novel: From Defoe to Scott* (Philadelphia, PN: University of Pennsylvania Press, 1997), p. 177.

25 Brown, *Institutions of the English Novel*, xvii–xviii, p. 183.

26 Watt, *The Rise of the Novel*, p. 32.

27 Terry Eagleton, *The English Novel: An Introduction* (Oxford: Blackwell, 2005), pp. 10, 11, 28.

28 M.M. Bakhtin, *The Dialogic Imagination: Four Essays*, ed. Michael Holquist, trans. Caryl Emerson and Michael Holquist (Austin, TX: University of Texas Press, 1981), pp. 18–20, 23, 34.

29 The term is used by G.J. Barker-Benfield in his valuable and comprehensive synthesis of this process, *The Culture of Sensibility: Sex and Society in Eighteenth-Century Britain* (Chicago, IL: University of Chicago Press, 1992). 'Commercial capitalism' comprises a network of interconnecting developments and practices ranging from naval strength ensuring trade routes and colonial success, improving internal communications infrastructure, agricultural breakthroughs enabling more plentiful supplies of cheaper food, to the emergence of a stable political regime, the new empirical science, the 'financial revolution', and the 1707 Act of Union.

30 Quoted from *The Poems of Alexander Pope*, ed. John Butt (London: Routledge, 1992), pp. 227–9 (Canto 3, ll. 25–28, 37–46, 65–66, 75–88).

31 Adapted from Hunter, *Before Novels*, pp. 23–5.

32 For a summary of the main traits of this fiction, which complements J. Paul Hunter's list of the characteristics of the novel, see Warner, *Licensing Entertainment*, pp. 111–16.

33 Catherine Ingrassia, *Authorship, Commerce, and Gender in Early Eighteenth-Century England: A Culture of Paper Credit* (Cambridge: Cambridge University Press, 1998), p. 81.

Chapter 2   Missing Parts: Fiction to Defoe

1 William Congreve, *Incognita; or, Love and Duty Reconcil'd* (London, 1692), preface to the Reader.
2 Aphra Behn, *Love-Letters between a Noble-Man and his Sister*, 3 vols (London, 1684–87), 1:139–40.
3 Hugh Thomas, *The Slave Trade: The History of the Atlantic Slave Trade 1440–1870* (London: Macmillan, 1997), p. 452.
4 Richard Kroll, ' "Tales of Love and Gallantry": The Politics of *Oroonoko*', *Huntington Library Quarterly*, 67:4 (December, 2004), 573–605 (p. 578).
5 Aphra Behn, *Oroonoko; or, The Royal Slave*, ed. Janet Todd (Harmondsworth: Penguin, 1992), p. 106.
6 For the most recent assessment of this matter, see Jane Spencer, *Aphra Behn's Afterlife* (Oxford: Oxford University Press, 2000), chapter 6.
7 Alan Sinfield, *Faultlines: Cultural Materialism and the Politics of Dissident Reading* (Oxford: Clarendon Press, 1992).
8 Catherine Gallagher, '*Oroonoko*'s Blackness', in *Aphra Behn Studies*, ed. Janet Todd (Cambridge: Cambridge University Press, 1996), pp. 235–58 (p. 240).
9 Olaudah Equiano, *The Interesting Narrative and other Writings*, ed. Vincent Carretta (New York: Penguin, 1995).
10 Delarivier Manley, *The New Atalantis*, ed. Rosalind Ballaster (Harmondsworth: Penguin, 1991), pp. 245–6.
11 Ros Ballaster, *Seductive Forms: Women's Amatory Fiction from 1684–1740* (Oxford: Clarendon Press, 1992).
12 John Richetti, *Popular Fiction before Richardson: Narrative Patterns, 1700–1739* (Oxford: Clarendon Press, 1969; repr. 1992), xxv–xxvi.
13 Daniel Defoe, *Roxana: The Fortunate Mistress*, ed. Jane Jack (Oxford: Oxford University Press, 1964; repr. 1976), pp. 1, 72.
14 Eliza Haywood, *Love in Excess; or, The Fatal Enquiry*, ed. David Oakleaf (Peterborough, Ontario: Broadview, 1994; repr. 1997), pp. 191–2.
15 Ballaster, *Seductive Forms*, pp. 167–8.
16 John Richetti, *The English Novel in History, 1700–1780* (London: Routledge, 1999), p. 22.
17 Daniel Defoe, *The Fortunes and Misfortunes of the Famous Moll Flanders*, ed. G.A. Starr (Oxford: Oxford University Press, 1981), p. 129.
18 Lincoln B. Faller, *Crime and Defoe: A New Kind of Writing* (Cambridge: Cambridge University Press, 1993), p. 125.
19 Defoe, *Roxana*, pp. 147–8.
20 Paul Langford, *A Polite and Commercial People: England 1727–1783* (Oxford: Oxford University Press, 1992), p. 483.

Chapter 3   Novels and Anti-novels: Contesting Fictions

1 Quoted in W.B. Carnochan, ' "A Matter *Discutable*": The Rise of the Novel', *Eighteenth-Century Fiction*, 12:2–3 (January–April, 2000), 167–84 (p. 171).

2 Henry James, 'The Art of Fiction', in *The Art of Fiction and Other Essays*, ed. Morris Roberts (New York: Oxford University Press, 1948), pp. 3–23 (pp. 3–5).

3 Pope, *The Poems of Alexander Pope*, p. 385 (Book 2, l. 150).

4 Michael McKeon, 'Watt's *Rise of the Novel* within the Tradition of the Rise of the Novel', *Eighteenth-Century Fiction*, 12:2–3 (January–April, 2000), 253–76 (p. 254).

5 Lewis Theobald, *The History of the Loves of Antiochus and Stratonice* (London, 1717), pp. x–xi.

6 Maximillian Novak, *Daniel Defoe: Master of Fictions* (Oxford: Oxford University Press, 2001), p. 389n.

7 Novak, *Daniel Defoe*, pp. 538ff.

8 Daniel Defoe, *The Life and Adventures of Robinson Crusoe*, ed. Angus Ross (Harmondsworth: Penguin, 1965), p. 37.

9 Novak, *Daniel Defoe*, pp. 527–8.

10 Quoted by Scott Paul Gordon, *The Power of the Passive Self in English Literature, 1640–1770* (Cambridge: Cambridge University Press, 2002), p. 46.

11 See Homi K. Bhabha, 'Of Mimicry and Man: The Ambivalence of Colonial Discourse', *October*, 28 (1984), 125–33 (p. 129): '... this process by which the look of surveillance returns as the displacing gaze of the disciplined, where the observer becomes the observed ...'.

12 *The Poems of Alexander Pope*, p. 515 (Epistle 1, ll. 289–94).

13 Carol Houlihan Flynn, *The Body in Swift and Defoe* (Cambridge: Cambridge University Press, 1990), p. 62.

14 Jonathan Swift, *Gulliver's Travels*, ed. Paul Turner (Oxford: Oxford University Press, 1986), pp. 53–4.

15 Margaret Anne Doody, 'Swift and Romance', in *Walking Naboth's Vineyard: New Studies of Swift*, ed. Christopher Fox and Brenda Tooley (Notre Dame: University of Notre Dame Press, 1995), pp. 98–126 (p. 120).

16 Declan Kiberd, *Irish Classics* (London: Granta, 2001), p. 87.

17 Jonathan Swift, *A Tale of a Tub*, ed. Herbert Davis (Oxford: Blackwell, 1965), p. 21.

18 J. Paul Hunter, *Before Novels: The Cultural Contexts of Eighteenth-Century English Fiction* (New York: Norton, 1990), p. 108.

19 Michael Seidel, '*Gulliver's Travels* and the Contracts of Fiction', in *The Cambridge Companion to the Eighteenth-Century Novel*, ed. John Richetti (Cambridge: Cambridge University Press, 1996), pp. 72–89 (p. 78).

20 Defoe, *Robinson Crusoe*, p. 209.

21 Defoe, *Robinson Crusoe*, p. 178.

22 Defoe, *Robinson Crusoe*, pp. 240–1.

23 J. Paul Hunter, '*Gulliver's Travels* and the Novel', in *The Genres of 'Gulliver's Travels'*, ed. Frederik N. Smith (Newark, DE: University of Delaware Press, 1990), pp. 56–74 (p. 69).

Chapter 4   Teaching Readers to Read: Richardson and Fielding

1 On this movement, see Henry D. Rack, *Reasonable Enthusiast: John Wesley and the Rise of Methodism*, 3rd edn (London: Epworth Press, 2002).

2   Tobias Smollett, *The Expedition of Humphry Clinker*, ed. Lewis M. Knapp (Oxford: Oxford University Press, 1966; rev. edn, 1984), pp. 137, 138.

3   James Grantham Turner, 'Novel Panic: Picture and Performance in the Reception of Richardson's *Pamela*', *Representations*, 48 (Autumn, 1994), 70–96 (p. 71).

4   T.C. Duncan Eaves and Ben D. Kimpel, *Samuel Richardson: A Biography* (Oxford: Clarendon Press, 1971), pp. 121–4.

5   Quoted by Christine Gerrard, *Aaron Hill: The Muses' Projector, 1685–1750* (Oxford: Oxford University Press, 2003), p. 207.

6   Samuel Richardson, *Pamela; or, Virtue Rewarded*, ed. Peter Sabor (Harmondsworth: Penguin, 1980; repr. 1985), pp. 371–2. References to *Pamela* are to this edition except where otherwise stated.

7   J. Paul Hunter, *Before Novels: The Cultural Contexts of Eighteenth-Century English Fiction* (New York: Norton, 1990), pp. 54–7, 91–4, 225–47.

8   Quoted in Eaves and Kimpel, *Samuel Richardson*, p. 120.

9   [Peter Shaw], *The Reflector* (1750), p. 14; quoted by Richard Gooding, '*Pamela, Shamela*, and the Politics of the *Pamela* Vogue', *Eighteenth-Century Fiction*, 7:2 (1994–95), 109–30 (p. 109).

10 Samuel Richardson, *Pamela; or, Virtue Rewarded*, ed. Mark Kinkead-Weekes, 2 vols (London: Dent, 1914; repr. 1965), 2:454.

11 Samuel Richardson, *Clarissa; or, The History of a Young Lady*, ed. John Butt, 4 vols (London: Dent, 1962), 1: xiv–xv. All further references to *Clarissa* are to the Penguin edition, ed. Angus Ross (Harmondsworth: Penguin, 1985). Subsequent references to *Clarissa* are to the letter number and to the page number in this edition.

12 Pope, *The Poems of Alexander Pope*, p. 231 (Canto 3, l. 144).

13 Richardson, *Pamela*, ed. Kinkead-Weekes, 1:203.

14 Thomas Keymer, *Richardson's 'Clarissa' and the Eighteenth-Century Reader* (Cambridge: Cambridge University Press, 1992), p. 21.

15 See for example Janet Altman, *Epistolarity: Approaches to a Form* (Columbus, OH: Ohio State University Press, 1981).

16 Terry Castle, *Clarissa's Ciphers: Meaning and Disruption in Richardson's 'Clarissa'* (Ithaca, NY: Cornell University Press, 1982), pp. 168, 24–5.

17 Terry Eagleton, *The English Novel: An Introduction* (Oxford: Blackwell, 2005), p. 70. See also Eagleton's *The Rape of Clarissa: Writing, Sexuality and Class Struggle in Samuel Richardson* (Oxford: Basil Blackwell, 1982).

18 Henry Fielding, '*The History of the Adventures of Joseph Andrews and of his Friend Mr. Abraham Andrews*' and '*An Apology for the Life of Mrs. Shamela Andrews*', ed. Douglas Brooks-Davies, rev. Thomas Keymer (Oxford: Oxford University Press, 1999), p. 314.

19 Ian A. Bell, *Henry Fielding: Authorship and Authority* (London: Longman, 1994), p. 68.

20 Judith Frank, *Common Ground: Eighteenth-Century English Satiric Fiction and the Poor* (Stanford, CA: Stanford University Press, 1997), p. 49.

21 Jill Campbell, *Natural Masques: Gender and Identity in Fielding's Plays and Novels* (Stanford, CA: Stanford University Press, 1995), chapter 2.

22 *A Series of Letters between Mrs Elizabeth Carter and Miss Catherine Talbot from the year 1741 to 1770*, 2 vols (London, 1808), 1:207 (20 June 1749).

23 *Selected Letters of Samuel Richardson*, ed. John Carroll (Oxford: Clarendon Press, 1964), pp. 92, 99.
24 Quoted in Eaves and Kimpel, *Samuel Richardson*, p. 295.
25 Richardson, *Pamela*, p. 172.
26 Quoted by Gerrard, *Aaron Hill*, p. 221.
27 Henry Fielding, *The History of Tom Jones*, ed. R.P.C. Mutter (Harmondsworth: Penguin, 1966; repr. 1975), p. 695.

Chapter 5 Renewing the Novel: Novelty, Originality and New Directions

1 James Raven, *Judging New Wealth: Popular Publishing and Responses to Commerce in England, 1750–1800* (Oxford: Clarendon Press, 1992), chapter 2.
2 Horace Walpole, *Correspondence*, ed. W.S. Lewis, vol. 35 (New Haven, CT: Yale University Press, 1973), p. 200 (24 December 1754).
3 Lance Bertelsen, *Henry Fielding at Work: Magistrate, Businessman, Writer* (New York: Palgrave, 2000), chapter 5.
4 Edward Young, 'Conjectures on Original Composition: In a Letter to the Author of *Sir Charles Grandison*', in *English Critical Essays (Sixteenth, Seventeenth, and Eighteenth Centuries)*, ed. Edmund D. Jones (London: Oxford University Press, 1922), pp. 315 64 (p. 316), *Journal of a Tour to the Hebrides with Samuel Johnson, LL.D.*, The Yale Editions of the Private Papers of James Boswell (Melbourne: William Heinemann, 1963), p. 234 (30 September 1773).
5 Young, 'Conjectures', p. 348.
6 Young, 'Conjectures', pp. 323, 324, 319.
7 Thomas Keymer, *Sterne, the Moderns, and the Novel* (Oxford: Oxford University Press, 2002), chapter 2.
8 James Boswell, *The Life of Samuel Johnson, LL.D.*, ed. Angus Ross (Ware: Wordsworth, 1999), p. 278.
9 *Boswell for the Defence*, ed. William K. Wimsatt, Jr. and Frederick A. Pottle, The Yale Editions of the Private Papers of James Boswell (Melbourne: William Heinemann, 1960), p. 84 (31 March 1772).
10 John Cleland, *Fanny Hill; or, Memoirs of a Woman of Pleasure*, ed. Peter Wagner (Harmondsworth: Penguin, 1985), pp. 41, 105, 220. While Cleland's novel is popularly known as *Fanny Hill*, that title properly belongs only to a later, expurgated version, which was first published in 1750.
11 Bradford K. Mudge, *The Whore's Story: Women, Pornography, and the British Novel, 1684–1830* (Oxford: Oxford University Press, 2000), pp. 203, 208.
12 'Goats and monkeys' is an allusion to *Othello*, Act 4, scene 1.
13 Peter Wagner, *Eros Revived: Erotica of the Enlightenment in England and America* (London: Secker & Warburg, 1988), p. 237.
14 Extracted in *Venus Unmasked; or, An Inquiry into the Nature and Origin of the Passion of Love*, ed. Leonard De Vries and Peter Fryer (London: Arthur Baker, 1967), p. 116.
15 *Venus Unmasked*, p. 21.

16 Randolph Trumbach, 'Modern Prostitution and Gender in *Fanny Hill*: Libertine and Domesticated Fantasy', in *Sexual Underworlds of the Enlightenment*, ed. G.S. Rousseau and Roy Porter (Manchester: Manchester University Press, 1987), pp. 69–85.

17 Wagner, *Eros Revived*, p. 218.

18 Christopher Flint, 'Speaking Objects: The Circulation of Stories in Eighteenth-Century Prose Fiction', *PMLA*, 113 (1998), 212–26; Deidre Lynch, 'Personal Effects and Sentimental Fictions', *Eighteenth-Century Fiction*, 12 (1999–2000), 345–68 (p. 361n).

19 Wayne C. Booth, 'The Self-Conscious Narrator in Comic Fiction before *Tristram Shandy*', *PMLA*, 67 (1952), 163–85 (p. 180).

20 Francis Coventry, *The History of Pompey the Little; or, The Life and Adventures of a Lap-Dog*, ed. Robert Adams Day (London: Oxford University Press, 1974), pp. 68–69, 22, 45, 190, 107.

21 Henry Fielding, *'The History of the Adventures of Joseph Andrews and of his Friend Mr. Abraham Andrews' and 'An Apology for the Life of Mrs. Shamela Andrews'*, ed. Douglas Brooks-Davies, rev. Thomas Keymer (Oxford: Oxford University Press, 1999), p. 137.

22 Liz Bellamy, *Commerce, Morality and the Eighteenth-Century Novel* (Cambridge: Cambridge University Press, 1998), p. 120.

23 Bellamy, *Commerce*, p. 126.

24 *The Monthly Review*, 4 (February, 1751), p. 317.

25 Ronald Paulson, *Don Quixote in England: The Aesthetics of Laughter* (Baltimore, MD: Johns Hopkins University Press, 1998), p. 174.

26 Charlotte Lennox, *The Female Quixote; or, The Adventures of Arabella*, ed. Margaret Dalziel (London: Oxford University Press, 1970), pp. 7, 5.

27 Catherine Gallagher, *Nobody's Story: The Vanishing Acts of Women Writers in the Marketplace, 1670–1820* (Berkeley, CA: University of California Press, 1994), p. 179.

28 Wendy Motooka, *The Age of Reasons: Quixotism, Sentimentalism, and Political Economy in Eighteenth Century Britain* (London: Routledge, 1998), p. 126.

29 Amanda Vickery, *The Gentleman's Daughter: Women's Lives in Georgian England* (New Haven, CT: Yale University Press, 1998).

30 Horace Walpole, *The Castle of Otranto: A Gothic Story*, ed. W.S. Lewis, rev. E.J. Clery (Oxford: Oxford University Press, 1998), p. 19.

31 Samuel Johnson, *The Rambler*, ed. W.J. Bate and Albrecht Strauss, The Yale Edition of the Works of Samuel Johnson, vols 3–5 (New Haven, CT: Yale University Press, 1969), 3:19.

32 Edmund Burke, *A Philosophical Enquiry into the Origin of our Ideas of the Sublime and Beautiful*, ed. Adam Phillips (Oxford: Oxford University Press, 1990), pp. 36–7.

33 *The Monthly Review*, 32 (May, 1765), p. 394.

34 Cited in Terry Eagleton, *The English Novel: An Introduction* (Oxford: Blackwell, 2005), p. 73.

35 E.J. Clery, *The Rise of Supernatural Fiction, 1762–1800* (Cambridge: Cambridge University Press, 1995), p. 79.

36 James Watt, *Contesting the Gothic: Fiction, Genre and Cultural Conflict, 1764–1832* (Cambridge: Cambridge University Press, 1999), p. 34.

37 Burke, *A Philosophical Enquiry*, p. 54.

38 Markman Ellis, *The History of Gothic Fiction* (Edinburgh: Edinburgh University Press, 2000), chapter 1.
39 Clery, *The Rise of Supernatural Fiction*, pp. 83–4.

Chapter 6 The Sympathetic Strain: Sterne and Sentimental Fiction

1   James Boswell, 'A Poetical Epistle to Doctor Sterne, Parson Yorick, and Tristram Shandy' (1760), as extracted in *Sterne: The Critical Heritage*, ed. Alan B. Howes (London: Routledge & Kegan Paul, 1974), p. 82.
2   *Sterne: The Critical Heritage*, pp. 52, 46–8.
3   Laurence Sterne, *The Life and Opinions of Tristram Shandy, Gentleman*, ed. Melvyn New and Joan New (Harmondsworth: Penguin, 1997), 1:22, 58. References to *Tristram Shandy* are to the volume and chapter numbers and to the page number in the Penguin edition.
4   This ruse would also be echoed in the second preface to *The Castle of Otranto*, in which Walpole claims to have assumed the authority to 'lay down what rules I thought fit' in composing his work (p. 14).
5   Edward Young, 'Conjectures on Original Composition: In a Letter to the Author of *Sir Charles Grandison*', in *English Critical Essays (Sixteenth, Seventeenth and Eighteenth Centuries)*, ed. Edmund D. Jones (London: Oxford University Press, 1922), pp. 315–64 (p. 324). Also noteworthy here is Sterne's observation that, in *A Sentimental Journey*, he would be offering the public 'something new, quite out of the beaten track': *Letters of Laurence Sterne*, ed. Lewis Perry Curtis (Oxford: Clarendon Press, 1935), p. 301 (23 February 1767).
6   Michael Rosenblum, 'The Sermon, the King of Bohemia, and the Art of Interpolation in *Tristram Shandy*', *Studies in Philology*, 75 (1978), 472–91 (pp. 475, 488–9).
7   *Memoirs of the Extraordinary Life, Works, and Discoveries of Martinus Scriblerus*, ed. Charles Kerby-Miller (New Haven, CT: Yale University Press, 1950; repr. New York: Oxford University Press, 1988), pp. 96–7.
8   *Memoirs of the Extraordinary Life, Works, and Discoveries of Martinus Scriblerus*, p. 100.
9   Ignatius Sancho, *Letters of the Late Ignatius Sancho, An African*, ed. Vincent Carretta (Harmondsworth: Penguin, 1998), p. 125.
10 *Sterne: The Critical Heritage*, pp. 166, 167–8.
11 Tobias Smollett, *The Expedition of Humphry Clinker*, ed. Lewis M. Knapp (Oxford: Oxford University Press, 1966; rev. edn, 1984), p. 128.
12 Terry Eagleton, *The Rape of Clarissa: Writing, Sexuality and Class Struggle in Samuel Richardson* (Oxford: Basil Blackwell, 1982), p. 13.
13 Sarah Scott, *A Description of Millenium Hall*, ed. Gary Kelly (Toronto: Broadview, 1995), p. 169.
14 Dorice Williams Elliott, 'Sarah Scott's *Millenium Hall* and Female Philanthropy', *Studies in English Literature*, 35 (1995), 535–53 (p. 536 and *passim*).
15 Betty A. Schellenberg, *The Conversational Circle: Rereading the English Novel, 1740–1775* (Lexington, KY: University Press of Kentucky, 1996), p. 92.

16 John Mullan, *Sentiment and Sociability: The Language of Feeling in the Eighteenth Century* (Oxford: Clarendon Press, 1988), p. 124.

17 James Boswell, *The Life of Samuel Johnson, LL.D.*, ed. Angus Ross (Ware: Wordsworth, 1999), p. 199.

18 Markman Ellis, *The Politics of Sensibility: Race, Gender and Commerce in the Sentimental Novel* (Cambridge: Cambridge University Press, 1996), p. 24.

19 Thomas Hobbes, *The Elements of Law Natural and Politic: Part I Human Nature Part II De Corpore Politico With Three Lives*, ed. J.C.A. Gaskin (Oxford: Oxford University Press, 1994), pp. 59, 53.

20 Mullan, *Sentiment and Sociability*, pp. 34, 40.

21 Henry Mackenzie, *The Man of Feeling*, ed. Brian Vickers, new edn (Oxford: Oxford University Press, 2001), p. 14.

22 Oliver Goldsmith, *The Vicar of Wakefield*, ed. Stephen Coote (Harmondsworth: Penguin, 1982), pp. 83, 92.

23 Ann Jessie Van Sant, *Eighteenth-Century Sensibility and the Novel: The Senses in Social Context* (Cambridge: Cambridge University Press, 1993), p. 101.

24 This essay is included as appendix 1 in the Oxford World's Classics edition of the novel; our quotations are from pp. 102–3.

25 Laurence Sterne, *A Sentimental Journey though France and Italy by Mr. Yorick*, ed. Paul Goring (London: Penguin, 2001), p. 22.

26 John Brown, *An Estimate of the Manners and Principles of the Times*, 2 vols (London, 1757–58), 2:40.

27 *Letters of Laurence Sterne*, p. 411 (9 February 1768).

28 Adam Smith, *The Theory of Moral Sentiments* (London, 1759), p. 36.

29 Roland Barthes, *The Pleasure of the Text*, trans. Richard Miller (New York: Noonday Press, 1975), p. 22 and *passim*.

30 Janet Todd, *Sensibility: An Introduction* (London: Methuen, 1986), p. 90.

31 Mary Wollstonecraft, *A Vindication of the Rights of Woman*, ed. Ashley Tauchert (London: Everyman, 1995), pp. 11–12.

32 Mary Wollstonecraft and Mary Shelley, *Mary, Maria, Matilda*, ed. Janet Todd (Harmondsworth: Penguin, 1992), pp. [3], 35.

33 Sterne, *Tristram Shandy*, 2:12, 92.

Chapter 7 Narrating the Nation: Leisure, Luxury and Politeness

1 John Brewer, *The Pleasures of the Imagination: English Culture in the Eighteenth Century* (New York: Farrar, Straus and Giroux, 1997); Roy Porter, 'Material Pleasures in the Consumer Society', in *Pleasure in the Eighteenth Century*, ed. Roy Porter and Marie Mulvey Roberts (Basingstoke: Macmillan, 1996), pp. 19–35 (p. 23).

2 James Boswell, *The Life of Samuel Johnson, LL.D.*, ed. Angus Ross (Ware: Wordsworth, 1999), p. 135; Frances Burney, *Journals and Letters*, ed. Peter Sabor and Lars E. Troide (Harmondsworth: Penguin, 2001), p. 25.

3 Diana Donald, *The Age of Caricature: Satirical Prints in the Reign of George III* (New Haven, CT: Yale University Press, 1996), p. 96.

4   For perceptions of the aristocracy during the 1770s, see chapter 12 of Paul Langford, *A Polite and Commercial People: England 1727–1783* (Oxford: Oxford University Press, 1992).

5   Oliver Goldsmith, *She Stoops to Conquer*, ed. Tom Davis (London: A & C Black; New York: Norton, 1979), p. 42 (2:1, ll. 520–5).

6   Tobias Smollett, *The Expedition of Humphry Clinker*, ed. Lewis M. Knapp (Oxford: Oxford University Press, 1966; rev. edn, 1984), p. 109.

7   Frances Burney, *Evelina; or, The History of a Young Lady's Entrance into the World*, ed. Margaret Anne Doody (Harmondsworth: Penguin, 1994), p. 28.

8   Richardson, *Pamela* (1980), p. 266.

9   Gerald Newman, *The Rise of English Nationalism: A Cultural History, 1740–1830* (London: Weidenfeld and Nicolson, 1987), p. 136; Julia Epstein, *The Iron Pen: Frances Burney and the Politics of Women's Writing* (Madison, WI: University of Wisconsin Press, 1989), pp. 100–2.

10 Lord Chesterfield, *Letters*, ed. David Roberts (Oxford: Oxford University Press, 1992), p. 98.

11 William Hazlitt, *Lectures on the English Comic Writers* (London: Dent, 1900), p. 179.

12 Henry Fielding, *'The History of the Adventures of Joseph Andrews and of his Friend Mr. Abraham Andrews' and 'An Apology for the Life of Mrs. Shamela Andrews'*, ed. Douglas Brooks-Davies, rev. Thomas Keymer (Oxford: Oxford University Press, 1999), pp. 21, 28, 244. Slipslop's sloppy verbal slip here is a *spelling* error, we might note, which, while it registers for the reader of the printed page, could not be apparent during Slipslop's actual *conversation* with Lady Booby.

13 Linda Colley, *Britons: Forging the Nation 1707–1837* (New Haven, CT: Yale University Press, 1992), pp. 121–2.

14 Thomas Pennant, *The Literary Life of the Late Thomas Pennant, Esq., by Himself* (London, 1793), p. 13; quoted in Colley, *Britons*, p. 116.

15 Jean Bernard Le Blanc, *Letters on the English and French Nations*, trans., 2 vols (London, 1747), 2:89.

16 David M. Weed, 'Sentimental Misogyny and Medicine in *Humphry Clinker*', *Studies in English Literature*, 37 (1997), 535–52.

17 Peter Borsay, *The English Urban Renaissance: Culture and Society in the Provincial Town, 1660–1770* (Oxford: Clarendon Press, 1989).

18 Susan L. Jacobsen, ' "The Tinsel of the Times": Smollett's Argument Against Conspicuous Consumption in *Humphry Clinker*', *Eighteenth-Century Fiction*, 9 (1996–97), 71–88 (pp. 80, 88).

19 Aileen Douglas, *Uneasy Sensations: Smollett and the Body* (Chicago, IL: University of Chicago Press, 1995), p. 180.

20 While this was the 26-year-old Burney's first published novel, it was not the first that she had actually written. On her fifteenth birthday, Burney burnt everything that she had written previously, which included poems, plays, and *The History of Caroline Evelyn*, a novel about Evelina's mother, who we learn about in the opening pages of *Evelina* itself.

21 Smollett, *Humphry Clinker*, pp. 8, 12, 92, 91.

22 Amanda Vickery, *The Gentleman's Daughter: Women's Lives in Georgian England* (New Haven, CT: Yale University Press, 1998), p. 8.

23 *The Macaroni, Scavoir Vivre, and Theatrical Magazine* (August, 1773), pp. 481–2.

24 Barbara Zonitch, *Familiar Violence: Gender and Social Upheaval in the Novels of Frances Burney* (Newark, DE: University of Delaware Press; London: Associated University Presses, 1997), p. 40.

25 Donald, *The Age of Caricature*, p. 83.

26 Fielding, *Joseph Andrews*, pp. 22, 111.

27 On the anti-aristocratic aspect of later eighteenth-century Gallophobia, see Newman, *The Rise of English Nationalism.*

28 Smollett, *Humphry Clinker*, p. 208.

29 Burney, *Journals and Letters*, p. 69.

30 Margaret Anne Doody, *Frances Burney: The Life in the Works* (New Brunswick, NJ: Rutgers University Press, 1988), p. 52.

31 Kristina Straub, *Divided Fictions: Fanny Burney and Feminine Strategy* (Lexington, KY: University Press of Kentucky, 1987), p. 50.

32 Straub, *Divided Fictions*, p. 20.

33 Zonitch, *Familiar Violence*, pp. 48, 31.

Chapter 8 Conclusion: Making the Novel, Reading the Novel

1 Terry Eagleton, *The English Novel: An Introduction* (Oxford: Blackwell, 2005), p. ix.

2 Terry Belanger, 'Publishers and Writers in Eighteenth-Century England', in *Books and their Readers in Eighteenth-Century England*, ed. Isabel Rivers (Leicester: Leicester University Press, 1982), pp. 5–25 (p. 6).

3 James Raven, *Judging New Wealth: Popular Publishing and Responses to Commerce in England, 1750–1800* (Oxford: Clarendon Press, 1992), pp. 33, 38–9.

4 Cheryl Turner, *Living by the Pen: Women Writers of the Eighteenth Century* (London: Routledge, 1992), p. 114.

5 Henry Fielding, '*The History of the Adventures of Joseph Andrews and of his Friend Mr. Abraham Andrews*' and '*An Apology for the Life of Mrs. Shamela Andrews*', ed. Douglas Brooks-Davies, rev. Thomas Keymer (Oxford: Oxford University Press, 1999), p. 3.

6 *Tobias Smollett: The Critical Heritage*, ed. Lionel Kelly (London: Routledge & Kegan Paul, 1987), p. 51.

7 Frances Sheridan, *Memoirs of Miss Sidney Bidulph*, ed. Patricia Köster and Jean Coates Cleary (Oxford: Oxford University Press, 1995), p. 399.

8 Frances Burney, *Evelina; or, The History of a Young Lady's Entrance into the World*, ed. Margaret Anne Doody (Harmondsworth: Penguin, 1994), pp. 7, 8.

9 Roy Porter, *English Society in the Eighteenth Century* (Harmondsworth: Penguin, 1982), p. 253.

10 Henry Mackenzie, *The Man of Feeling*, ed. Brian Vickers, new edn (Oxford: Oxford University Press, 2001), p. 103.

11 Tobias Smollett, *The Expedition of Humphry Clinker*, ed. Lewis M. Knapp (Oxford: Oxford University Press, 1966; rev. edn, 1984), p. 12.

12 Quoted from *Sheridan's Plays*, ed. Cecil Price (London: Oxford University Press, 1975), pp. 15–16 (1:2, ll. 1–26).

13 Fielding, *Shamela*, p. 332.

14 *Sheridan's Plays*, p. 21 (1:2, ll. 194–8).

15 Frank Donoghue, 'Colonizing Readers: Review Criticism and the Formation of a Reading Public', in *The Consumption of Culture, 1600–1800: Image, Object, Text*, ed. Ann Bermingham and John Brewer (London: Routledge, 1995), pp. 54–74 (p. 55).

16 Joseph F. Bartolomeo, *A New Species of Criticism: Eighteenth-Century Discourse on the Novel* (Newark, DE: University of Delaware Press; London: Associated University Presses, 1994), p. 115.

17 *The Critical Review*, 2 (November, 1756), p. 379.

18 Sterne, *Tristram Shandy*, 1:13, 32; 3:4, 132–3; Richard Graves, *The Spiritual Quixote; or, The Summer's Ramble of Mr. Geoffry Wildgoose*, ed. Clarence Tracy (London: Oxford University Press, 1967), p. 5.

19 Burney, *Evelina*, pp. 4–5.

20 Clara Reeve, *The Progress of Romance*, 2 vols (Colchester, 1785), 1:111.

21 Markman Ellis, *The Politics of Sensibility: Race, Gender and Commerce in the Sentimental Novel* (Cambridge: Cambridge University Press, 1996), p. 198.

22 Robert Burns to John Murdoch, 15 January 1783, from *The Letters of Robert Burns*, 2nd edn, ed. G. Ross Roy, 2 vols (Oxford: Clarendon Press, 1985), 1:17–18.

23 *The British Critic*, 8 (November, 1796), pp. 527–8.

24 Thomas J. Mathias, *The Pursuits of Literature: A Satirical Poem in Dialogue*, 3rd edn (London, 1797), pt. 4, p. 87n.

25 Claudia L. Johnson, ' "Let me Make the Novels of a Country": Barbauld's *The British Novelists* (1810/1820)', *Novel*, 34:2 (Spring, 2001), 163–79 (p. 166).

26 *The British Novelists*, ed. Anna Barbauld, 50 vols (London, 1810), 1:37–8.

27 *The Monthly Review*, 2nd ser., 5 (July, 1791), pp. 337–8.

28 *The British Novelists*, 1:37.

Bibliography

Primary Works

Arbuthnot, John and others, *Memoirs of the Extraordinary Life, Works, and Discoveries of Martinus Scriblerus*, ed. Charles Kerby-Miller (New Haven, CT: Yale University Press, 1950; repr. New York: Oxford University Press, 1988).

Barbauld, Anna, ed., *The British Novelists*, 50 vols (London, 1810).

Behn, Aphra, *Love-Letters between a Noble-Man and his Sister*, 3 vols (London, 1684–87).

Behn, Aphra, *Oroonoko; or, The Royal Slave*, ed. Janet Todd (Harmondsworth: Penguin, 1992).

Boswell, James, *Boswell for the Defence*, ed. William K. Wimsatt, Jr. and Frederick A. Pottle, The Yale Editions of the Private Papers of James Boswell (Melbourne: William Heinemann, 1960).

Boswell, James, *Journal of a Tour to the Hebrides with Samuel Johnson, LL.D.*, The Yale Editions of the Private Papers of James Boswell (Melbourne: William Heinemann, 1963).

Boswell, James, *The Life of Samuel Johnson, LL.D.*, ed. Angus Ross (Ware: Wordsworth, 1999).

Brown, John, *An Estimate of the Manners and Principles of the Times*, 2 vols (London, 1757–58).

Burke, Edmund, *A Philosophical Enquiry into the Origin of our Ideas of the Sublime and Beautiful*, ed. Adam Phillips (Oxford: Oxford University Press, 1990).

Burney, Frances, *Evelina; or, The History of a Young Lady's Entrance into the World*, ed. Margaret Anne Doody (Harmondsworth: Penguin, 1994).

Burney, Frances, *Journals and Letters*, ed. Peter Sabor and Lars E. Troide (Harmondsworth: Penguin, 2001).

Burns, Robert, *The Letters of Robert Burns*, 2nd edn, ed. G. Ross Roy, 2 vols (Oxford: Clarendon Press, 1985).

Chesterfield, Lord, *Letters*, ed. David Roberts (Oxford: Oxford University Press, 1992).

Cleland, John, *Fanny Hill; or, Memoirs of a Woman of Pleasure*, ed. Peter Wagner (Harmondsworth: Penguin, 1985).

Congreve, William, *Incognita; or, Love and Duty Reconcil'd* (London, 1692).

Coventry, Francis, *The History of Pompey the Little; or, The Life and Adventures of a Lap-Dog*, ed. Robert Adams Day (London: Oxford University Press, 1974).

Defoe, Daniel, *The Life and Adventures of Robinson Crusoe*, ed. Angus Ross (Harmondsworth: Penguin, 1965).

Defoe, Daniel, *Roxana: The Fortunate Mistress*, ed. Jane Jack (Oxford: Oxford University Press, 1964; repr. 1976).

Defoe, Daniel, *The Fortunes and Misfortunes of the Famous Moll Flanders*, ed. G.A. Starr (Oxford: Oxford University Press, 1981).

Equiano, Olaudah, *The Interesting Narrative and other Writings*, ed. Vincent Carretta (New York: Penguin, 1995).

Fielding, Henry, *The History of Tom Jones*, ed. R.P.C. Mutter (Harmondsworth: Penguin, 1966; repr. 1975).

Fielding, Henry, *'The History of the Adventures of Joseph Andrews and of his Friend Mr. Abraham Andrews' and 'An Apology for the Life of Mrs. Shamela Andrews'*, ed. Douglas Brooks-Davies, rev. Thomas Keymer (Oxford: Oxford University Press, 1999).

Goldsmith, Oliver, *She Stoops to Conquer*, ed. Tom Davis (London: A & C Black; New York: Norton, 1979).

Goldsmith, Oliver, *The Vicar of Wakefield*, ed. Stephen Coote (Harmondsworth: Penguin, 1982).

Graves, Richard, *The Spiritual Quixote; or, The Summer's Ramble of Mr. Geoffry Wildgoose*, ed. Clarence Tracy (London: Oxford University Press, 1967).

Haywood, Eliza, *Idalia; or, The Unfortunate Mistress* (London, 1723).

Haywood, Eliza, *Love in Excess; or, The Fatal Enquiry*, ed. David Oakleaf (Peterborough, Ontario: Broadview, 1994; repr. 1997).

Hazlitt, William, *Lectures on the English Comic Writers* (London: Dent, 1900).

Hobbes, Thomas, *The Elements of Law Natural and Politic. Part I Human Nature Part II De Corpore Politico With Three Lives*, ed. J.C.A. Gaskin (Oxford: Oxford University Press, 1994).

James, Henry, 'The Art of Fiction', in *The Art of Fiction and Other Essays*, ed. Morris Roberts (New York: Oxford University Press, 1948), pp. 3–23.

Johnson, Samuel, *The Rambler*, ed. W.J. Bate and Albrecht Strauss, The Yale Edition of the Works of Samuel Johnson, vols 3–5 (New Haven, CT: Yale University Press, 1969).

Lawrence, D.H., 'Why the Novel Matters', in *English Critical Texts*, ed. D.J. Enright and Ernst de Chickera (London: Oxford University Press, 1962), pp. 286–92.

Le Blanc, Jean Bernard, *Letters on the English and French Nations*, trans., 2 vols (London, 1747).

Lennox, Charlotte, *The Female Quixote; or, The Adventures of Arabella*, ed. Margaret Dalziel (London: Oxford University Press, 1970).

The Macaroni, Scavoir Vivre, and Theatrical Magazine (August, 1773).

Mackenzie, Henry, *The Man of Feeling*, ed. Brian Vickers, new edn (Oxford: Oxford University Press, 2001).

Manley, Delarivier, *The New Atalantis*, ed. Rosalind Ballaster (Harmondsworth: Penguin, 1991).

Mathias, Thomas J., *The Pursuits of Literature: A Satirical Poem in Dialogue*, 3rd edn (London, 1797).

Pennant, Thomas, *The Literary Life of the Late Thomas Pennant, Esq., by Himself* (London, 1793).

Pope, Alexander, *The Poems of Alexander Pope*, ed. John Butt (London: Routledge, 1992).

Reeve, Clara, *The Progress of Romance*, 2 vols (Colchester, 1785).
Richardson, Samuel, *Pamela; or, Virtue Rewarded*, ed. Mark Kinkead-Weekes, 2 vols (London: Dent, 1914; repr. 1965).
Richardson, Samuel, *Clarissa; or, The History of a Young Lady*, ed. John Butt, 4 vols (London: Dent, 1962).
Richardson, Samuel, *Selected Letters of Samuel Richardson*, ed. John Carroll (Oxford: Clarendon Press, 1964).
Richardson, Samuel, *Pamela; or, Virtue Rewarded*, ed. Peter Sabor (Harmondsworth: Penguin, 1980; repr. 1985).
Richardson, Samuel, *Clarissa; or, The History of a Young Lady*, ed. Angus Ross (Harmondsworth: Penguin, 1985).
Sancho, Ignatius, *Letters of the Late Ignatius Sancho, An African*, ed. Vincent Carretta (Harmondsworth: Penguin, 1998).
Scott, Sarah, *A Description of Millenium Hall*, ed. Gary Kelly (Toronto: Broadview, 1995).
A Series of Letters between Mrs Elizabeth Carter and Miss Catherine Talbot from the year 1741 to 1770, 2 vols (London, 1808).
Sheridan, Frances, *Memoirs of Miss Sidney Bidulph*, ed. Patricia Köster and Jean Coates Cleary (Oxford: Oxford University Press, 1995).
Sheridan, Richard Brinsley, *Sheridan's Plays*, ed. Cecil Price (London: Oxford University Press, 1975).
Smith, Adam, *The Theory of Moral Sentiments* (London, 1759).
Smollett, Tobias, *The Expedition of Humphry Clinker*, ed. Lewis M. Knapp (Oxford: Oxford University Press, 1966; rev. edn, 1984).
Sterne, Laurence, *Letters of Laurence Sterne*, ed. Lewis Perry Curtis (Oxford: Clarendon Press, 1935).
Sterne, Laurence, *The Life and Opinions of Tristram Shandy, Gentleman*, ed. Melvyn New and Joan New (Harmondsworth: Penguin, 1997).
Sterne, Laurence, *A Sentimental Journey though France and Italy by Mr. Yorick*, ed. Paul Goring (London: Penguin, 2001).
Swift, Jonathan, *A Tale of a Tub*, ed. Herbert Davis (Oxford: Blackwell, 1965).
Swift, Jonathan, *Gulliver's Travels*, ed. Paul Turner (Oxford: Oxford University Press, 1986).
Theobald, Lewis, *The History of the Loves of Antiochus and Stratonice* (London, 1717).
Venus Unmasked; or, An Inquiry into the Nature and Origin of the Passion of Love, ed. Leonard De Vries and Peter Fryer (London: Arthur Baker, 1967).
Walpole, Horace, *Correspondence*, ed. W.S. Lewis, vol. 35 (New Haven, CT: Yale University Press, 1973).
Walpole, Horace, *The Castle of Otranto: A Gothic Story*, ed. W.S. Lewis, rev. E.J. Clery (Oxford: Oxford University Press, 1998).
Wollstonecraft, Mary, *A Vindication of the Rights of Woman*, ed. Ashley Tauchert (London: Everyman, 1995).
Wollstonecraft, Mary and Mary Shelley, *Mary, Maria, Matilda*, ed. Janet Todd (Harmondsworth: Penguin, 1992).
Young, Edward, 'Conjectures on Original Composition: In a Letter to the Author of *Sir Charles Grandison*', in *English Critical Essays (Sixteenth, Seventeenth, and Eighteenth Centuries)*, ed. Edmund D. Jones (London: Oxford University Press, 1922), pp. 315–64.

Secondary Works

Altman, Janet, *Epistolarity: Approaches to a Form* (Columbus, OH: Ohio State University Press, 1981).

Armstrong, Nancy, *Desire and Domestic Fiction: A Political History of the Novel* (New York: Oxford University Press, 1987).

Bakhtin, M.M., *The Dialogic Imagination: Four Essays*, ed. Michael Holquist, trans. Caryl Emerson and Michael Holquist (Austin, TX: University of Texas Press, 1981).

Ballaster, Ros, *Seductive Forms: Women's Amatory Fiction from 1684–1740* (Oxford: Clarendon Press, 1992).

Barker-Benfield, G.J., *The Culture of Sensibility: Sex and Society in Eighteenth-Century Britain* (Chicago, IL: University of Chicago Press, 1992).

Barthes, Roland, *The Pleasure of the Text*, trans. Richard Miller (New York: Noonday Press, 1975).

Bartolomeo, Joseph F., *A New Species of Criticism: Eighteenth-Century Discourse on the Novel* (Newark, DE: University of Delaware Press; London: Associated University Presses, 1994).

Battestin, Martin C., *A Henry Fielding Companion* (Westport, CT: Greenwood Press, 2000).

Belanger, Terry, 'Publishers and Writers in Eighteenth-Century England', in *Books and their Readers in Eighteenth-Century England*, ed. Isabel Rivers (Leicester: Leicester University Press, 1982), pp. 5–25.

Bell, Ian A., *Henry Fielding: Authorship and Authority* (London: Longman, 1994).

Bellamy, Liz, *Commerce, Morality and the Eighteenth-Century Novel* (Cambridge: Cambridge University Press, 1998).

Bertelsen, Lance, *Henry Fielding at Work: Magistrate, Businessman, Writer* (New York: Palgrave, 2000).

Bhabha, Homi K., 'Of Mimicry and Man: The Ambivalence of Colonial Discourse', *October*, 28 (1984), 125–33.

Booth, Wayne C., 'The Self-Conscious Narrator in Comic Fiction before *Tristram Shandy*', *PMLA*, 67 (1952), 163–85.

Borsay, Peter, *The English Urban Renaissance: Culture and Society in the Provincial Town, 1660–1770* (Oxford: Clarendon Press, 1989).

Brewer, John, *The Pleasures of the Imagination: English Culture in the Eighteenth Century* (New York: Farrar, Straus and Giroux, 1997).

Brown, Homer Obed, *Institutions of the English Novel: From Defoe to Scott* (Philadelphia, PN: University of Pennsylvania Press, 1997).

Campbell, Jill, *Natural Masques: Gender and Identity in Fielding's Plays and Novels* (Stanford, CA: Stanford University Press, 1995).

Carnochan, W.B., ' "A Matter *Discutable*": The Rise of the Novel', *Eighteenth-Century Fiction*, 12:2–3 (January–April, 2000), 167–84.

Cash, Arthur H., *Laurence Sterne: The Later Years* (London: Methuen, 1986).

Castle, Terry, *Clarissa's Ciphers: Meaning and Disruption in Richardson's 'Clarissa'* (Ithaca, NY: Cornell University Press, 1982).

Clark, J.C.D., *English Society 1688–1832: Ideology, Social Structure and Political Practice during the Ancien Regime* (Cambridge: Cambridge University Press, 1985).

Clery, E.J., *The Rise of Supernatural Fiction, 1762–1800* (Cambridge: Cambridge University Press, 1995).

Clute, John and Peter Nichols, eds, *The Encyclopaedia of Science Fiction* (London: Orbit, 1993).

Colley, Linda, *Britons: Forging the Nation 1707–1837* (New Haven, CT: Yale University Press, 1992).

Davis, Lennard J., 'Dialectics on the Loose: The History of the Novel in Infinite Regress', *The Eighteenth Century*, 30:3 (Autumn, 1989), 43–50.

Davis, Lennard J., *Factual Fictions: The Origins of the English Novel* (New York: Columbia University Press, 1983).

Donald, Diana, *The Age of Caricature: Satirical Prints in the Reign of George III* (New Haven, CT: Yale University Press, 1996).

Donoghue, Frank, 'Colonizing Readers: Review Criticism and the Formation of a Reading Public', in *The Consumption of Culture, 1600–1800: Image, Object, Text*, ed. Ann Bermingham and John Brewer (London: Routledge, 1995), pp. 54–74.

Doody, Margaret Anne, *Frances Burney: The Life in the Works* (New Brunswick, NJ: Rutgers University Press, 1988).

Doody, Margaret Anne, 'Swift and Romance', in *Walking Naboth's Vineyard: New Studies of Swift*, ed. Christopher Fox and Brenda Tooley (Notre Dame: University of Notre Dame Press, 1995), pp. 98–126.

Doody, Margaret Anne, *The True Story of the Novel* (New Brunswick, NJ: Rutgers University Press, 1996).

Douglas, Aileen, *Uneasy Sensations: Smollett and the Body* (Chicago, IL: University of Chicago Press, 1995).

Downie, J.A., 'The Making of the English Novel', *Eighteenth-Century Fiction*, 9 (1996–97), 249–66.

Downie, J.A., 'Mary Davys's "Probable Feign'd Stories" and Critical Shibboleths about "The Rise of the Novel" ', *Eighteenth-Century Fiction*, 12:2–3 (January–April, 2000), 309–26.

Eagleton, Terry, *The Rape of Clarissa: Writing, Sexuality and Class Struggle in Samuel Richardson* (Oxford: Basil Blackwell, 1982).

Eagleton, Terry, *The English Novel: An Introduction* (Oxford: Blackwell, 2005).

Eaves, T.C. Duncan and Ben D. Kimpel, *Samuel Richardson: A Biography* (Oxford: Clarendon Press, 1971).

Elliott, Dorice Williams, 'Sarah Scott's *Millenium Hall* and Female Philanthropy', *Studies in English Literature*, 35 (1995), 535–53.

Ellis, Markman, *The Politics of Sensibility: Race, Gender and Commerce in the Sentimental Novel* (Cambridge: Cambridge University Press, 1996).

Ellis, Markman, *The History of Gothic Fiction* (Edinburgh: Edinburgh University Press, 2000).

Epstein, Julia, *The Iron Pen: Frances Burney and the Politics of Women's Writing* (Madison, WI: University of Wisconsin Press, 1989).

Faller, Lincoln B., *Crime and Defoe: A New Kind of Writing* (Cambridge: Cambridge University Press, 1993).

Flint, Christopher, 'Speaking Objects: The Circulation of Stories in Eighteenth-Century Prose Fiction', *PMLA*, 113 (1998), 212–26.

Flynn, Carol Houlihan, *The Body in Swift and Defoe* (Cambridge: Cambridge University Press, 1990).

Forster, Antonia, 'Review Journals and the Reading Public', in *Books and their Readers in Eighteenth-Century England: New Essays*, ed. Isabel Rivers (London: Continuum, 2001), pp. 171–90.

Frank, Judith, *Common Ground: Eighteenth-Century English Satiric Fiction and the Poor* (Stanford, CA: Stanford University Press, 1997).

Gallagher, Catherine, *Nobody's Story: The Vanishing Acts of Women Writers in the Marketplace, 1670–1820* (Berkeley, CA: University of California Press, 1994).

Gallagher, Catherine, '*Oroonoko*'s Blackness', in *Aphra Behn Studies*, ed. Janet Todd (Cambridge: Cambridge University Press, 1996), pp. 235–58.

Gerrard, Christine, *Aaron Hill: The Muses' Projector, 1685–1750* (Oxford: Oxford University Press, 2003).

Gooding, Richard, '*Pamela, Shamela*, and the Politics of the *Pamela* Vogue', *Eighteenth-Century Fiction*, 7 (1994–95), 109–30.

Gordon, Scott Paul, *The Power of the Passive Self in English Literature, 1640–1770* (Cambridge: Cambridge University Press, 2002).

Grundy, Isobel, 'Restoration and Eighteenth Century', in *The Oxford Illustrated History of English Literature*, ed. Pat Rogers (Oxford: Oxford University Press, 1987), pp. 214–73.

Howes, Alan B., ed., *Sterne: The Critical Heritage* (London: Routledge & Kegan Paul, 1974).

Hunter, J. Paul, *Before Novels: The Cultural Contexts of Eighteenth-Century English Fiction* (New York: Norton, 1990).

Hunter, J. Paul, '*Gulliver's Travels* and the Novel', in *The Genres of 'Gulliver's Travels'*, ed. Frederik N. Smith (Newark, DE: University of Delaware Press, 1990), pp. 56–74.

Ingrassia, Catherine, *Authorship, Commerce, and Gender in Early Eighteenth-Century England: A Culture of Paper Credit* (Cambridge: Cambridge University Press, 1998).

Jacobsen, Susan L., ' "The Tinsel of the Times": Smollett's Argument Against Conspicuous Consumption in *Humphry Clinker*', *Eighteenth-Century Fiction*, 9 (1996–97), 71–88.

Johnson, Claudia L., ' "Let me Make the Novels of a Country": Barbauld's *The British Novelists* (1810/1820)', *Novel*, 34:2 (Spring, 2001), 163–79.

Kelly, Lionel, ed., *Tobias Smollett: The Critical Heritage* (London: Routledge & Kegan Paul, 1987).

Keymer, Thomas, *Richardson's 'Clarissa' and the Eighteenth-Century Reader* (Cambridge: Cambridge University Press, 1992).

Keymer, Thomas, *Sterne, the Moderns, and the Novel* (Oxford: Oxford University Press, 2002).

Kiberd, Declan, *Irish Classics* (London: Granta, 2001).

Kroll, Richard, ' "Tales of Love and Gallantry": The Politics of *Oroonoko*', *Huntington Library Quarterly*, 67:4 (December, 2004), 573–605.

Langbauer, Laurie, *Women and Romance: The Consolations of Gender in the English Novel* (Ithaca, NY: Cornell University Press, 1990).

Langford, Paul, *A Polite and Commercial People: England 1727–1783* (Oxford: Oxford University Press, 1992).

Lynch, Deidre, 'Personal Effects and Sentimental Fictions', *Eighteenth-Century Fiction*, 12 (1999–2000), 345–68.

Mayer, Robert, *History and the Early English Novel: Matters of Fact from Bacon to Defoe* (Cambridge: Cambridge University Press, 1997).

McKeon, Michael, *The Origins of the English Novel, 1600–1740* (Baltimore, MD: Johns Hopkins University Press, 1987).

McKeon, Michael, 'Watt's *Rise of the Novel* within the Tradition of the Rise of the Novel', *Eighteenth-Century Fiction*, 12:2–3 (January–April, 2000), 253–76.

Motooka, Wendy, *The Age of Reasons: Quixotism, Sentimentalism, and Political Economy in Eighteenth Century Britain* (London: Routledge, 1998).

Mudge, Bradford K., *The Whore's Story: Women, Pornography, and the British Novel, 1684–1830* (Oxford: Oxford University Press, 2000).

Mullan, John, *Sentiment and Sociability: The Language of Feeling in the Eighteenth Century* (Oxford: Clarendon Press, 1988).

Newman, Gerald, *The Rise of English Nationalism: A Cultural History, 1740–1830* (London: Weidenfeld and Nicolson, 1987).

Novak, Maximillian, *Daniel Defoe: Master of Fictions* (Oxford: Oxford University Press, 2001).

Paulson, Ronald, *Don Quixote in England: The Aesthetics of Laughter* (Baltimore, MD: Johns Hopkins University Press, 1998).

Porter, Roy, *English Society in the Eighteenth Century* (Harmondsworth: Penguin, 1982).

Porter, Roy, 'Material Pleasures in the Consumer Society', in *Pleasure in the Eighteenth Century*, ed. Roy Porter and Marie Mulvey Roberts (Basingstoke: Macmillan, 1996), pp. 19–35.

Rack, Henry D., *Reasonable Enthusiast: John Wesley and the Rise of Methodism*, 3rd edn (London: Epworth Press, 2002).

Raven, James, *Judging New Wealth: Popular Publishing and Responses to Commerce in England, 1750–1800* (Oxford: Clarendon Press, 1992).

Richetti, John, *Popular Fiction before Richardson: Narrative Patterns, 1700–1739* (Oxford: Clarendon Press, 1969; repr. 1992).

Richetti, John, *The English Novel in History, 1700–1780* (London: Routledge, 1999)

Rosenblum, Michael, 'The Sermon, the King of Bohemia, and the Art of Interpolation in *Tristram Shandy*', *Studies in Philology*, 75 (1978), 472–91.

Ross, Deborah, *The Excellence of Falsehood: Romance, Realism, and Women's Contribution to the Novel* (Lexington, KY: University Press of Kentucky, 1991).

Schellenberg, Betty A., *The Conversational Circle: Rereading the English Novel, 1740–1775* (Lexington, KY: University Press of Kentucky, 1996).

Seidel, Michael, '*Gulliver's Travels* and the Contracts of Fiction', in *The Cambridge Companion to the Eighteenth-Century Novel*, ed. John Richetti (Cambridge: Cambridge University Press, 1996), pp. 72–89.

Shevelow, Kathryn, *Women and Print Culture: The Construction of Femininity in the Early Periodical* (London: Routledge, 1989).

Sinfield, Alan, *Faultlines: Cultural Materialism and the Politics of Dissident Reading* (Oxford: Clarendon Press, 1992).

Spencer, Jane, *The Rise of the Woman Novelist: From Aphra Behn to Jane Austen* (Oxford: Blackwell, 1986).

Spencer, Jane, *Aphra Behn's Afterlife* (Oxford: Oxford University Press, 2000).

Straub, Kristina, *Divided Fictions: Fanny Burney and Feminine Strategy* (Lexington, KY: University Press of Kentucky, 1987).

Thomas, Hugh, *The Slave Trade: The History of the Atlantic Slave Trade 1440–1870* (London: Macmillan, 1997).

Todd, Janet, *Sensibility: An Introduction* (London: Methuen, 1986).

Trumbach, Randolph, 'Modern Prostitution and Gender in *Fanny Hill*: Libertine and Domesticated Fantasy', in *Sexual Underworlds of the Enlightenment*, ed. G.S. Rousseau and Roy Porter (Manchester: Manchester University Press, 1987), pp. 69–85.

Turner, Cheryl, *Living by the Pen: Women Writers of the Eighteenth Century* (London: Routledge, 1992).

Turner, James Grantham, 'Novel Panic: Picture and Performance in the Reception of Richardson's *Pamela*', *Representations*, 48 (Autumn, 1994), 70–96.

Van Sant, Ann Jessie, *Eighteenth-Century Sensibility and the Novel: The Senses in Social Context* (Cambridge: Cambridge University Press, 1993).

Vickery, Amanda, *The Gentleman's Daughter: Women's Lives in Georgian England* (New Haven, CT: Yale University Press, 1998).

Wagner, Peter, *Eros Revived: Erotica of the Enlightenment in England and America* (London: Secker & Warburg, 1988).

Warner, William B., *Licensing Entertainment: The Elevation of Novel Reading in Britain, 1684–1750* (Berkeley, CA: University of California Press, 1998).

Watt, Ian, *The Rise of the Novel. Studies in Defoe, Richardson, and Fielding* (London: Chatto & Windus, 1957).

Watt, Ian, 'Flat-Footed and Fly-Blown: The Realities of Realism', *Eighteenth-Century Fiction*, 12:2–3 (January–April, 2000), 147–66.

Watt, James, *Contesting the Gothic: Fiction, Genre and Cultural Conflict, 1764–1832* (Cambridge: Cambridge University Press, 1999).

Weed, David M., 'Sentimental Misogyny and Medicine in *Humphry Clinker*', *Studies in English Literature*, 37 (1997), 535–52.

Zonitch, Barbara, *Familiar Violence: Gender and Social Upheaval in the Novels of Frances Burney* (Newark, DE: University of Delaware Press; London: Associated University Presses, 1997).

Index